VIKING

A HOUSE DIVIDED

The Untold Story of
the McCain Family

PAUL WALDIE

with
KATE JENNISON

VIKING

VIKING

Published by the Penguin Group

Penguin Books Canada Ltd, 10 Alcorn Avenue, Toronto, Ontario,
Canada M4V 3B2
Penguin Books Ltd, 27 Wrights Lane, London W8 5TZ, England
Viking Penguin, a division of Penguin Books USA Inc., 375 Hudson Street,
New York, New York 10014, U.S.A.
Penguin Books Australia Ltd, Ringwood, Victoria, Australia
Penguin Books (NZ) Ltd, 182–190 Wairau Road, Auckland 10, New Zealand

Penguin Books Ltd, Registered Offices: Harmondsworth, Middlesex, England

First published 1996
1 3 5 7 9 10 8 6 4 2

Printed and bound in Canada on acid free paper ∞

Canadian Cataloguing in Publication Data

Waldie, Paul, 1960-
A house divided: the untold story of the McCain family

ISBN 0-670-86453-6

1. McCain, H. Harrison, 1927–   . 2. McCain, Wallace. 3. McCain family.
4. McCain Foods Limited. I. Title.

HD9217.C34M337 1996   338.7'66402853'0922   C96-930327-0

For my grandmother Norma Simpson
and my daughter Augusta

PREFACE

"This is really good," Mike Babad said as he looked over at me and waved a pink telephone message slip. It was early afternoon on August 23, 1993. I had been a reporter at the *Financial Post* for less than a year. Because I was new to the *Post*, and business reporting in general, my job consisted largely of putting company earnings on a table that ran every day in the paper. Babad was the *Post's* assignment editor and he knew I was eager for any real reporting assignment. "I guarantee you, this is good," he said still waving the slip as I walked over to his desk. "Sure it is," I said skeptically before quickly grabbing the slip. The name John Lute was scrawled across the top along with a phone number. "Something is up between the McCain brothers," Babad said as I returned to my desk wondering who the McCain brothers were. I called Lute. He said he was a spokesman for Wallace McCain and that Wallace was about to sue his brother Harrison over the future of McCain Foods Ltd.

From then on, the McCains became a permanent beat for me. I attended every public court hearing, poured over thousands of pages of court documents and developed contacts with dozens of lawyers, company workers and family friends. I also came to know many family members and watched as they struggled to understand what was happening to their family. My contacts with the family weren't always friendly. After one story on a McCain board meeting, I received a call from Harrison's assistant, Marilyn Strong. "I've got Harrison McCain for you," she said briskly. After a short pause, Harrison was on the line blasting away at the offending piece noting that I had got the time of the meeting wrong and made him look bad for implying that he cut short a meeting with Wallace. "I read this this morning and I just was disappointed as hell," he said. "I said, 'Jesus Christ, Paul's got fed that god damn stuff by [Wallace's public relations firm] and he sucks it in, my God.' All the board meetings we have start at 10 o'clock and it's on the program for that day at 10 o'clock. I just really think Paul, you're a good fellow, but you're just fucking naïve. You're just fucking naïve." But that kind of call was rare and indeed a few weeks later, Harrison was joking with me about his daughter Gillian's plans to write a book on the history of punk rock.

My initial reporting was hampered by the lack of any useful written material on the McCains or McCain Foods Ltd. The company has always been privately held and rarely releases public information. There had been several newspaper and magazine articles on the family and McCain Foods but they offered few insights and often contained contradictory information. Like most journalists, I ended up relying heavily on the faded memories of friends and a family genealogy that was done in the 1980s by a relative. I learned later that the genealogy was even more inaccurate than some of the newspaper and magazine articles.

In the fall of 1994, I met with Meg Masters at Penguin Books and agreed to do a book on the family. Over the next two years, I began to learn far more about the family and the company. Several McCains, including some who had never spoken to the press before, spent countless hours with me providing a rare look inside the family and the company. Wallace, Harrison and their sister Marie were especially helpful. As were Margaret, Rosemary, Andrew, Michael, Scott and Eleanor.

Many current and former McCain Foods executives also provided invaluable background on the business. They include Carl Morris, Carl Ash, Alden Lunn, Ralph Orr, Tim Bliss and Archie McLean. I also thank many other employees and family friends including Donald Trafford, Jim Coutts, Richard O'Hagan, Louis Robichaud, Charles Gallagher, Reg Gilbert, Claude Bursill, Mary Walters, Gordon Hill, Joe Palmer, William Smith, Ernie Ellis and Bev O'Keefe. Several McCain critics also deserve thanks, especially Bert Deveaux, Skip Hambling, David Malcolm, Bob Cowan and Gerry McAuliffe.

I am also indebted to a variety of McCain lawyers, consultants and advisers. Lawyers Jack Petch, Alan Lenczner, John Campion and Gary Girvan spent many hours helping me understand legal issues in the family's lawsuits. Doug Morrison helped me sort out the Bodine's case and figure out the Chicago court system. Public relations consultants Pat McGee, David MacNaughton and John Lute always kept me aware of the family's moves and helped arrange interviews. Tom Muir took me through the financial details of the Maple Leaf Foods takeover. Family business experts John Ward and Leon Danco helped me better understand the McCain family dynamics.

I also thank the staff at several archives who always went out of their way to help me find mine. The staff at the Provincial Archives in New Brunswick were especially helpful and generous with their time. Archivists at Mount Allison University and Acadia University were also extraordinary. Thanks as well to the National Archives of Canada and the staff at the Harriet Irving Library at the University of New Brunswick. Donegal Ancestry in Donegal, Ireland was also an important resource in sorting out the McCain family history.

I also worked with several colleagues at the *Post* over the years on various McCain stories. Paul Brent and Eric Reguly generously gave me their notes and insights.

Thanks as well to Meg Masters and everyone at Penguin Books. A big thank you also goes to my parents, my in-laws and Donna, Gordon and their family for their support throughout this project. My family saw me through many difficult periods and accepted that for the last three years I have been able to think of little else but the McCains.

Finally, I also want to thank my wife Kate Jennison who sorted through stacks of material and helped keep the story focused. Together we pooled our insights and brainstormed our way through many passages of the book.

Paul Waldie

CHAPTER ONE

J ack Petch looked out the car window and tried to make out the farmhouses as they streaked by. He couldn't see much. It was dusk, and the houses were set back from the road, hidden by thick stands of trees. He'd been to New Brunswick a few times before but never this far out in the countryside, and from what he could see it looked beautiful. They were travelling down a dark stretch of road between Moncton and Fredericton. The road wound through lush farms and small forests. Up ahead, the Saint John River flowed as wide as a lake, and the road hugged the shoreline winding its way into Fredericton.

Petch leaned back in his seat to stretch his long legs. He was tired and rumpled from another long day in court. He brushed his dark hair out of his eyes and leaned his head back to stretch his neck. The law student driving the car said this was a shortcut, but they still had an hour to go to Fredericton, and another hour and a half after that to get to Florenceville. The kid looked a bit excited and nervous. Who wouldn't be? Petch thought. It's not every day that you get to crash a private meeting of the McCain family.

With a fortune worth more than $2.3 billion, the McCains were one of the most prominent and successful families ever to come out of New Brunswick. Their food empire stretched across Canada and through more than forty countries around the world. They were also intensely private. No outsider had ever attended a family meeting, and Petch knew tomorrow's meeting would be no ordinary gathering.

The family was about to vote on the removal of Wallace

McCain as co-chief executive of McCain Foods Ltd. Petch was supposed to try to stop them, or at least make the proceedings as unpleasant as possible. He hadn't been invited to the meeting and he didn't yet know what his strategy would be. He closed his eyes for a moment and tried to think.

It had all started four years earlier on a fall day in 1990. Petch was sitting in his corner office high above King Street in the heart of Toronto's financial district, flipping through some paperwork, when his secretary put through a call from Australia. Petch was a senior partner at Osler Hoskin & Harcourt, one of Canada's oldest and biggest corporate law firms. He'd been practising law for nearly thirty years and had handled some of the firm's biggest clients. Petch was wondering who he knew in Australia as he picked up the receiver.

"It's Wallace McCain in Australia," a sharp voice announced over the phone. Petch rolled the name over in his mind. He knew something about McCain Foods and he'd vaguely heard of the family, but he thought the guy in charge was named Harrison McCain. Who the hell was Wallace? Petch barely had time to say hello before the caller asked for an appointment.

A few days later, Wallace McCain stepped into Petch's office. Petch was impressed. Wallace was over six feet tall and more tanned and fit than any sixty-year-old Petch had ever seen. He had thick, shock-white hair, a long nose and piercing eyes that stared straight at Petch as they talked. Wallace sat down and launched into a lengthy tale of family discord. He told Petch that he ran McCain Foods with his older brother Harrison. Everything had been fine for years but recently they'd been unable to agree on how to involve their sons and nephews in the company. Succession was also a problem, Wallace said, and he wanted some legal advice in order to protect his family's interests.

Petch wasn't surprised. He'd worked on similar problems with hundreds of family-owned companies. Few made it past the founder stage because of disputes over succession. After listening to Wallace for a while, he concluded that the McCain situation was reasonably straightforward. Wallace and Harrison each owned one-third of McCain, so as long as they could agree on a few changes, the problem would be solved. It wouldn't take more than a few months, Petch told Wallace.

Now, as he opened his eyes and watched the car approach the exit for Florenceville, Petch wondered how he could ever have been so naïve. It was now September 12, 1994, and four years, two lawsuits and two hostile takeover bids later, the family didn't seem any closer to solving its problems. Petch was beginning to doubt that it ever would.

As the car rounded the turn from the exit ramp, Petch saw the huge McCain plant to his right. Steam poured out from all sides and the air had the distinct odour of peeled potato skins. On top was a faded yellow star, the company's symbol for nearly forty years. They turned left at the stop sign near the company's gates and drove down a small road that ran beside the Saint John River. It was Main Street, Florenceville.

Not much here, Petch thought as he looked around. They passed an Irving gas station, a Sears catalogue store, another store called Buckingham's and a couple of churches. A third church looked as if it had just been converted into a McCain office, with a McCain sign out front just beside a small graveyard. The town was full of McCain buildings. There was a McCain recreation centre on one street, a McCain seniors' complex on another and a McCain library at the corner of McCain Street and Main.

When they came to the McCain Produce Co. building, the student turned right and drove over a narrow wooden bridge to the west side of the Saint John River. From there they made a sharp right and then a left and climbed up a steep hill that wound around to another road called Riverview Drive. The road ran parallel to the river and cut across the middle of a long hill that rose up from the bank. It was lined with houses, some large and some barely farmhouses, each with a panoramic view of the village, the valley and the McCain plant on the other side. Wallace had mentioned something about growing up in a house along here, Petch remembered as he looked at the homes.

After a few minutes, Petch saw Wallace's home off to the right, and set back into the rising hillside. It was a white, two-storey house with black shutters and six white pillars in front. Petch could now see why everyone said it reminded them of something from *Gone with the Wind.* As he stepped out of the car, Petch looked over to the house next door. Two lots, two fences and a row of tall trees separated the houses, but Petch could just make out the long, low, Cape Cod style home. It belonged to Harrison. Wonder what he'll say when he sees me tomorrow, Petch thought.

"What the hell are *you* doing here?" boomed Harrison. Petch had just walked into the boardroom on the third floor of McCain's world headquarters, a building attached to the plant. He smiled good-naturedly at Harrison and waved hello to the other family members standing and sitting around a long conference table. The room was small for a company with more than $3 billion in sales, but it reflected the McCains' no-nonsense style. One wall was made of glass bricks that set the room off from an open office area. The other walls were bare, except for a large map of the world. Petch deliberately sat down across from Harrison. He wasn't going to be intimidated. The law student sat next to him, still a bit shaken by the hostile greeting they'd received.

At first glance, it would be hard to tell that Harrison was Wallace's brother. Harrison was about six inches shorter than Wallace and had a round, rugged face. Most of his hair had long since receded, but there was still a scattering of fine grey wisps on either side of his forehead. Harrison was wearing a dark suit, a sure sign something important was happening. No one at McCain's head office, not even Harrison or Wallace, wore a suit unless he had some very important business to take care of.

Petch looked around the room and counted about fifteen other family members. Most were staring at him and not saying a word. The company had only twenty-three shareholders in total, the members of four McCain families—Harrison's, Wallace's and those of their older brothers Andrew and Bob, who had died years before.

Sitting at the head of the table, just to Harrison's right, was Andrew McCain, Bob's oldest son. Andrew had never worked for McCain Foods beyond a few summer jobs, but three years earlier the family had appointed him chairman of a new family board made up of six sons, representing each of the four families. The board was supposed to represent the family's interests in the company, but in the last few months it had become a pit of anger, jealousy and open warfare. The fight was mainly over who should succeed Harrison and Wallace as McCain's chief executive, and the battle lines were clearly drawn. Wallace and his sons were on one side; Harrison, Andrew and the remaining family members were on the other. Today's meeting had been called by Harrison's forces, and if they were successful, Wallace would be demoted to a figurehead position in the company after almost forty years of hard work.

"I've got a few proxies." Petch rummaged through his briefcase for the legal documents that represented Wallace's family's voting shares. "And l think you all know what they are."

Andrew looked anxiously at Harrison. They were both hoping this would be a short meeting. They had only one resolution for the family to consider: a motion to give the directors of Andrew's board the power to remove Wallace. This was the third time they had tried to pass this sort of resolution, but each time Wallace had taken the family to court.

"As you know, Wallace can't be here because of the court hearing in Moncton," Petch said, referring to the latest court fight. "So, I would like to ask for an adjournment so that he can attend the meeting and make a statement on his own behalf."

"No goddamn way," Harrison snapped. "You've known about this meeting for a long time."

Andrew then began the meeting by explaining why the resolution was necessary. Harrison and Wallace were no longer working together, Andrew said. Wallace had tried two hostile takeover bids for McCain Foods and the family had gone through a wrenching eight-month private arbitration. The board believed the only solution was for Wallace to step down. Harrison would remain in charge until a new chief executive could be found.

Petch interjected. There were rumours, he said, that Andrew had told people this meeting would last only ten minutes. If that was true, Andrew should step down as chairman because his remarks suggested that he didn't want a full debate on the resolution. He again asked for a delay so that Wallace would have a chance to defend himself. Andrew scoffed at the suggestion and asked for a vote to determine if he should continue as chairman.

Everyone voted in favour, except Petch, on behalf of Wallace.

Finally, the vote was called on the resolution. Once again, with the exception of Petch's proxy votes, everyone voted in favour, effectively cutting Wallace out of the company he had helped to found, the company that bore his family's name.

Just after the vote count was announced, Petch interjected again. There were all kinds of irregularities in the voting procedures, he said. Then he demanded to examine every proxy and every ballot.

"We don't run our meetings that way," said Harrison, dismissing the request. "You're being frivolous."

Petch demanded an apology—Harrison's comments were unfair and uncalled for. Harrison shook his head and refused to apologize. Petch was just wasting everyone's time, he said. Petch turned to Andrew and asked for a ruling from the chair. Not sure what to do, Andrew finally agreed only to strike Harrison's comments from the minutes, and with that, he adjourned the meeting.

A small tray of sandwiches was brought in and Harrison asked Petch icily, "Are you staying for lunch?"

Petch smiled. "Sure." He was about to ask if he could join Harrison for a ride back to the court hearing in Moncton on the company's private plane, but he caught himself. That would be pushing it, he thought.

As the family left the McCain headquarters they were met by a team of reporters. Andrew stepped into the crowd and gave a terse statement indicating that the family as shareholders had approved the motion to remove Wallace as co-chief executive. Then he left for the McCain plane with Harrison.

After Andrew left, a reporter asked Petch for a comment. He hesitated for a moment and then ripped into Andrew and the others for holding such an unfair and one-sided meeting. "Wallace deserved a chance to be here," Petch said angrily. There were all kinds of problems in the balloting, he added, and then he hinted that he might challenge the vote in court. Petch knew his comments would be front-page news the next day. At least the trip wasn't a total loss, he thought as he went off to find a phone.

Calling Wallace in Moncton was a sad task. Wallace had been fighting to keep his job for three years. He didn't want to step down from McCain, and he felt he was being forced to leave so that Harrison could control the succession process. Now the family had voted to remove Wallace from the one job he loved. Wallace thanked Petch for his efforts. He added that he wasn't surprised by the results—he'd been losing every family vote for years—but Petch could sense disappointment in his voice.

Petch hung up, jumped back in the car with the law student and they drove back to Moncton. It was early afternoon, and he could see the scenery now. It was beautiful. The leaves on the trees were already changing, turning colours and drifting to the ground.

The vote on that September day formally severed one of the most successful business relationships in Canadian history.

Wallace and Harrison McCain had started McCain Foods Ltd. in 1956 with nothing but an empty cow pasture in Florenceville, a $100,000 inheritance from their father and the help and advice of their older brothers. Over the next four decades, the McCains created the largest potato processor in the world. McCain Foods now has more than twelve thousand employees in nearly seventy plants at forty-four locations around the world. McCain French fries are sold worldwide from Tokyo to Toronto and Auckland to Alaska. McCain has become so international in scope that nearly 80 percent of its sales are generated outside Canada. Nearly half of all the French fries eaten in Canada, Australia, Britain, France, Brazil, Chile and Argentina are made by McCain, and the company dominates markets in Germany, Japan and much of western Europe. Soon, McCain fries will be on sale in India and across eastern Europe, and the company is looking at Turkey, South Africa and China as well.

From the day the first skinny fry rolled off the conveyor belt in Florenceville, McCain Foods has never lost money. The company's profit jumped 13 percent to $130 million in 1995 and sales topped a record $4 billion. Even bad economic times haven't slowed down McCain. Between 1989 and 1993, while other companies were struggling through a prolonged recession,

McCain's annual profit more than doubled, from $35.5 million to $76 million.

Through it all, the brothers' relationship survived almost every obstacle, from battles with McDonald's Corp. and the Australian government to death threats and near-fatal illnesses. Together, they were ruthless competitors. "I haven't run into anyone who likes them," says Bob Cowan, former head of Lamb-Weston Inc., McCain's biggest competitor worldwide.

For years, Harrison and Wallace avoided the conflicts and power struggles that crush many family businesses. Their secret was in a relationship that had been cultivated since childhood. Wallace adored and respected his older brother Harrison and wanted his approval. Whenever Harrison insisted, Wallace backed down. Wallace's loyalty to Harrison was so strong that at times it made him turn a deaf ear to the advice of his own wife and put his own position in the company at risk.

As their own children grew up, Wallace saw in his youngest son, Michael, the same drive and talent that had made his partnership with Harrison so successful. Wallace encouraged Michael's ambition in the hope that he would one day run McCain Foods. But Harrison found the idea intolerable. He didn't like Michael. In his eyes, Michael compromised his relationship with Wallace and represented a future that excluded him. Ironically, the strengths that Wallace saw in Michael were the same ones he admired in Harrison, a sharp mind and a fierce determination that were unmatched in the family.

When Wallace felt Harrison was actively impeding Michael's advancement within the company, he fought back. For the first time, when Harrison insisted, Wallace didn't back down. Harrison pushed harder and Wallace was forced to choose between his brother and his son. In the end, Wallace made the only choice he felt he could, his son. That choice destroyed a lifelong relationship with Harrison and completely alienated Wallace from the rest of the McCain family. The brothers turned the power they'd used to build McCain Foods against each another. In doing so they destroyed a family legacy one hundred and fifty years in the making.

CHAPTER TWO

It took only ten minutes to walk from the three-room school-house to the McCain home, but Wallace liked to dawdle. He was a tall, wiry twelve-year-old with big ears that stuck out from his short dark hair. As he walked, he kept his hands in his pockets and his eyes firmly trained on the ground. He was thinking about his next cigarette. Wallace usually stole the smokes from his brothers' coat pockets. Sometimes he sold a couple of eggs from the few chickens his family kept to Dolf Lovely's store and used the money to buy a pack. Maybe he should see if old Charlie Antworth had a spare smoke, Wallace thought as he kicked up some dust along the dirt road. He liked Antworth, and Wallace knew he'd never tell his dad.

Charlie Antworth's house was across the road and down a bit from the McCains'. Like all the homes on the road, it was built high up on the sloping banks of the Saint John River. As he sat on the porch taking long drags on his cigarette, Wallace looked out at the valley and the rolling hills that sprawled out in every direction.

It was spring 1942, and the trees were taking on a light green as new leaves emerged from swollen buds. Farmers were already preparing their small plots for the year's potato crop. "Tubers" had always been the biggest crop in Carleton County and Carleton had always been the biggest potato county in New Brunswick.

Things were looking up, Wallace thought. The Depression hadn't touched his family, but he remembered seeing a lot of his friends on "the parish," a kind of local charity that provided meagre help to the destitute. It was the war that had really turned things around. Wallace followed the news from overseas as best he could. A lot of local boys had signed up to go over, and now that the federal government's referendum on conscription had been approved there was no telling how many more would go. Wallace was ready. He was already attending summer cadet camp, and if the war continued, he was joining the navy. That is, if his father would let him.

From where he sat, Wallace could see his father's business across the river in East Florenceville. McCain Produce Co. Ltd. was right in the middle of Main Street. Wallace's dad was Andrew Davis McCain, and he ran one of the biggest businesses in town. Everyone called him "A.D." or "Mr. McCain," never Andrew. A.D. was the local Liberal Party heavyweight, the school board chairman and a member of the Baptist regional committee. His business was dealing potatoes and he'd been doing that for decades, just like his father.

As Wallace looked at the long, low McCain Produce building, he thought about the time it had caught fire in 1933, nearly wiping out the business. Wallace was only three years old when it happened, but people around town still talked about it. The fire had started in one of the offices in A.D.'s building and quickly spread. By the time it was out, seven buildings along Main Street had burned down. There wasn't much anyone could do, since East Florenceville didn't have a fire truck at the time. The volunteer fire brigade could only watch as the buildings burned. It was rumoured that someone in town might have set the blaze, but nothing was ever proven.

A few doors from McCain Produce was the town's most prominent feature, the Exchange Hotel. Though the three-storey building hadn't been used as a hotel for years, in its day it had offered both an elegant dining room and a rowdy bar. Then, when the Baptists opened two churches in town, all the village's bars were closed. Jim Davis bought the hotel, turned the main floor into a general store and rented out the rest of the rooms. It wasn't as grand as it used to be, but the building was still the first thing anyone noticed in East Florenceville.

Davis's was the main store in town, and he let just about anyone run a tab. He sold clothes, hardware and a few groceries.

He was big enough to be part of the Maritime Merchants Alliance, and he printed up a two-page flyer every couple of weeks listing his latest supplies and prices. Wallace preferred Lovely's store across the street. It was smaller and sold ice cream, candy and cigarettes.

Not far from Davis's store was the the office of A.D.'s old rival, Benjamin Franklin Smith. Smith was another produce dealer, and he was also the local Conservative Party operative. Wallace didn't know much about politics, but he knew that in his father's home the Tories were the enemy. A.D. had hung a huge portrait of Liberal Prime Minister William Lyon Mackenzie King in the family dining room just in case anyone forgot. Down from Smith's was Green's Theatre. The cinema was a popular place, especially on Saturday nights when they showed westerns. Wallace's best friend, Alden Lunn, worked there with his father. Alden usually worked in the back with his dad while his mom sold tickets out front.

Wallace didn't go over to East Florenceville very often. No one on the west side of the river did. Some people were still upset that the east side had developed at the expense of the original settlement on the west side. Called Buttermilk Creek, the village was renamed in 1855 to honour Florence Nightingale. Then in the 1870s the government decided to put the railway over on the east side, which was called Cornsilk Flats. Everyone in Florenceville was furious because as soon as the railway opened most of the village's businesses, including McCain Produce, moved across the river. Then the government built a bridge to make it easier for farmers to get their produce to the train station. It was one of the few bridges this side of Fredericton, about ninety miles south. Cornsilk Flats grew at a great rate and changed its name to East Florenceville in 1908. Those left in Florenceville made a brief show of independence— they had their own school, church, post office and even a small café—but it was a futile gesture.

Wallace liked to linger at Charlie Antworth's as long as he could. He knew as soon as he got home he'd have to pick potatoes at his Aunt Hazel's farm or do some chores around the house. Wallace hated chores. But after a few smokes he decided to head home, slowly.

His full name was George Wallace Ferguson McCain. His parents were hoping for a girl when he was born, and they were all set to name the baby Helen, after a cousin who was going to help with the delivery. But when the baby turned out to be a boy, they decided to name him after his grandfather, George, and give him his grandmother's maiden name, Ferguson. They also wanted to recognize Helen somehow so they put her last name, Wallace, in between, and that became the name everyone used.

Wallace was the youngest of six children. He wasn't very close to most of his older brothers and sisters. Marie was ten years older, and Andrew, Bob and Eleanor were off at university while Wallace was growing up. Wallace hadn't been sorry to see Eleanor go. He was still mad about the time last year when she'd finked on him for drinking—a serious crime in their strict Baptist household. He had gone for a ride with Bill Kennett, who owned the village taxi. Kennett stopped to buy a case of beer and offered Wallace a drink. Wallace didn't like beer but took a few swigs anyway. When he got home Eleanor was sitting in the kitchen. She caught a whiff of Wallace's breath and yelled as loud as she could, "Wallace has been drinking!" For a year, Wallace was allowed to go out only with his friend Alden Lunn, because Wallace's mother knew he didn't drink.

Harrison would never get into a mess like that, Wallace thought. He was just three years older than Wallace and every bit his hero. Harrison drank and smoked all the time and never got caught. "Harrison always gets what he wants," Wallace moaned to his friends.

Their father even let Harrison milk the family cow when Bob and Andrew were away at school. A.D. had only one cow and he used it to teach his boys a good business lesson. Whichever son was milking the cow could sell the milk and keep all the proceeds. If the cow had a calf, he could sell that, too, and keep the money. Of course, by the time it was Harrison's turn at the cow, Wallace wanted a cow to milk too. He always wanted to do whatever his big brother was doing. When his dad relented and finally bought Wallace a cow, he discovered that he hated the work. Then Harrison went off to university and Wallace was stuck milking both cows.

He got some consolation when one of the cows had a calf. Wallace fattened the calf for weeks and eventually called the local rover, who roamed from farm to farm looking for calves or pigs to buy and then resell to the slaughterhouse. When the rover finally showed up, A.D. told Wallace to do the selling. As the rover sized up the calf, Wallace put on his best sales routine. "It's a fine calf," he kept saying as the man examined the animal and kicked it gently in the belly. "I'll give you twenty-five dollars," the rover finally said. "No way," said Wallace, not knowing how much the calf was really worth but figuring he had to turn down the first offer. "I want thirty." Wallace kept talking and haggling and the rover finally relented. "I'll give you twenty-seven," he said. Wallace smiled and stuck the bills in his pocket. Then he went out and bought himself a new bike.

Harrison's full name was Harold Harrison McCain, the names coming from two of his father's business associates. Harrison was shorter than Wallace but had a quick smile and his father's crisp blue eyes. Even as a kid, Harrison carried himself with rare self-assurance. When Murray Butler, the local hockey coach, wanted a new hockey rink for the village, Harrison organized a fund-raising drive and helped get the rink built, even though he was only fourteen and didn't even play on the hockey team. Wallace was the hockey player, star right-winger, but Harrison was the McCain kid people remembered.

Harrison wasn't universally loved, however. There were those in the village who thought he was arrogant. His best friend growing up, Don Trafford, remembers how Harrison refused to play with one boy because he came from a poor family.

"I felt sorry for the kid," recalls Trafford, now a stocky farmer who still lives on his family's farm outside Florenceville. "I remember getting in fights with Harrison because he didn't want the Foster boy playing scrub with us. [Harrison's] mother once called my mother because he came home with his shirt ripped up. Fighting is how we eventually became friends."

Trafford also remembers bailing Harrison out of trouble at countless dances. Trafford, Harrison and their buddy Fraser

Stephenson went to all the dances together. They started in nearby Centreville on Thursdays and ended at Ginn's across the border in Maine by Saturday, with stops in Hartland and at the Florenceville Legion along the way. Harrison was a real ladies' man, Trafford recalls, and he had no qualms about asking a girl to dance even if her boyfriend was standing right beside her. "Harrison was very domineering. He never backed down from a fight," remembers Trafford. Sometimes, just getting Harrison home was a chore. "I didn't drink at all. But I remember showing him the stairs more than a few times after a dance because he was so drunk."

At school, Harrison did just about as little work as possible but always passed with ease. Not Wallace. He wouldn't have graduated high school if it hadn't been for a teacher named Dorothy Stickney. She was a former major in the Canadian army and she kept Wallace and his classmates after school for months one year to prepare them for the provincial exams. Every day at 4:00 she made a pot of tea and handed out cigarettes to convince them to stay for the extra instruction. Wallace hated her at the time and had to be dragged to school. But when exam time came, he graduated at the top of his class.

For most of their childhood, Wallace and Harrison were the only McCain children around the house, but they still shared a room and even a double bed. In the McCain household, the only person who didn't share a room was the maid. The McCains were one of the few families around that almost always had live-in help. The "hired girl" lived upstairs in a small bedroom just off a porch that was down the hall from the children's rooms. The McCains usually hired young girls from nearby farms. Mrs. McCain hoped the extra cash would help the maid's family to send her to university, but few ever went. It cost up to one-third of an average yearly salary to send a child to university, and few families around Florenceville earned average salaries.

The McCains were about the only family around that could afford it. A.D. sent all six of his children to university, and at one point he was paying for four children to be in university at the same time. The McCains also had cars, a rarity in an area where many farms didn't even have electricity. A.D. started with a green

Oldsmobile, then a couple of Buicks, a Ford and then a black Cadillac—the first in town.

"Wallace could always get a nice car to drive," recalls Alden Lunn. "When we were going off to dances he would drive five times and I would drive maybe once because I couldn't get the family car very often. It used to bother me a little."

The McCain house was originally the Catholic church rectory, but it was sold to A.D., a devout Baptist, when the church closed. Like many houses in the area it was once covered with metal siding that was later replaced with clapboard. It was white with green shutters and had a small, enclosed verandah. The back yard sloped steeply down to the river, and tucked in one back corner was a small chicken coop.

There were two doors at the front of the house. The door on the left led into a small sitting area and living room. The living room had a smoky fireplace and a beautiful piano. A.D. was a pretty good tenor and sometimes sang to his wife's accompaniment. Off to one side was a small den and an elegant dining room with a plate rail that displayed Wallace's mother's fine china plates.

The other front door led straight into the kitchen. That was the door Wallace, Harrison and nearly every visitor used. The kitchen was dominated by a massive wood stove that always made the room warm and welcoming. In the corner was a big walk-in pantry, which their mother kept well stocked with preserves. A long couch ran against a wall and a variety of chairs were scattered throughout the room to accommodate the family's many visitors.

Whenever they came home, Wallace and Harrison would almost always find their mother in the kitchen cooking. She was usually sitting in the rocking chair near the doorway to the dining room, peeling potatoes with a porcelain bowl sandwiched between her knees. Periodically, she'd get up and open the heavy metal door to the oven. If it was too hot she'd get a small pan of cold water, place it on a rack inside and leave the big door open.

Laura McCain was a small, vibrant woman who ran a tight household. Every day was organized around a strict meal schedule. Breakfast was at eight, lunch at noon and supper at

six—sharp. Only A.D. was allowed to be late to the table.
Wallace and Harrison always knew if they ever got out of line
they would have answer to their mother, not their father. One of
Laura's favourite discipline tactics was to threaten her kids with a
stint in a Catholic reformatory if they didn't behave. Marie and
Eleanor were put on midnight curfew until the day they were
married. "If I was ever late I had to give a full account of my
whereabouts," recalls Marie.

Laura wasn't from Florenceville, but she fit in well. She was
born Laura Blanche Perley in Maugerville, a small town just east
of Fredericton. She came to Florenceville in 1916 as a twenty-
five-year-old teacher. In 1909 she got her education certificate
from the provincial normal school and she went on to spend a
few years teaching in Alberta, where her sister Mary lived. In
1915, she went to Mount Allison Ladies' College in Sackville,
New Brunswick, and took a one-year course for teachers who
wanted to specialize in teaching household science, which in
those days included laundry, sewing and waitressing as well as
the basics of home economics, dietetics and home nursing. Life
at the college was strict. Like all students, Laura had to wear a
bulky uniform and wasn't allowed to be alone with students from
Mount Allison University, the co-ed institution that was affili-
ated with the college. Every visitor to the Ladies' College had to
have a letter of introduction, and students could have their mail
restricted at any time at the request of their parents.

After graduating from college, Laura applied for a job in
Florenceville teaching grades one to three and household science.
She was hired by A.D. who was the school board chairman at the
time. They married two years later. Laura quit teaching after the
wedding and was pregnant with their first child within a month.
She loved telling her children that the wedding had almost not
happened. A.D. had wanted Laura to be rebaptized in the
Baptist church, but Laura refused. Her family was staunch
Anglican. "I've been baptized once and that is enough," she told
A.D. "If you don't like it, then the marriage is off." A.D. relented
when Laura agreed to attend the Baptist church. She even taught
Sunday school, which was one way to make sure her children,
especially the boys, attended church. Not that there was much to

do on Sundays around Florenceville anyway. Things got so boring that Marie often went to the Anglican church service in the afternoon with her friends just for something to do.

As long as A.D. was alive, Laura's focus was strictly on her children and her husband. In fact, the McCains barely knew Laura's family. They seldom went to Maugerville because the journey took nearly a day. Laura didn't have many relatives. Her father, George Perley, died before Wallace was born and her only sister still lived in Alberta. Laura had a brother, William, but he was fifteen years older and was the son of George's first wife, who'd died of consumption.

In fact, Laura came from a long line of indomitable and spirited people. From the McCains' point of view, however, they had one strike against them: they were Tories. Her grandfather, William Edward Perley, spent forty-four years in the New Brunswick legislature, and for a long time he was one of the few legislators to support New Brunswick's entry into Confederation. He was so popular in his home county of Sunbury that in one election he received every vote. One of Laura's cousins, George H. Perley, held several federal cabinet posts, including Secretary of State and Minister of Overseas Forces during World War I. He was also Canada's high commissioner in London and a delegate to the Paris Peace Conference in 1919 and the League of Nations in 1921. Another Perley, Moses Henry Perley, trained as a lawyer in Saint John in 1839 and later became a businessman, surveyor, immigration official and naturalist whose charitable works included setting up a home for orphans.

Perhaps Laura's most famous relative was her great-great-grandfather, Israel Perley, who helped establish Maugerville as one of the first English settlements in New Brunswick in 1763 when he led a band of discharged American soldiers into what was then called Nova Scotia in search of land to settle. Israel was from Boxford, Massachusetts, where his ancestors had lived since they'd arrived in America in 1630 from Wales with the Puritans. His great-grandfather, Thomas, was Boxford's only jurist. He once condemned a local woman to death for being a witch but spared her life when she recanted.

During the American Revolution, Israel's sympathies were

with his American cousins. Most of his family back home was fighting the British, and Perley was eager to help. He and a group of others organized a "liberation army" of New Brunswick settlers and vowed to take Halifax for the Americans. But the rag-tag army Perley supported was crushed by the British at Fort Cumberland. Eventually, they were forced at gunpoint to take the oath of allegiance to the Crown. At the same time, in Massachusetts, Israel's father was part of a delegation of town representatives that was meeting to consider a constitution for their newly liberated country. Ironically, years later, Israel Perley himself was elected to the Nova Scotia legislature.

If Laura was the disciplinarian of the McCain house, A.D. was the quiet taskmaster. A.D. was difficult to get to know well. He was a careful man who always went to work in a dark three-piece suit, stiff white collar and black dress shoes, even if he was heading out to meet a local farmer. A.D. enjoyed walking alone to his office with the family's spaniel, Mike, trailing behind. He also insisted that the family eat dinner together in the dining room every evening, and he never spoke about business at home. He didn't talk about much of anything, but just one word could silence the household. "Whenever he got irritated with Mrs. McCain, he used to just clear his throat and say, 'That's enough, Laura,' and that was it," recalls Harrison's friend Don Trafford.

A.D. was forty years old when he married Laura and was already well established in his business. He started his produce company on August 10, 1909, with his father, Hugh Henderson McCain, and two other investors. The business was first called McCain Prime Co. Ltd. to include the name of one of the other investors, Livingstone C. Prime, a wealthy Saint John merchant. A.D. and his father bought the other investors out on September 16, 1914, and changed the name to McCain Produce Co. Ltd.

Hugh Henderson McCain died six years later of a heart attack on June 1, 1920, at the age of sixty-seven. None of A.D.'s children got to know their grandfather well, but A.D. always had plenty of pictures of his father around the house, and the town was full of stories about "Henry."

Henry was a tall man with a bushy moustache and a natural gift for business. He was the youngest of eight children and an orphan by the time he was twelve. His parents had come to New Brunswick from around Castlefin, Ireland, in the early 1830s. Andrew McCain, Henry's father, was a Presbyterian from the village of Meenahoney in the county of Donegal. Family legend has it that Andrew and his family were driven out of Ireland because of poverty and famine, but this heart-warming story of their struggle to succeed in the New World isn't strictly true.

Andrew's family were well off in Ireland and were likely important local figures. His father, John, was a landowner who had enough money to send his four children to a local school, an unheard of extravagance in a predominantly rural county. Given the history of the area, John McCain's ancestors must have received their land for their support of Oliver Cromwell in his revolt against King Charles I of England in the 1600s. Historically the McCains—meaning "son of John"—are Scottish, and many of Cromwell's strongest supporters were Presbyterian Scots who were rewarded for their loyalty with land in Ireland and a role in helping to settle the Catholic countryside. Andrew is believed to have made a trip back to Ireland after his first trip to Canada in 1826, which suggests he was anything but a pauper. According to one story, Andrew met his wife, Margaret Ferguson, during the second crossing in 1834, and the two married within days of arriving in New Brunswick.

Andrew was twenty-one years old when he made his way up the Saint John River to the Florenceville area in search of good farmland. He bought one hundred acres with a friend, David Bell, on the west side of the river. Like all farmers in the area, many of whom were also from Ireland, Andrew grew potatoes, hay and a few other vegetables. He died on August 2, 1865, seven years after the death of his wife Margaret at the age of forty-seven. When Andrew died, his eight children wrote a short poem in his memory: "Dearest father, thou hast left us, here thy loss we deeply feel. But 'tis God that hath bereft us, He can all our sorrows heal."

Henry took over the farm after his father died and bought up hundreds more acres. At the age of twenty-four, he married Frances Jane Kirkpatrick, the daughter of Joseph Kirkpatrick, another local farmer. Nine years later, Henry bought his brother

John's struggling produce business. Henry was a natural entrepreneur. He quickly turned the company into a large distributor
of hay, oats, pork, poultry, butter and "farm produce of all
kinds," according to his letterhead. He set up a small store and
was one of the first local merchants to pay farmers in cash for
their produce instead of simply bartering goods.

Henry's thriving business caught the attention of Frank
Carvell, a lawyer from nearby Woodstock and Carleton County's
Liberal power broker. In 1895, the provincial government
increased the number of representatives from Carleton County
from two to three. With an election approaching, Carvell started
looking for a bright young candidate to add to the Liberal slate.
He approached Henry, who was thrilled to accept the nomination. Henry knew politicians enjoyed a prominent position in
the community. More important, MLAs had access to lucrative
government contracts, which was good for business.

The Liberals won a big majority in 1895 and all three Liberal
candidates in Carleton County were elected. In 1899 Henry was
reelected on the wave of an even bigger majority, and the
Liberals' hold on power seemed unshakable. Henry's years in the
legislature were undistinguished, however. He went entire ses-
sions without saying a word, and when he did speak it was usually on one of two issues—the evil of alcohol or the evil of giving
women the vote. His only real contribution as a lawmaker was
in ensuring that a government bill regulating the size of farm
fences was adopted.

Outside the legislature, on the other hand, where politics and
business met, Henry was a professional. He mastered the art of
pork-barrelling and swinging government projects to Carleton
County. One of his biggest coups came in the late 1890s. Henry
had been lobbying the government for years to build a new toll
bridge at Hartland, a few miles south of Florenceville. Farmers,
he said, needed another bridge to get across the Saint John River
so they could get their produce on trains to market. The government finally agreed and awarded the contract to the newly
formed Hartland Bridge Co.—a local company that just happened to be partly owned by Henry McCain, Frank Carvell and a
few other local Liberals. The government also gave the company

the contract to collect the tolls. And Henry managed to ensure that it was exempt from all provincial and local taxes. The covered bridge, considered the world's longest, still stands as one of Hartland's major tourist attractions.

Eventually the political payoffs became too tempting for Henry, and by his second term in office he became downright greedy. At the beginning of the Boer War in the late 1800s, the Liberal government in Ottawa announced plans to send hay and other produce to support the British army. Henry managed to get a huge contract to supply hay for the project. He quickly expanded his operations and soon had two steam presses, the first in the county, and more than thirty employees working double shifts. He made so much money in the first year of the contract that other produce dealers, especially Liberals, began to gripe. Why couldn't they get a piece of the action? they complained to Carvell, who was still considered the political godfather of the county.

Carvell was sympathetic and began lobbying Ottawa to divide up the contract more generously. He also asked Henry to spread some of his good fortune among some of the other party faithful. But Henry refused. It was his deal and his business. Tension mounted, and soon the issue spilled over to the Liberal nomination meeting for the federal election. Henry had been considered front-runner for the nomination and he badly wanted the federal seat; members of Parliament had even more prestige and more lucrative business connections. But the angry produce dealers swung the nomination to Carvell.

Furious, Henry refused to contribute any money to Carvell's campaign. That irritated party officials in Ottawa, who were getting tired of all the bickering in New Brunswick. Henry was told that if he wanted to keep his hay contract, he'd better cough up a donation. Still Henry refused, and the party and Carvell felt it was time to teach him a lesson. Carvell set up a company called the New Brunswick Hay Co. Ltd. and Ottawa gave him the contract. Henry retaliated by trying to buy up as much hay as possible in order to force Carvell to deal with him. As Henry started buying up hay, Carvell turned to B.F. Smith of Florenceville, the only other large hay producer in the county, and the two cut a deal. Smith, who was a Tory and knew he had no chance at the federal contract, was delighted by the chance to knock down his cross-town rival.

As both McCain and Carvell were madly buying up hay, the war suddenly ended and the federal government cancelled the program. Henry was stuck with a mountain of hay and massive debts. He had to call A.D. home from the prestigious Horton Academy in Wolfville, Nova Scotia, because he couldn't afford the fees any more and he needed his only son to help sort out the mess. It was the ultimate humiliation for the McCains. The fact that A.D. was even attending a school as well regarded as Horton was big news in the village, and his every trip home was dutifully reported in the local paper. Meanwhile, Carvell escaped with only minor losses because McCain had been buying up much more hay. He also won the seat in the federal election and represented the county in Ottawa for years. Henry and A.D. slowly managed to pull out of the financial ruin Carvell had caused but they never forgot. Henry was so outraged at his fellow Liberals that he didn't stand for reelection in the provincial elections of 1903, although it's doubtful he would have been nominated.

Revenge for the McCains came during the 1908 provincial elections. The Liberals were facing their first defeat in sixteen years and Carvell turned to the McCains for help. No chance, Henry and A.D. said. They refused to do anything unless the party reimbursed them for some of the losses from the hay contract. Carvell balked and neither side budged. Finally, early on election day, a mysterious package arrived for the McCains on the mail train. No one knows what was in the package but, according to *The Daily Gleaner* of Fredericton: "The result was that ten minutes after the delivery of the mail Henry and Andrew were in their team making for the poll. They cast solid Liberal votes, and from that day to this Carvell and the McCains have been reconciled." Whatever the payoff was, it wasn't enough. The Tories were swept into office with a wide majority.

A.D. never went back to school after the hay fiasco. Instead, he vowed to reestablish his father's produce business. By the time Henry died in 1920, A.D. had accomplished that goal. He had set up McCain Produce and established himself as every bit the shrewd, tough dealer his father was. He had to be. By the 1920s, the produce business had changed dramatically. In 1922, the American government moved to protect its own growers and slapped huge tariffs on potatoes imported from Canada. That crippled Carleton County farmers, who relied on potatoes for their biggest source of income. McCain, like all dealers, had to look elsewhere for markets. Within a year, he was shipping potatoes to Cuba, but it wasn't easy. A.D. had to find Cuban brokers, hire ships and then compete with cheaper U.S. imports. The competition was brutal.

Fred Hatfield recalls the time his father Hebert and a group of dealers went to Boston to salvage a shipment of potatoes. Potato prices had fallen suddenly and the dealers' spuds were stuck in rail cars along the dockside. The railway was demanding payment for storage and Hatfield, A.D. and the other dealers jumped in a car and headed to Boston. While they were driving, a frost hit parts of the United States and potato prices jumped back up, but A.D. and the other dealers had no way of knowing. As they started a late-night poker game at their hotel, a phone call came from a buyer looking for as many potatoes as possible. By chance, Hatfield took the call and made a deal to sell all of his potatoes stuck on the rail cars. He returned to the poker game without saying a word. He then suggested that instead of betting money, the men should play for their potatoes. Feeling they had little to lose, the others agreed. Hatfield cleaned up. When the others found out about the price increase the next day, Hatfield smiled and promised to pay expenses for the trip home.

A.D. ran a tight business and was always looking for ways to cut costs or at least ensure stable prices. One of the best ways to do both was to co-operate with other dealers. By working together as a group they could buy in bulk and have more clout against the large operators when it came to making deals. But A.D. didn't trust many of his competitors and they didn't trust him. Alliances between dealers were routinely formed and broken when one dealer couldn't resist undercutting his partners. A.D. once broke a complicated arrangement with Guy Porter Co. of Perth, one of the biggest dealers in the county. Under the deal, both companies were to take turns guaranteeing each other's sales in Cuba. Whenever it was A.D.'s turn to win the sale, Porter would purposely bid ten cents a barrel higher; when it was Porter's turn, A.D. would bid higher. But the deal fell apart after a few shipments when A.D. undercut Porter for a quick sale.

The government tried for years to figure out what the dealers were doing and if it was legal. The federal Department of Labour even started an investigation in 1925 to determine the extent of the price-fixing and collusion. After months of hearings, all the investigators could conclude was that the dealers were price-fixing but doing it so ineffectively that they were hurting both themselves and the farmers.

Relations between dealers and farmers were never very good. Whenever a group of dealers did manage to fix prices the added profits were rarely passed on. When a group of local farmers set up a co-operative to arrange their own sales to Cuba, A.D. and the other dealers drove them out of business. "It is evident that the potato situation in New Brunswick is absolutely controlled by the shippers and that the potato growers receive practically no benefit from market advantages," the federal report said.

A.D., like many dealers, held a tight financial grip on farmers. He sold farmers fertilizer and equipment in the spring in return for potatoes in the fall. The arrangement left many farmers perpetually in debt to A.D. Moreover, few farmers had heated storage space, which meant they had to sell their crop as soon as it was harvested. That provided an instant glut for A.D. and the other dealers, who could snap up cheap potatoes and then rent heated storage space and sell the spuds later at a higher price.

Once, A.D. took over the collection of farm loans from a friend who'd died. As A.D. leaned on the farmers to pay, one man near Bristol gave up. He packed up his family and drove to A.D.'s office. "He handed him the keys, and A.D. said, 'It's not really worth that much,'" says the farmer's son, who still fears reprisals from the McCains if he is identified. "My father reached over the desk and began choking him. I had to pull him off or he would have killed him. That farm was all my dad had."

Like other dealers, A.D. also controlled a large acreage of farmland, leaving little room for smaller producers. "There are some of those big fellows like McCain who will put in one hundred or one hundred and twenty-five acres and he runs the little fellow out," testified a farmer named Upton Squires during the federal investigation. "He raised over eleven thousand barrels this year, they tell me. That isn't right. He is killing off the little fellows."

For all A.D.'s power, he was just a bit player compared to Guy Porter in Perth, William Pirie in Grand Falls, Hebert Hatfield in Hartland (whose son Richard would later become premier) or even his old rival B.F. Smith. In order to fly higher, A.D. knew he'd have to enter the political arena. Like his father, A.D. knew the importance of political office, and he tried desperately to get elected. But this wasn't the 1800s, when a tap on the shoulder by Carvell was enough to ensure a loyal and obedient Liberal a long political career. The Tories ran things in Carleton County now, and A.D. was going to have to scrap.

His first and biggest political fight was against B.F. Smith in 1916. The race was actually a by-election but it became one of the most notorious battles in New Brunswick history. Smith had just been appointed Minister of Public Works by Premier James Kidd Flemming, who was also from Carleton County. At the time, cabinet nominees had to stand for reelection in their riding before officially joining cabinet. Reelection was usually just a formality, but this time the Liberals had the Tories on the ropes and were hoping to use Smith's cabinet nomination as a referendum on the government's performance. The Tories were plagued by scandals, including a bizarre project to help the British army in World War I by donating potatoes. What should have been a noble gesture had turned into a political nightmare when it was discovered that the government was buying potatoes only from Tory farmers. A.D. blasted Smith and Flemming throughout the campaign over the scandal. His picture was on the front page of *The Carleton Sentinel* every week. The paper was blatantly Liberal and it didn't hurt A.D. that his father had been one of its co-owners. In spite of the scandals, however, Smith won easily.

The two met again a few months later in the general election, and even though the Liberals won a huge majority provincially, Smith won again in Carleton County. That was A.D.'s last campaign. If he couldn't win a seat in a Liberal landslide, he knew he could never win. Besides, two defeats were enough for the local party establishment, and they looked for a new face. Smith, meanwhile, went on to become a senator and built the biggest house in East Florenceville.

His losses notwithstanding, A.D.'s run at politics still gave him rare standing in the community, and he was long considered the local Liberal power broker. In many ways he became something like a permanent mayor of Florenceville. Villages didn't have mayors at the time because the local government was run by the county council, but A.D. served as school board chairman for over forty years, he co-ordinated assistance for people in need during the Depression, and he was always looking for a new business to back. A.D. was also often called on to help the town deal with the provincial government. Reg Tweedale remembers meeting A.D. after World War II to negotiate the sale of the village's tiny power station. The government had created a provincial power agency and was trying to bring all of the small rural stations under its control. Tweedale had just been hired to co-ordinate the purchases. A.D. "was a tough bargainer," recalls Tweedale. "He wanted a lot of money considering it was a makeshift operation and not worth very much. He walked away two or three times. He had all the angles and he worked them. I think we finally bought it for a few thousand dollars but it was a good price for the town."

The prestige and position conferred on him by the town were important to A.D., and he liked to throw his weight around a little. He would routinely show up at the bank a few minutes after it closed to avoid standing in line, relishing the fact that the bank manager would always be pleased to open the door and serve him.

A.D. hoped that his sons would climb higher than he had, and his particular wish was that one of them would become a doctor. That had been his own dream until he was called home because of his father's bankruptcy. In A.D.'s eyes, medicine was a real profession, while produce dealing was just a business.

His first hope was his oldest son. Andrew dutifully tried a couple of brief stints at the University of New Brunswick and Acadia but eventually dropped out and took a job with McCain Produce. Andrew had been born with a serious heart condition that prevented him from engaging in any vigorous physical activity. A.D. was afraid to push him, and so Andrew became the only McCain child not to graduate from university. A good-looking, charming man, Andrew was always considered the closest thing Florenceville had to a playboy. He joined all the local clubs—from the Masons and Elks to the curling club—and he spent most of his time chasing women, playing poker with his buddies and drinking, lots of drinking.

"If there was a town drunk, he was it," said Alan Morris, who grew up with Andrew's kids. "People like him gave me a bad impression about drinking."

On July 26, 1947, Andrew married a farmer's daughter, Marjorie Luella Pearson, who worked as a secretary at McCain Produce. The two had six children, but that never slowed Andrew down. He kept up the life of a "dandy" right up until the night he died.

Knowing Andrew's limitations, A.D. pushed his ambition on to his second son, Bob. Bob would come the closest to realizing his father's goal.

CHAPTER THREE

Bob McCain sat brooding on a train to Sussex, New Brunswick. It was Sunday, May 21, 1944, and Bob was on his way to spend fifteen days training at a military base, a compulsory service for all university students. This was Bob's first camp, and he wasn't sure what to expect. All he knew was that no one liked the training camp, not the students or the military. The military were contemptuous of college students— kids with a lot of attitude and no common sense—the students saw the military as overbearing, oppressive and pointless.

Bob was a medical student at Dalhousie University in Halifax, Nova Scotia, and students were supposed to attend camps in the same province as their university. But Bob had heard that the Sussex camp was easier than the Nova Scotia camps and he'd asked the military if he could switch. Since he'd attended the University of New Brunswick before going to medical school, the army, after a lot of wrangling and paperwork, reluctantly agreed.

Bob quickly discovered that his information about Sussex was wrong. Sussex was one of the toughest camps in the Maritimes. Students were taken on night marches with full packs, did countless hours of drill and took part in intensive weapons training. Part of that training involved firing mortar guns, and Bob was among the first group to take mortar training that spring. There was little if any preparation for the training: students were simply marched out to a line of mortar guns along an embankment and told to fire.

Bob took the first gun in line that day with his friend, Walter

Ross. He tossed the mortar shell into the gun and hunched over beside it. Ross pulled the trigger. But something went wrong— the shell blasted out of the gun and exploded less than a foot out of the barrel. The explosion boomed across the valley. In a second Bob was knocked sideways. Shrapnel ripped through his left arm and hand. Ross was blown backwards. His chest was blown apart, and shrapnel shredded his arms. Behind them a line of students screamed out as bits of the bomb sprayed out from the blast.

As Ross lay slumped near the gun, Bob struggled to his feet to help him. Donal Baird, who was manning the gun beside them, staggered to his feet to help while dozens of soldiers and students ran over. It seemed to take forever for the ambulance to get up the embankment to the scene.

"Bob was standing there with his arm just hanging loose," recalls Baird. "I didn't think he would live."

Bob and Ross were taken to the Sussex Military Hospital. Ross died two days later. Bob was luckier—he survived. Extensive surgery on his arm and hand meant months of confinement while he recovered in hospital. The accident left him with partial use of his left hand and serious injuries to his left forearm. He would also have periodic seizures for the rest of his life.

The accident was a horrible twist of fate. Without the use of his hand, Bob's plans to become a surgeon were crushed. A successful student, he was always considered the McCain with the brightest future. Now, without the full use of his left hand, Bob could see no reason to continue in medical school, and Dalhousie's medical teaching staff agreed. Shortly after returning home, Bob received a letter from the school telling him that, in light of his recent accident, they saw no reason for him to return.

The accident devastated A.D., who had great hopes for Bob. In spite of his sentiments, however, A.D. was first and foremost a realist. If his son wasn't going to medical school then he was going to work for the family business. A.D. gave Bob a job at McCain Produce for forty-five dollars a week, the same wage given to every other employee. The job turned out to be Bob's true calling—perhaps the accident had been a blessing in disguise. He found that he loved farming, horses and cattle and was happy to be back home. He also became a champion horse and cattle breeder. Bob's instincts for farming and the business of farming were respected throughout the county, and he was often asked to serve on provincial committees dealing with agricultural issues.

Being at home also improved Bob's health. His recuperation was overseen by his old friend Dr. John Lockhart, who ran a clinic in nearby Bath. Bob and Lockhart were avid followers of the local political scene. Bob was a die-hard Liberal like his father, while Lockhart was a true-blue Tory, and they routinely bet on the elections. In 1948, when the Tories won the provincial election seat in Carleton County, Bob had to pay up by taking Lockhart and his wife out for dinner in Maine.

Unbeknownst to Bob, Lockhart had invited along a young nurse who had just started working for him at the clinic. Her name was Isobel Rosemary Baird, but she introduced herself to Bob as Rosemary. She was twenty-three years old and had only been in the area a few weeks. She'd come from Saint John, New Brunswick, and had trained under her father, a physician at Saint John General Hospital. A nursing colleague had told her about a job at Lockhart's clinic in Bath and Rosemary had jumped at the opportunity. She thought it would give her some independence and the chance to break away from her father's watchful eye.

Rosemary was one of the most interesting women Bob had ever met. To be working in a tiny community so far from home at the age of twenty-three was an unusual act of independence at that time. It was a move that concerned Rosemary's mother, who wondered why her daughter would want to leave home and move to a place where she didn't know anyone. But Rosemary was a Baird, and she felt she had a lot to live up to. Her father, Dr. Kenneth Baird, was one of the most skilled and innovative physicians in Saint John. He was constantly challenging the medical establishment and experimenting with new treatments.

Before Rosemary was born, her father had spent five years working in remote parts of China as a medical missionary. Rosemary's mother gave birth to three of her six children in China and Rosemary would have been born there as well, but the family returned to Saint John, New Brunswick, just before her birth. After Rosemary was born, her father bought an old sea captain's home near the dockyards. The men who worked there often couldn't afford medical services, the work was hazardous, and their injuries were often so severe that even if they could get medical attention it was usually too late. Rosemary remembers many evenings as a child when an injured dock worker would show up at the Baird home bleeding from a vicious wound. Her father never turned anyone away and would accept any form of payment, which was more often than not a basket of food.

Bob was taken with Rosemary's altruistic approach to the world. He was a great believer in contributing to the community and serving others, and he was impressed with the selfless values Rosemary had grown up with.

Rosemary was in love with Bob from the first time she saw him. But there was a catch. She was already engaged to a doctor in Nova Scotia. That made both Rosemary and Bob hesitant. However, the two continued to see a lot of each other because of Bob's regular trips to Lockhart for treatment. Four months later, Rosemary fell sick and returned to Saint John for an appendectomy. Bob found he missed her so much that he visited her nearly every weekend. After she recovered, she broke off the engagement and the two decided to marry as quickly as possible.

Three months later, on December 28, 1949, their wedding was held in the Bairds' old sea captain's house in Saint John. Bob asked his older brother, Andrew, to be his best man. The wedding was anything but a huge success, though. Unfortunately for Bob and Rosemary, their families regarded one another with suspicion. The Bairds thought the McCains were farmers; Bob was an unsuitable match for Rosemary, the daughter of a prominent physician. "They weren't professional, and that kind of marriage was difficult in those days," recalls Donal Baird, Rosemary's brother, who was also with Bob at the time of his mortar accident. For their part, the McCains were insulted by the Bairds' condescending attitude. Bob was the family hero, and the McCains found the idea that they were not in the same social class as Bob's bride intolerable.

Things only got worse when, after a short honeymoon in Quebec, Bob and Rosemary moved into a small house in Florenceville across from A.D. and Laura. Rosemary's strong personality irritated the McCains. She battled with her mother-in-law over everything from child-rearing to housekeeping. "I would just tell her that's not what I am doing, and I don't think she liked that too much," recalls Rosemary.

For Rosemary, the McCains were overwhelming. They were everywhere. Her husband worked at McCain Produce, she spent most holidays with her in-laws and their home was owned by her father-in-law, who held the $4,500 mortgage. But Rosemary did what she could to preserve her own identity. She kept up her membership in the United Church in spite of the fact that the McCains were devout Baptists. And she worked hard to keep in touch with her own family, in spit of the difficulty. Rosemary remembers only a few times when the McCains were supportive of her need to see her family. Once, three years after she married Bob, Rosemary caught a rare form of polio and was desperate to get home to her father. She knew his innovative treatments would arrest the disease in its early stages. To Rosemary's surprise, her father-in-law pulled up outside her house in his Cadillac. The Cadillac was A.D.'s pride and joy and no one else ever touched it. But A.D. was anxious to get Rosemary home to her father and the Cadillac was the quickest way he knew how. Rosemary was grateful and never forgot the gesture of support.

Rosemary's strained relationships with her in-laws compounded her feelings of isolation. The only in-law Rosemary really liked was A.D. To this day she has fond memories of him bouncing her daughter on his knee and taking the children for drives in his Cadillac. But she didn't get along with Bob's brothers. The way she saw it, Andrew was little more than a "gofer" for his father. She was undecided about Wallace at first, but the two would later clash bitterly, and she argued constantly with Harrison. Fortunately, Harrison and Wallace were away at university most of the time.

Neither Harrison nor Wallace had wanted to go to university. Wallace had told all of his school friends he was going to join the navy, and Harrison wanted to drive a truck. But with Bob unable to finish his schooling, A.D. put the pressure on his youngest sons to earn a degree, preferably in medicine. Without discussing it with them, A.D. enrolled both boys at Acadia University.

"I didn't even know I was going until three or four days before I left," remembers Harrison. "He just said, 'You're enrolled, the tuition is paid and you are going.'"

Acadia University, in Wolfville, Nova Scotia, had a formidable reputation. It had been a Baptist college for more than a hundred years and, more importantly, had an affiliation with A.D.'s old school, the prestigious Horton Academy. Academic standards were high and students were expected to keep up, even when some of the textbooks were written in German. It was a popular choice for well-connected families. New Brunswick oil tycoon K.C. Irving sent his kids to Acadia, as did A.D.'s old business nemesis and rival Hebert Hatfield.

Harrison started his freshman year in the fall of 1945. It was quite a time to be at any university in Canada. Campuses were suddenly a sea of khaki as returning soldiers took advantage of the government's free tuition offer and inundated university programs. Acadia's student population more than doubled to about a thousand that year. The added students put pressure on the university's resources. Hotels in Wolfville were leased to the school for student residence and the school even commandeered some army homes to house more students and to use as classrooms. The university also rushed construction of a new four-storey dormitory that was supposed to house 150 students. Though only one floor was finished in September 1945, a makeshift roof was put on and Harrison, along with other freshmen, was assigned to a two-man room. The long low building was officially called the War Memorial Residence but everyone called it the "Barrax."

The soldiers dramatically changed campus life and gave Wolfville a vibrancy it had never known before. Most were far older than the other incoming freshmen and had a vastly different outlook on life. For a seventeen-year-old kid like Harrison, who'd rarely been away from Florenceville, it must have seemed incredible to meet young men who only months earlier had been fighting in Europe. "The veterans worked hard and they played hard," recalls Stuart Eagles, a classmate of Harrison's.

Playing hard wasn't easy at Acadia. The university was still run by the Northern Baptist Institute and alcohol was forbidden on campus. That didn't sit well with the veterans, who quickly organized trips to nearby Kentville, where beer was twenty cents a bottle. Every Friday, scores of parched Acadia "Axemen" lined the road to Kentville trying to hitch a ride. Sometimes they'd buy a couple of cases of beer or a drum of rum. With so many veterans on campus, school officials often gave up trying to enforce the rules.

"I remember hitchhiking back from Kentville once and the president drove by," said Eagles. "I had just bought three cases of beer. He stopped, opened his trunk and helped me put the beer in. Then he gave me a ride to the Barrax."

Harrison fit right in. He joined the soccer team, the pre-med club and was a fixture at school pep rallies. Everyone was wild about "Harri."

"Confidence and initiative are a good portion of the personality that is Harri's," said the school yearbook the year he graduated. "Perhaps it's an inter class hockey game or perhaps it's a union meeting, whatever, he's in there with all the scrap and love of a square deal that he can muster."

"He was a real leader," recalls Eagles. "You could see it then. He had this booming voice and you could always hear him coming."

Eagles says Harrison could almost always be found in the middle of a group of friends smoking and talking at "Mom's," an old house that was converted into a café. Mom's was a popular hangout for students, in part because the owner let the kids run a tab. If he wasn't at Mom's, Harrison was organizing excursions to Kentville for a case of beer or hiding empty bottles in his room from the dean of men. The motto he chose for his graduation picture said it all: "Get thee behind me, Satan...and push."

In spite of his heavy socializing, Harrison always managed to keep up his schoolwork and pass every course. But he was no academic, and he gave up any aspirations to become a doctor after his first year.

In the fall of his senior year Harrison led a group of students in a project to build a student union building. Acadian students had talked about the project for nearly ten years but nothing had ever happened. Harrison felt the students had waited long enough.

"You had to go off campus to get a cup of coffee or have a ciga-rette," he remembers. "So a group of us talked it over one day and we said what we should do is build a student union building."

Just as he had when he built the hockey rink in Florenceville, Harrison became the chief organizer. He coaxed students to donate whatever they could and sent hundreds of letters to par-ents asking for donations. He persuaded the university to fund part of the project. Within a few months, enough money was raised to pay for architectural drawings, and by the fall of 1950, Acadia's two-storey, brick Students' Union Building was finished. It cost $30,000, and nearly all of the money had come from Harrison's fund-raising drive.

Harrison had graduated by the time the building was finally completed, and he was invited back as a special guest for the opening ceremonies. He didn't go. Seeing the completed building didn't interest him. It was the process that counted, not the result. He'd enjoyed shaping and creating the project, and he was satisfied that he'd left his mark, but he had long since moved on to other things.

Wallace arrived at Acadia when Harrison was starting his third year, but, unlike his brother, Wallace didn't fit in. He was a shy kid who had never strayed far from Florenceville, and now he was terribly homesick. The freedom of university seemed almost too much. Wallace seemed destined to remain on the periphery. He joined the football team not as a player but as the manager. It was a job that was always assigned to an incoming freshman because no one else wanted to do it. Wallace hated the job and he grudgingly hauled water for players, sorted equip-ment and made sure everyone had all the gear they needed before every game. He was later put on the school's athletic council, an administrative body that oversaw campus sports. It was the kind of detail job Wallace would have all his life.

One thing that hadn't changed from Florenceville was Wallace's longing to keep up with his big brother. He moved into the "Barrax" in his second year to be close to Harrison. He joined the sophomore hockey team, and he discovered from Harrison that drinking was one way to make friends. He'd never been very interested in drinking as a kid in Florenceville, but at

Acadia, with hundreds of veterans around, someone who didn't drink might as well have had leprosy. Soon, Wallace became the organizer for the trips to Kentville, and his room was littered with empty beer bottles and under constant surveillance by the dean. His strategy worked. Wallace and Harrison became closer than ever and were often side by side.

Unlike Harrison, however, Wallace couldn't mix good times and schoolwork. He failed two out of five courses in his first year and was on the verge of being expelled. He failed three out of five the next year. Harrison was constantly trying to coax Wallace to do just enough work to pass.

"Well, you're down there, the bill is all paid," Harrison used to tell his little brother. "You don't have to lead the class but you'd better try and get through the courses."

Harrison graduated in 1949 with no idea what he would do next. He didn't feel there was room for him at McCain Produce since his older brothers, Andrew and Bob, were working there full time. So he started looking through employment ads in the Halifax newspaper. He came across one from a drug company called Mowat and Moore. The company was looking for "detail men" to keep druggists and doctors supplied with the latest drugs. The ad said company executives would be in Halifax for interviews the next week. Harrison borrowed a car from a friend and headed to Halifax to talk his way into an interview.

"They said, 'You can't get this job, you've got to be in chemistry, you've had no pharmacology, you're not a graduate in pharmacy. So you know you can't do this job,'" recalls Harrison. "I said I'm exactly the right man for the job."

Displaying the chutzpah that would catapult him to the top of the business world in later years, Harrison made the company a deal. He would work for free for six months. If the company wasn't satisfied, it could fire him. If they were satisfied, they would hire him and give him the back pay. "It won't cost you a nickel," Harrison told them. He got the job. "They didn't ask me to do that deal," he recalls. "They just thought I was so cheeky that I got the job."

Harrison was given eastern Ontario as his territory. He was kept on after the six-month period, but the job bored him and he left after about two years. "The hours were awful short," he remembers. "You couldn't see a druggist before nine-thirty in the morning because he was doing his cash from the night before. Then you start to see the doctors around one-thirty and you are all through by four-thirty." The offices were also closed Wednesday afternoons and Saturdays.

Harrison left to take a job with K.C. Irving's Irving Oil. From a single gas station in a tiny New Brunswick town, Irving would create one of the biggest corporate empires in the Maritimes. His gas stations lined highways across the region and his business tentacles reached into shipping and later forest products and newspapers. Harrison knew K.C. Irving's sons from Acadia and kept in touch with them after graduating. The Irving boys encouraged their dad to take a look at this McCain kid.

"They were telling their dad what a great salesman I was," says Harrison. "So he must have believed them. A general manager [from Irving] called me a couple of times. I didn't want to go back to New Brunswick. Mr. Irving called me and came up [to Ontario] and saw me."

Irving didn't usually interview potential employees, but he made an exception for Harrison. He must have decided the McCain kid was worth the trip, because he offered him a job as a salesman, and Harrison accepted. Harrison grew to admire Irving and his way of doing business. Even now he refers to him always as "Mr. Irving." Working for K.C. was a business lesson no school could have ever taught him. Irving had started with next to nothing and by the 1950s had built up a small empire through fierce determination and a work ethic that bordered on maniacal.

K.C. was a perfectionist who fretted over every detail. Irving constantly pushed Harrison's limits. Once, Harrison was desperately trying to sell Irving fuel to a large power station. Finally, after eighteen months, he closed the deal and called Irving to give him the good news. "I got the fuel contract," Harrison said excitedly. Irving paused and then quietly asked, "What about the lubricating oil?"

"Mr. Irving wasn't satisfied if you got 95 percent," says Harrison. "He'd be intensely worried about the other 5 percent."

Along with his business acumen, Harrison also admired the

way Irving managed his public image. Though he owned virtually every media outlet in New Brunswick, K.C. rarely spoke to the press. Throughout the years, Irving had created an image as a tireless, shrewd and sometimes rough businessman, but Harrison told friends that much of Irving's image was phony. Rumour had it that Irving got to work by 7:00 a.m. but Harrison discovered that this wasn't true. More often than not, Irving simply called staff members early from home just to keep them on their toes. It was a trick that worked. His staff was always at the office by 7:00.

"I'd say Irving was the man Harrison most admires," says Harrison's friend Jim Coutts, former principal secretary to Pierre Trudeau. Harrison "thought K.C. had built a good image of himself. Irving was careful to establish certain theories about himself. That really impressed Harrison."

While Harrison was enjoying success and promotion at Irving Oil, Wallace was facing expulsion from Acadia. It was the end of his second year. He had failed most of his courses and was constantly in trouble with school officials for drinking. Being expelled didn't matter to Wallace. He hated school and he didn't want to go back. But he was afraid of his father's reaction.

In a desperate attempt to resolve the situation Wallace decided to tell his father that Acadia had assigned him an awful dorm room. He practised his pitch for days before finally getting up enough nerve to try it out on A.D. Wallace walked into his father's office one afternoon and sat down in front of A.D.'s desk. With his eyes firmly fixed on the floor, he informed his father about the dorm assignment. He explained that the room was so intolerable and would have such a detrimental effect on both his ability to study and his life at Acadia that he really thought it would be in his best interests not to return. In fact, it would be best all around, Wallace told his father, if he just stayed home.

A.D. was shocked and shook his head in disgust. "Don't worry," he told Wallace. "I'll phone the dean right now." Before Wallace could respond, his father was angrily reproaching the dean on the phone for assigning Wallace such an unacceptable dorm room. His father was barely two minutes into his rant when the dean said something that silenced him. Wallace felt the blood drain out of his face. The next ten minutes felt like an hour. All he heard his father say was, "I see…is that right…I understand." His father hung up the phone and looked at Wallace for a long time without saying a word. Then to his surprise and delight, Wallace heard his father say, "I think it's best if you don't go back to Acadia."

But A.D. wasn't going to let Wallace off the hook that easily. He insisted that Wallace finish his degree somewhere else. And he enrolled Wallace in the University of New Brunswick that fall.

Wallace didn't have any more success concentrating on his studies at UNB than he'd had at Acadia. "I remember the first time I saw him [at UNB]," recalls Tim Bliss, a close friend and former executive at McCain Foods. "Wallace was drunk and raising hell at a football game."

At UNB Wallace finally got his chance to take a crack at the navy. He joined the University Naval Training Division and spent a summer on a supply ship sailing from British Columbia to Halifax via the Panama Canal. It was a wonderful experience, and it made him realize how desperate he was to get into the real world. He finally figured out that the quickest way to get out of school was to pass his courses. He successfully completed the year at UNB and even took a course over the summer to make up lost ground. He then discovered that he could graduate a semester earlier if he switched to Mount Allison University in Sackville, and so he enrolled there in the fall of 1950.

When he arrived in Sackville, Wallace deliberately chose a room off campus in the hopes that it would prevent him from being distracted. He couldn't, however, bring himself to miss the first fall dance. Wallace was new on campus and felt the dance might be a good way to meet people, especially women. As he stood near the wall overlooking the crowd, a young girl caught his eye. She was standing talking with a group of friends at the far end of the dance hall. It was her expression that captured Wallace's attention: she looked as uncomfortable as he felt. Wallace found out that her name was Margaret Laura Anne Norrie. She was in her first year at Mount Allison and she was just fifteen years old. She'd come to Mount A. after graduating from Havergal College, a prestigious private girls' school in Toronto.

As the first dance started, Wallace walked up to the group

and managed to get himself introduced to Margaret by a mutual friend. The introductions over, Wallace asked her if she would like to dance. "Well, I just said I was going to dance with Bob," Margaret replied politely. She would have gladly danced with Wallace later but her manners wouldn't permit her to go back on her promise. His discomfort heightened, Wallace abruptly turned away. "Fine," he said. "I won't ask you again, then." It was an empty threat. Wallace did ask Margaret out again, but it wasn't for another four years.

Wallace wasn't the only one to have his head turned by an attractive woman that fall. A few months after the dance, Harrison called Wallace and announced that he was coming for a visit. Wallace soon discovered that Harrison had ulterior motives. He was coming to meet the daughter of the premier of New Brunswick, Marion MacGregor McNair, known to everyone as "Billie." Harrison had heard that Billie was attending Mount Allison and he was curious to meet her. Just as he would be years later, Harrison was interested in powerful people in a way that Wallace never would be. Harrison was even more eager to meet her after Wallace told him she was the best-looking girl on campus. "Get me a date," Harrison told his little brother.

Harrison was not disappointed when he met Billie. She was both beautiful and elegant. Just twenty-three years old, she had a sophistication beyond her years. At the time they met, Billie was a senior, studying fine arts. Her childhood had taught her to be quiet and reserved about her feelings. And Harrison, a dynamic extrovert, was intrigued.

Perhaps the attraction was rooted in their differences. Harrison's childhood had encouraged him to go out into the world and take it on. Billie's had taught her to shy away from it. She had been forced early on in childhood to create an acceptable public persona and never rock the boat or embarrass the family. Her father was a Rhodes scholar, a successful lawyer who served as the provincial Minister of Justice, party leader and then premier. Her mother was mentally ill and spent much of Billie's childhood in and out of hospitals. As a result, Billie was left in the care of housekeepers, her older brother and her grandmother. It was while she was under the care of her grandmother that she was given the nickname "Billie": her grandmother thought she looked more like a boy than a girl.

Even in the family's private moments, Billie would find herself on a public stage. Her brother John remembers when she was a young girl and went on a fishing trip with her father. She caught a huge salmon and was grinning from ear to ear with delight. To celebrate Billie's success a photograph was taken of her proudly holding the fish. "It was one of the few times she was truly exuberant," John says. The photo, which in any other home would simply have gone into the family album, ended up on every provincial tourism pamphlet in New Brunswick.

When Harrison met Billie he was very much aware of the public image that accompanied success. As a child he had watched his father create a social and business profile that was feared and respected. The man he worked for, K.C. Irving, had spent a lifetime cultivating a social and business image that made him a legend in the Maritimes. Billie's father had done the same thing through his political success. And because her mother's illness had kept her out of the public eye, Billie had been an important part of her father's political image. Her connections, experience and social skills heightened Billie's appeal to Harrison. She could open the door to a world he'd never encountered in Florenceville. And she did, when she took him home to meet her father.

The rapport between Harrison and Billie's father was mutual. John McNair admired Harrison's vitality and energy and welcomed him as an equal. He was convinced Harrison would be a success. "Dad got a real kick out of Harrison," says Billie's brother John. "Harrison would come to our home and just be bouncing off the walls. Dad would sit and smile and just shake his head."

The Honourable John McNair was thrilled when his daughter and Harrison announced their engagement. And his enthusiasm for his future son-in-law was visible to everyone on their wedding day, October 4, 1952. John McNair turned their wedding into a huge public event. Saint Andrew's Presbyterian Church in Fredericton was filled with hundreds of supporters, politicians, dignitaries and members of the media. McNair was determined that nothing, not even the fact that he'd been defeated as premier just two weeks earlier, would ruin his daughter's wedding day.

If Wallace admired his older brother before the wedding, he thought Harrison could walk on water after it. Wallace was Harrison's best man, and he had never attended such an impressive social event in his life. There were just three years between the brothers but on that day, it felt like a lifetime to Wallace. Harrison had graduated easily from university, he had started a successful career at Irving Oil, and he was now marrying the daughter of a former premier in what had become the biggest social gathering since the provincial election.

Wallace had just graduated from Mount Allison the spring before. He'd been slated to graduate a year earlier and had even been photographed for the university yearbook, but he'd failed a French course and had to make it up over the summer through a correspondence course.

With his degree finally in hand and no definite career plans, Wallace returned home. Whenever he got the chance, he'd go to Sackville to visit Anne Reid, his college sweetheart. But no McCain could live in Florenceville for long without sooner or later working for the family business. And so, after a few days, Wallace found himself working for his father's business for forty-five dollars a week. It wasn't a pleasant experience.

His father and his two older brothers Andrew and Bob had fixed ways of doing business. Any attempt by Wallace to do things differently was greeted with disdain. Wallace found he was spending more time arguing with his father and brothers than he was working. One night, Wallace ruined a shed full of potatoes by forgetting to close the door. It was a serious offence at McCain Produce, but Wallace was resolutely unapologetic. The incident had brought home to him the frustrating fact that one of the most responsible parts of his job was tucking the potatoes into bed at night! Was this what his father and brothers really thought of his abilities? After just six months, Wallace began applying for jobs advertised in the Woodstock paper.

Wallace was quickly offered a job with a bank but it didn't interest him. He then landed a job as a salesman for Green Cross, selling insecticide and other chemicals to farmers. His territory included most of the Saint John River valley. Wallace was finally doing something that he could do on his own and in his own way. He became a tenacious salesman, badgering, hounding, cajoling every potential client. He was in his early twenties, over six feet tall, with a thick head of hair and his mother's hawk-like eyes. Clients found they couldn't resist him or the powerful non-stop voice that extolled the virtues of the latest fertilizer or bug-killer.

Despite Wallace's skill at hard selling, one business always seemed out of reach. Even after dozens of calls and countless sales pitches, Wallace couldn't make a sale with Thorne's Hardware, a chain of stores based in Saint John. Then one day he got a call from the company president. Wallace was thrilled. Finally, he thought, I can sign them up. To his surprise, the president offered Wallace a job. K.C. Irving, who had bought the company years earlier, wanted to make it a province-wide industrial supply business. The new management at Thorne's was looking for a young upstart to help turn the business around, and Wallace looked like the perfect candidate. He was offered the job of general manager for one hundred dollars a week. It wasn't till he'd accepted the offer that he discovered there was a hitch: the company wanted him to fire the man he was replacing. Wallace didn't have the heart to tell someone more than twice his age that he had to leave; the man had been with Thorne's for years. So Wallace decided to work around him. He named himself sales manager and the general manager kept his job. He was still there when Wallace left four years later.

One of the big attractions of the Thorne's job was its location. Wallace would be based in Saint John, which was currently the home of his big brother Harrison. Wallace rented a room on Union Street only blocks from Harrison's house, and the two were constantly together. Although Wallace's room came with meals, he ate almost every dinner with Harrison and Billie.

Wallace set a torrid pace at Thorne's. He would often work fourteen hours a day, seven days a week. He was thrilled with his new responsibilities and enjoyed the hands-on decision-making the job required. But he was also terrified of failing. A part of him knew he was in over his head. His only work experience was selling pesticides for a few months, and now he was in charge of a sales team with a mandate to expand across the province. The fear and exhilaration only made Wallace work harder. Within a few years, he'd successfully expanded the company from a local building depot to a major industrial supplier. When Wallace started, the company had sixteen salesmen; by the time he left, there were twenty-five.

"I wasn't sure about him when he started," recalls Charles Levesque, who was a regional sales manager at Thorne's at the time. "He was ten years younger than me and I wasn't sure he knew what he was doing. But that didn't last long. He impressed me from the first time I saw him. He was a driver."

Levesque remembers dozens of sales trips with Wallace through the Gaspé Peninsula. The two would pile into Levesque's car and stack boxes of valves, bolts and tools in the back seat. Wallace would take the wheel and leave Levesque nearly white with fear as the car tore up the winding roads. They finished most days in the nearest bar drinking until late at night, but they never missed the first light of morning for the trip to the next town.

February 8, 1953, was a typical winter day in Florenceville. The hills were piled with snow and the ice was thick on the Saint John River. Inside the McCain house, Laura was hounding her husband about a doctor's appointment. Ever since A.D. had had a heart attack a few years earlier Laura had been relentless about his checkups. Tired of the badgering, A.D. finally turned to his wife and said, "I'll go if you go for a checkup, too." Laura agreed and the two went together to the clinic in Fredericton.

A.D. was told he was in fine health. He laughed and returned home with Laura to Florenceville. Shortly after they got home, he began planning a trip to South America to check up on some seeds he'd sold. "He wanted to see his potatoes growing," recalls his daughter Marie who was at home at the time and helped her father pack for the trip.

That night, with his bags packed for the trip, A.D. had a massive heart attack. The family summoned a doctor from Fredericton. Bob's wife Rosemary also rushed over to help. Although Rosemary was a nurse, Laura wasn't thrilled to see her.

"She resented me taking care of A.D.," says Rosemary. "But I was a nurse, and I was the only one around who had the training."

A.D. was alive but weak and barely conscious. There wasn't much point in sending him to the nearest major hospital in Woodstock; it was clear to everyone that he didn't have long to live. He died ten days later at the age of seventy-four. "I remember coming down the stairs to tell them," says Rosemary. "They were all sitting in the kitchen. It was awful."

A.D.'s funeral was held at the small Baptist church across from his house. Despite freezing weather and icy roads, dozens of cars lined the road in front of the church. It was a massive show of respect. His death put the entire village of Florenceville into a state of mourning. A.D. was buried in the family's small cemetery, just down the road from where he'd been born.

A.D. had died without a will. As the McCain family struggled to unravel what exactly had been left, they were amazed at what they discovered. By the time he had died, A.D. had amassed a small fortune through a series of investments in the stock market. His holdings were worth about $400,000, a huge amount in 1953. No one in the family, not even Laura, had any idea he'd been playing the stock market. They were also startled by the complexity and scope of A.D.'s landholdings. He held title to dozens of farms across the county, mainly because the owners had defaulted on his loans. But the records for many were sketchy, and Laura would wrestle with tax officials for years over the value of A.D.'s properties.

Without a will, the ownership of McCain Produce was split by law. Laura automatically received one-third of everything A.D. owned, including the company. The remainder was divided equally among the six children, which meant each received about one-ninth of the stocks and ownership in McCain Produce. The stocks worked out to a value of about $40,000 per child.

Throughout her married life, Laura had devoted herself to maintaining the McCain family name and the prestige and respectability that accompanied it. When A.D. was alive she had done that by dutifully fulfilling her role as his wife and mother to his children, and by keeping his secrets. For years, A.D. had a mistress who lived in a house right beside his office. The woman's husband worked for A.D., so he always knew when she would be alone. When the man went off to work, A.D. would sneak out the back door of his office and run over to her house. No one talked about it much, but "everyone in town knew what was going on," says Mary Walters, whose father ran the office beside A.D.'s. "Mrs. McCain must have known too. But what could she do?" Laura had overlooked A.D.'s repeated unfaithfulness and rarely challenged his need for privacy in business and personal matters. She loved him. When A.D. died, Laura became his staunchest defender. The McCain name and everything A.D. had built was not going to end just because he did. She was determined to keep the McCain culture and legend alive. A big part of that culture was McCain Produce, and Laura insisted that none of her children sell their stake in the company. It would remain a McCain family business.

Laura knew nothing about the business but named herself president and moved into A.D.'s old office. It was a remarkable move at the time. Few women owned or managed businesses, and A.D. had never involved his wife in the company. Andrew and Bob became vice presidents and ran much of the day-to-day operations. But Laura was no figurehead. She learned the business and took an active role in overseeing shipments. She eventually became a shrewd businesswoman and investor, successfully managing her own portfolio of stocks until well into her eighties.

"She'd call me up all the time about some issue or government policy," says Charles Gallagher, a former New Brunswick Minister of Agriculture. "If a month went by without a call from Mrs. McCain I would be very surprised."

Along with running the business, she took part in a host of community activities. She started a Boy Scout troop, published a cookbook to raise money for local projects and founded a local library by badgering residents to donate books. She was a charter member of the Women's Institute and helped establish twenty chapters across the province. She was proud of the organization's work, especially in education. She enjoyed reminding people that the Institute pushed for laws on compulsory school attendance and also forced the government to allow women to be elected to local school boards. Laura returned to the Anglican Church after

A.D.'s death and was the first woman ever elected to the synod of Fredericton.

Laura was also determined not to let the sexism prevalent at the time interfere with her community work. She refused to allow the fact that she was a woman to prevent her from doing things that she felt needed to be done. "Some men will talk to you as if you don't have a brain just because you're a woman," she sharply told a reporter in the late 1960s.

Laura lived in the family home until her death. For many in town, she was a local charity quick to lend some old clothing or make a meal for a sick friend. For years she held regular rummage sales but kept them private so anyone stopping in to buy something wouldn't be noticed by the community. She was anxious to protect people from the stigma attached to buying second-hand clothes.

Laura's work and community involvement didn't go unnoticed. In 1974, she received the Order of Canada. In keeping with her frugal style, Laura refused to buy a new pair of shoes for the ceremony. Instead, she decided to borrow an old pair of silver shoes Billie had turned in to the rummage sale.

"She was stomping around the kitchen and Billie said to her, 'why are you wearing my silver shoes?'" remembers Wallace's wife Margaret. "And she said, 'These are the ones I've decided to wear when I get the Order of Canada.' And Billie said, 'But I wear a size nine and you wear a size seven.' 'That's all right,' Laura said, 'I've got the toes all stuffed. I'm not spending the money on a new pair of shoes for one night.'"

Billie tried to coax her into a new pair of shoes and even bought several pairs for her to try on, but Laura had decided, and that was that. She would be wearing the size-nine silver shoes at the Order of Canada ceremony in the Governor General's residence in Ottawa.

The ceremony over, and the shoes an apparent success, Laura decided to save herself some more money by taking a bus back to her hotel. As she triumphantly stepped off the bus, she momentarily lost control of the size-nine silver shoes. She slipped and fell hard on the pavement, breaking her elbow. Billie was to spend a lot of time regretting that she'd ever turned those shoes in to the rummage sale.

Laura's children were surprised by their mother's tireless activity after A.D.'s death. Growing up, they had never seen that side of her. Their father had always been such a strong presence in the family and the community that there had been little room for Laura's personality. It was only after he died that they glimpsed the qualities that had spurred him to marry her: her independence, her drive and her indomitable spirit. The McCains had many dreams and more than enough drive and ambition to achieve them. It was to become a point of pride that when push came to shove they could adapt to any situation or circumstance. And they could always be counted on to marshal ruthless survival instincts when it came to business. They discovered that their mother was going to try to keep them on the straight and narrow with the same adamant resolve their father once had.

CHAPTER FOUR

Wallace pulled his car into the parking lot of a hotel in Truro, Nova Scotia. It was a cool Sunday evening in May 1954, and Wallace was on another sales trip for Thorne's. He planned to spend a week in the area calling on stores and other potential customers. After checking in, Wallace did what he always did on a sales trip, he went looking for an attractive girl to take out on a date.

He had a few buddies in Truro from his naval training days at Mount Allison, but female companions didn't immediately come to mind. Then he remembered Margaret Norrie, the pretty fifteen-year old girl he'd met at the fall dance at Mount A. four years before. Wallace flipped through Truro's small phone book, called Margaret and asked her if she wanted to go out for a cup of coffee that evening.

Margaret was leery of Wallace when he called. She knew some of Wallace's university friends in town and had heard stories about his raucous days at school. She agreed to go out, but she made a pact with herself: if Wallace made one false move she was heading home in a hurry.

When Margaret opened the door, Wallace was taken aback. She wasn't the teenager he'd remembered from Mount Allison; she was an attractive young woman. Wallace drove nervously to the local coffee shop. As they sat down across from one another, Wallace tried to make small talk with Margaret. It fell flat. He had too much on his mind. Then, without knowing why or how he'd got started, Wallace found himself telling Margaret about the last year. He talked about his father's death, about the months it had taken him and Harrison to sort out the will, about getting his mother started at McCain Produce, about the $40,000 inheritance, about his anxiety over what to do with the money. He told her that all his life he had grown up watching his father run his own business and watching all the other farmers and owners of small businesses in Florenceville. His world as a child had been filled with entrepreneurs. Self-employment and self-reliance were as firmly planted in his upbringing as potatoes in the summer. He told her he was frustrated at Thorne's and that his brother Harrison was feeling unchallenged at Irving Oil. He told her that he knew from working with his father that he wasn't cut out for taking orders.

Wallace didn't stop there. He told Margaret about his past relationships with other women and about Anne Reid, with whom he had just broken up after a two-year relationship. He told her about his failures at school and his drinking. After months of keeping his thoughts contained, Wallace found himself pouring his heart out to a woman he'd just met.

Margaret was overwhelmed. She'd never met a man as chatty and open as Wallace before. And she knew he was taking a huge risk. This was, after all, the 1950s, and there were very strict social taboos surrounding relations between men and women. But the more Wallace told her, the more she realized how much they had in common. Both had grown up in small towns, both their fathers had died, and both had strong mothers. Margaret was surprised by her feelings for Wallace. Normally she was extremely cautious about the men she dated, but she felt his respect and found herself instinctively trusting him.

Wallace was determined to see Margaret again. Although he was scheduled to leave Truro the next day, he cancelled his appointments and took Margaret to a movie instead. He scrapped his schedule again the next day and spent it with Margaret. Wallace had never changed his schedule before for anyone or anything that didn't relate to a sale.

Four months later, on Thanksgiving weekend, Wallace and Margaret were engaged. Ten months later, in August 1955, they got married in the United Church in Truro. Harrison was Wallace's best man. Brothers Bob and Andrew were ushers along with Wallace's best friend from Acadia, Arthur Irving, son of K.C. Irving. After the wedding ceremony everyone headed to the church basement for a reception. Margaret's family had strong religious convictions and kept the reception a sober affair—no drinking and no dancing. "Just afternoon tea with sandwiches and cupcakes," recalls Margaret.

After a brief honeymoon in Bermuda, Wallace and Margaret moved into a small one-bedroom apartment in Saint John. The flat was only a few blocks from Harrison and Billie, and the couples were constantly together.

Married life wasn't easy for Margaret. She had a hard time adjusting to the McCain family culture. Wallace had been raised in a house where women stayed home and looked after the needs of their husbands and children. Margaret had been raised by her mother, a fiercely independent widow with eight children. Margaret's father had been a mining engineer, and the family lived in northern Quebec for years. He died when Margaret was eleven, and Margaret's mother took her children and returned to the family farm in Truro.

Margaret saw her mother as a passionate woman with resolute principles and beliefs. When Margaret's mother felt strongly about something there was no stopping her. She once led a protest against construction of a road through a wilderness area by jumping on a tractor and heading a small convoy. She also became involved in every community activity in Truro. Once a census taker came to the family farm with a questionnaire. Eventually he got to the question about Margaret's mother's occupation. "I assume we will put here 'housewife.'" he said. "I beg your pardon," she shot back, "I'm a Jersey breeder."

Margaret admired and respected her mother's independence and struggled daily with the fear that she might let her down. She never forgot that she had been named after her mother, and she knew that her mother expected her to put her life to good use within the community. But Margaret felt crippled by an intense shyness and feelings of insecurity. When she was at Mount Allison Margaret forced herself to become more outgoing by joining clubs and attending every campus social event. "I knew my shyness was a terrible handicap that I had to overcome.

When I went to university I said to myself, 'If it kills me, I am going to learn how to talk to people.' I thought, 'I am not going to miss one dance, no matter what I have to do. I am no longer going to be a wallflower,'" Margaret recalls. In her efforts to emulate her mother she joined the French club, the choral society and the cheerleading squad. She even won a school debating title in her senior year and attended a national Liberal convention with her mother.

After graduating Margaret went on to take a year-long course in social work at the University of Toronto. Now, at the age of twenty-one, she was a qualified social worker, and she'd just been offered a job in Saint John. But she was also a newlywed in the 1950s. Men had very different attitudes then. "Wallace didn't want me to work," says Margaret. "You can only do so much cleaning in a one-bedroom apartment. And so I got very bored. This wasn't what I wanted to do with the rest of my life."

In an effort to overcome her boredom, Margaret asked Wallace if she could join him on one of his sales trips. Wallace wasn't thrilled but agreed to take her. It was mid January and brutally cold when they hit the road for the Gaspé. Wallace and his cohort Charles Levesque sat up front while Margaret was relegated to the back. "I was beside a pile of brochures on hammers and saws and samples of nails," she remembers. "We drove around the Gaspé coast and we couldn't see out the windows because they were all frosted up. There I sat. And what did I listen to? I listened to a lecture on nails, hammers and bolts for the whole week. That's how he killed any desire for me to join him on business trips."

The regular contact with Billie and Harrison was a mixed blessing. Margaret liked Billie and the two got along well, but they didn't have a lot in common. Billie had two small children and was happily committed to staying home and raising them.

As for Harrison, Margaret was uncomfortable from the first time she met him. "I felt like a bulldozer had run over me," she says. To Margaret, Harrison was loud, self-centred and, at times, condescending. Margaret was still battling her shyness and often felt awkward in Harrison's company. Wallace could see that there would always be distance between his wife and his brother, and he knew that there were aspects of Margaret's personality that would always challenge Harrison.

"Margaret was competitive, I could smell it," Wallace recalls. "She's got some strong views. Some would say she's damned opinionated. She doesn't mind taking a stand and she'll tell you what's on her mind."

In spite of her uncertainty about Harrison, Margaret could see that the brothers were inseparable. Whenever the couples were together, Wallace and Harrison would spend hours talking about their jobs or some new business scheme, shutting out Margaret and Billie completely.

By the fall of 1955, Harrison was getting impatient to start his own business. Like Wallace, Harrison had seen his father run his own enterprise and had always wanted to follow that example. The job with Irving Oil had given Harrison a good lesson in how K.C. ran his companies, and Harrison wanted to try the techniques himself. But he knew he couldn't start a business while he was working full time as sales manager for New Brunswick, PEI and Newfoundland, so he quit Irving Oil to devote his time to looking for a business opportunity.

It was a risky move. Harrison had a young family to support and no idea what business to pursue. But the $40,000 inheritance from his father bolstered his instincts and ambitions. Wallace was welcome to come along, but Harrison wasn't waiting for his younger brother. "I didn't leave to find a business for Wallace and me," Harrison now says. "I left to find a business for myself."

Wallace was eager to join his brother in business. He still had a little brother's admiration for Harrison and dreamed of working with him. He got to work immediately trying to find something for them to get into.

From his work at Thorne's, Wallace knew that Douglas Allen, a hardware store owner in Amherst, Nova Scotia, was thinking about selling his business. Wallace suggested they buy the store. Margaret was thrilled. Amherst wasn't far from Truro, and it was a chance for her to be closer to her family. The brothers went to see Allen and he immediately liked their enthusiasm. He didn't have any other offers and he was ready to sell on the spot.

There was only one problem: Wallace wanted the deal

worked out in detail. He drew up a lengthy legal contract covering every aspect of the sale. Harrison's inclination was to keep the deal simple. That was his style. Get the deal done quickly with minimal hassle and move on. But Wallace needed the fine print first. That was the way he worked. Put it in writing so that if there were any problems later, there would always be something to fall back on. Wallace had inherited this healthy scepticism about business from his father, who had trusted no one. Like his father, Wallace took risks but he didn't take chances. Even the purchase of a hardware store in a small town had to be done properly.

Unfortunately, Wallace's thoroughness backfired. Allen was intimidated by the contract and felt the McCains were trying to pull something. Within days, he found another buyer and sold the business for virtually the same price. The new buyer had given Allen a one-sheet contract and settled the deal with a handshake. Harrison and Wallace were devastated.

With the hardware store gone, the brothers moved on to other ideas. They considered buying a seat on the Toronto Stock Exchange or the Montreal Exchange. Wallace wasn't interested in the stock market and suggested buying a bottling operation or a dry-cleaning business instead. In the winter of 1955, Harrison returned to Florenceville and from there took a truckload of Christmas trees to Florida. He sold the trees but made only enough to cover his expenses. He still had no idea what to do.

By now, their mother Laura was getting concerned. Wallace still had his job at Thorne's, but Harrison had no income and at this rate his inheritance wouldn't last long. He needed something to do. Laura began imploring Bob to help Harrison find some kind of business. It was a familiar role for Bob. He was the McCain most people, inside and outside the family, turned to for advice. Bob had a confident, easygoing nature and was respected across the county. He was generally considered the favourite among the McCain boys.

Bob did have an idea for Harrison. He noticed that General Foods Corp. had started packaging frozen vegetables just across the border in Maine under the Birds Eye label. They were also making frozen French fries. Bob didn't know much about frozen

French fries but he knew that most of the farmers in the county were shipping their potatoes to the Birds Eye plant to be processed. Bob had a feeling this new French fry idea might catch on. He wasn't alone.

Just a few months earlier, in March 1955, a Chicago salesman named Ray A. Kroc had incorporated McDonald's Systems Inc. Less than a year before, Kroc had met two brothers, Richard and Maurice McDonald, in San Bernardino, California. Kroc was national sales manager for Multimixer, a brand of milk shake machines. He'd heard about the McDonald brothers' remarkably successful restaurant, predictably called McDonald's. The McDonalds were buying so many of Kroc's Multimixers that he made a special trip to California to see what they were up to.

Dick and Mac, as they were called, had stumbled into the restaurant business eighteen years earlier. They'd come to Hollywood from New Hampshire in 1930 with visions of making it in the movies. Their father had worked in a shoe factory, and the boys figured any job was better than that. After years of pushing sets around movie lots for next to nothing, they managed a theatre. When that went under, they opened a hot dog stand. Then, in 1937, they decided to cash in on the latest craze sweeping California—drive-in restaurants. The idea of getting a quick meal without leaving your car became more and more popular as automobiles began to crowd California roads.

The brothers bought their first drive-in in Pasadena, but by 1940 they'd moved to a bigger drive-in in San Bernardino, a desert town about sixty miles east of Los Angeles.

At first, the McDonald's drive-in was a huge success. It was the only drive-in in town and it immediately attracted hordes of teenagers. But soon competitors popped up and the McDonalds began to realize that the drive-in was not a competitive proposition. The noisy crowds of teenagers began to turn off the family market. Service was slower then at regular restaurants, which meant fewer customers passing through. The staff turnover was high, and drive-ins began competing with each other for carhops. The carhops who stayed were more interested in chatting up customers and the cook than serving food. "The fry cooks were always trying to date the carhops," Dick McDonald told *The Wall Street Journal* in 1991. "Oh, what a headache they were." If the carhop snubbed the cook, he would fill her orders last, and the customers complained.

In 1948, the brothers decided to close the drive-in and reopen a takeout under a new format. They trimmed the menu from twenty-five items to nine, cut the price of a burger to fifteen cents from thirty cents and pledged to serve customers as quickly as possible. "If we'd let people start saying 'Hold the onion,' our system was dead in the water," McDonald told the paper. The whole concept was speed, low prices and volume. They also enclosed the restaurant almost entirely in glass so that a sceptical customer, worried that a cheap burger meant cheap quality as well, could see the preparation process. That became almost as much of a selling point as the low prices. They called it the Speedy Service System. Dick also decided that the brothers needed a new sign for their restaurant and he sketched a design involving two giant golden arches in the shape of an "M." When Dick showed the drawings to an architect, he laughed and called it a dumb idea. But Dick insisted, and the arches stayed.

Soon after McDonald's opened it became famous for its fifteen-cent burgers and ten-cent bags of fries. News of the remarkable restaurant spread across the state and soon imitators sprang up. The brothers licensed a few franchises but had no interest in establishing a national chain. Enter Ray Kroc, a lifelong salesman eager to get out of the milk shake business.

Kroc was fascinated by the McDonald's concept from the time he pulled into the parking lot on a hot July morning and saw a line-up at the takeout counter. He realized immediately that the Speedy Service System would revolutionize the food service business. He was also confident that he could quickly establish McDonald's outlets nationwide through franchising, since it cost just $75,000 to set up a McDonald's compared to $300,000 to open a drive-in. "He was more enthused about the prospects than my brother and me," Dick McDonald told *The Wall Street Journal.*

Kroc opened a McDonald's in Des Plaines, Illinois, a month after joining McDonald's, and within a year he had more than thirty restaurants. But the success of McDonald's was being copied by other fast-food businesses, which were also expanding wildly. By 1955, Chicken Delight was moving across America. That same year, an Indiana farm boy named Harland Sanders was also having huge success with his Kentucky Fried Chicken restaurant, and he started franchising. InstaBurger King, later shortened to Burger King, was also getting underway in Florida with its famous "Whopper." And then there were the existing chains, such as A&W (which started in the 1920s as a soda stand and was now a drive-in chain), Dairy Queen and Tastee Freeze.

The growth of the fast-food industry led to innovations in food preparation as well. By 1955, Kroc and others were already working on foods that would be quicker to prepare. Frozen French fries were one of the first innovations. McDonald's, like most restaurants, was preparing fries from fresh potatoes, but that required them to keep a large stash of potatoes on hand, and precious time was lost in the preparation. Freeze-dried potatoes had been around since World War II and that laid some of the ground work for developing frozen fries.

Among the early pioneers was John Simplot, a rugged Idaho farmer who dropped out of high school to start a produce business called J.R. Simplot Co. He was one of the main suppliers of freeze-dried potatoes to the U.S. Army during the war. Shortly after the war ended, a chemist told Simplot about an idea he had for frozen French fries. "He told me, 'If you buy me a freeze box I think I can come up with a new product that will sell,'" recalls Simplot, who still lives on the same farm in Idaho. "I said, 'Hell, if you freeze a potato you've got a barrel of mush.'" But the chemist insisted, Simplot bought the freeze box, "and, we got a patent on [frozen] French fries."

Simplot wasn't the only one working on frozen French fries at the time. Kroc put his own team of researchers on similar ideas soon after joining McDonald's. Lamb-Weston Inc. in Oregon, a rival of Simplot's, was also working on a similar project. And some food processors at General Foods' Birds Eye plant, in the heart of Maine's potato country, were playing around with the idea too.

Bob McCain had probably never heard of Kroc, McDonald's or Burger King in the summer of 1955 as he watched what the

Birds Eye plant was doing. Canada was an untapped market for the U.S. fast-food chains. But whatever Birds Eye was producing it looked intriguing. Why should New Brunswick farmers ship fresh potatoes over to a processing plant in Maine? Bob thought. Why not build the plant here? The plant would have a huge advantage in its home market because Canada had a 17.5 percent duty on processed potatoes imported from the United States.

Bob told Harrison about the idea. Harrison wasn't sure—he was considering a few other options—but he trusted Bob's intuition and agreed to take a look. He decided to call Wallace to see if he was interested in the venture.

It was January 1956, and Wallace and Margaret were spending a weekend in the Lord Beaverbrook Hotel in Fredericton.

"I told him what I was going to do," Harrison now says. "And he said, 'Well, you go ahead and start that and we'll see how it goes. I'll help you all I can, I'll put some money in and see if it's big enough for two of us, and I'll see what I'm going to do.' I said, 'No, come right now. Come right now. Don't fool around, just make up your mind.'"

To Harrison, who wanted an instant commitment, Wallace's reaction might have seemed hesitant, but as Margaret remembers it, Wallace was enthusiastic and eager to go. He hung up the phone barely able to contain his excitement about the idea. "Oh God," she thought to herself, "I don't want to go to Florenceville and spend the rest of my life there." But Wallace tried to reassure her that it would only be temporary. "Don't worry, Margie," he told her. "If we do this, you know, we'd probably get started and move the head office to Montreal or Toronto."

Wallace told his colleagues at Thorne's a few days later that he would be quitting in six months to start a frozen French fry business with his brother. Charles Levesque shook his head at Wallace and urged him to stay. It wouldn't work, he told him. And he was a fool to walk away from a good career at Thorne's. But Wallace was convinced and submitted his resignation.

While Wallace spent his last six months at Thorne's, Harrison and Bob tried to gather as much information as possible about frozen French fries. They went to New York to see officials at Seabrook Farms Co., one of the largest frozen-food producers in the United States. They travelled to Toronto and Montreal to meet with distributors and they read everything they could on the business.

Everyone they talked to gave them the same advice: don't do it. You'll never be able to compete with Simplot or Lamb-Weston. Big food processors like General Foods are also going to get into the game. Besides, frozen fries are popular out west with McDonald's, but not here.

Frozen fries hadn't caught on in Canada. In fact, Harrison's research found that while Americans were consuming 13 pounds of frozen fries per capita every year, Canadians were gulping down barely 2.5 pounds per capita. In addition, nearly 20 percent of the entire U.S. potato crop was used in some form of processing, compared to barely 4 percent in Canada.

"Everyone said we were stupid to go into it," Harrison recalls. "It was the wrong thing to do, but I think the more negatives we heard, the more positive we became that we wanted to go into it."

Whether it was stubbornness or a need to do something, Harrison never thought twice about building the plant. Bob had convinced him that the idea would work and Bob knew agriculture better than anyone else in the family. Harrison trusted him and trusted his own instincts. By the spring of 1956, Wallace had left Thorne's and was ready to help with the details. He was also completely sold on the idea.

Bob, Harrison, Wallace and their older brother Andrew decided to pool their inheritance to get the business started. It would be run by Harrison and Wallace, while Bob and Andrew stayed with their mother at McCain Produce. Bob and Harrison thought each brother should kick in $25,000, but Wallace balked. He remembered trying to work with his father and older brothers in the family business just after he'd graduated, and he wanted more control over this operation. Wallace said that since he and Harrison were going to run the new business, they should invest more and have a larger ownership stake. Bob and Andrew agreed and Wallace and Harrison put up $30,000 each and received one-third ownership in the new business. Bob and

Andrew each put in $20,000 for roughly one-sixth ownership in the company. That ownership structure would never vary.

The brothers never even considered including their mother or their sisters in the new company, even though Laura was running McCain Produce, and Eleanor and Marie each had the same $40,000 inheritance. Women simply didn't start businesses in rural New Brunswick in 1956. Marie bears no resentment about the exclusion. Her involvement "was never considered and I never asked," Marie says. She accepts that given the attitudes at the time, it would have been inconceivable for the brothers to have involved their sisters in the company.

With the ownership sorted out, the brothers needed to incorporate the company. They turned for help to Harrison's brother-in-law, John McNair, who was a lawyer in Fredericton. With McNair's help, McCain Foods Ltd. was incorporated on May 24, 1956. Harrison was named president and Wallace secretary-treasurer. Although there was no legal tie, the new business was seen as an extension of McCain Produce, so there was no need to give Bob and Andrew titles since they were already vice presidents there.

All four brothers were also named company directors. But they decided that the board should have an odd number to break any tie votes. They thought of asking Eleanor's husband Patrick Johnson to join the board.

Eleanor had married Johnson, a dashing, twenty-eight-year-old, Oxford-educated Englishman, just two years earlier. He'd been born in India and loved to tell the story of how he'd nearly died at three days of age when a snake crawled into his crib. Johnson had met Eleanor at Graham Eckes School, a private school in West Palm Beach, Florida, where they were both teaching. After the wedding, they'd moved to England, where Johnson took up another teaching position.

The McCain boys decided that as long as Johnson was living in England he was too far away to play a meaningful role on the board. So their next choice was Marie's husband, Jed Sutherland. He was a big, rugged man with a passion for horses. Sutherland was a dentist who'd served briefly as an army dentist during the war. After marrying Marie in 1940, Sutherland had bought a practice in Woodstock. He also bred horses with Bob and later ran a bottling operation in Woodstock. Sutherland agreed to join the board, putting the final piece in the company's incorporation.

Now that the company was official, at least on paper, the brothers had to figure out how to build a French fry plant. Despite Bob and Harrison's research, the McCains had never seen the inside of a potato processing factory. They soon realized that, in addition to a plant, they would also needed a cold storage warehouse to store their frozen fries until they could be shipped. But where would they get the money to build a warehouse? They had already put up $100,000 for the processing plant.

As luck would have it, the federal government had a program at that time that provided grants to companies for the construction of cold storage warehouses in rural areas as a way of helping farmers. The grants were made under what was then called the Cold Storage Act, which was administered by the Department of Agriculture. In return for a grant, the government required the company to set aside a certain amount of space for public lockers for local farmers to store their own meat and produce.

The McCains knew they needed one of the grants to get their warehouse built. So, within a month of incorporating McCain Foods, they incorporated a company called Carleton Cold Storage Co. Ltd. Unlike McCain Foods, which was owned entirely by the brothers, Carleton Cold Storage was incorporated as a public company. That would make their application for the grant even more appealing to the Department of Agriculture. The brothers rounded up about eight local farmers as shareholders and split 7,500 shares among them. Wallace was named president of the new entity and the application was filed. It worked. The government approved the application and Carleton Cold Storage received an $87,000 grant.

By June 1956, both companies were established and Wallace and Harrison were ready to move to Florenceville to start construction. Wallace and Margaret were the first to move. They rented a small, drafty house across the road from the McCain family home. It was owned by Laura, who had inherited it from one of A.D.'s many business dealings, and she rented it to her son for forty dollars a month; there was no free ride from Laura the businesswoman. The house was also next door to Bob and Rosemary.

Harrison and Billie moved a few weeks later. They rented a small house in East Florenceville just down from the gas station. The house was tiny and had just two bedrooms—a tight squeeze since Harrison and Billie already had two children.

For Margaret and Billie, moving to Florenceville required a huge adjustment. Billie had been raised in Fredericton, the daughter of the premier. She'd grown up in a stimulating environment and must have found the thought of living in a village of five hundred people impossible. But she wasn't in a position to argue or complain—Harrison didn't tolerate whiners or complainers. "You get on with Harrison by making sure he has his own way," his good friend Claude Bursill now says. "He would be a difficult person to live with. You'd have to adjust yourself."

Billie would never have more than a few close friends in Florenceville and she never played more than a minor role in community activities. "Billie was modest to an extreme extent," remembers Bursill. "Her shyness appeared to be a diffidence that became almost a self-effacement." She wasn't as outgoing as Margaret and friends say she found small-town life difficult. "You didn't just walk up to her house for coffee uninvited," says Connie Bliss, who lived a few doors down from Billie and Harrison.

Despite her small-town surroundings, Billie would always cling to her one great passion—art. Her favourite outing was to call up her one close friend in Florenceville and go to Gagetown to visit the craft shows. Later, she studied antiques in London, England, and sponsored an art competition at the Beaverbrook Gallery in Fredericton. She even turned a room in her house in Florenceville into a small studio for her painting. "But I never once saw her put any of her paintings on the wall," says one of her closest friends. "She said Harrison didn't care for them."

Margaret was used to small-town life, having been raised in northern Quebec and rural Nova Scotia, but she wasn't eager to embrace it again at the age of twenty-two. She'd always planned to have her own career, but that wouldn't be possible now in Florenceville.

There were family pressures as well in the McCain home town. From the day they moved to Florenceville, Margaret and Billie had no choice but to become a part of the McCain family culture. The McCains had always been the most prominent people in town, and the prospect of McCain Foods only heightened that. Their mother-in-law also made it clear to Billie and Margaret that their first priority was to their husbands. They found themselves in the same position as Rosemary. Laura was a constant presence in their lives, offering advice on raising children, housekeeping, cooking and family life in general. The wives knew that Harrison and Wallace adored their mother, so challenging her was out of the question. Margaret also felt she was often pitted against Billie and never seemed to measure up to Billie's impeccable standards. "Nothing was ever out of place at Billie's house," recalls Margaret. "And she was always immaculately dressed. It didn't matter what time of day it was."

The more Billie and Margaret tried to settle in Florenceville, the more they grew apart. Margaret jumped into community life and developed a group of close friends. She played the organ at the Anglican church and started her mornings with a group of friends at the lunch counter of Buckingham's, the local store.

Margaret was still pushing herself to live up to the example set by her mother, who was as active as ever. In 1956, Margaret's mother won the local Liberal nomination for the provincial election. One of her opponents in the dual-member riding was a young Truro lawyer who had taken over the moribund Conservative Party. His name was Robert Stanfield. He won the riding easily and the Tories put an end to twenty-three years of Liberal rule.

There was distance as well between Margaret and Bob's wife Rosemary, even though they were neighbours. Rosemary had her own circle of friends in the village and her own interests. And she kept it that way. Although for years Wallace and Bob and their families shared Christmas together, relations between Rosemary and Margaret were cool. Rosemary found Margaret arrogant and preoccupied with her family's interests. Margaret was uncomfortable with Rosemary's values and felt Rosemary encouraged her children to bank on the McCain name.

Wallace and Harrison, however, were too busy to concern themselves with domestic rifts. They needed far more than the federal cold storage grant and the $100,000 inheritance money to get their business going. Fortunately for them, the New Brunswick government had been desperate for years to find some kind of economic boost for Carleton County. It was also an election year, and the premier, Hugh John Flemming, represented the county in the legislature. Supporting a new plant that could create hundreds of jobs in a depressed county would certainly be a big campaign boost. Flemming's government had been trying to entice General Foods and Salada-Shirrif-Horsey Co. to locate vegetable processing plants in the region but was having no success. So, when Harrison and Wallace made their pitch to Flemming for some government support for their new business, he was as excited as they were. "The business was going to be in his riding," Wallace recalls. "He was going to be a hero."

Flemming was so eager to help the McCains that he even ignored their dyed-in-the-wool Liberal affiliations, no small feat in politically sensitive New Brunswick. After all, Flemming was from one of the bluest Tory families in the county. His father was James Kidd Flemming, who'd been premier when A.D. McCain ran for the Liberals in two bitterly contested provincial elections. But none of that mattered to Hugh John Flemming in the spring of 1956. These McCain boys were promising jobs and there was an election on the line. Flemming promised to guarantee a $280,000 bond issue for the new company within months. More money would come later. "We are convinced that this new industry will help to provide new and profitable markets for farmers over a wide area of New Brunswick," Flemming told reporters as he announced support for the McCain project. A few weeks later, on June 18, the Tories won a huge majority.

Just as the provincial financing was arranged, the brothers got another boost. Bob was elected to Carleton County council as a representative from Florenceville. New Brunswick's counties had tremendous power at the time. There were no mayors or city halls, and county councils ran most local services. In many ways they were more powerful than the provincial government. For one thing, the councils had the power to grant tax concessions to businesses.

Desperate for any way to save money, Wallace and Harrison headed to the council chamber in Woodstock on June 26, 1956, to ask for a tax break for McCain Foods. It was an audacious move. They had no factory, no employees and no product—but they did have a brother sitting on council. The brothers agreed that Harrison would make the presentation and Wallace would be ready to answer any detailed questions. The brothers sat and waited in the council chambers as a county official made a presentation on a new $205,000 nurses' residence at the Carleton Memorial Hospital. Then the county tax collector filed a report on tax receipts. Shortly before noon, Harrison was given the floor. He sat up straight, cleared his throat and began reading a prepared statement in a clear, confident tone. It was vintage Harrison. He began by challenging the council and then offering McCain as a solution to the problems that beset the area.

"For the past two years, we have learned, much to our sorrow, that our principal agricultural crop of potatoes is becoming a liability rather than an asset to the economy of our county," he said. He continued for fifteen minutes, talking about the huge contributions McCain Foods would make to Carleton County. The company would create sixty jobs immediately and two hundred jobs within five years, he said, and twenty new homes would be built for them. That was an extraordinary promise for a business in a village of barely five hundred people. He also said McCain would buy $213,000 worth of vegetables from local farmers in the first year of operation and $667,000 within five years. Those were enormous sums considering the council's entire budget at the time was around $500,000.

"We have been working on this proposition for the past two years," Harrison continued, "and now that it is to become a reality we find that after reviewing our indebtedness, which is a long-term commitment, we must have considerable financial consideration on some of our local problems." Those problems, naturally, included local taxes and the county's fees for power and water. Harrison ended his presentation by noting that a company in Ontario, presumably Salada-Shirrif-Horsey Co., which was planning a plant in Alliston, Ontario, had received a twenty-year "free taxation grant before building the same type of plant as ours. Therefore, if these obstacles are to be overcome, we must have tax concessions to allow us to pay the producer a fair price and still be able to sell the volume markets as cheaply as the Central Canadian processor can."

Councillors were impressed. Here was a twenty-eight-year-old man and his twenty-five-year-old brother essentially asking for a twenty-year exemption from local taxes to help a business they hadn't even started. But the McCain name meant a lot to many councillors, some of whom were farmers who had been selling potatoes to McCain Produce for years. "I am sure every member of council realizes how important and beneficial this is to the province," councillor James Davis told reporters at the time, after noting the McCain family's contribution to the county. The council agreed to appoint a committee to consider the request and report back at its next meeting in January.

While council was considering the tax concession, the brothers started looking for a place to build their plant and warehouse. They wanted a site close to the Saint John River to provide a plentiful source of water. They knew that French fry plants needed lots of water for steam-peelers, potato-cleaners and boilers. The brothers looked at sites in the villages of Bath and Bristol, which were near Florenceville. Then they came across a 5.3-acre strip of farmland right on the edge of the river in East Florenceville.

The land was perfect. It was in the McCains' home town and it ran between Highway 2, which followed the Saint John River south to Fredericton, and the CPR tracks. Ironically, it was owned by Frank Smith, a relative of A.D. McCain's old rival B.F. Smith. Wallace and Harrison wanted the land and Smith, surprised that any non-farmer would want to buy his property, sold it to them in early July.

Now that they had a site, the McCains were finally ready to build their plant. But how? Wallace and Harrison didn't know where to start, and neither did Bob. "Our only experience with French fries at the time was eating them," remembers Wallace.

Luck was with the McCains again. The man who'd helped Birds Eye build its plant in Maine was living just a few miles away. Olof Pierson, or O.P. to everyone who knew him, was a hard-drinking, absent-minded inventor who'd been born with a knack for figuring out how things worked. Years earlier he'd decided to take up flying, and on his very first lesson a stone got caught in the joystick. The instructor decided to dislodge the rock by doing a quick roll, but he'd forgotten to fasten his seat belt and fell out of the open-air cockpit over a harbour. Pierson, who had done up his belt, managed to land the plane while his instructor was treading water in the harbour.

Harrison and Wallace hired O.P. and his assistant, Franklin Hickling, to build the McCain plant. But the McCains quickly found out that inventors don't always appreciate the business side of a project. O.P. once invented a harvesting machine but didn't bother to patent the idea. Friends say it was copied by a rival who produced it on a large scale and made a small fortune. O.P. didn't care much for the detailed designs or strict timetables that were crucial to the McCains. He often scratched out drawings for the McCain plant on envelopes, napkins or any other scrap of paper he had handy when an idea struck. The McCains could hardly push O.P. Everyone knew he was an extraordinarily gifted designer; he was credited with helping build one of the first potato processing plants for the John Baxter Co. in Maine. But his lack of business sense frustrated the brothers.

When O.P. did manage to come up with a plan for the factory, the brothers took the drawings to George McLaughlin, a contractor in nearby Perth. He looked at the assorted scribbles and asked, "But how high do you want the roof?" Wallace went back to O.P. who just looked at him blankly and said, "Well, how high do you think it should be?"

By the end of August, O.P. had finally put the plans in place and about seventy builders were hired to start construction. As the ground was broken, Wallace and Harrison put up a huge sign along the road to the site: "The New Home of McCain Foods Ltd., Flavor Frozen Foods From Canada's Most Modern Plant."

Based on Pierson's scribbled plans, the cold storage building would be 87,000 cubic feet. It would also include two hundred public lockers to meet the conditions of the federal grant. The processing plant would be 100 feet long, 128 feet wide and include a small office, lunch room, potato-conditioning area, processing line, packing area and a small laboratory.

The processing plant would cost about $500,000 to build and the Carleton Cold Storage warehouse would cost $260,000, but the brothers had enough financing in place. Fortunately, the provincial government was backing the $280,000 company bond issue as promised and was also preparing to ante up another $140,000 in loans. The brothers had arranged a $100,000 line of credit from the Bank of Nova Scotia, as well. At first the loan manager in Fredericton had refused to give them the money, fearing the project was too risky. But just as the brothers were leaving the bank, a senior manager who'd been an old friend of their father's spotted them. He overruled the loan manager and granted Harrison and Wallace the line of credit. A.D. had always paid his bills, the senior manager told the loan manager, and these boys would too.

Once construction began more problems arose. O.P. had designed conveyor belts that turned out to be too small. He'd also forgotten a crucial element. "How do you drive the belt?" Wallace asked O.P. "I guess you need a motor," Pierson replied. "Okay. What size, what speed?" asked Wallace. Pierson shrugged and said, "I think five horsepower and different speeds, I guess."

Pierson might have been scatterbrained, but he did manage to come up with some innovative equipment for the factory. He designed a steam-peeler based on a concept that is still used today. Pierson's contraption was fairly simple. Potatoes were put in a 200-gallon tank and steam was pumped in from either end. The rising pressure and temperature literally blasted the skin off the potato. Once the potatoes were peeled they were dumped into a trough of running hot water for cleaning. Then they were dumped onto another contraption Pierson called the "trimming table." It was a round, stainless-steel table that looked like an airport baggage carousel, and it rotated the potatoes as they rolled down. Workers would sit around the table and check the potatoes as they sped by, removing eyes, buds or any remaining peel.

There was only one problem with Pierson's design. The bolts on the portholes of the steam-peeler often couldn't take the pressure that built up inside. They would burst off the machine and fly through the plant like bullets. The peeler managed to stay together but workers would have to scramble to put the bolts back on. "I remember sitting here in my office and you would hear this *ping, ping,* as the bolts flew off and bounced off other machines," says Carl Morris, a long-time McCain vice president.

While construction proceeded in fits and starts, the brothers began scouring North America for boilers, freezing equipment and a machine to cut up the potatoes. They managed to find some boilers in Napanee, Ontario, that looked like the right size for a French fry plant. They found the right freezing equipment for the cold storage at Linde Hall Refrigeration Co. in Montreal. Most of the other machines had to be shipped in from California. Some of the machinery was designed to process frozen vegetables and had to be adapted by Pierson to the French fry line.

Finding the right equipment and sorting out the construction problems delayed the plant opening. Wallace and Harrison had hoped to open the plant in October or mid November at the latest, to coincide with the potato harvest, but the buildings weren't finished until late December. Once construction was finished, they spent the next few weeks installing machines and testing the line. They didn't manage their first test runs until early January 1957, about three months behind schedule and long after the potato harvest.

Then came good news from the county. Council had approved their request for tax concessions and voted to exempt McCain Foods and Carleton Cold Storage from all local taxes for 1957 and 1958. The council would consider further tax exemptions in 1959. It wasn't the twenty-year tax break Harrison wanted, but it was a big boost and it would save the brothers thousands of dollars in taxes.

And they were lucky to get it. Later that winter, Carleton County council received a letter from Ewin Allen, the Deputy Minister of Municipal Affairs. Allen explained that the council's two-year tax exemption for McCain was illegal. Under provincial law, Ewin wrote, county councils weren't allowed to exempt companies from all local taxes. "I do not think that the provisions of section 4 of the Municipal Tax Act ever intended to cover complete exemption," he wrote. "Someone has suggested to me that the properties might be omitted from the assessment list and roll altogether on the grounds that the industries were in the process of being constructed. I would hesitate to do this since some taxpayers or lawyer might very well pick this up and trouble or embarrassment might result.

Allen wasn't trying to undo the concession. The provincial government was completely behind the McCain enterprise, and Allen's job was to see that nothing impeded the company. He was warning the council that the tax concessions as structured were a potential scandal. But he had a solution. Instead of a complete exemption, Allen suggested the council charge McCain and Carleton Cold Storage a nominal amount of tax. "In other words, it would be possible to set a percentage so low that the tax would be practically nothing," he advised. Council took his advice and set McCain's taxes to virtually zero in 1957 and 1958.

With the tax concessions sorted out, Wallace and Harrison hired their first employees. Forty people took their places on the first production run, instantly making McCain Foods one of the largest employers in town. Most of the new staff were from Florenceville or farms nearby, and none had ever worked in a factory before. But then again, neither had Wallace or Harrison. The brothers paid their new employees between sixty and seventy cents an hour, about the same as the local sawmill. Thirty-five of the first employees were women. Most were farm wives, eager for some extra family income, and they would remain the backbone of McCain Foods for years. It was an ironic twist that the McCain boys, who generally believed that a woman's place was in the home, would become the largest employers of women in the county.

With their employees in place and the test runs a success, the McCains were ready for business. What they needed now was a grand opening to let everyone know that McCain Foods had arrived.

Finally, on February 23, 1957, they were ready. It was a typical winter day in Florenceville. Snow was piled high around the low white McCain Foods and Carleton Cold Storage buildings. A seventy-five-foot-long red ribbon fluttered in the slight breeze as a couple of men tried to attach it to both buildings. Inside the processing plant, newly hired women brushed lint off the white uniforms and white hats that had "McCain Foods Ltd." printed across the front. Not far away, in the village's Masonic Hall, Bill Kennett, the man who'd given Wallace a ride and a sip of beer when he was twelve, rushed madly to set up the last of dozens of tables for refreshments. Beside the plant, hundreds of people shook off the cold and the snow and filed into the auditorium of the new Florenceville Regional High School.

Reporters from the Fredericton and Saint John newspapers were in town and their editors back home were finishing up huge special features on the new plant. The *Daily Gleaner* in Fredericton was preparing a five-page spread on the opening, including dozens of ads from New Brunswick businesses wishing the McCains success. "People like the McCain family keep the Maritimes growing," said an ad from Harrison's old employer, Irving Oil. "We are pleased and proud to have been associated with the construction of New Brunswick's newest industry," said an ad from Wallace's employer, Thorne's Hardware. Florenceville merchants, including many who had once competed with A.D. McCain, placed dozens of small ads that simply said "Congratulations." One was from Gordon Lovely, who still ran the store where Wallace used to barter food for cigarettes as a twelve-year-old.

At 2:00 p.m. sharp, Wallace McCain strode across a small stage to a podium and nervously looked out at a thousand faces. His mother Laura was sitting right in front wearing a bright corsage and her best Sunday morning hat. Behind her sat K.C. Irving and his wife Harriet. Harrison, Andrew and Bob stood near the stage in their best suits. Next to them was Premier Hugh John Flemming. Next to the Premier were the federal Minister of Labour, the provincial Minister of Agriculture, the Deputy Minister of Industry and Development, the Reverend Hubert Doody and Fred McCain, the local MLA and a distant relative. As he approached the podium, Wallace took a deep breath. With a strong but slightly nervous voice, he welcomed the crowd to the official opening of McCain Foods Ltd. and Carleton Cold Storage.

The politicians spoke next and praised the plant and the brothers for their industriousness. Harrison was the last speaker. He thanked everyone for their support and offered a special salute to his mother. Then the dignitaries went outside, cut the long red ribbon and went on a tour of the plant. Harrison watched for a moment as every piece of the ribbon was cut up for souvenirs. As he stood in the plant, Harrison spoke briefly to a local reporter about A.D. It had been four years nearly to the day since the McCains had buried their father. If only he could see his boys now. None of them were doctors, as A.D. had hoped, but Harrison knew his father would have been proud.

The next day newspapers across the province carried the company's first advertisements: "McCain French Fried Potatoes are the World's Best, 8 ounce package, 39 cents."

CHAPTER FIVE

It was supposed to take thirty-five minutes for a potato plucked from a nearby farm to become a frozen French fry. The potatoes arrived at the plant in huge wooden barrels. They were then washed and dumped into one of eight Pierson steam-peelers. Next, the peeled potatoes rolled on to the trimming table, where workers cut off any imperfections. From the trimming table, the spuds were thrown into a cylinder that sped them around and shot them through a series of knives. The sliced pieces moved along a conveyor belt to a drum for a blanching process that removed bacteria and gave the fries a golden-brown look. After that, the slices were cooked in cottonseed oil in a fryer that was twenty-five feet long and six feet wide. Once cooked, the fries went to the cold storage area where they were blast-frozen at minus 40 degrees (F), packed in thirty-pound cartons and stacked in a separate room at minus 10 degrees.

The process looked simple enough on paper. But the plant rarely operated so smoothly. Wallace and Harrison spent nearly all their time keeping the factory's one shift running six days a week.

There was never enough power to run all the equipment at the same time. When the McCains started processing frozen peas, they had to stop the French fry line, remove the wiring and hook it up to the pea line. Most of the machinery was second-hand and there was always something in need of repair. Boilers routinely broke, and during one breakdown of the freezer system harmful gases leaked out for days before a repairman could be flown in from Montreal. As machines went down, Harrison went from garage to garage in the county, asking mechanics if they could do a quick repair. Employees were encouraged to bring tools and other equipment from home to save the company money. Sometimes employees even lent Wallace and Harrison money to buy a new piece of equipment. "You always got it back, sometimes with interest," says Charlie Russell, an early employee.

Working conditions were arduous. Women performed most of the line work, which was by far the most tedious in the plant. Many could stand it for only a few months a year, and the turnover rate was high. "I couldn't do that job on the trimming table," says Ken Antworth, one of the company's first employees. "The conveyor belts made me dizzy. And they couldn't talk or socialize very much because they had to concentrate on what they were doing." Even Harrison once described the trimming table job as "bloody awful boring."

Because the cold storage area had public lockers, farmers, hunters and fishermen would often tramp through the McCain plant with their latest hunting trophies or some other fresh meat for storage. Sometimes workers in the cold storage had to stop what they were doing to help someone find his locker.

There were plenty of problems outside the plant, too. One of the biggest was transportation. The McCains wanted to get their fries to Montreal and Toronto, the major markets, as quickly as possible. Before the plant opened, they'd lined up food brokers in both cities and rented warehouse space. If the warehouses were kept stocked with regular shipments, brokers could then place their orders with the warehouse and McCain would make the delivery to the customer.

Unfortunately, there weren't many truckers in Carleton County who could handle McCain's requirements. Most local trucking companies did little more than haul produce to market for farmers. McCain worked with one of the few that had a licence to operate in Ontario and Quebec, Maine Maritime Express. McCain also hired a small trucking firm called Day & Ross, which was started in nearby Hartland in 1950 by Albert Day and Walter Ross. Day & Ross handled most of their shipments within the Maritimes.

Another major problem facing the brothers from the start was the quantity and quality of the local potatoes. Carleton County was too rocky and hilly for farmers to grow more than a few acres of potatoes, which meant that most farms were too small to support the demands of a factory. In the late 1950s, the average farmer grew thirty-eight acres of potatoes, thirteen acres below what was then considered the minimum acreage for an efficient potato farm operation.

Not only were the farms small, the farmers didn't grow the right kind of potato for making French fries. For more than a century, farmers in Carleton County had grown Kennebec, Green Mountains and Keswicks. They all were excellent table stock but they were too small and round to make the long fries that restaurants wanted.

U.S. processors had discovered that the best potato for making French fries was the Russet Burbank. It is larger than most potato varieties and has an oval, uniform shape that makes perfect fries. The Russet had been around for nearly a century and was already marketed as the best potato for baking. Thanks to a brilliant marketing job by the state of Idaho, the Russet was eventually commonly known as the Idaho potato. As the potato processing industry grew, the Russet quickly became so popular that for years McDonald's required that all of its French fries had to be made from Russets.

Farmers in New Brunswick couldn't grow Russets very well because the province's growing season was too short. The McCains would have to make do with their local varieties and try to convince major buyers that New Brunswick potatoes were just as good.

Despite all the problems, Harrison and Wallace were happy to be in business at last. "How did we keep going?" Wallace now asks with a wry smile. "We just didn't know any better." They thrived on the daily challenge of keeping the plant running. The brothers worked late into the night, every night, and then headed back before the first workers arrived in the morning. Part of their time was spent in a tiny office not far from the potato line with nothing but two metal desks, two telephones and one ashtray that was piled high with the remainders of what had become a two-pack-a-day habit for both of them. "They could work from 7:00 a.m. until 7:00 p.m., drink and talk business until 3:00 a.m. and be back at work by 7:00 the next morning," recalls Joe Palmer, who worked for and later ran Day & Ross.

Bob and Andrew were also available for help and encouragement. The older brothers mainly stuck to running McCain Produce with their mother, but all four brothers met regularly to talk about the new business. Sometimes it was around the table in one brother's kitchen or in A.D.'s old office. During many of those impromptu meetings, Bob was an especially important resource. The company had been Bob's idea and he still knew far more about agriculture and agribusiness than his other brothers. He also helped inside the plant. His wife Rosemary remembers Bob swiping kitchen knives from home and taking them to the plant to experiment with the slicing machine. Another of Bob's contributions was a makeshift communications system that linked every McCain truck, office and house. "We had this big radio tower in our backyard," remembers Rosemary. "And, in the closet behind our bed was the base station for the radio." Their mother's home was also on the radio and she would often interject over the airwaves to chastise one of her sons for his foul language.

Bob was in many ways a mentor to the others. He had always been the most easygoing McCain and the one everyone could come to for sound advice. When a reporter asked Andrew in 1959 to name the organizational genius of the McCain family, Andrew didn't hesitate—"Bob."

Wallace worked mainly out in the fields. McCain Foods needed thousands of acres of potatoes, and the brothers developed a contract system to ensure a steady supply. Under the system, farmers signed a contract with McCain, usually in the spring, agreeing to deliver a specified quantity of potatoes at a fixed price. Terms of the contract dictated the price and when delivery would be required. Farmers were responsible for storing the potatoes until the delivery date. The final price also depended on the quality of the produce. The grades for processing weren't as strict as for potatoes sold to groceries stores, but all the grading was done by McCain employees.

For McCain, the contract was a way of guaranteeing supply and fixing costs. For the farmers, the contract meant a guaranteed income. But there were risks. If the price of potatoes dropped over the summer, the company would lose money because it had to pay farmers the contract price. However, if the price increased, the company saved money and the farmers were stuck with the lower contract price.

The contract was a new way of doing business for many farmers, and Wallace wanted them all to know it was a legal document. Just as he had with Douglas Allen's hardware store, Wallace made sure every detail was covered in the contract.

He explained to farmers that McCain's price wouldn't be the highest, but it was a guaranteed price and it would provide an important safety net. "A grower isn't going to make his fortune selling to us," he told a reporter in 1969. "But a contract with a processor for a moderate price is safe and it's the growers with that kind of a market who have survived best during [price slumps]."

Wallace and Harrison also began buying up farmland to grow their own potatoes. They had no intention of growing enough to supply their plant, they just wanted to see how much it cost farmers to grow potatoes in order to set a price for the McCain contract. They soon owned about four hundred acres of potatoes, not including about five thousand acres owned by McCain Produce.

Wallace also tackled the transportation problem. He pushed Day & Ross and Maine Maritime hard, demanding cut rates and prompt service. He pushed so hard that at one point he nearly put them out of business. Day & Ross "and other truckers were having problems keeping up with our growth," says Wallace now. "I looked after freight and maybe I pushed too hard. [Day and Ross] had trouble and couldn't buy equipment."

In between everything else, Wallace and Harrison loaded their cars with samples and hit the road to restaurants, school lunch rooms, hospital cafeterias, roadside canteens and anyone else who might be interested in buying their new frozen French fries. They also won an important contract with the Birds Eye plant in Maine to process frozen vegetables. The contract wasn't big, but Wallace and Harrison were desperate for any sale that would give them an early boost. Ironically, within a few years they would drive the Birds Eye plant out of business.

Because the plant hadn't opened until February, Wallace and

Harrison knew they wouldn't be able to keep production going for long. Farmers couldn't store potatoes for more than a few months, and by April the potatoes from the previous fall's harvest wouldn't be any good for processing. They decided to close the plant in April and reopen in October. Though most of the workers had to be laid off, the downtime would give the brothers a chance to repair equipment and try to make some sales.

Wallace and Harrison's frantic energy created an air of excitement about the new venture. Long-time friends couldn't resist getting involved. Harrison's pals Don Trafford and Fraser Stephenson were among the first farmers to contract with McCain. Wallace's college chum Tim Bliss joined McCain shortly after graduating from engineering school. He quit a job at the Irving company to work for McCain. Wallace's childhood buddy Alden Lunn even cut short his honeymoon to run the cold storage warehouse, even though he'd never seen a freezer before.

A big coup for the brothers was luring Carl Morris from his job at Birds Eye. Morris was second in command at the Birds Eye plant and had negotiated the processing contract with McCain. He was so impressed with the young entrepreneurs that he agreed to leave Birds Eye to become McCain's plant manager. His experience was crucial in helping the brothers keep the plant going. "We learned everything we know about making French fries from Carl Morris," says Wallace.

Sadly, struggling to keep the business going left the brothers with little time for their growing families. By 1957, Wallace and Margaret had a son, James Scott. Harrison and Billie had three children: two boys, Mark and Peter, and a daughter, Ann. Bob and Rosemary had a son, Andrew, and a daughter, Elizabeth. And Andrew and his wife Marjorie had three girls, Linda, Kathy and Margaret, along with a son named Allison.

Harrison and Wallace's families were most affected by the burgeoning new enterprise. Margaret remembers going days without seeing Wallace. Often after a long day at work, Wallace would head to Harrison's for a drink and then both would go back to work. Nearly every weekend was taken up with work, and neither brother had much time for holidays. Indeed, for all of the McCain wives, at times it was almost as if they were single parents.

Margaret "looked after things at home," Wallace recalls. "She looked after the kids. She disciplined them. I did a little, but damned little. To be honest, she raised them." As their families grew, the issue would become even more important to Margaret.

In the summer of 1957, the McCains sank even more time into the company with their decision to expand their line to include frozen peas. McCain contracted sixty-five farmers to grow about nine hundred acres. For the farmers, the peas provided not only an extra cash crop, but a rotation crop. Ideally, potato fields should be rotated every three years to avoid exhausting the soil, but few farmers in Carleton County could afford even minimal rotation. Peas weren't the best alternate crop, but they at least provided some change.

At the outset of the pea venture, Wallace and Harrison split up. Wallace worked in the fields while Harrison stayed at the plant with their plant manager, Franklin Hickling, who rigged up a pea-processing line. But processing peas turned out to be tougher than potatoes.

Peas ripen in a very short time. Twelve hours can mean the difference between grade A and grade B. That meant farmers had to follow a rigid growing schedule. Once the peas were ripe, Wallace had to move quickly from farm to farm with the harvesting equipment. Every vine had to be cut, stacked and fed into one of several viners that the McCains had bought second-hand. The viners separated the peas from their pods and dumped them into fifty-pound boxes. Once the peas were at the plant, Harrison took over. The peas were cleaned in boiling water, graded and pumped into a packaging machine. They were then sent off to cold storage for freezing.

Just as they got the system underway that summer, they were hit with a big drop in price because of a sudden glut of peas on the market. Rather than cut their losses by selling quickly, the brothers decided to store their peas and hope prices would go back up.

In October 1957, the plant reopened and French fries again rolled off the line. At the end of its first year in business, McCain Foods had revenues of $152,678, thanks largely to the Birds Eye contract. Wallace and Harrison even turned a tiny profit. They paid themselves a minimal salary and plowed all the rest into much-needed equipment and expansion.

Over the winter of 1957 and into the spring of 1958, the brothers kept up their ferocious pace. One evening, after another gruelling day, Wallace began to feel some sharp pains in his abdomen. At first he ignored the pain. He was too busy to be laid up by some stomach problem, he told himself. But the pain persisted, and soon he was too weak to work. He was losing weight but local doctors were mystified about the cause. K.C. Irving heard about Wallace's problems and sent a plane to take him to the Lahey Clinic near Boston. It was one of the best clinics on the east coast; Irving himself had gone there for medical treatment.

Luckily for Wallace, the clinic was home to Dr. Sara Jordan, nearly seventy-five years old but one of the leading experts in intestinal illness. Jordan diagnosed Wallace's problem as ulcerative colitis, an inflammatory bowel disease. The disease can normally be controlled with medication, she told Wallace, but his was in an acute phase. Dr. Jordan believed that the only way to save Wallace was to remove his large intestine. That procedure, however, was still new at the time and had first been attempted only six months earlier in England. Along with removing the large intestine, Jordan would have to run the small intestine through Wallace's abdomen to provide some way of excretion.

The surgery took several hours and no one was sure Wallace would live. "It was horrendous," Margaret recalls. She was nearly nine months pregnant at the time, which only added to the stress. To her relief, the operation was a success and Wallace came home a month later. The doctors showed him how to attach a small bag to his abdomen to clear the small intestine. Today, Wallace is one of the oldest living patients of the operation.

While Wallace was ill, Harrison was back before the county council looking for another tax break. The initial two-year concession was due to expire at the end of 1958, and Harrison wanted to start lobbying as early as possible for a new round of concessions. He knew the company wouldn't get a complete exemption from taxes again, but he wanted some long-term commitment to keep McCain Foods' taxes low. On June 18, he asked council to fix McCain's taxes at $1,000 a year for twenty years. The rate was less than half what the company was supposed to pay. Harrison also wanted an exemption from a county supplementary tax that was assessed against businesses to help pay for local schools.

It was an ambitious request and it put the council in a difficult position. There was no way the council could grant a twenty-year tax exemption. That would not only cut off an important source of tax revenue, it would also encourage other businesses to ask for similar exemptions. A local farmer's market was asking for tax concessions at the same time and the councillors had turned them down. How could they now turn around and give McCain Foods an extremely generous tax break?

The council still wanted to help McCain, however, and Bob's input no doubt persuaded any dissenters. The day after Harrison's presentation, the councillors agreed to give McCain a ten-year fixed tax rate. Under the plan, McCain was to pay $1,200 a year for the first five years and then $2,000 a year for the next five years. The company would also be assessed at a fixed rate of $100,000 a year for the supplementary school tax. Harrison wasn't happy. He felt McCain needed a twenty-year concession plan, and he planned to fight the council's proposal. However, he would have to wait until the next council meeting in January. Besides, another, more pressing problem had emerged.

After two years in business, Wallace and Harrison could see that their distribution system wasn't working. The cost of shipping, storing and delivering their products in Ontario and Quebec was mounting. Competition was starting to increase, especially in Ontario, where Salada-Shirrif had opened a plant in Alliston. The McCains figured they would be priced out of the market if they didn't find a way to cut their transportation costs. There were also logistical problems: they never knew how much of a particular product they had to keep in the warehouse, and they were forever trying to second-guess their brokers.

The brothers worked on the problem for months. The distribution system they were using was the one used by every major food processor in the United States, and there didn't seem to be any alternative. Wallace also thought he'd gone as far as he could in wringing cheap rates out of Day & Ross and Maine Maritime.

But they were still paying more than four dollars a pound to get their fries to market in Ontario. Instead of trying to fix their distribution system, they were going to have to change it.

What if they scrapped the warehouses and delivered directly to the brokers, or even to the customer? That would eliminate the cost of renting warehouses and shipping product twice, once to the warehouse and once to the final customer. They also wouldn't have to worry about how much of each product they had to ship to the warehouse since they would just fill orders from Florenceville as they came in. Overall, McCain could cut its transportation costs by one-third. But they would have to lean on their truckers to make quick, unscheduled trips. Brokers would also have to be convinced to place orders large enough to merit sending a truck from New Brunswick. And, with no regional warehouses, the brothers would have to make Carleton Cold Storage big enough to handle all the company's storage.

Putting the plan in place was a slow process. Day & Ross had just four trucks and six trailers at the time, giving them little flexibility to meet such a demanding schedule. Wallace bought three trucks to augment the shipping Day & Ross could handle. The brothers also drew up plans to expand Carleton Cold Storage and started slowly to convince brokers to take larger shipments. As the overall plan fell into place, costs fell and McCain was able to compete with anyone in Montreal and Toronto. "That decision to change the distribution system," Wallace now recalls, "was the single most important reason for our success. No one was doing it that way at the time."

The McCains still wanted more control over the system. For two years, Wallace and Harrison had done almost all the selling, with brokers picking up the ongoing orders. Now, they decided to use fewer brokers and develop their own sales team. The first step was to hire a sales manager.

A buyer at Dominion Stores had told Harrison about a hot young salesman named Ralph Orr. He was a tall, boisterous Halifax native who was working in New Brunswick for a company called Puritan Foods. Harrison was convinced that Orr was perfect for McCain and he quickly spread the word among restaurants and stores that Orr was about to join the company.

In fact, Orr recalls being told he was joining McCain by a Puritan customer. "I was making the rounds up the Saint John valley and I called some people around Edmonston," says Orr. "One guy said to me, 'So, I hear you're going to McCain.' I hadn't even *met* Harrison McCain."

Orr called Harrison to find out what was going on. Harrison said he was looking for a sales manager and asked if Orr could come to Florenceville the next day to talk about the job. Orr was interested. He'd been offered a national sales position with Puritan in Vancouver but neither he nor his wife wanted to leave New Brunswick, so the McCain job sounded enticing.

Orr drove up to the McCain plant early the next morning. As he got out of his car, he took a long look at the small, white building. He really wasn't sure what McCain made but it didn't look like a very big operation. Orr was having second thoughts as he sat down in the small office to talk to Harrison, but an hour or so later, he agreed to join the company and move to Florenceville. "I don't know how Harrison talked me into it," Orr recalls with a laugh. "I moved into a hotel and then rented a tiny house. My wife nearly died. There was nothing to do in that town."

Orr was immediately put in charge of sales for the Maritimes while Wallace and Harrison fanned out to other provinces trying to find customers. From the day he started, Orr knew that selling McCain's frozen fries was going to be tough. Frozen fries and fast food still hadn't caught on in Canada the way they had in the United States. Few restaurant owners wanted to switch from making their own fries out of fresh potatoes. It didn't help that McCain's frozen fries were far more expensive than fresh potatoes.

"Our fries were costing about eighteen cents a pound while [a restaurant owner] could get fresh potatoes at about three cents a pound," recalls Orr. How did he get them to switch? "We had to use charm, bullshit, anything that would work."

Orr remembers walking up and down streets across the Atlantic provinces talking to every cook in every greasy spoon and trying to show them the benefits of a product that was more expensive and completely unknown to most of them. "It was a bastard. I knew a lot of these guys from my former job and they'd say, 'Orr, you're a good fellow but you must be mad.'"

The McCain salesmen found that even if they made a sale and convinced a restaurant to use McCain's frozen fries, the cook would switch back to fresh potatoes a week or two later. "You'd sell two or three cases of prepared product and you'd go back two weeks later and say, 'How is it working out?' and he'd say 'I've gone back to fresh,' and you'd start to sell him all over again," recalls Bev O'Keefe, who worked as a McCain salesman for a while. "I remember every goddamn night—Harrison might be in B.C. and Wallace might be in Saskatchewan and I might be in Halifax and we'd talk to one another on the damn telephone every night and say 'Who did you get today for an account?'"

Wallace and Harrison knew they needed a clever pitch. Restaurant owners agreed the frozen fries were convenient, but convenience wasn't enough when the owner had a bottom line to worry about. The brothers had to compete on price, and they came up with a sales pitch that purported to show how McCain fries were competitive with fresh potatoes. The pitch was summarized in a company pamphlet. According to McCain, 100 pounds of potatoes cost $3.00 (3 cents a pound). But the restaurant owner lost half the potato in trimming, peeling and cutting up for French fries. That increased the cost to $6.00 for 100 pounds. Taking into account the cost of fat for cooking, the total came to $9.64, which was the same as 53 pounds of McCain frozen fries.

Timing, however, proved to be their biggest sales asset. As 1958 wore on, the fast-food phenomenon started building. Ray Kroc had established over one hundred McDonald's restaurants across the United States. Burger King was a close second, and Kentucky Fried Chicken was spreading quickly as well, along with a host of copycat chains. Canadians were also finally getting into the act. In Edmonton, Leroy Russell, a Montana native, was setting up the first of many A&W drive-ins. And, every fast-food restaurant owner was discovering that French fries were their second-most-profitable item, after soft drinks.

McCain's frozen fries were the perfect fit. Soon, Wallace and Harrison could barely keep up with orders as new fast-food restaurants opened up. They signed up nearly fifty restaurants in Toronto and dozens more across the Maritimes. While restaurants were McCain's biggest customers, grocery stores were also eager to stock McCain products mainly because of the fast food craze. By the end of 1958, McCain fries and peas were on the shelves of every Sobey's store in the Maritimes, and more than three hundred Dominion stores in Quebec and Atlantic Canada. The business soon "was growing like hell," says Bev O'Keefe. "We were witnessing growth of 50, 60, 70, 80 percent a year."

After just two years in operation, employment at McCain's plant more than doubled to ninety-four. Another one hundred workers were employed during peak pea and potato harvest season. The brothers now had 1,300 acres of peas under contract and were packaging three million pounds of frozen peas a year. They also put an addition on the cold storage building that nearly doubled its size, and they installed a new $105,000 freezer.

Harrison and Wallace were making small inroads into markets in western Canada as well. They trucked fries to Toronto and put them on a train for Winnipeg, where they'd rented warehouses. Local brokers did the rest, with Wallace or Harrison making frequent sales trips. Sales were also getting so widespread that the brothers bought a second-hand airplane to stretch their reach even further. They flew out of Fredericton or Maine or any open field that was clear enough.

In the fall of 1958, the brothers even lucked out on the pea crop they had stored a year earlier when prices plunged. Bad weather ruined pea crops throughout the region and prices soared. McCain sold their stored peas and turned a healthy profit from a crop that only twelve months earlier had seemed to be a write-off. But they weren't always so lucky. Their plans to package frozen strawberries and carrots fell flat, mainly because of production problems. And there was still the matter of tax concessions from the county council.

On January 21, 1959, Harrison and Wallace headed to Woodstock. Harrison still wasn't happy with the council's proposed ten-year tax break. The brothers said that they had reviewed the proposed concessions and had found them "quite frankly inadequate and not providing the necessary assistance." The difference between their plan—fixing McCain taxes at $1,000 a year for twenty years—and what the council proposed amounted to $1,500 a year for ten years. "Is this such a large amount to be concerned about? It could rightly be said that this amount of money means a great deal to both the company and the municipality, but to whose greater advantage would this difference of $1,500 be?"

The company, they argued, had contributed more than $560,000 to the county in two years through wages and purchases of produce from farmers. On the other hand, McCain's operating costs were high because of its location, they argued. The company also paid more for transportation and power than companies in Ontario, and McCain provided its own water supply, which saved the county money. Giving McCain a higher tax break would help the company expand, and that would provide benefits to the community, they argued. "This difference of $1,500 means a great deal in the operations of the company and it is respectfully submitted that the same amount of money does not have the same meaning to the municipality."

The tough presentation, along with a few well-chosen words from Bob, who was still a councillor, worked. Three days later, council agreed to rescind its June resolution and grant McCain a twenty-year tax break. McCain was to pay $1,500 a year for ten years. The company's taxes would increase to $2,000 a year for the next five years and $2,500 a year in the last five years. The plan would be reviewed after the first five-year period, which gave the brothers a chance to negotiate a new deal. Overall, the council's plan was about twice what McCain had hoped to pay, but the brothers had managed to win a twenty-year tax concession with a chance to renegotiate in five years. It was a rare and lucrative arrangement at the time.

The council's tax concessions had to be approved by the provincial government. It gladly agreed and legislation was passed in April 1959 outlining McCain's tax schedule with the county.

With the concessions sorted out and sales booming, Wallace and Harrison began to think about expansion. They were already convinced that they would soon conquer the Canadian market. But that wasn't enough. They had to go farther. The brothers had watched their father expand his business to Cuba and Europe. Foreign markets were crucial to his business and the brothers knew they were important to McCain Foods. But where should they go?

The United States was the most logical option, but J.R. Simplot and a few other large processors were well established there. Wallace and Harrison knew they couldn't compete with them and didn't want to lose a lot of money trying. With the United States ruled out, the brothers turned to Britain and Australia, largely because they were English-speaking. (They also considered South Africa but eventually ruled it out because of the growing political problems.) After some research they discovered that Britain and Australia were untapped markets for frozen French fries. None of the big American processors had expanded beyond the United States since it was providing more than enough business for them. There were some major food processors in Britain and Australia, including Unilever and Nestlé's, but those companies had virtually no frozen French fry production because the American fast-food phenomenon had yet to take hold.

"They really weren't basic in the [French fry] business," Harrison once said. "They didn't own really good factories. They bought most of the product they sold and they had a huge number of other products to sell. So, they didn't really have much deep commitment to the potato business."

The brothers decided both countries were easy prey for a company that specialized in French fries. Besides, it was only a matter of time before Brits and Aussies got their first taste of fast food, and the McCains wanted to be there first to cash in. Eventually that became the motto for McCain's expansion around the world—get there first and then dominate the market.

Harrison and Wallace decided to tackle Britain first since it was closer. In the fall of 1959, they contacted distributors in Britain to get a feel for the market and the importing process. Their first sale was a load of frozen peas to Smedley's Ltd. Within a few months, McCain was supplying frozen fries and potato products to half a dozen other British food companies. It was a small start, but it gave the McCains a sense of how to operate in another country and how to co-ordinate overseas shipping.

By 1960, Wallace and Harrison felt the business was established enough that they could move out of their rented homes and find something more suitable for their growing families. Harrison and Billie were especially keen to get out of the tiny two-bedroom house, since they now had four children.

Harrison started looking for a place to build a new, larger home. He picked a site on the west side of the river, across the road and a few doors down from the McCain family home, where his mother still lived. The McCain plant was just to the north-east. The lot was enormous, stretching up from the road that he and Wallace used to walk down to get to school. Harrison built a Cape Cod style house with white clapboard siding. The setting was beautiful—the front porch had a spectacular view of the rich farmland of the river valley.

Wallace built his house shortly after his brother. He chose a site next to Harrison's, divided from it by only a small field. "I always thought Harrison took the best view in the village," remembers Wallace. "And this was the second-best spot." Margaret hired an architect from Saint John to design the two-storey white house with black shutters. Wallace's contribution were the six pillars that ran along the front of the house and, years later, a small tower in the back yard. From there he could see across much of the valley, and on a quiet evening it was one of his favourite places.

Building their houses side by side might have been a coincidence but it reflected the closeness of their relationship at the time. Wallace and Harrison spent nearly all their hours together, working every day and most nights at the plant. On the occasional summer Sunday afternoon they would round up the office staff, who always worked weekends, for a game of golf. In the few hours they had off, the brothers would often play tennis together.

Their personalities complemented each other when it came to running the business. Harrison was the overall planner who enjoyed working on the big moves, such as co-ordinating the expansion into Britain. His name appears on nearly all early correspondence to England about arranging the first shipments and brokers. He also had a way of making people do almost anything for his approval. "Harrison has a great capacity for finding good people and working with them," says Harrison's long-time friend Jim Coutts. "He's a recruiter."

Harrison liked to play a big brother role with the staff. He could often be remarkably generous, writing out cheques for thousands of dollars to support a local cause. He once gave an executive $7,000 to start a group home for young people without seeing any plans for the project. Florenceville is also full of stories of sick people being offered the McCain plane to fly to hospital in Fredericton. In many ways, Harrison enjoyed the role of protector and benefactor for all of Florenceville.

Harrison McCain was not necessarily an easy man to work for, though. Ralph Orr remembers how Harrison would play off Wallace with employees. "Wallace would give someone shit and then Harrison would come in to try to smooth things over," Orr says. "Harrison was more of a schemer. He would wait for someone to hang themselves before he fired them."

Harrison also had a temperamental side that often shocked friends. His friend Claude Bursill remembers Harrison blowing up at an office worker once for making an innocuous joke about lawyers. "Harrison leapt out at this comment and said he wanted details," remembers Bursill. "He was banging on his desk. It was astonishing anybody would do this. The fellow drove me to the airport in Fredericton and barely said a word, he was so shaken up. Harrison had a temper, and he could lose it and be very rough."

Even close friends were kept at arm's length. Harrison rarely opened up to friends emotionally and never spoke in detail about the company's affairs. "He doesn't want anybody to know about the business beyond a certain point," says Jim Coutts.

While Harrison played the patriarch, Wallace kept the plant humming. He was even more of the detail man now than when he and Harrison first began looking for a business. He spent endless hours trying to cut costs and fretting over the intricacies of the plant. "Wallace was dedicated more to the business details," says Coutts.

Wallace became shameless about finding out what McCain's competitors where doing. For years, Wallace and his friend and company engineer, Tim Bliss, travelled to French fry plants in the United States and talked their way in for a tour. "We run a small potato processing plant in Canada and we'd appreciate a chance to see how it's really done," Wallace would tell the plant manager. The manager would usually reply, "Canada? You can't process potatoes up there." Then he would throw open the doors and give the Canadians a guided tour. Once they got home, Wallace and Bliss would write down everything they had seen and copy it for McCain's plant. The "tours" helped immeasurably, and McCain was always on top of the latest techniques. As a testament to how important the visits were to McCain's development, the brothers never let anyone into their plant, including their biggest customers.

Wallace was also more demanding of employees, especially the sales staff. He didn't care about being liked, he wanted results, and if someone couldn't deliver they were fired. "His favourite expression was 'Fuck him, fire him,'" says Orr, who adds that Wallace's toughness was one reason he left McCain in the late 1960s. Wallace "was always looking for perfection. And it made me uncomfortable how quickly he fired people."

On the other hand, Wallace also inspired intense loyalties. He respected employees who proved themselves, and he forged lifelong friendships with some of the senior staff. He was also honest, almost to a fault, telling suppliers, farmers or even customers exactly what he thought. Wallace was never afraid to question his own work. If he made a mistake, he admitted it and didn't try to blame an underling. He once gave a speech to an industry association that was giving McCain an award, outlining in detail some major mistakes he had made in McCain's Australian operations.

The brothers had few if any major disagreements. Wallace can remember only one argument they could not resolve. It was over publicity. From the start, Harrison was eager to promote the company. Breaking with the practices of his mentor, K.C. Irving, Harrison wanted to take a high public profile to help get the company's name recognized. To Harrison, publicity was the only way a small company in rural New Brunswick would get noticed by the major players in central Canada. It was also free advertising. But on this point Wallace agreed with Irving; he wanted the company to guard its privacy and keep a low profile. The two argued over the issue for years before asking Carl Morris, Tim Bliss and some other managers what they thought. Wallace remembers both brothers putting forward their thoughts. The group agreed with Harrison. "So, I dropped it," Wallace recalls.

Wallace and Harrison's business relationship was getting results. By the early 1960s, the fast-food business was well established in Canada and McCain was striking it rich. In 1961, Harland Sanders finally franchised his Kentucky Fried Chicken restaurants and dozens of his restaurants were set up in Canada using only McCain fries. "I knew the guy in Halifax who had the Atlantic Canada franchise for Kentucky Fried Chicken," recalls Ralph Orr. "He told me he wanted to keep using fresh potatoes, I said 'You're crazy.' He later bought McCain fries and became a good way into other Kentucky Fried Chicken restaurants."

Canada still had a long way to go before matching the expansion of fast food that was underway in the United States at the time. By 1961, McDonald's had more than two hundred restaurants across the United States and its main rival, Burger King, was close behind. Dozens of other chains were also springing up as well, and it was only a matter of time before those chains headed north.

By 1964, McCain's sales had hit $2.5 million. The company was selling sixteen different products, including various cuts of French fries and several versions of instant potatoes, such as flaked potatoes, potato patties, potato crystals, potato puffs and even potato chips. Their frozen vegetables also included peas, broccoli and Brussels sprouts. The plant was running two ten-hour shifts year round and employed more than seven hundred people at peak season. It had also been completely renovated, which helped cut production costs by 40 percent. McCain could now process in one hour what it had taken a year to process in 1957. The cold storage area had also been more than doubled and was now around 1.3 million cubic feet.

Sales were going so well in Toronto that the brothers hired a full-time sales manager for Ontario. Richard McWhirter was thirty years old and full of frenetic energy. He'd left his home in Apple River, Nova Scotia, at the age of eighteen to find a career in Toronto. After getting a job at a bank, he quit when he was transferred to Halifax. He'd always wanted to get into sales and he landed a job with a food broker. Every day his boss gave him a sampling of products and a streetcar pass and told him to cover the city. His success landed him a sales job with Kellogg Co. in Hamilton, Ontario. Like Ralph Orr, McWhirter found McCain fries a tough sell in the late 1950s until the fast-food chains arrived. "Selling [McCain] in the early days was tougher than selling insurance," he said in a company profile in 1968. But soon he had signed up restaurants and grocery stores across the province, and Ontario became McCain's biggest market.

By the early 1960s, Wallace had given up running McCain's own trucks, and the brothers bought Day & Ross in 1965. By then Day & Ross had grown into a good-sized trucking company with twenty tractors and thirty trailers. But the other carrier McCain used, Maine Maritime, which had a licence to haul to Ontario, was in dire financial shape and was facing bankruptcy. McCain had already pumped considerable money into the company to help keep it going but nothing seemed to be working. Just as Maine Maritime was about to go under, the McCains decided to buy it in order to get the Ontario licence. But they had to move fast. Once the company was in bankruptcy the licence would be cancelled. The brothers managed to close the deal barely twenty-four hours before the licence was due to expire. They merged Maine Maritime's few trucks into Day & Ross, and Joe Palmer, who was by now a partner in Day & Ross, was named president. The McCains now owned one of the biggest trucking companies in the Maritimes.

With their distribution system in the Maritimes, Quebec and Ontario working well, they still faced some difficulties in getting McCain products to western Canada. To make matters worse, by 1963 the company was also facing new competition in the west. Simplot had built a plant in southern Manitoba's rich potato country. In Alberta, Sun-Alta Potato Processors Ltd. had opened a new $1-million French fry plant in Taber, and several local processors were popping up around Vancouver. The competition was making it hard if not impossible for McCain to stay competitive in western Canada, which was a lucrative market. McCain had to ship its fries by train to Winnipeg, Edmonton, Calgary and Vancouver and store them in warehouses. "It took two weeks or a month sometimes," Wallace remembers. "And our stuff would arrive defrosted." Once orders were filled they had to truck the fries to the customer. It was a carbon copy of the costly distribution system they had once used in eastern Canada.

Just as it appeared that the company might have to write off the west, the brothers noticed an interesting phenomenon. In the United States, American railways were moving carloads of agricultural products from west to east but were heading back west virtually empty. The McCains talked to the U.S. railways, who said they would gladly haul McCain fries west for a fraction of the rate CP and CN were charging. But it wouldn't be as easy as loading on the CP cars outside the Florenceville plant. To get their fries to Vancouver, Wallace and Harrison would have to truck them across the Maine border to Mars Hill, load them onto a train for Boston, transfer to a train headed to Seattle and then truck them up to Vancouver. Even with that circuitous route, however, the brothers figured they could cut their transportation costs by half. They decided to use the cheaper U.S. rates as leverage with the Canadian railways. Harrison began to badger, cajole and harass CP: if they didn't cut their rates, the company would use the U.S. railways.

"He was a great salesman," said Stuart Eagles, Harrison's friend from Acadia who was working at CP Rail's head office at the time. "He'd convince CP to cut its freight rates. He'd go right in to see Ian Sinclair, who was vice president of CPR at the time. I remember Sinclair saying, 'God damn, here comes Harrison again.'"

"CP caved in," says Wallace. "And so did CNR. And that saved our ass in the west."

Just as the western transportation issue was solved, a potential disaster flared up on an unexpected front. In early 1963, some county councillors were beginning to have second thoughts about the twenty-year tax concession the county had granted McCain. While McCain was providing significant benefits to the county and had strong support around Florenceville, there were those who were beginning to resent the McCains' growing power.

The McCain family now ran three of the biggest companies in the county, McCain Foods, Carleton Cold Storage and

McCain Produce. McCain Foods had more than three hundred farmers under contract and owned thousands of acres of farmland. The company was also the biggest purchaser of local farm produce, buying $2.75 million a year in potatoes and other vegetables. Why did McCain Foods still need a tax break?

In January 1963, the detractors got their chance to take on McCain. The company's tax concession was up for its five-year renewal and a group of councillors were ready to pounce. Bob was still on council and kept Harrison and Wallace posted on the opposition to the concession. In an attempt to head off the detractors, Wallace and Harrison headed to council on January 16 to make their pitch again.

It was a compelling case. Before McCain, the county had been a basket case of rural depression. Throughout the 1950s, the government had been desperate to attract any investment. Parts of the area didn't even have electricity until after World War II. Now, thanks largely to McCain, farmers had a buffer to fluctuating potato prices and farm wives and other non-farm workers had an opportunity to work. Florenceville had virtually no unemployment, and the region's average income level was approaching the provincial average for the first time. The McCains had also made enormous contributions to the village, donating money for countless community projects including a hockey arena, curling rink and library. Wallace and Harrison felt the donations were part of their responsibility as owners of the town's largest employer.

On the down side, the McCains were now perceived as feudal landlords, living in a castle on the hill and owning almost everything around it. While the McCains contributed to many community projects, they also seemed to be balking at paying taxes that benefited the community. It was as if the McCains wanted to control whom they supported and how, instead of bolstering the local government with their tax dollars.

A day after the presentation by Harrison and Wallace, a group of ten councillors moved a resolution to cancel McCain's tax concessions. They argued that while the council was grateful for the prosperity McCain provided, the county couldn't afford the concession any longer. It was also unfair to farmers and other local businesses who were paying much higher taxes. Furthermore, the county was getting insufficient help from the provincial government to pay for social services and needed the tax revenue from McCain.

Because of the sensitivity of the vote—most councillors had family or friends who worked for McCain or grew potatoes for the company—council agreed to hold a secret ballot on the motion. It was defeated fifteen to ten, a remarkably close vote considering how supportive the council had been to McCain just four years earlier. After two more days of debate, council gave interim approval to a five-year tax break for McCain based on a complicated formula that worked out to around $8,000 a year. It was a victory for McCain's opponents because under the original tax plan the company was slated to pay $1,500 a year for the next five years. But opponents of the tax break still had one more card to play.

The new rate was to take effect in 1964, but council put a notice in the local papers asking for public comment before holding a final vote on the tax break. When council met six months later for the final vote, councillors were presented with a petition signed by 248 people asking the county not to proceed with any concessions for McCain. It was a large number of people considering that the vast majority of families in the county must have had either a family member or relative working for McCain Foods or McCain Produce. The McCains had never faced that kind of public opposition before, and it must have come as a shock to the family, considering that they had always considered themselves part of the community. But clearly there was animosity among people who were still living on meagre incomes while the McCains amassed huge wealth. McCain Foods was booming, but many people in Carleton County didn't see the benefits of that growth flowing down to them. The area was more prosperous because of McCain, but how much more prosperous might it be if the company paid its fair share of taxes? they asked.

The outcry didn't work. Despite the petition, and a call by one councillor to put off the final vote, council approved the revised tax concession. Once again, Bob's role on council was pivotal not only as a key vote but in lining up support for

McCain. It was the last time the company would have to con-front council for tax breaks; the provincial government abolished county councils in 1965 as part of a sweeping reform of munic-ipal government.

Resentment towards McCain persisted. Some farmers began grumbling about the company's control over nearly every aspect of farming. Those feelings were exacerbated in 1964 when McCain bought Thomas Equipment.

Emery Thomas had been running a small blacksmith shop for twenty years just down the road from Florenceville in the vil-lage of Centreville. Thomas was an inventor, someone who liked to tinker with anything mechanical. By the early 1960s, Thomas had created a new contraption for harvesting potatoes. The McCains liked the idea but could see that Thomas would never be able to mass-produce his machine since he had only two employees, so Wallace and Harrison bought his company for about $75,000 and made him head of the research team. They had big dreams for Thomas Equipment. If the harvester and some of Thomas's other ideas worked out, the McCains hoped to make Thomas Equipment a major farm machinery company. That would be a nice bit of diversification.

Perhaps more importantly, Thomas Equipment was another rung on McCain's ladder of vertical integration. McCain Produce grew potato seeds, Thomas Equipment machines har-vested the ripe potatoes and McCain Foods processed them. In the mid 1960s, the brothers would also start a fertilizer company, further tightening their grip.

There were complaints that farmers who signed contracts with McCain were also forced to buy Thomas Equipment and other supplies from McCain. Both Wallace and Harrison denied it, but Harrison's friend Don Trafford says the pressure was there, even if it was subtle. Farmers, he remembers, were often asked what fertilizer they would be using as they signed their annual McCain contract. "What would you say?" he asks.

In 1964, two farmers openly challenged the company. Euclide Ouellette and Louis Guy Desjardins, both from neigh-bouring Victoria County, defied the McCain contract and sold their potatoes elsewhere. Desjardins further challenged McCain by saying that the company hadn't honoured its pea contract with him because it had not taken delivery of the entire crop.

The McCains fought back, hard. In what might be seen as a forerunner to the ruthless legal assault they would launch on each other in the 1990s, Harrison and Wallace hit both farmers with crushing lawsuits. In separate statements of claim, McCain demanded Ouellette pay $15,602 as a reimbursement for the potatoes plus 1 percent interest a month for the nine months since the contract had been signed. The company also wanted $3,812.42 for fertilizer they had advanced Ouellette against the contract. The total claim was $19,033.18, a massive amount for any farmer at the time. As for Desjardins, McCain demanded $4,500 for the potatoes.

The brothers were determined to show Ouellette, Desjardins and other farmers that the McCain contract was a legally binding document. Wallace had set out the terms of the contract in detail and he expected it to be honoured. He knew it was tough but this was business. "The contract is written for dishonest people," Wallace once said in a documentary about the company. "It's a tough contract. There isn't any question about it. And the contract, I agree, is one-sided." The company won both suits and the farmers were ordered to pay.

Harrison's friend Don Trafford says the McCains had other ways to keep farmers in line. "I used to haul potatoes for them as a way of making some extra money," he said. "Once, I started criticizing them too much, and I was told they wouldn't be hiring my truck that year. It was just their way of making a point. If a group of farmers didn't like their contract, McCain would go over to Maine for potatoes just to teach them a lesson."

While there were critics, many thought the McCains were tough but fair. Numerous farmers contracted with McCain for decades and earned a good living. Even Don Trafford concedes that the McCains treated farmers reasonably. "Their price was all right but no one was going to get rich off it," he says. The key, however, was to always play by McCain's rules.

CHAPTER SIX

Ralph Orr staggered into his hotel room in New Glasgow, Nova Scotia, and collapsed on the bed. He was exhausted from another tough day of selling McCain fries to every greasy spoon, truck stop and lunch counter in town. His hands ached from lugging the McCain samples around and his head pounded from another long day of reciting the benefits of frozen French fries. It was March 1964, and even though the company was booming Orr still found the sales calls gruelling. He'd been McCain's sales manager for about five years and still found the work tougher than his old job at Puritan Foods.

Just as Orr put his feet up on the bed the phone rang. It was Harrison. "We're sending you to England for some trade shows," Harrison barked into the phone. Orr thought maybe he was having a bad dream. He'd had a vague idea that Harrison and Wallace were planning to expand to England, but Orr thought that was a long way off. He'd also never been to England and had no idea if they even ate French fries there. Orr tried tactfully to bow out of the British invasion. "I don't know a pence from a pound," he said. Harrison laughed and replied, "Everything will be fine," before quickly hanging up.

Orr was on a flight to London a few days later. His assignment was to manage a McCain booth at two major trade shows for Canadian companies. The shows were in Manchester for one week and Glasgow the next week, and about a hundred companies were expected to display their products. He was worried. He had no idea how to manage the booth or even where it would be set up. He also had no local support, since McCain had only a few local brokers selling its fries.

Orr decided to ask for some assistance at the the Canadian high commission. A trade official explained the format of the shows and told Orr where to set up the McCain booth. He also suggested that Orr hire some demonstrators to hand out samples of McCain fries. Orr thought that was an excellent idea and he hired fifty demonstrators from an agency recommended by the high commission. Feeling somewhat in control at last, he headed to Manchester to set up the booth.

The next day, as he sorted out the McCain products, Orr noticed a group of fifty women walking towards the booth. They were all young, gorgeous and dressed in tight skirts. He gulped. He wasn't sure this was the image Harrison wanted to project, but there was nothing he could do now.

As the show began, the product and the demonstrators turned out to be a huge hit. The McCain booth was constantly surrounded, causing a huge traffic jam in the hall. Orr was handing out samples and lining up distributors non-stop. "Our products were the most popular by far," he recalls. "We started selling samples even though we weren't supposed to."

Then, about halfway through the first show, Orr discovered that some of the men crowding around his booth were after more than frozen French fries. Some of his demonstrators were prostitutes. "I found that out when one of them propositioned me," he recalls. Now he was really worried. If word got out that McCain had hired hookers to work a trade show, the company might be mired in scandal before it even got a foothold in Britain. Orr was near panic. "Sick, really sick," he scrawled in his diary after one long day at the show. Orr headed nervously off to Glasgow for the second show, where the fries and the friendly demonstrators were just as big a hit.

The true profession of some of the demonstrators remained a secret, but word of McCain's frozen fries spread across Britain. Orders poured in and the company's sales soared from $50,000 to $1 million within about a year. Sales were growing so fast that the McCains decided to buy a distributor. They settled on Caterpac Ltd., which in just ten years had become Britain's largest food importer. McCain bought Caterpac in September

1965 and moved its head office from London two hundred miles north to Grimsby to take advantage of cheaper port facilities. The McCains then hired a young executive named Charles "Mac" McCarthy, who had worked at Eskimo Foods Ltd. in Britain, to run Caterpac. After just five years, the McCains had already established their primary goal in Britain: they were the first major French fry maker in the country. Now they had to dominate the market.

Back home, the McCain business was growing in several directions. By 1966, the brothers had started a fertilizer business called McCain Fertilizer Ltd. and built a $150,000 plant in Florenceville, with plans for a second plant of similar size in Grand Falls. Additions were also being made to the processing plant and the cold storage area, and they were planning to start production of boil-in-bag vegetables and shoestring-cut French fries. Up the road in Centreville, the McCains were also preparing a 37,000-square-foot factory to make potato harvesters for Thomas Equipment.

Rapid expansion and changes in the company were beginning to change the relationship between Harrison and Wallace. In business terms, they still made all major decisions jointly and were in constant contact. But on a personal level, the two started growing apart. At one point, according to Wallace's wife Margaret, Harrison suggested that the families keep their distance socially because he and Wallace spent so much time together at work and needed to develop other contacts. As if to emphasize his point, Harrison planted a row of tall pine trees between his house and Wallace's in the early 1960s, which Margaret started calling "the Berlin Wall." By the late 1960s, the families were spending almost no time together. "I don't remember going over there very much at all," says Wallace's daughter Eleanor. "I'm sure we did for big events, but nothing really stands out."

McCain Foods was becoming more established and the brothers were no longer so absorbed in keeping the plant running that they were inseparable. They now had more freedom to become involved in other interests. Their choices would accentuate their personal differences.

Much of Harrison's time was spent creating a public image for himself and McCain. He'd always believed that a strong public profile would help McCain and open new contacts. Soon, Harrison became the only McCain quoted in most news reports and profiles of the company. He also began offering views on public issues and even advocated the union of the Atlantic provinces and a free trade pact between the Maritimes and the New England states.

Harrison also became a good friend of Premier Louis Robichaud after his surprising victory for the Liberals in the 1960 provincial election. Robichaud was just thirty-four years old when he became premier, and he'd been Liberal leader for only two years. Harrison knew the importance of political contacts. After all, McCain had received more than $1.3 million in federal and provincial loans, grants and guarantees, along with untold thousands in local tax concessions. But Harrison also honestly admired Robichaud and was one of his biggest supporters in the business community.

Harrison was one of the few businessmen to publicly back Robichaud's sweeping "Program of Equal Opportunity." Launched in 1965, the program was one of the biggest reforms of municipal government ever attempted in Canada. It involved abolishing county councils, handing more power to the provincial government, thereby standardizing social services across the province and putting an end to local tax concessions. Many business leaders criticized the program, including K.C. Irving, who bitterly attacked Robichaud. But Harrison openly supported the premier, believing such reform was long overdue. Perhaps it was his mother's charitable nature, but Harrison was a social liberal at heart. He believed strongly in social programs and felt New Brunswick had fallen behind. Harrison also publicly endorsed Robichaud's call for official bilingualism, a proposition not popular with business people at the time. Harrison and Robichaud became close personal friends. They flew to hockey games in Boston together on McCain's plane, and sometimes Harrison even lent the plane to Robichaud for government business.

In 1966, Robichaud gave Harrison an impressive platform to

develop his own ideas for improving the province's economy. Harrison was appointed to the New Brunswick Development Corp, which had been created in 1963 as part of a government initiative to develop new industry in the province. The board was made up of seven New Brunswick business people, including Harrison, who advised the government. It was headed by a flamboyant Englishman named James Addison. Harrison and Addison were a perfect match and became close friends. Both were dreamers who had big plans for New Brunswick. "He was probably the most progressive member of the board," Addison says today.

Addison's plans were enormous, and Harrison was one of his biggest boosters. He proposed building a massive, multiple-industry complex filled with companies selected by the corporation. Addison predicted the complex would employ twenty thousand people within eight years. He even spent $500,000 (US) for studies by British and Italian consultants. But the project was too grand for New Brunswick's government and it never got past the planning stage. Undeterred, Addison later proposed building a new a deep-water port near Saint John. The port would include an industrial complex that would be dedicated as a free trade zone. Addison spent $242,000 to study the idea plus $25,000 for a public relations campaign. He then approached one hundred companies around the world to see if they would locate in the new complex. None would commit, and the project was dropped. The failures created a cloud around the development corporation, and it was wound up in the early 1970s.

Addison spent money recklessly, says Reg Tweedale, who was Deputy Minister of Industry at the time. "I don't think [the corporation] had any real lasting effect."

Harrison also became enamoured with developing contacts beyond New Brunswick. He would often invite writers, bankers and other business people to his home for dinners and weekends. He even built a small guest house for his many visitors and hired a full-time chef and butler. A swimming pool and tennis court were added later as well. One McCain executive remembers Harrison returning from a trip to Asia and proudly displaying a new shirt. "Know where I got this?" Harrison asked the executive. "Marcos gave it to me." Harrison saw the contacts as advancing McCain's worldwide image. He was also fascinated by other successful people, and friends say he had a curiosity about ideas, world events and other business leaders.

By 1966, Harrison and Billie had two sons, Mark and Peter, and three daughters, Laura, Ann and Gillian. His business schedule kept him on the road for about six months every year, and his rare evenings and weekends at home were filled with visitors or more work. The pressures on him were enormous. He once told Margaret, "When I come home I want the kids ready for bed. I'll have a short period of time with them and I expect total obedience."

Billie rarely complained about Harrison's schedule, but friends say it did affect her. "'You know, Harrison has been away 265 days this year,'" Billie once told a close friend. "That's all she said about it, but it bothered her."

Aside from coping with her husband's absence, Billie was also expected to keep the house in immaculate condition. Harrison would call last-minute dinner parties and Billie would have only a few hours' notice to whip up an extravagant meal. To keep the house clean at all times, she insisted that the children play only in their rooms.

"Harrison divorced his family for the company," says one former McCain executive.

While Harrison built a public profile, Wallace chose to shy away from the limelight. Like Harrison, he was appointed to some government advisory councils, and he also endorsed most of Robichaud's policies, but he rarely offered his views in public and the councils he joined were low-profile. Wallace was cynical about politics. He never forgot the time as a child when his father had made him hand out five-dollar bills to Liberal supporters heading to the polls on election day in Florenceville.

Wallace's shyness kept him away from Harrison's social events. He was also somewhat suspicious and sceptical of most public figures. He wasn't impressed by or interested in them. To many of Harrison's friends, that made Wallace appear cold and distant. "We used to go over to see Wallace occasionally," says Claude Bursill. "He was pleasant. But Wallace never seemed to me to be a nice bloke."

Outside of McCain Foods, Wallace's focus was his family. Like Harrison, Wallace put in a swimming pool and tennis court, but there was no guest house, and social events were rare at Wallace's home. His illness and near death in 1958 made him aware of his own mortality: he couldn't take anything for granted.

Margaret believed that if her children were to develop properly they needed mothering and fathering. She was respectful of the demands McCain's made on Wallace's time and accepted that he too was on the road half the year. What she wouldn't accept was Wallace spending what free time he did have with anyone but their children. "I could work twelve days straight but if I had the next three days off [Margaret] filled them with hockey practices, swim meets and time with the children," says Wallace. "There was no way we were going off skiing or to some party."

"I remember Wallace rushing out of a meeting saying he had to go off to his son's hockey game," said Tim Bliss, Wallace's friend and a McCain vice president. "I coached the kids for a while and I remember him attending quite a few games. Harrison's kids also played for me but he wasn't there as much."

While Harrison tried to present a polished, professional image, Wallace tended to be a bit more homespun. Even late into his career Margaret would have to match up his suits and ties, numbering them so that Wallace could easily see which ones went together.

In spite of Wallace's efforts to become a family man, Margaret was still frustrated. Michael, a brother for Scott, had been born in November 1958, just three weeks after Wallace's life-saving operation. The doctors had told Margaret then that because of Wallace's illness, there was little chance that they would be able to have more children. The news was devastating. Margaret had come from a large family and had expected to have one herself. In particular, she'd always hoped to recapture the relationship she had with her mother by having a daughter of her own. So, in 1966, Margaret and Wallace adopted a baby girl called Martha. Then, three years later, the doctors were proved wrong and Margaret was delighted to give birth to a daughter, whom they named Eleanor, after Wallace's sister.

It wasn't always easy for Wallace to keep up his family responsibilities. Once, when Scott and Michael were young, Wallace suggested taking the family on a business trip. "I said 'There is no way I'm going,'" remembers Margaret. "'You'll just go off to your meetings and leave me to look after them. It will just be like at home. You take them with you and you spend time with them.' He did it, and really enjoyed it."

As the company grew, McCain Foods became less and less a family project and more the private concern of Harrison and Wallace. Bob and Andrew became gradually less involved, until their participation was practically nonexistent. Harrison and Wallace didn't need to consult their other brothers. The company was no longer a start-up enterprise and the younger brothers knew what they were doing. They weren't rookies who needed Bob's sage advice any more. Both older brothers got most of their news about McCain Foods from the newspaper. "We absolutely never consulted them," Wallace said later in court. "In fact, I think eventually it became a bit of a sore point...because they hated like heck reading in the newspaper that we just bought a new company."

At one point, in the mid-1960s, Harrison and Wallace rearranged their finances for tax reasons and created a holding company to shelter some of their income. "At that time, there was no effective board of directors, and I truly don't remember whether Bob and Andrew knew that Wallace and I owned [the holding company] or not," Harrison said.

Andrew and Bob were still directors of McCain Foods, along with brother-in-law Jed Sutherland. They were also co-owners of the company, holding almost one-third of the company's shares between them. But the McCain Foods board never met. Wallace and Harrison had no interest in consulting the directors or the shareholders. According to court documents filed during their later legal battle, many McCain Foods documents were written as though they had board approval when no board meeting ever took place. On one occasion, a batch of board resolutions purportedly passed by the directors was signed by Mac McCarthy, head of British operations, even though he wasn't a member of the board. At other times, Wallace and Harrison would meet together and approve various board resolutions, even though the company's by-laws required a quorum of three directors for any board meeting to be official. On other occasions, the younger brothers took actions that by law required shareholder approval.

Although the older brothers had rights under provincial legislation to information and consultation, none of the infractions was ever enough of an issue to inspire more than quiet grumbling from Bob and Andrew. They knew from the start that Harrison and Wallace would run McCain Foods while they stuck to running McCain Produce. Later, it was Bob's wife Rosemary who was really annoyed. She would often complain that Harrison and Wallace never gave Bob credit for the role he played in the company.

However serious the family divisions were at the time, they did nothing to slow down the company. In February 1967, the brothers celebrated McCain Food's tenth year in business. Sales were now well over $20 million a year and the company was the largest frozen vegetable processor in Canada and the fourth-largest French fry maker in the world. The popularity of fast food was still pushing McCain's growth. McDonald's had more than three hundred restaurants across the United States and plans were underway to open stores in Canada and Japan. There were also more than six hundred Kentucky Fried Chicken restaurants, including more than one hundred in Canada. A&W was nearly as big as Kentucky Fried Chicken and was also expanding rapidly. McCain was supplying both Kentucky Fried Chicken and A&W in Canada and hoped to get McDonald's when it moved north. McCain was also supplying hundreds of other restaurants, cafeterias and canteens. Even the restaurant in the Seattle Space Needle was serving New Brunswick fiddleheads packaged by McCain.

Wallace and Harrison now employed about 1,300 people. They pumped $4 million every year into the county in salaries, making McCain the most important employer in the county. They also built forty homes in Florenceville and sold them to company staff for $13,000 to $15,000, just covering the cost of construction. McCain's importance wasn't lost on Premier Robichaud. His government had guaranteed a $250,000 McCain bond issue in 1963, a $500,000 bond issue in 1964 and a $1-million bond issue in 1966. As a mark of the company's success, Harrison was invited to Ottawa for a dinner with the Queen to honour outstanding young Canadians. The event was part of the Queen's visit to celebrate Canada's centennial year.

While the public image of McCain showed a company enjoying enormous success, the day-to-day operations were far from problem-free. Transportation was once again causing headaches in the late 1960s. McCain's trucking company, Day & Ross, had expanded enormously since McCain bought it in 1965. By the late 1960s, Day & Ross had four hundred trucks and five hundred employees compared to just twelve trucks and fifteen workers in 1960. But Day & Ross was losing money. In fact, the company hadn't made a dime since it was bought by McCain, according to court documents. Company president Joe Palmer tried to keep Day & Ross as independent of McCain as possible by lining up other customers, but it wasn't working, and the losses were becoming intolerable for Wallace and Harrison. After poring over the books, the brothers came up with an idea to pull Day & Ross out of the red.

The trucking company was pouring money every year into enormous fines for unsafe equipment, speeding and violating other assorted provincial laws. They paid $254.65 in fines in 1966, then $9,016 in 1967; $8,703 in 1968; $15,956 in 1969; $16,733 in 1970; and $19,490 in 1971. Rather than simply trying to improve the company's poor driving and safety record, Wallace and Harrison decided to claim the fines as a business expense and deducted them for tax purposes. That would cut Day & Ross's tax bill and generate some needed cash for the business. But Revenue Canada balked at the claims and took the company to court in 1976. The trial lasted weeks, but in the end, the McCains won over the judge and Day & Ross was permitted to claim the fines as a legitimate cost of doing business.

Thomas Equipment was also becoming a disappointment by the end of the 1960s. The new plant was turning out about a thousand harvesters a day. Sales were fairly strong at first, but after a couple of good years the harvesters ran into warranty problems that kept profits down. The business never became the huge player in farm machinery that the brothers had hoped.

Then, in 1966, the McCains came face to face with another problem that they'd been trying to ignore for a decade. Dr. John Bates, chairman of the New Brunswick Water Authority, told Woodstock's town council that McCain was the second-largest polluter on the Saint John River, accounting for 10 percent of the pollution. He was backed up a year later by a report from the province's Department of Natural Resources that also singled out McCain as one of the province's biggest polluters. "This serious pollution on the Saint John River has been going on for a long time and is now a matter of general public concern," the Natural Resources report said, pointing to McCain as well as Irving Oil and Fraser Pulp and Paper.

Wallace and Harrison had always known that pollution would eventually become an issue—an expensive issue to solve. "Unofficial notice has been given by both Provincial and Federal authorities that sewage disposal into New Brunswick rivers may be stopped," the brothers told Carleton County council in a brief in 1959. "This expenditure must be made within the next few years. It is obvious to any of those who have examined this situation that these costs are extreme and would allow only a slight margin of profit, if any." In fact, before building the French fry plant, they'd calculated that it would cost $90,000 to put in a waste-treatment facility and they'd decided to hold off.

They knew they couldn't ignore the Water Authority much longer. It was already threatening to order companies, including McCain, to clean up. So, the McCains signed an agreement with the Water Authority promising to build a treatment plant to meet their requirements, a promise that would cost them at least $1 million to keep. Wallace and Harrison decided to ask for some government assistance. Hoping for a grant, they approached the Atlantic Development Board, an agency formed in 1963 by the federal government to help promote economic development in Atlantic Canada. The McCains weren't disappointed. The ADB agreed to help finance a $435,000 filtration system as the first step in the company's water-treatment program.

Just as they were sorting out the company's pollution problems, the brothers' attention was diverted to politics. Louis
Robichaud had called a provincial election for October 23, 1967,
hoping for his third straight victory. The election was also going
to be a test of support for his "Program of Equal Opportunity,"
which had been launched during the previous legislative session.
Robichaud wanted Harrison to run for the Liberals in Carleton
County. Harrison would be an ideal candidate. The county's
three seats had gone Tory for decades. Who better to wrest a seat
from the Tories than the head of the county's biggest employer?
But Harrison wasn't interested. Friends say Harrison declined in
part because he preferred business to politics, but he also had an
innate fear of public speaking. Robichaud also tried asking
Wallace, who, not surprisingly, turned him down.

Robichaud then asked Bob to run. The premier knew Bob
was tremendously popular in the county. He also had political
experience, having served on the county council for nearly a
decade. Having a former county councillor as a candidate would
also be a good way for the Liberals to fend off criticism concerning their abolishment of county councils. Carleton Council
had passed a resolution condemning the policy, but with Bob as
a Liberal candidate that resolution would lose some of its impact.

It wasn't hard for Robichaud to persuade Bob to run. Bob
had always been the most politically active of A.D.'s children and
had worked on local campaigns for years. When the time came,
he was easily nominated to the slate of three Liberal candidates,
which also included Hugh Tait and Christine Young.

Despite having a McCain on the ticket, the Liberals faced
long odds in Carleton County. The three incumbent Tories
would be tough to beat, and they had their own McCain—Fred
McCain, a distant cousin to Wallace and Harrison and the
former principal of the school they'd attended as kids. The other
Tory candidates included Edison Stairs and Richard Hatfield, a
young up-and-coming politician from nearby Hartland whose
father Hebert had competed with A.D. McCain in the potato
business.

Knowing he couldn't win the election strictly on political
affiliation, Bob decided to run a low-key campaign that focused

on his personal popularity among farmers. The strategy worked, and as the campaign wore on, local Liberals started thinking Bob might win. But with only a week left in the campaign, Bob caught pneumonia and was bed-ridden.

Wallace and Harrison dropped everything to rescue their brother's campaign. They knew Bob was close to winning and they wanted to keep his momentum building. They decided to help the only way they knew how: by turning the campaign into a McCain-run business. They opened new campaign offices and saturated the county with Bob's campaign literature. McCain workers were not so subtly told who to vote for, and campaign volunteers were pushed to their limits.

But the high-profile style backfired. Though he led the Liberal ticket and was the closest any Liberal had come in decades to winning a seat in Carleton County, Bob lost by 977 votes. Some Liberals and a few Tories blamed Harrison and Wallace's show of force for the defeat.

"I don't think people appreciated the campaigning in the last week," said Charles Gallagher, a local Tory who later represented the county in the legislature as a cabinet minister. "Bob was doing well with a low-key campaign and people respected that. Then here come these two guys who run McCain Foods and they start making a show. I don't think people appreciated being told how to vote by McCain Foods."

The loss was disappointing for all of them, but Bob never blamed his brothers. Even within the family he would only say that if the campaign had lasted one more week he would have won. He was touched that his brothers dropped everything to help. For their part, Harrison and Wallace were consoled by the fact that the Liberals were returned to office and their friend Louis Robichaud was still premier. That year, the province backed $850,000 worth of McCain bonds.

After the election was over, Wallace and Harrison got back to business and started planning another international expansion. With Britain now well established, they turned their attention to Australia. They were delighted to discover that getting their products to Australia wouldn't be hard. "All these Australian boats were returning home from Canada half empty so they were eager to find something to take back," remembers Wallace. Once the shipments were lined up, the McCains hired a broker in Australia to sell their products. When he died unexpectedly a few months later, the brothers decided that someone needed to fly to Australia to scout out the market. Harrison was busy with Britain so Wallace made the trip.

Shortly after arriving, Wallace met Ernie Ellis, a young Englishman who was working for a British fish importer. "Wallace invited me to join McCain and we started up in July 1968," recalls Ellis. Within six months, Ellis had opened an office in Sydney and built up a sales staff across Australia. Unknown to Wallace, Ellis's staff consisted mainly of his relatives.

The company was getting off to a shaky start. McCain's crates were arriving in port smashed or stacked so high the bottom cases were crushed. Solving that problem meant coming up with new containers and working out a better relationship with port officials. Sales were also slow, and the fledgling Australian operation was losing money. Wallace soon found he was spending more and more time in Australia trying to sort out the troubles.

Meanwhile, Harrison was in London overseeing what was becoming a booming market in Britain. By 1968, Caterpac's annual sales had climbed to $3.5 million from 1965's $1 million. Caterpac had also given McCain a gateway to Europe, and sales were growing in new export markets such as West Germany, Italy and Scandinavia.

Harrison understood instinctively how to do business in Britain's class-conscious society. He always stayed in a suite at the Savoy in London, the city's most exclusive hotel. The only place more exclusive was Buckingham Palace. Queen Elizabeth's Coronation Ball was held at the Savoy in 1953. "It was a smart business tactic," recalls Ralph Orr. "If you called someone and left a message that you were staying at the Savoy, it looked good." During one trip, Tim Bliss remembers getting ready to check out of the hotel with Harrison. "He said, 'I'll look after the tips,'" says Bliss. "We got to the lobby and there were about eight people lined up, and Harrison just started peeling off bills." The Savoy would remain a regular British haven for both brothers for years.

Exports to Britain were getting big enough that Wallace and Harrison began making plans to build a factory. They had been mulling over the project for months when one night, during a trip to London, Harrison turned on the television to catch the news. The first item involved a government announcement to devalue the British pound by 14 percent. Harrison knew they had to get a factory built fast, before the devalued pound priced McCain's French fries out of the market.

Harrison and Wallace, together with Tim Bliss and Carl Morris, began scouring the countryside looking for a place to build a plant. Their first choice was near the company's office in Grimsby, in the heart of Britain's potato country. But when a proper site around Grimsby couldn't be found, they looked at Scarborough, on the edge of the potato region. They'd designed a 102,000-square-foot plant by late January 1968 and had it ready for production that fall. Because they were using the same direct-to-customer distribution system as in Canada, they added a 525,000-square-foot cold storage area. The building cost $2.6 million and looked like an airplane hangar. Mac McCarthy was named managing director of overall operations while his brother James was hired as plant manager, overseeing about three hundred people.

The plant and the McCains were big news in Scarborough. More than three hundred locals attended the opening ceremonies on March 21, 1969. The McCains also flew twenty-six people over from Florenceville, including Bob, Andrew and their mother Laura, who was seventy-eight at the time. During the opening ceremonies, Mrs. McCain unlocked the plant door and said: "May God bless this factory and all who work in it."

Wallace didn't have long to celebrate the British plant opening. Things in Australia weren't getting better. McCain might have been the first French fry company in Australia, but the company there was still losing money. Wallace headed off again to find out what was going wrong.

One day, when he was once again immersed in the company's books, he got a call from an Australian customs official, who accused McCain of "dumping" product—selling at a lower price in Australia than in Canada in order to undercut local competition. Wallace was livid: he denied the charges and blasted the official for making such an accusation. But then he checked with Ellis.

In fact, his staff had been routinely changing receiving documents. The price the Australian office was paying McCain Canada for fries and other products was lowered to cut import taxes and duties. The change was made to cut costs, but the Australian customs officials had every right to call it dumping. The government had caught on to the arrangement through some duplicate copies of invoices. Ellis filled out one copy showing the lower Australian price but the duplicate, showing the Canadian price, also ended up at customs.

Ellis defended his staff to Wallace. He said the Australian business was under pressure because of stiff competition from Birds Eye, which had the largest market share for frozen food in Australia and was making a push into the French fry business. He also blamed the Canadian office. McCain "had a second-grade product, called Carleton Farms or something, that was being sold obviously at a lower price than their McCain brand. So what they did to get the price down in Australia [was] put the first-grade product in the second-grade boxes," Ellis recalls. "And that's what caused the trouble, price-wise, with customs here. They were packaging good product in their second-grade box."

Who was to blame didn't matter to Australian customs officials. They fined McCain about $30,000 and threatened to put a tariff on the company's products. Wallace knew any tariff would price McCain out of business in Australia and the only way to avoid it was to set up a plant in the country. But where and how? Wallace began searching the countryside for something, anything, to buy to keep the company going. But after a few weeks he had to put the search on hold and return to New Brunswick, where a bigger project was ready to go.

The brothers had been thinking about building a new plant in New Brunswick for some time. The Florenceville plant had been expanded as much as it could and sales were growing fast enough to sustain a new facility. Robichaud's reelection also made it a good time to move on the idea. They went to see Bob Higgins, the Minister Responsible for Economic Development.

According to Reg Tweedale, Higgins's deputy minister, Wallace and Harrison told Higgins that McCain had been offered substantial tax concessions by officials in Maine to build the plant just across the border in Aroostook County. They added that it was an attractive offer because it would help the company expand into the United States.

"They had a pretty good story about opening markets in the U.S.," recalls Tweedale. "It was an important issue. Higgins felt processing of potatoes was economically important and if it was lost to Maine it would be a real detriment to New Brunswick. McCain used this to their advantage."

The McCains also approached the federal government for help. Fortunately for them, the government had just created a new Department of Regional Economic Expansion (DREE) only months earlier. The McCains had excellent contacts in the federal government. Harrison and Wallace were among the early backers of Pierre Trudeau's leadership in 1968. Both brothers admired Trudeau, and Wallace even put aside his usual scepticism and worked tirelessly on Trudeau's campaign; to this day, a picture of Trudeau is among the few non-family photos in Wallace's house. Harrison was just as impressed by Trudeau and also made lasting friends with some of Trudeau's senior staff, including Jim Coutts. Those contacts no doubt helped as the brothers lined up financial support for the new plant.

Within a few months, the provincial and federal government offered support. On August 27, 1969, the McCains, Robichaud and Higgins announced that the company would build a new 168,000-square-foot plant in Grand Falls, about ninety miles north of Florenceville. The plant would cost $5.6 million and, most important to the politicians, provide four hundred local jobs. "The only effective method of establishing worthwhile and viable industries in the province is through a cooperative blend of industry and all levels of government," Robichaud said after announcing the plant's construction.

In return for building the plant in New Brunswick, McCain received the first grant awarded by the new federal Department of Regional Economic Expansion, to the tune of $3.4 million, the largest allowable grant under the program at the time. The provincial government also provided money for a pollution-control system and agreed to guarantee a $5.2-million McCain bond issue.

Harrison made no apologies for the government support. It was just good business sense to him. "The new federal Department of Regional Economic Expansion—a most impressive group, with a real go-ahead attitude—is the best thing that has ever happened to the Maritimes," he said after the announcement. Harrison was so impressed with DREE that he later hired away George McClure, the department's regional officer in Atlantic Canada, to be a vice president at McCain.

Tweedale never begrudged the government support for McCain. "It was a good deal. Without it, the plant would have gone to Maine," he says.

With the Grand Falls plant safely underway, Wallace returned as quickly as possible to Australia. He was still scrambling to find a factory to buy to keep McCain afloat. In the fall of 1970, he heard about an old potato processing factory available in a tiny village called Daylesford about 125 miles west of Melbourne. The village had barely five hundred residents but it was in the heart of Australia's potato-growing region. Wallace drove up to the small white building and cringed. The "factory" consisted of a dilapidated shed and a worn-out potato line that could barely produce two hundred pounds of French fries an hour—about what the Florenceville plant produced when it first opened. "It would have been the worst potato line I ever saw in my life anywhere in the world," Wallace recalled. The building also had no heat and had been used as a shell factory during the war.

Wallace, disheartened, was about to leave when he spotted a group of local farmers. He decided to ask them about growing conditions in the area. The farmers told Wallace that they could grow potatoes twelve months of the year. Wallace was stunned. Farmers in New Brunswick were lucky to get one good harvest in the fall and could only work their land for six months of the year. To be able to harvest every month of the year was incredible to Wallace. This made buying the factory worthwhile. McCain wouldn't have to build any storage facilities or worry about a constant supply of fresh potatoes. He rushed to a phone to call

Harrison. "This factory would be a hell of an acquisition for us," he said, barely able to contain his excitement. Not only would McCain be able to beat the tariffs and stay in business in Australia, he added, "Just think, we can store potatoes in the ground for twelve months of the year."

Harrison was just as excited as Wallace and the brothers agreed that Wallace should buy the old factory right away. Wallace hung up, found the owner and offered him $200,000. Although he was leery about Ernie Ellis because of the customs problems, Wallace needed him right now and told Ellis to keep pushing sales as hard as possible. Meanwhile, Harrison told Olof Pierson's assistant, Franklin Hickling, who still worked for McCain in Florenceville, to get on a plane to Australia. He had a plant to sort out.

A few weeks before Wallace closed the Daylesford deal, the brothers were faced with an unexpected political change in New Brunswick. On October 26, 1970, Robichaud lost to the Conservatives led by Richard Hatfield. The Liberals received more votes than the Tories but the distribution of the vote managed to give the Conservatives a six-seat majority.

Although the McCains were die-hard Liberals, they weren't overly concerned about continued provincial support from the new premier. Hatfield was from Hartland, just a few miles from Florenceville, and he represented Carleton County in the legislature. Hatfield's family was also in the potato processing business, and though his father and A.D. had once been competitors, Hatfield would become as big a booster of McCain Foods as Robichaud. "There is more overall benefit, to the overall economy, and I would say more direct benefit to the agricultural economy, by supporting a food processing industry like McCain," he once told a reporter.

A few months after the election, Robichaud stepped down and the party called a leadership convention for October 1971 in Fredericton. Harrison was determined to play a role in choosing the next Liberal leader. Few thought Hatfield would remain in power for long and Harrison likely wanted to make sure the next Liberal premier was a McCain supporter.

From the start, the leadership campaign became a bitter battle between the party's old guard and the young reformers. One young politico was thirty-six-year-old Deputy Justice Minister John Bryden. He had quit his job when Hatfield was elected and decided to run for the Liberal leadership, even though he had never been involved in party politics. "I did not believe anybody was capable of running the party so I decided to run," recalls Bryden. "I didn't know anybody in the Liberal Party."

As Bryden started making the rounds of Liberal Party workers he was told that he should talk to the McCains. Not only was the family considered one of the biggest Liberal heavyweights in New Brunswick, but they were shopping around for a candidate to back. Bryden called McCain Foods and made an appointment to see Harrison. He drove up to Florenceville a few days later and was promptly ushered into Harrison's office.

Harrison was on the phone and waved at Bryden to sit down. Through a small doorway, Bryden could hear Wallace, who was back briefly from Australia, in a neighbouring office, barking orders over the telephone. As Bryden sat waiting, he watched as Harrison fielded several calls at the same time and shouted instructions to Wallace in the next room. Wallace was handling just as many calls and yelling back orders to Harrison. Bryden grew more and more uncomfortable.

"They were negotiating some deal, and while the deal is going on they are clearing with each other by hollering back and forth as to whether Harrison agreed with the position Wallace was taking and vice versa," recalls Bryden. "And sometimes the language was not absolutely pure. It got just a little blue."

Eventually, Harrison hung up and asked Bryden what he wanted. Bryden didn't mince words: he explained that he was running for the Liberal leadership and he hoped for the McCains' support. Just as he finished, Wallace walked in and sat down on a nearby chair. "Well Jesus Christ, young man, you haven't even got a constituency," Harrison said, brushing aside Bryden's comments. But Wallace was intrigued and told Harrison to back off.

"They were very, very good at playing the bad cop, good cop roles," remembers Bryden. "They were about as good at it as anybody I have ever met, and you never knew who was who until you got into the middle of it. On that day, Harrison was sort of the bad cop and Wallace was the good cop."

The conversation lasted an hour with no firm commitment from Harrison or Wallace, but Harrison promised to let Bryden know who they would support. A few weeks later, Bryden got a call from Harrison at midnight. Harrison said the family was backing former industry minister Robert Higgins for leader.

The choice made sense for the McCains since Higgins had been responsible for the provincial support for the Grand Falls plant. But he was also considered one of the so-called old guard, who were losing favour in the party now that it had been defeated. The McCains knew it would be a tough fight and they gave Higgins substantial support. Harrison did some fund-raising and Bob McCain helped run the campaign. Wallace didn't get involved as much; he had to get back to Australia to get the Daylesford plant running.

On the eve of the leadership vote, Harrison arrived at the Lord Beaverbrook Hotel in Fredericton ready to take charge of the Higgins campaign. He ordered a gathering of the campaign staff in his suite and began poring over the work that had been done to identify supporters. There were now five candidates, Higgins, Bryden, Norbert Thériault and Bud Williamson, both former Robichaud cabinet ministers, and Maurice Harquail, the deputy mayor of Campbellton. Higgins was considered a front-runner, along with Bryden, but the race was close.

Harrison "came in as though he was chairman of everything," says a former Higgins worker. Harrison also wanted to know if the campaign staff had lined up a list of candidates to run for the party's executive positions. He knew those positions would be critical to a new leader because they would help ensure that he maintained the backing of the party's rank and file.

"We said we didn't care about that," says the Higgins worker. But Harrison did care and he suggested that his brother Andrew should be given the job of party treasurer. Andrew "was sitting at the back of the room by the bar working on his third double at the time," says a campaign worker. No one was enthusiastic about Andrew as treasurer but no one wanted to argue with

Harrison. Besides, maybe having a McCain as treasurer would keep the coffers full.

Harrison then said they needed to figure out a way to get Norbert Thériault out of the leadership race. Thériault was running third but was expected to back Bryden in later balloting. If Thériault withdrew maybe Higgins would have a better chance. Harrison suggested they offer Thériault the position of party president.

The convention began the next day, and it was clear that Bryden's campaign was gathering steam. As expected, Higgins led after the first ballot, but Bryden was within a hundred votes. Thériault was third and had enough votes to give either Bryden or Higgins a majority. Bryden was feeling confident as delegates prepared for the second ballot. But just before the voting was to start, Thériault announced that he was withdrawing from the campaign and supporting Higgins. Bryden was stunned, and some of Thériault's supporters stormed out in anger. Higgins won on the next ballot, and Thériault was named party president. For the first time ever the party decided to pay the president a salary. Andrew McCain was named party treasurer.

"The deal that was made was that Norbert would withdraw and become the president of the Liberal Party and be paid a stipend which had never been done before," says Bryden, now a senator, who credits Harrison for orchestrating a clever political move. "It's quite clear that a deal was done to get Norbert out so it did not go the extra ballot. And to get him to support Bob Higgins."

While Harrison savoured the political victory, Wallace was facing more problems in Australia. The farmers who had told him that it was possible to grow potatoes twelve months a year hadn't told him one crucial detail: it rained in Daylesford from mid June to mid September. Few if any potatoes could be picked during those months, and the spuds that were pulled out were so waterlogged they were black. "I remember seeing potatoes as black as the ace of spades in August or September," Wallace recalls.

So much for not having to build a storage facility, Wallace thought. But despite the setback, he and Hickling managed to get the small plant operational, and McCain cranked out enough French fries to supply its customers. Meanwhile, Harrison and Carl Ash, McCain's chief financial officer, flew in to meet Australian customs officials, who were still pondering punishing tariffs on McCain.

"I remember they were all dressed in dark suits and were very serious," says Ash. "I made a presentation and then Harrison spoke. These guys never once even smiled." The McCains managed to talk their way out of the tariffs, and they even got the $30,000 fine lowered thanks to their tenacious lawyer.

Just as Australia got going again, the company opened up another international market. In 1969, Wallace joined twenty-nine other food industry executives on a trade mission to Asia sponsored by the federal Department of Industry, Trade and Commerce. While in Japan he met representatives from Nichirei, a large frozen-food company. Wallace signed a deal to ship some McCain product to Nichirei. But, just as in Australia, most of the crates in the first shipment were destroyed en route and the Japanese importers complained. Wallace was tied up with Australia and turned the problem over to Carl Morris, who was running McCain's plants.

Morris solved the shipping problems and started slowly building McCain's business in Japan. It was the first non-English-speaking country McCain had penetrated, and it was rare at the time for any Canadian company to export into Japan.

As the 1970s began, McCain was operating on three continents. Sales had more than doubled in three years and they reached $50 million in 1970. As profits poured in they were plowed immediately back into expansion. Wallace and Harrison were beginning to feel almost invincible.

CHAPTER SEVEN

Wallace was standing in line getting jostled by the crowd outside a small takeout restaurant in Richmond, B.C., a Vancouver suburb. The line-up stretched down the block. It was spring 1967, the year of Expo and Canada's centennial. It was a time of optimism and confidence in Canada, and McDonald's was cashing in. The Richmond restaurant was the first McDonald's to open in Canada. It looked just like any one of the more than eight hundred McDonald's that Ray Kroc had opened by that time. The restaurant had glass walls and Dick McDonald's now famous golden arches bending over the roof.

When he finally got inside, Wallace wondered what all the fuss was about. "It looked like a fifth-class fast-food place compared to what you would see today," he recalls. The restaurant was smaller than other fast-food places Wallace had seen. There were few seats and the place didn't seem as organized as a Kentucky Fried Chicken, A&W or any of the other major drive-ins. But Wallace did notice that the cook was making French fries out of fresh potatoes. Might as well make a pitch for McCain fries, he thought and asked to see the owner.

The owner was George Tidball, a young entrepreneur who had bought the rights to McDonald's for all of western Canada. He'd paid $70,000 (US) plus 1 percent of sales for the right to open ten restaurants—a fraction of what Kroc was charging for franchises in the United States. The low fee reflected what some McDonald's executives felt about foreign expansion. The franchises in Canada were the second attempt by McDonald's to expand into a foreign country. The first try had come a few years earlier when franchise rights were sold to a group in the Caribbean, a venture that had ended miserably because of poor local management. Many executives in McDonald's head office were leery about another foreign venture, but Kroc was sold on Canada. It was a similar culture to the States, and he was impressed with Canadian cities. Tidball wasn't the only franchise-holder in Canada. McDonald's had sold rights in eastern Canada to George Cohon, a transplanted Chicagoan, and his partner Ted Tannebaum. They were planning to open their first restaurant in London, Ontario, in 1968.

Wallace was impressed by Tidball, even if his McDonald's wasn't the best-looking restaurant around. The two talked about the industry and Wallace did his best to convince the young owner to buy McCain fries. But Tidball wasn't interested. He preferred making fries out of fresh potatoes and didn't believe frozen fries could ever taste as good. Wallace shrugged and left.

Wallace and Harrison weren't so sure that missing out on Tidball's business was such a great loss. From what he'd seen, Wallace didn't think McDonald's was going to be a huge hit in Canada. Besides, McCain had Kentucky Fried Chicken and A&W—the two biggest players in the Canadian fast-food business—and they were going after other new chains, including Burger Chef, Chicken Delight, Smitty's, Heavenly Chicken, Dog 'n Suds, Red Barn, White Spot, Dairy Queen and Frostop Stores. McCain would do just fine without McDonald's.

Wallace was right. McDonald's was far from taking Canada by storm in 1967. According to John Love's book *McDonald's: Behind the Arches,* both Tidball and Cohon were losing $1 million (US) a year at first. But Kroc could see the potential in the Canadian market, and he almost immediately regretted the cheap franchise fee he'd charged. On the day Cohon's first restaurants opened in London, Kroc arrived offering to buy back the franchise rights for $1 million. Cohon didn't sell. He figured if Kroc was offering that much, the franchise must be worth a lot more. But soon both Tidball and Cohon recognized that they didn't have the resources to take advantage of their franchise rights. The business required volume and neither owner could build his restaurants quickly enough to raise McDonald's visibility and develop a solid customer base. By 1971, both had sold their franchise rights back to McDonald's for a combined $15 million.

Tidball went on to other restaurant ventures, including opening another chain called The Keg. But Kroc asked Cohon to stay in charge of McDonald's Canadian operations. Kroc knew that while Canada was similar to the United States, there were enough differences that the Canadian franchise couldn't be run out of McDonald's head office in Chicago. Kroc gave Cohon the freedom and resources to run his own show. With that kind of backing, Cohon could now expand McDonald's quickly across Canada. But simply building more restaurants wasn't enough. He also slashed prices by 20 percent to entice Canadians into the new takeouts. The price cut worked. Per-restaurant sales jumped by 25 percent in one year. Full prices were restored two years later, but by then McDonald's sales were booming.

By 1974, McDonald's had surpassed Kentucky Fried Chicken and A&W as the number-one fast-food chain in Canada, with about $110 million in sales. Cohon would soon have more than two hundred restaurants across Canada and he'd open a new outlet almost every week. McDonald's was becoming so dominant in Canada that its biggest U.S. rival, Burger King, gave up on the Canadian market after setting up a dozen restaurants in the late 1960s. (Burger King wouldn't return to Canada in a big way until the 1980s.)

The McCains couldn't ignore McDonald's any longer. The chain the brothers had dismissed as insignificant a few years earlier was now moving into every suburb in Canada. McDonald's had also stopped using fresh potatoes for French fries and was using frozen fries. The brothers knew it was time to close in. But they faced an enormous obstacle.

Two years before Wallace ventured into Tidball's restaurant, John Simplot of J.R. Simplot Co. had a historic meeting with Ray Kroc. At the time, Kroc was plagued with problems supplying his booming chain with fresh potatoes for French fries. Co-ordinating potato shipments to every restaurant was becoming a nightmare as the chain sprawled out across North America. Things were worst in summer when scorching heat ruined the spuds before they arrived.

Simplot's company was one of McDonald's major potato suppliers. At the time, he was working on a new rail transport system that involved shipping the potatoes in specially designed refrigerated boxcars. But Simplot's first shipment was a disaster. His high-tech cars didn't work, and the potatoes shrivelled up in the scorching heat. Simplot gave up the transportation idea and decided to tell McDonald's officials about the frozen fries his chemist had come up with a few years earlier. Simplot had been selling a few cases of the fries, but he didn't have a big enough clientele to merit a huge investment in the product. If McDonald's liked the idea, he'd be set. Simplot met Steve Barnes, a McDonald's vice president, at a food service convention and told Barnes about the frozen fries.

"I got him here to Idaho and showed him what we were doing, and he took a few pounds back," Simplot recalls. "We made him a few million pounds and he tried them in his stores."

The experiment was a hit. Packages of frozen fries were a hell of a lot easier to ship than boxcars of potatoes. And, as Barnes discovered, the frozen fries tasted just as good as the freshly made ones. McDonald's customers wouldn't notice a thing, except maybe faster service since the fries took only a couple of minutes to cook. Barnes took Simplot's idea to Kroc, who was also excited. Kroc had been fretting over the fresh potato problem for years and was already at work developing McDonald's own frozen French fries. Kroc had even approached Simplot's main rival, Lamb-Weston Inc., about developing a new frozen French fry for McDonald's, but officials at Lamb-Weston had thought it was too risky. So, when Kroc heard about Simplot, he was ready to strike a deal.

Kroc invited Simplot to California for a meeting. "I spent three or four days at his place and when I got ready to go, he said, 'Okay Jack, you get your plant and I'll put my restaurants on as fast as you can process potatoes.' We shook hands and that's the only [French fry] contract I've ever had with McDonald's," Simplot recalls. He invested $3.5 million in a new French fry plant, and J.R. Simplot Co. has remained McDonald's largest single French fry supplier ever since.

By the time Wallace and Harrison were approaching McDonald's about McCain fries, nearly all the McDonald's restaurants were being supplied by Simplot. He had two plants in the United States by 1972 and one in Manitoba that eventually became a joint venture with Carnation. Simplot was so firmly entrenched in the McDonald's culture that he sat on the company's board of directors for years.

Simplot's dominance left little room for the McCains. But Wallace and Harrison were still confident that they could win over some of the McDonald's business. After all, McDonald's was buying up to one-quarter of the total frozen French fry production in the United States and even Simplot couldn't keep up with that demand. The McCains were also encouraged by Cohon, who was trying to create a strong Canadian image for McDonald's by using as many Canadian suppliers as possible. But McDonald's wasn't going to make it easy. They played hard ball and made the McCains wait.

The relationship that McDonald's had forged with Simplot was critical in many ways. The restaurant chain had a loyal, lifelong supplier, but it never relinquished control. Kroc liked doing business that way. Control was important to McDonald's success, and the company built its entire supply system on that premise. McDonald's demanded close, co-operative relations with its suppliers and went so far as to call them "McFamily." Kroc generally preferred to use smaller suppliers because they were more willing to work closely with the company. In that way, McDonald's had developed a vast network of dedicated suppliers who understood that the relationship was a two-way street. McDonald's wouldn't cut loose a supplier just because someone else offered a better price. But in return, McDonald's demanded access to suppliers' financial records and production plants to help find ways of cutting costs.

Suppliers were also expected to keep McDonald's a top priority, even if they had their own retail brand. H.J. Heinz Co. learned that lesson the hard way in 1973. Heinz officials told McDonald's vice president of purchasing, Lynal Root, that because of a tomato shortage Heinz would have to cut its ketchup supplies to McDonald's. When Root found out that

Heinz hadn't cut back on any of the ketchup it sold in stores in order to protect its brand name, Heinz went from supplying 90 percent of McDonald's ketchup to virtually zero. Heinz has since regained some of McDonald's business, but it has taken more than twenty years.

McDonald's supplier philosophy didn't suit Wallace and Harrison. They didn't want to "partner" with anyone and they were damned if they were going to put any customer ahead of the McCain brand. They'd spent years battling to convince restaurant owners to try, and then stick with, frozen fries. And they had serious doubts that they could maintain a long-term relationship with any one client.

From the outset, the McCains and McDonald's did not get along. "I remember meeting [McDonald's representatives] in a small room right over there," recalls McCain vice president Carl Morris as he points to a tiny room near his office in the McCain plant in Florenceville. "They wanted to see the rest of the plant and we said, 'No way, this is as far as you get.'"

The McCains were traders, not partners. They made deals based on price, quality and supply. They had no expectations beyond each written contract and always assumed that if someone came along with a better price the restaurant owner would switch suppliers. That's the way K.C. Irving had taught them business, and it was the way their father ran McCain Produce.

The brothers would also never agree to show anyone their factory or their finances; privacy was as important as profits to the McCains. For years, the brothers wouldn't even tell Statistics Canada how many French fries they made. Even the annual reports of Carleton Cold Storage, which was a public company until 1973, were filed secretly with the government. "We always filed them as late as possible, after the third or fourth warning," says Carl Ash, McCain's former chief financial officer. "And we would ask the official in the Department of Industry who took the report just to stick it in some filing cabinet and keep it away from the public." There were sound practical reasons for the McCains' secrecy. The brothers worried that widespread reporting of McCain's profits—which were breaking records every year in the 1960s—would attract other competitors, especially K.C. Irving.

By the mid 1970s there were good business reasons for McCain's and McDonald's to co-operate. After all, both were becoming world leaders in their respective businesses, businesses that complemented one another perfectly. Could there be a more obvious team than the world's biggest fast-food chain and the world's biggest French fry producer? Issues of partnership, secrecy and control kept the two apart, but it became a highly personal dispute as well. "We were arrogant sellers and they were arrogant buyers," recalls Wallace. "They would only do business with us if there was absolutely no one else to deal with." McDonald's long-time chief executive Fred Turner, Kroc's right-hand man, "didn't like Wallace and Harrison," says a source close to Turner. Turner so despised the brothers that he was willing to inconvenience his own company just to stick it to the McCains. On one of his first meetings with Tom Albrecht, one of McDonald's European managers, Turner admitted that his first job was to try to diversify away from McCain fries, even though McCain was the biggest supplier around. Turner also considered shipping frozen fries from Simplot's plant in Idaho to McDonald's restaurants in Britain even though McCain had finished its plant in Scarborough, England. McDonald's didn't go ahead with the plan, in part because of a strike by dock workers. With nowhere else to turn, the restaurant chain had no choice but to deal with McCain. Fortunately for McCain, its British manager, Mac McCarthy, handled McDonald's account and his jovial manner helped smooth out relations. But it didn't come easily, especially if Harrison was around. McCain vice president Tim Bliss remembers McCarthy telling him about meetings with Harrison and McDonald's executives in Britain. "Harrison's blood pressure used to just soar during the meetings," Bliss recalled. "Mac would sit right beside him just so he could kick Harrison under the table if he got too angry."

Relations between the two companies gradually improved, but it took years of hands-on, personal attention from Wallace and Harrison. The effort eventually paid off. In Canada and Australia, McCain now has about one-third of McDonald's business. In western Europe, McCain supplies about 80 percent of McDonald's restaurants, although McDonald's has little choice since McCain is the only major French fry producer there. McDonald's is currently encouraging McCain rival Lamb-Weston to set up plants in Europe to act as a counter to McCain's dominance, but it's unlikely that Lamb-Weston will ever challenge McCain's position.

However, in the United States, which is McDonald's biggest market by far, McCain is still virtually shut out. In fact, McCain didn't sell a single French fry to an American McDonald's restaurant until 1991. Even then, the company managed to supply only a few restaurants around Norfolk, Virginia. Today, McCain has grabbed about 6 percent of McDonald's U.S. business. That isn't bad considering that McDonald's total French fry purchases in the United States are roughly equal to the entire Canadian market. But McCain's biggest rivals, Simplot and Lamb-Weston, have 45 percent and 25 percent respectively of McDonald's U.S. business.

The early battles with McDonald's showed that Wallace and Harrison were prepared to fight hard for their way of doing business. They were arrogant, cocky and self-assured—with good reason. They had one of the fastest-growing companies in Canada; they were leaders in a trend that was sweeping the nation. But sometimes their aggressiveness backfired. One of the biggest debacles came in the mid 1960s, during a meeting with Gilbert Lamb.

Wallace and Harrison met Lamb at a frozen food convention in New York around 1965. The McCain boys were eager to visit the man who was considered a pioneer in the food processing industry. Lamb had been just eighteen years old when he took over his family's small fruit and vegetable business in Oregon after his father's death. He expanded the business into frozen vegetables and French fries in the early 1960s and renamed the company Lamb-Weston Inc., after the site of his first processing plant in Weston, Oregon. Lamb soon built up a sizeable food service clientele and had a strong business making French fries for grocery stores under their own labels.

Lamb was forever coming up with new gadgets for his plant—he'd always been more of an inventor than a CEO. One of his most famous inventions was a potato-cutting machine called the Lamb Gun. The machine fired potatoes through a long tube filled with water and into a series of knives, which could be adjusted to any cut of French fry. The gun immediately became an industry standard and was used by virtually every French fry producer, including McCain.

When Wallace and Harrison arrived in the hotel suite to meet Lamb, he introduced them to company president Ed Watson and Bob Cowan, who was in charge of Lamb-Weston's sales at the time. After some idle pleasantries, Harrison and Cowan got into a lengthy discussion about sales and overall business strategy. Soon Harrison was critiquing Lamb-Weston's private-label business and suggesting that Lamb-Weston was making a mistake by concentrating on private-label business instead of developing its own brand name. Cowan was taken aback. He'd barely met Harrison and this upstart from Canada was already telling Lamb-Weston how to run its business. Cowan started challenging Harrison, and the two ended up in a shouting match.

"Harrison just wouldn't quit," remembers Wallace. "I agreed with everything he was saying but he just kept harping on it and getting more aggressive. And Cowan is just like Harrison so the two start going at it. Finally, Harrison says to Cowan, 'You're nothing but a stupid fucking farmer.'"

Cowan went on to become president of Lamb-Weston, but he never forgot the insult. "I remember that meeting in New York very well," Cowan recalls angrily. "And I made sure they paid for that, every word." In fact, his retaliation would nearly cripple McCain's business in the United States in the 1980s.

Arrogance got Wallace and Harrison into another major scrap in the 1960s that left lasting bitterness, this time with their old employer and mentor, K.C. Irving. By the late 1960s, Irving dominated New Brunswick's economy with interests in oil, pulp and paper, newspapers and shipping. At the same time, McCain's trucking company, Day & Ross, was losing buckets of money and the brothers were scrambling to cut costs. With that in mind, the brothers decided to review the company's fuel contract with Irving Oil. Every year, the McCains had put out tenders for Day & Ross's fuel and oil contract, and every year, Irving submitted the highest bid. No one dared say no to Irving, so

Wallace and Harrison would talk to Irving Oil officials and ask them to cut their price.

"They'd say, 'What price do you want?' and we'd tell them and they'd do it," recalls Wallace. But the next year Irving would submit the same high price and the McCains had to make the same request.

In 1967, Wallace and Harrison decided they'd had enough and they took a lower bidder. It was a daring move. Wallace and Harrison were snubbing not only the most powerful company in the province but also family friends and their former boss.

Former McCain executive Bev O'Keefe says the decision infuriated the Irvings, who thought they had a long-term arrangement with Day & Ross. Relations between the Irvings and McCains worsened when Irving decided to start a trucking company called Midland Transport Ltd., and Day & Ross opposed Midland's application for a licence. O'Keefe and others say Irving's decision to go into trucking was in part prompted by the cancellation of the contract with Day & Ross, but Wallace disagrees and argues that Irving would have gone into trucking some day anyway. "Did that cause them to get into trucking? I doubt it," he says.

The trucking issue wouldn't be the last time the two businesses fought. In 1979, Irving decided to compete with McCain head-on in the French fry business. The Irvings could see how lucrative the business had been for the McCains and wanted a piece of the action. Irving acquired Prince Edward Island-based C.M. McLean Ltd., a small but pesky competitor of McCain's. Within weeks of the deal, McCain hit Irving with a lawsuit over the Lamb Gun. McCain had bought the Canadian rights for the potato-cutter from Lamb-Weston but Irving had come up with a copycat version. The McCains wanted a court order stopping Irving from using its gun because the design was a copy of the Lamb Gun. McCain lost the case, mainly because of flaws in Gilbert Lamb's patent. McCain threatened another suit against Irving in 1980 over changes to its trademark that made it appear similar to McCain's. That case was settled out of court.

CHAPTER EIGHT

Gordon Hill nervously checked his tie as he knocked on the door in Toronto's Royal York Hotel. Harrison McCain welcomed him in and gave him a strong handshake and a big hello before introducing him to Wallace, who was finishing off a drink near a makeshift bar in the corner. The room looked like a college dorm. Clothes were strewn about and the beds had been pushed to one side to make more room for the boxes of McCain product samples piled up against a wall.

It was May 1969, and Wallace and Harrison were in town for the Canadian Restaurant Show, the biggest food service event of the year. The McCain booth had been a huge hit during the show, attracting more than twelve thousand visitors. To help draw a crowd the brothers had set up a special slot machine that gave away transistor radios and vouchers for McCain food as its jackpots. Each night during the show, the brothers turned their hotel room into a hospitality suite and invited restaurant executives up for a drink. It had been a week of non-stop selling and schmoozing.

Hill had been eager to meet the McCains ever since a friend in New Brunswick told him Harrison was looking for someone to handle McCain's advertising. Hill had been in the advertising business since leaving the army at the end of the war and was now building up his own ad agency. Now, as he sat on the corner of a bed, Harrison and Wallace told him what they were after.

By the late 1960s, McCain had secured a dominant position in the food service business, but their frozen oven-baked fries were still unknown to most grocery store shoppers outside Atlantic

Canada. The McCains needed more exposure for their product, the brothers told Hill. And the key to that was television.

Television had already transformed the food industry. As families rushed home to watch their favourite TV programs, restaurants adapted by introducing more fast-food takeouts and delivery services. In the late 1960s, McDonald's became the first restaurant to advertise on national network television in the United States. Cooking at home was also being simplified with TV dinners and a host of other frozen, crystallized, canned and freeze-dried products. Television was speeding up the whole pace of life, and the way the brothers saw it, McCain's frozen oven-baked fries would fit right in.

McCain had done some local television advertising but without any noticeable results. Harrison and Wallace felt it was time to go national. They asked Hill to draw up some sample TV ads for McCain. "But keep it cheap," they told Hill as he left.

Hill was stumped. He wasn't sure how to introduce and sell such a new concept in a thirty-second ad. He needed some kind of focus for the pitch, so he rounded up his staff for some primitive market research. "We opened up the phone book and called every twentieth name. We asked if they ever ate French fries when they went out and if they ever made them at home."

What Hill discovered was that few people made French fries at home because fryers were big, expensive and messy. Even those who did tackle the challenge were rarely satisfied: the homemade fries took a long time to make and usually turned out oily, not crispy like restaurant fare. With that, Hill decided on his pitch: McCain fries were easy to cook and tasted just as good as restaurant-made.

"I came up with a slogan that said, 'French fries that taste so good you'll think you are eating out.' No oil and no smoke," remembers Hill. He made a sample of the ad and flew out to Florenceville with an assistant to show Harrison and Wallace.

Hill had worked in New Brunswick before—he'd helped run a few Liberal election campaigns—but he wasn't prepared for Florenceville or the barebones McCain headquarters. "I remember we stayed at the Cheerio Motel right beside the plant," Hill recalls. "They put us in a cottage about two feet from the railroad tracks. We couldn't see the tracks when we arrived, but the place shook like hell when the early morning train went by."

After the wake-up call, Hill walked across an open field to the McCain building. He stepped into Harrison and Wallace's tiny office on the main floor and realized there wasn't enough room for his presentation. Harrison suggested they head to the Legion Hall down the road. Hill suppressed a laugh, but within a few minutes he was standing behind a table in the middle of the hall trying to concentrate on his presentation—showing slides, discussing market surveys, selling the slogan—as a stream of Legionnaires shuffled in for a quick beer. The presentation worked, and Hill was hired to produce a series of ads.

McCain's first major television ad campaign was an instant success. The simple message worked so well that grocery stores could barely keep their shelves stocked with McCain fries. Now that the McCains had discovered the power of television, they were ready for a blitzkrieg. Over three years they increased their ad budget from $75,000 to $500,000 and flooded the airwaves with low-budget ads proclaiming Hill's simple message. Hill was given most of the McCain advertising work and spent nearly all of his time on the McCain account. The success of the McCain ads boosted his own business and he opened a new office in Montreal.

Once their TV ads hit screens across Canada, McCain went through a period of unparalleled growth. Between 1970 and 1974, sales more than tripled to over $100 million. They bought a second airplane, a new Mitsubishi turboprop, which at the time was the top executive aircraft. Later they built a mile-long runway on a hill behind their houses and erected a two-plane hanger. The Grand Falls plant began production in 1971 and the Florenceville plant went through a $1.4-million expansion. In 1975, another plant was added in Portage la Prairie, Manitoba, to feed the growing demand in western Canada. In Britain, the fast-food phenomenon was just getting started, but already McCain sales were rising so fast that in 1974 Wallace and Harrison announced plans to build a new $16-million plant in Whittlesey, England. European sales were also picking up enough that the brothers bought a plant in Spain in 1976 and two plants in Holland, the heart of Europe's potato country. After a few years they expanded one of the Dutch plants and bought another one.

Even in Australia things were looking up. Wallace had finally sorted out the problems in the Daylesford plant by 1971 and put it through a $400,000 renovation. Sales improved enough that by 1975, the Daylesford plant was scrapped and a new one was built in nearby Ballarat. Relations with the Australian government had also improved—so much so that the government gave McCain a low-interest loan to help build the new plant. "It was the sort of loan that Harrison said he would never pay off it was so cheap," recalls Ernie Ellis, the former manager of McCain's Australian operations. "If interest rates were around 18 percent to 19 percent at the time, we got it for around 7 percent. If the plant cost $3.5 million, we probably got $1.5 million in government assistance."

There were still some problems in Australia. Just before the plant opened, Ellis committed an unpardonable crime, for which he had to be dismissed: he had allowed the formation of a union at the plant. The McCains weren't big fans of unions and had done their best to discourage them. In 1973, they fired Renald Desrosiers, a twenty-three-year-old worker at the Grand Falls plant, after he began a union drive. To further thwart the movement, the company began a seasonal layoff at the plant a month early. When the layoff was over, the plant managers refused to rehire sixty-three people who had signed union cards. Desrosiers took his firing to the New Brunswick Industrial Relations Board and won. McCain was ordered to rehire him and pay him back wages. But Desrosiers was laid off a few weeks later, and workers at the plant were so intimidated that a union was never organized.

The brothers also sued a union in Newfoundland after it refused to stop representing workers at a local trucking company bought by Day & Ross. The McCains fought the union all the way to the provincial supreme court, claiming that it had no right to represent the workers because Day & Ross was not unionized in New Brunswick. However, they lost that battle as well.

Needless to say, when Wallace found out that Ellis had permitted a union to form in Australia, he was as good as gone. Even worse, as far as Wallace was concerned, the union was led by the head of the local Communist Party. "Wallace and I didn't see eye to eye on different matters here in Australia," Ellis recalls tactfully. "I was sort of an independent character and that didn't suit Wallace at different times. We crossed swords and agreed to disagree and go our separate ways."

Just when they thought business couldn't grow any faster, the brothers got another major boost back home. Scientists at the Department of Agriculture research station near Fredericton came up with a new potato variety called the Shepody. It was the first potato ever bred exclusively for the processing industry, and it was a miracle for the McCains.

Ever since they had cut their first French fry, Wallace and Harrison had had to fight the impression that eastern potato varieties didn't measure up to the Russet Burbanks for making fries. The Russet grew best out west and was the variety used by McCain's biggest competitors, including Simplot and Lamb-Weston. McDonald's was one of many restaurants that preferred Russets for all its fries.

Luckily for the McCains, the provincial government had been as troubled by the problem as they were. In the early 1960s, two large U.S. processors, General Foods and Salada-Shirrif, decided not to establish French fry plants in New Brunswick mainly because local farmers couldn't grow Russet Burbanks. The loss of jobs prompted the provincial government to press agricultural researchers to develop a processing potato that could grow in New Brunswick. After years of mixing and matching genes from dozens of potatoes, Dr. Donald Young, a researcher at Agriculture Canada, hit on a cross that worked. The Shepody, named after a small river near the Bay of Fundy, was as big, long and smooth as the Russet but took about a month less to mature.

The McCains were so excited by the new potato that they offered Young acres of land to grow and test the Shepody. They also opened the doors of their plant and let researchers in to test the potato's processing characteristics. All the help from the McCains sped up testing and the Shepody was introduced on a wide scale within a few years of its discovery. It wasn't long before the new spud rivalled the Russet as the industry standard. Today, the Shepody is the third most common variety grown in Canada and the United States. In fact, the variety is so well accepted that even Simplot and Lamb-Weston use it to make their fries.

With a new potato variety to take on their competitors and a successful television campaign pulling in customers, the McCains seemed unstoppable. But the success of their oven-baked fries soon began to attract competitors. The brothers knew they were vulnerable to a better product because McCain's oven fries had a tendency to turn out soggy. So, when they heard that Heinz was developing a frozen French fry that baked with deep-fried crispiness, the brothers knew they had to come up with a better product soon or they would lose a huge chunk of their market. They handed the job to their new marketing manager, Archie McLean.

McLean had only just been hired in 1972 when he went to work on one of the biggest McCain projects ever. His experience was with Quaker Oats in Ontario. A big, gregarious man with a huge smile and strong religious convictions, McLean used to teach Sunday school and often opened business meetings with a prayer. He was the fourth marketing manager the brothers had hired in four years. All the others had quit after a few months because Wallace and Harrison insisted on running most of the marketing themselves. McLean nearly threw in the towel as well after a week on the job. Instead, he sent Wallace and Harrison a long letter telling them to back off and to let him do his job. Afraid to lose another manager, the McCains agreed to step away.

With some room to manoeuvre, McLean got to work on the new French fry project with Carl Morris, vice president of production, and Tim Bliss, vice president of engineering. Morris had been fiddling with his own ideas on how to improve the oven fries by the time McLean arrived, and, within a few months, he'd drawn up plans for a new processing system. His idea was to cut the fries thicker and coat them lightly with an oil that would make them crispy once baked. After a year of tests, Morris patented the design and McLean came up with a name.

"We called them Superfries because I loved the word 'super,'" recalls McLean with a chuckle. McCain's Superfries beat Heinz to market and became the number-one-selling oven fry almost over night. "The market grew 30 percent almost immediately," recalls McLean. By 1978, McCain was selling Superfries in Canada, Europe, Britain and Australia, and the product is still the company's top money-maker.

The rush to get Superfries onto the market taught the brothers that they had to diversify and keep introducing new products. Although they had introduced frozen vegetables and fruit pies in 1969, they had scrapped their small potato chip business because it was too costly, and they were still too focused on one product. They needed a broader base, so they turned to McLean for some ideas.

Fortunately for the brothers, before he came to McCain, McLean was working on a frozen pizza for Quaker Oats. Quaker had been marketing a frozen pizza in the United States but had yet to introduce one in Canada. McLean saw an opportunity. He got Morris and Bliss involved in designing ovens and a pizza line. He also arranged for a company in Toronto to package the products. A year later, the first McCain frozen pizza rolled off the line, and once again the company had an instant hit.

"We doubled the national consumption of frozen pizza within a year and had half the business," recalls McLean. Business grew so fast that the packaging company couldn't keep up with the orders and McCain had to build its own packaging line in Florenceville. Two years later, McCain built a new $2.5-million pizza plant in Grand Falls, with the help of a $1.5-million provincial loan. The plant hit full capacity within a year and was doubled in size by 1978. More plants were added around the world and McCain bought a couple of other pizza-makers including Gusto Pizza from Nestlé Canada and Ellio's Pizza in the United States.

"Borrowing" ideas from competitors like Quaker Oats became a McCain hallmark. The company developed an expertise at taking other people's ideas and making them an even bigger success. For years, the McCain "research department" consisted of McLean flipping through trade magazines. But whatever McCain lacked in inventiveness it more than made up for in innovation. For example, when Pillsbury came out with Pizza Pops—rolled dough stuffed with pizza toppings—consumers loved the idea but didn't like the Pops' tendency to leak. McCain took the idea and created its own no-leak Pizza Pocket. Then they launched a massive ad campaign with the slogan: "No leaks, no mess." It worked. Within a year, McCain had doubled the market and owned half the business. Pizza Pockets were later introduced in France, Australia and the United States and have become the second most profitable product for McCain, next to Superfries. Pillsbury has improved its product but still lags behind McCain in sales.

Not every McCain innovation succeeded, however. The company tried a line of frozen yogurt once, which fizzled miserably. A frozen bread flopped when the company discovered that as the dough thawed the yeast died and the bread wouldn't rise when baked. Frozen doughnuts also bombed and were taken off the market after just a month. And frozen entrees have been a struggle for the company in many countries for years. But the setbacks were small compared to the success of Superfries, pizza products and other innovations, such as frozen desserts. In most cases, McCain's products became big sellers in Canada and around the world.

All of the company's success was starting to pay off personally for Harrison and Wallace. But just as the threads of the business were being successfully woven together, relations between the brothers continued to unravel. Both were on the road about half the year and when one was home the other was usually away. Wallace and Harrison's interests outside the company were also growing further apart. Harrison continued to build a public profile outside McCain. He kept up a demanding schedule, balancing company business and private functions with business leaders and other dignitaries. Louis Robichaud, who had been appointed to the federal Senate, remembers the morning just before Christmas one year when he got a call at his home in Ottawa from Harrison. "Harrison asked me what I was doing that afternoon and I said not much. So he said, 'Billie and I will be right over.' They flew out from Florenceville for the afternoon."

Harrison got a huge boost in 1971 when he was appointed to the board of the Bank of Nova Scotia. Bank boards are coveted positions in the business world. It was a dream job for Harrison, who had spent years trying to develop contacts across other industries. Wallace, meanwhile, continued to shun public attention and directorships. He balanced his business schedule with his family schedule and shied away from public events.

In 1971, the brothers changed their titles. Harrison became chairman instead of president and Wallace was named president instead of vice president. The titles meant little in terms of overall authority; Wallace and Harrison continued to make all company decisions together. But the titles were a reflection of how each brother met the different needs of the company. The chairman's job involved overall planning and the future direction of the company: it was the perfect position for Harrison, who considered himself the visionary. The president, however, ran the day-to-day operations: exactly the kind of detail job Wallace had been doing since McCain started.

The titles, however, cemented the perception of each brother within the company and the family. Even though they had equal day-to-day authority, there was an assumption by most employees that Harrison was in charge. To many executives, Harrison was somebody they felt they worked for, whereas Wallace was somebody they worked with. Tim Bliss recalls that at many executive meetings Harrison would automatically sit at the head of the table while Wallace took a seat with the others. At company functions, Harrison was almost always the only brother to give a speech. While the brothers treated each other as equals in decision-making, they were often treated by others as though they occupied different positions in a real hierarchy of power. Wallace "sometimes looked just as subservient as the rest of us," recalls Bliss. "He wasn't. But Harrison sometimes made it appear that way. Even at Christmas parties or other company functions, Wallace would always let Harrison have the limelight."

Family members also began deferring to Harrison as the company grew. For many he became what his son Mark later called the "guiding spirit" of the McCains. To have Harrison as a guest was considered a great family honour. Wallace's daughter Eleanor recalls a visit to her Aunt Eleanor's home in Toronto. Her aunt gave her one of the two bedrooms on the main floor because it had a telephone and she would be able to call her fiancé in private. After leaving for a few hours one day, Eleanor returned to her aunt's home to find her bags packed and sitting on the stairs. Harrison had made a surprise visit, she was told, and would she mind taking a room upstairs, even though it didn't have a phone, so that Harrison could have the ground floor of the house to himself? Throughout the rest of her visit, young Eleanor said she felt out of place as her aunt raced around to cater to Harrison's wishes.

Resentment was beginning to surface by the mid 1970s. Wallace didn't agree with Harrison's appointment to the bank board and resisted Harrison's suggestion that Wallace join a bank board as well. "We'd made a deal not to serve on outside boards because it would take time away from McCain," Wallace recalled. "But Harrison did anyway." After years of coaxing from Harrison, Wallace caved in and took a seat on the board of the Royal Bank of Canada in 1986. As it turns out, it was the best advice Harrison ever gave Wallace: the board position proved to be an invaluable resource in his later battle with Harrison and other family members.

Distrust between Wallace and Harrison only grew when they, along with Bob and Andrew, made plans to put their McCain holdings in a family trust. It was mainly a way to save on taxes but the trusts would also keep McCain's ownership in the family by passing it on to the next generation. Each brother appointed another to head his trust after he died. Harrison, however, was the one brother who was against putting all his holdings into a family trust. "Harrison said, 'Don't do it,'" Wallace recalls. "Don't trust your wife or your kids,' All my life, Harrison has been telling me, 'Don't trust people.'"

If maintaining the appearance of unity was important to the business, it was the hallmark of the McCain family culture. Margaret was becoming restless and uncomfortable, weary of maintaining the façade. She was growing tired of the McCain's unwritten rule requiring members to protect the family's name at any cost. As an aunt she often felt powerless when she saw the turbulent lives of her teenaged nieces and nephews. The pressures on the young McCains were fierce, and those pressures were sometimes manifested in self-destruction and abuse. Some of the children were exhibiting symptoms of anorexia and alcoholism. But because of the family culture these problems could never be admitted to or addressed. Emotional support simply wasn't there. "We worshipped at the altar of the McCains," she recalls. "Nothing could ever sully the family name or cause controversy."

Margaret came from a large, open and caring family. Throughout her married life she missed that warmth and intimacy. She found living with the McCains lonely and the family very insular. Spouses were often left with the sense that they were not, and never would be, real McCains. There would always be family matters that they were not privy to and issues that were just plain none of their business.

Just as the McCains did not open up to in-laws, they were horrified if in-laws opened up to them. Margaret became painfully aware of this when she was trying to help her sister through a troubled marriage. "The McCain family didn't want to hear about it," she says. "They were willing to provide financial support but they didn't want to talk about what was going on."

Women also had very rigid and constricted roles within the McCain family, and while this had been barely acceptable to Margaret in her twenties, it was positively suffocating to her now that she was in her mid forties. It was the 1970s, and women's roles had changed so much in the outside world that a family culture insisting that women refrain from blue jeans and eye shadow just didn't make any sense to Margaret.

As Margaret's misery grew, she began to seriously question her marriage. She saw little of her husband, and she was frustrated that the values she had grown up with, and so anxiously wanted to pass on to her children, conflicted with the values of the McCains. She wanted to create a family life with Wallace that would enable her four children to grow into well-adjusted, successful adults, but she just didn't see how this was possible in her current circumstances.

During one of her blackest moments, she wrote two lists: one outlined the reasons why she should stay and the other the reasons why she should go. After much soul-searching Margaret decided to keep the name McCain and remain in her marriage. But in order to do this she knew she had to make some serious changes—changes to meet her own needs and the needs of her children. She was going to have to find a way of articulating those needs to her husband and asking that they be met. And she was going to have to wrestle with the intense control that her husband and her husband's family expected to have over people they were involved with. She began her fight with a small but symbolic battle by taking on the McCain clothing code. She told Wallace she was going to wear what she felt like, when she felt like it. And if that meant blue jeans and eye shadow, then so be it.

Bob's wife Rosemary was also wrestling with the insular nature of the McCain family. In 1973, Bob became seriously ill after a business trip to South America for McCain Produce. The illness persisted, and Bob seemed to need more and more rest. Soon he was too ill to walk, and then one day in October he fell unconscious. Rosemary rushed him to the McCain airstrip and Bob was flown to a hospital in Montreal on the company plane. One of his kidneys had failed and he was put on emergency dialysis. The doctors had no idea why the kidney failed or how to treat him. They told Rosemary he wouldn't live out the week. Miraculously, Bob's condition stabilized enough over the next few days for the doctors to attempt a transplant. Their hopes collapsed once again, however, when the new kidney failed within two weeks, and Bob was put back on dialysis.

As soon as he was well enough to live outside the hospital, Bob and Rosemary rented an apartment in Montreal for several months to be near the dialysis. When his condition stabilized and it became clear that dialysis was going to become a way of life, they made arrangements to have a dialysis machine installed in their home in Florenceville.

Rosemary knew that Bob didn't have long to live. The pressure was enormous. It took all of Rosemary's time and attention just to keep Bob alive. She sent her two teenaged children to boarding school; she wanted to protect them from their father's illness, which prevented her from meeting their needs. Like Margaret, Rosemary felt lonely. She felt taken for granted, unsupported and exploited by some of the McCains, who, in spite of the family's wealth, seemed to expect her to put her own life aside in order to be a twenty-four-hour nurse to Bob. When Rosemary's own father died in 1976, she was so preoccupied with Bob's illness that she wasn't able to grieve or properly mourn his death.

As she came face to face daily with Bob's mortality, she became more and more angry with the McCains. She felt that the family had never fully recognized Bob's talent and creativity and his role in getting McCain Foods started. In her eyes, Bob was the founder of the company. Without him there simply would not have been a McCain Foods. It was his idea, his research, his energy and his instincts that had put Wallace and Harrison on the track to becoming millionaires.

By 1976, Bob had for many years been no more than a token director and now, in the final days of his life, it seemed to Rosemary that Harrison and Wallace were more interested in making their next million than they were in the fact that he was dying. Bob had never been financially rewarded for his contribution to McCain. Harrison and Wallace were not paying dividends to Bob or Andrew, even though together they owned one-third of the company. Rosemary felt Bob had created a legacy, a legacy she was concerned their four children might never be able to share in because of Harrison and Wallace's selfishness.

CHAPTER NINE

Wallace took a seat onstage and tugged at his black gown. It was May 5, 1973, and he had been invited to receive an honorary degree from Mount Allison University. As he looked out at the faces of hundreds of students and their families, Wallace smiled to himself at the irony. Here he was, a below-average student at three universities, about to receive an honorary degree at the age of forty-three. His mother, Laura, had been given an honorary degree a year earlier by Mount Allison. Wallace could understand the school recognizing his mother's accomplishments in business and volunteer work, but he wasn't sure quite why he was being honoured in this way.

The graduation ceremonies began and Wallace listened as university president L.H. Cragg gave a brief address. Cragg then introduced Steven Heckbert, the graduating class's valedictorian. Heckbert sauntered to the stage with a look of defiance. He had long hair, no socks and a T-shirt under his gown.

The next thing Wallace heard was the shrill, deafening sound of a whistle being blown into a microphone. He thought he was going to have a heart attack. When he recovered from the shock, what he heard was Heckbert shouting abuse and accusations about McCain Foods. Apparently, Wallace and his brother Harrison were guilty of a greed that bordered on the criminal. They were personally responsible for the destruction of family farms, grossly exploiting their employees and polluting the environment. Wallace also learned that the only reason he was being given the honorary degree was because the university saw it as a cheap and easy way to get a donation out of McCain. Just to keep his audience on their toes, Heckbert punctuated his tirade by repeatedly blowing his whistle into the microphone. Wallace was becoming afraid for his safety—who knew, maybe he was going to pull out a gun.

Fortunately for Wallace, a visibly shaken President Cragg got up and pulled Heckbert by the arm away from the podium. "Mr. Heckbert," he told the crowd, "I would like to thank you for the sincerity with which you have brought your concerns before us. But I must remind you that, though the university is a proper place for debate, the university's convocation is not the proper place, and it certainly is not a proper occasion for personal attacks." Confused and deflated, Heckbert left the podium and sat down as Cragg awarded Wallace his degree. Wallace never forgot the experience. It was the first in a series of humiliating public attacks on McCain in the 1970s.

With the protests of the '60s still ringing in its ears, Canada's government in the '70s was becoming increasingly socially conscious and in response the federal government began funding a variety of health, education and welfare programs. Since most people in rural areas had poor access to these programs, the federal government provided money to the provinces to set up agencies to investigate ways of bringing these resources into rural communities. "People power" was very much in vogue. In New Brunswick, the Department of Agriculture had embarked on a program to improve rural life. No one in the department really knew how rural life could be improved, but that didn't matter.

The task of organizing New Brunswick's new rural development branch fell to David Malcolm, an earnest young man who'd worked on and off in the department for a decade. Malcolm was an idealist who jumped at the chance to improve the lives of farm families. His convictions were based on a deep religious faith. Whenever he went on a business trip into rural areas, he always made sure the trunk of his car was full of Bibles so that he could leave them in hotel rooms along the way. He even looked like a missionary, thin, with a thick beard and piercing eyes. When the department gave him money to hire two assistants, Malcolm found his own idealism mirrored in two young men, Bert Deveaux and Skip Hambling. He hired both of them immediately.

Hambling was from Ottawa and had graduated from Acadia University in the late 1960s with a degree in arts and a major in protesting. He was a student radical who fought for socialism, co-operation and activism. He couldn't wait to take on every major corporate interest in New Brunswick, especially those "creepos" the McCains. Farmers were always a bit suspicious of Hambling at first because of his long pony-tail and dishevelled appearance, but as soon as they saw his quick smile and friendly nature, their scepticism faded. Deveaux was more reserved than Hambling. He was a practitioner who knew how to put social theory into real action. His father was a Cape Breton coal miner, and, like Hambling, Deveaux had grown up with a suspicion of all things corporate.

Hambling and Deveaux had known each other for years. They met while working together in a Company of Young Canadians program in Sydney, Nova Scotia, helping to organize community groups. When the program folded they headed to Montreal to work in a youth centre, but they were fired when it was discovered that the centre had been opened all night as a hangout for teens.

As soon as they hit McCain country, Malcolm, Hambling and Deveaux started a crusade encouraging farmers, lumberjacks and fishermen to organize and stand up to big corporations. No company was too big to tackle. "We had this Goliath idea," recalls Hambling. "The bigger they were the better."

The group homed in on McCain after Deveaux attended a small farmers' meeting one evening in Woodstock. He went to provide information on marketing boards and farmers' associations and came away with the strong impression of a growing resentment towards McCain. "They all felt screwed," Deveaux remembers. He was also told about two farmers McCain was suing for $32,000 in total for failing to fulfill terms of the McCain contract.

After the meeting, Deveaux talked with other McCain farmers, who complained that the company was paying pitiful amounts for produce. For example, farmers around Rogersville, an Acadian community in northeastern New Brunswick, told Deveaux that it cost them about $2,000 per acre to grow Brussels sprouts, including labour costs, but McCain was paying only about $2,100 per acre.

Deveaux, Hambling and Malcolm decided to help the farmers organize an association to negotiate with McCain over potato contracts. The company had opposed every attempt to organize farmers into a bargaining unit; Harrison liked to deal with a farmer individually and "look him in the eye." But Deveaux and Hambling were convinced the only way farmers could get higher prices for their produce was by working together.

Organizing farmers to take on McCain, especially in Carleton County, wasn't easy. Two groups were already trying: the National Farmers Union (NFU) and the New Brunswick Federation of Agriculture, an association of farmers. The NFU was founded in 1969 and led locally by farmer Harry Ebbett. Ebbett, worried about McCain's growing power, had already stopped selling potatoes to the company because he felt their price was too low. He was convinced that farmers had to organize and bargain as a collective. Deveaux thought the three should work together and he planned a series of public meetings dubbed a "Farmers' Inquiry." The inquiry would be a way for farmers to bring public attention to McCain's contract and the problems of agriculture in general. Harry Ebbett and the NFU were thrilled. They'd had no success organizing farmers and were ready to try almost anything. In a gesture of what was to come, the "inquiry" held its first organizational meeting in Florenceville, not far from the McCain plant.

Most of the briefs presented by farmers during the hearings were written by Hambling or Deveaux, and every one included a bitter attack on McCain. The theme was summarized in a twenty-two-page brief called "The Spider and the Web—Agribusiness and the Farmer. The way it really is." "Corporations and farmers are locked together in a spider and fly relationship—with no doubt as to who is the spider and who is the fly," the brief said. It went on to attack McCain's contract system, saying the company "owned the soul of the farmer." It also blasted McCain's vertical integration and said the company had complete control over farmers.

Soon, as many as one hundred farmers started attending the meetings, and the media began to take notice. So did some government officials. "The inquiry frightened the Department of

Agriculture because they had never seen anything like this," said Deveaux. It was turning into the biggest protest yet against McCain.

Wallace and Harrison managed to ignore most of the meetings and rants. Just a bunch of noisy radicals, they thought, representing a small minority of farmers. Harrison told a reporter at the time that the group was "a very vocal group. More vocal than thoughtful."

Undaunted, Deveaux and the others pressed on. Their first victory came when the farmers around Rogersville agreed to stop supplying McCain unless the company increased its prices. Because the region was mainly francophone, it was one of the few where McCain negotiated annual contracts with farmers as a group. The head of the local co-op, Jean Finnigan, was bilingual and he negotiated on everyone's behalf. It hadn't been much of a negotiation, however. The farmers weren't important McCain suppliers. There were only a couple of dozen and they grew just six hundred acres of Brussels sprouts. Wallace "was always fair and good to deal with," recalls Finnigan. "But I didn't have much to bargain with. What could I do? Refuse to take their offer and stop growing Brussels spouts? They would just get them from somewhere else." Complicating Finnigan's own role was the fact that he was also paid twenty-five dollars a week by McCain to act as a regional co-ordinator for the company.

The farmers had never really tried to find another buyer for their sprouts, but with a few months of Deveaux's help, they found other takers who were prepared to pay more than McCain. Deveaux also encouraged the farmers to build a greenhouse in order to grow their own bedding plants instead of buying them from McCain. It was a small protest, but it was the first time a group of farmers had openly challenged the company.

Wallace didn't just wait around to see if the farmers would find other buyers, he went out and found an opportunity for McCain to grow its own Brussels sprouts in nearby St. Leonard. "That gave McCain even more leverage over us," recalls Finnigan.

Meanwhile, Deveaux, Hambling and Malcolm's inquiry ended after three months with no official comment from McCain or the province. However, the government did set up a travelling committee on rural land use and ownership. Since the government hadn't responded to their inquiry, Malcolm, Deveaux and Hambling decided their next move was to present a brief to the legislative committee. On October 1, 1975, they delivered a blistering attack on McCain and Irving for buying up land and destroying the family farm. They also recommended that the province adopt a policy to prevent "non-farm corporations from being or becoming farmers. The same policy should also provide for immediate withdrawal of the McCain interests from producing products which they are purchasing from other farmers, and their eventual total withdrawal from the production of agricultural products," they told the committee.

Committee members were shocked but the presentation went unnoticed by the media for more than a week. Then, on October 8, *The Telegraph-Journal* in St. John carried a story headed: "Irving, McCain Branded Potential Threats To The Family Farm." Harrison was livid and issued a terse response. "Any inference that we've been a predatory buyer…just bluntly isn't true," he told the paper.

Officials in the Department of Agriculture were also furious and embarrassed that two of their employees would attack one of the province's biggest employers. The government was still backing McCain with millions of dollars in bond guarantees, and criticism of the company couldn't be tolerated. "Before the day was out, I had a call from the Minister of Agriculture saying he wanted to see me," recalls Malcolm. "And so I went, and I was told that we should not have presented a brief."

Malcolm insisted that they were speaking as individuals and not as representatives of the government. He explained that they had presented the brief after hours to avoid any appearance that they were speaking on behalf of the department. But that didn't matter. "I was told I'd be given a new job," he recalls. Deveaux and Hambling were also reassigned, but a few months later all three quit and started a tiny weekly newspaper in Fredericton called *The Plaindealer*. It was filled with stories of corporate greed, political scandal, farmers' rights and the McCains, but it never reached more than a handful of readers.

Just when the McCains thought they were finally rid of the

pesky trio and safely out of the spotlight, a producer from the CBC television program "The Fifth Estate" started poking around New Brunswick in the fall of 1976 for some information on McCain. His research led him to Deveaux, Hambling and Malcolm, who were eager to share their stories and contacts.

The producer was Gerry McAuliffe, a gruff, driven newsman whose mandate was to produce three documentaries a year, "but they all had to be ball-busters," he says with a smile. "The Fifth Estate" had been on the air for only a year but it had already acquired a reputation as a hard-hitting investigative program. McAuliffe had taken an interest in McCain after receiving a press release from the company in September announcing the construction of the new $12-million plant in Portage la Prairie, Manitoba. McAuliffe was struck by the amount of government money going into the project. More than half the cost—$7 million—was coming from the federal government and the Manitoba Development Corporation. David Lewis and the federal New Democratic Party had made "corporate welfare bums" a hot issue at the time, and McAuliffe smelled a scandal. "The McCain story had never been done on television before," he remembers. "And they were getting a shit-load of government money."

With the help of Deveaux, Hambling and Malcolm, McAuliffe got to work. He interviewed angry farmers about McCain's contract system and profiled the family of a young boy who had died working one of McCain's machines. He also found out about the failed union drive in Grand Falls, and he calculated that McCain had so far raked in more than $21.5 million in government handouts. He taped an interview with David Malcolm about losing his job after criticizing McCain and his crew got lots of shots of empty pesticide barrels outside McCain's plant. It was shaping up to be another ball-buster. The only thing missing was an interview with one of the McCain brothers.

McAuliffe contacted both Wallace and Harrison to ask for an interview. Wallace was more than a little nervous. "I knew what this program was like and I told Harrison to forget it," remembers Wallace. "I said, 'You're going to get burned.' But he wanted to do it." Harrison felt he had nothing to hide, and believing that some comment was better than none, he agreed to the interview. His only condition was that McAuliffe type up a list of questions and submit it in advance.

McAuliffe was thrilled, and the show's host, Adrienne Clarkson, flew out to interview Harrison outside the McCain plant. It would be the first time a McCain had been interviewed at length on national television, and McAuliffe wanted it to be unforgettable. When he felt Clarkson wasn't being tough enough, McAuliffe himself took over the interview and fired off dozens of brash questions about safety, money and pollution.

After interviewing Harrison for more than an hour, McAuliffe was confident he had the footage he needed, and the crew headed to Fredericton for an interview with Premier Richard Hatfield about the government's support for McCain. It was only then that McAuliffe realized the close co-operation between McCain and the premier. When he asked to use Hatfield's telephone, McAuliffe saw a notepad sitting next to the phone with some scribbled lines. It was a list of the questions he had fired at Harrison less than two hours earlier. With his interviews and research complete, McAuliffe returned to Toronto to put together the documentary. He was sure he had all the ammunition he needed to put McCain in the hot seat.

That fall, Wallace was once again sidelined by illness. For several weeks, he had been feeling periodic pains in his abdomen. Then one morning, just as he was preparing for a business trip, a stabbing pain shot through his side. He was petrified. He hadn't felt this kind of pain in nearly twenty years, since the doctors had removed his large intestine. He and Margaret rushed to the Lahey Clinic in Boston, where Wallace had undergone his intestinal surgery in 1958.

Doctors diagnosed the problem as a hernia and told him not to worry, it would be a simple operation—until they discovered that the hernia was constricting Wallace's small intestine, which was potentially fatal. They rushed him into surgery. Though it seemed successful at first, a few days later gangrene set in and doctors had to operate again. That operation triggered adhesions—a tissue that clings to bones and other organs. Doctors spent nine hours trying to remove the adhesions by clipping off bits of Wallace's small intestine and piecing together what was left. After weeks of recovering in Boston, Wallace returned home in December 1976 and immediately went back to work.

"I thought Wallace was going to die," remembers McCain vice president Carl Morris. "Then two days later I get a call from Wallace and he says in a faint, raspy voice: 'Carl, I'm coming in on Saturday. I want to see the plant.' So, I'm sitting here in my office Saturday morning and I see him walking up the sidewalk. He looks crumpled and hunched over like he's a hundred years old. I tell him, 'Look, go home, we can do this again another time.' But he just keeps going and does a short tour around the plant. The next day he came in again a little bit stronger and then day after day he kept getting stronger until he was back to normal."

While Wallace was still recovering at home, McAuliffe's documentary finally aired. It was December 8, 1976, and the program was worse than anything Wallace or Harrison could have imagined. Titled "Citizen McCain," the documentary was a tough, critical look at the company, highlighting all of McAuliffe's most damning research. Harrison looked defensive and uneasy in the interview; McAuliffe's questions had clearly caught him off guard. It was the first time McCain had received such fierce negative publicity, and the brothers were unprepared. "I just about died," recalls Wallace, who blasted Harrison for agreeing to the interview. "I said to Harrison, 'There's your P.R.' He was pissed off."

Harrison scrambled to repair the damage. McAuliffe says McCain threatened to pull its advertising from CBC. Harrison went on a counterattack and challenged the program's claims in a lengthy interview with a Maritime business magazine, but it had nothing like the national audience of the CBC broadcast.

Hatfield and several cabinet ministers also came to the aid of the company and publicly condemned the program as misleading and one-sided. Letters to the editor poured in to the *Telegraph-Journal*, some supporting the broadcast but most backing McCain and denouncing the CBC. The *Hartland Observer* wrote a front-page editorial saying simply: "McCains are the best thing ever to happen to agriculture in New Brunswick, and indeed, may well go down in history as being the best thing that ever happened to the Canadian agricultural industry."

Margaret's mother, who was now a Liberal senator, did her bit by launching a blistering attack in the normally sedate Senate against the program, the CBC and Clarkson, personally. "In my opinion, Miss Clarkson must have a perverted mind when she is able to work so hard to find such ugly things to say and insinuate about McCain Foods," Margaret Norrie told the Senate. She then demanded to know the full cost of the program. Other senators backed her up and one even questioned Clarkson's immigration status.

While the McCains battled back, many people came to the defence of the CBC and Clarkson. The United Church in New Brunswick wrote a letter supporting the allegations raised in the program. Others wrote Senator Norrie condemning her remarks and slamming McCain. "We are fortunate in Canada that we have men and women in the media who will keep us informed about what is happening in government and business," wrote one woman from Islington, Ontario. "It is the people's business to know what happens to grants or loans from our federal regional development money." Another writer was more direct: "Both you and the McCains are, like the dinosaurs, doomed to extinction."

Harrison and Wallace never fully recovered from the "Fifth Estate" experience. The program made them cautious about the press. Wallace refused nearly every interview request after the show aired, and both brothers became fierce defenders of the company's reputation. No one was going to humiliate them like that again.

A few weeks later on February 8, 1977, a small newspaper called *Farm and Country* published an editorial questioning the amount of government support given McCain Foods and the family's close ties to the Liberals. Most of the comments had already been raised by "The Fifth Estate," and compared to the CBC, *Farm and Country* had a minuscule audience (the paper was based in Toronto and sold just 80,000 copies nationally, including 30 in New Brunswick). But that didn't matter to the McCains. They weren't about to stand for another attack no matter how small the medium. The brothers decided to fight back as hard as they could. They filed a libel suit against the paper in New Brunswick, even though *Farm and Country* was based in Ontario. Wallace and Harrison obviously felt they would get a more sympathetic hearing at home. They were right. The court awarded McCain $60,000 in damages, exactly what Harrison had sought. It was one of the largest libel awards ever at the time and it nearly drove the paper out of business. The McCains had made their point.

Not long after the lawsuit, the other pockets of protest fizzled out. The newspaper Deveaux, Hambling and Malcolm started began to lose advertisers and folded. Hambling went to work for a union in Ottawa. Deveaux became a filmmaker in Toronto, and Malcolm joined CBC Radio in Fredericton as an agricultural reporter.

As for the farmers in Rogersville who were trying to find other buyers for their produce, the new orders never came through. One potential buyer went bankrupt after taking delivery of some Brussels sprouts, leaving the farmers' co-op with a substantial debt. The farmers reluctantly returned to contracting with McCain, and Finnigan later retired as co-op president. Successive presidents tried to take a tougher line with McCain, but with no success. The company continued to plant more of its own vegetables and recruited other growers.

"You could count on one hand the number of farmers around here today," says Finnigan as he looks out the window of his small home near Rogersville. He is retired now and suffers from Parkinson's disease, so he stays home most of the time. "Most people around here now work wherever they can to earn enough for unemployment insurance."

Wallace and Harrison came out of the 1970s bruised by the bad publicity and burned by the media. But in business terms, the decade was one of the most successful ever for McCain Foods. Thanks largely to the huge growth of fast-food franchises, Canadian restaurant sales hit more than $8.5 billion in 1979, compared to $1.2 billion in 1970. McCain's sales soared from $30 million in 1969 to $360 million as of June 30, 1979.

Fast food wasn't the only transformation affecting McCain in the 1970s. By the end of the decade, the next generation of McCains was beginning to take its place in the company. Wallace and Harrison had always expected that their children, especially their sons, would join the company one day. But they didn't have time to work out how, when or in what positions. And they couldn't sit still long enough to talk about which of their children, if any, might one day take over. They made the fatal mistake of assuming that everything would somehow fall into place.

CHAPTER TEN

Michael McCain walked as quickly as he could. He was trying to keep up with his older brother, Scott. It was a hot summer day and Michael was already sweating. The brothers were heading for an open field and another long afternoon of potato picking. Picking potatoes was not thirteen-year-old Michael's favourite pastime, and he never understood why Scott was in such a hurry to get going. But Scott was always eager to work. So far the two had spent one summer tarring the roof at the McCain plant and another working as masons' helpers. For Michael, those jobs had been nightmares. "There has to be a better way of earning spending money," Michael grumbled to himself as he looked at the potato field looming ahead.

There wasn't much else to do in Florenceville besides pick potatoes. The village's population was still barely six hundred people. The nearest movie theatre was twenty-five miles away in Woodstock. And in spite of a new Trans-Canada Highway, most families stuck pretty close to home. The McCain kids did have it a lot easier than other kids: they had private planes to take them on holidays, and swimming pools and tennis courts in their back yards. Of course there were those who resented them, but the McCains had been a prominent local family for so long that most people pretty much took their wealth for granted. Besides, the McCain kids spent most of their days doing the same things everyone else did. In winter they skated and played hockey on the outdoor rink (that is, until McCain Foods helped build a new arena). In summer they played baseball, went to bush parties and picked potatoes. Every teenager hitchhiked wherever they were going—it just wasn't cool to be seen walking. And the local diner was the only real hangout—until it nearly slid down the riverbank and had to be torn down. On Fridays, teenagers would pile into a car and head to a bar called The Halfway House just over the border in Maine, where strawberry wine was ninety-nine cents a glass and the drinking age was just eighteen, not twenty-one, the way it was in New Brunswick.

From a distance it was hard to tell that Michael and Scott were brothers. Scott was a tall, athletic kid with strong shoulders and a big smile. He was a stand-out winger on Florenceville's hockey team and had been considered one of the village's best players ever since he was a young boy. Born in 1956, Scott was the oldest of Wallace and Margaret's four children. His size and friendliness made him a popular child. Scott's mother called him the Pied Piper of Florenceville because so many kids followed him around.

Michael was two years younger than his brother. He was shorter, more compact and much more serious. He was always called Michael, never Mike. He was the kid who always seemed to be taking something apart and putting it back together. Although he wasn't as big as his brother, he had a remarkable toughness and tenacity. In hockey, while Scott was the flashy winger, Michael was a sturdy defenseman. Michael had a killer instinct and his teammates called him "Dim," after one of the thugs in *A Clockwork Orange*. Michael's focus was always unshakable. From the time he was a boy, he knew that McCain Foods was going to be his life. "He's been telling me since he was five years old that he wanted my job," recalls Wallace.

Michael and Scott were close growing up. They wrestled together, played sports and generally drove their mother Margaret crazy. When they got too rowdy, Margaret took after them with a fly-swatter. When they got completely out of hand, she called Wallace at work. "Wallace, I can't take it any more," she used to say. Within minutes, Scott and Michael would see a cloud of dust on the horizon as Wallace's car tore up the road to the house. "We could time it," remembers Michael. "It took him maybe two minutes to get down that road to our house. He came so fast down that road, it was like a rocket. Then he would come in, spank us and drive back to work just as fast. It was a ten-minute round trip, tops."

If there was ever any action in Florenceville, Scott was in the middle of it. But in spite of Scott's popularity, Michael felt protective towards his older brother. Somehow, he knew that Scott's genuineness made him vulnerable. It was the same genuineness, the same vulnerability, he saw in his dad. Some things just didn't seem to matter enough to his father. Take his Uncle Harrison. Whenever Michael read about McCain Foods in the newspaper or in a magazine, it was always Uncle Harrison photographed at the opening of a plant, it was always Uncle Harrison who'd been appointed to some new board or agency, and it was always Uncle Harrison who seemed to win awards. Michael's dad just didn't seem to care. He was happy to let Harrison take centre stage—he said he was good at it. But Michael knew there was more to it than his dad let on. He knew his dad and Uncle Harrison had once been as close as he was with Scott. They must have been close when he was born, thought Michael, because he was named Michael Harrison McCain, and Harrison was his godfather. But something had changed over the years. Maybe it's what happens when you grow older, thought Michael. Or maybe it was the business. Michael worried. He didn't want to stop being buddies with Scott just because he grew older.

Michael knew the growing tension between his dad and Uncle Harrison was the reason he didn't see much of his uncle's sons, Peter and Mark. Peter was two years older than Michael and finishing high school. Like Michael, he was awkward and uncomfortable around people. But Michael thought Peter didn't try hard enough. He didn't work hard at school. He seemed more interested in drinking. And he wouldn't stand up to his dad. Michael would see Harrison giving Peter a hard time and Peter would just take it. Michael knew *he* wouldn't take it if Harrison ever got on his back—he'd fight back. He remembered the time he'd once started asking Harrison questions about something. Harrison got fed up and told him to be quiet, but Michael didn't back away. He just stood there and fired off a few more questions.

Michael didn't know Peter's brother Mark that well because he was five years older. Mark wasn't around much anyway. He spent most of his summers with his Aunt Eleanor and Uncle Patrick in Toronto. But whenever Mark was around, Michael got a kick out of him.

Mark was crafty, bright and personable. He was also physically smaller than most of his cousins—his nickname was "Sparky"—and that forced him to live by his wits. But Mark's cheekiness seemed to always get him into trouble with Harrison. Once Mark phoned up McCain headquarters and asked for his father. Harrison didn't take many personal calls at work, especially from his children, so Mark pretended to be the RCMP. That got his father on the phone in a hurry, and it got Mark in hot water. When Mark was in grade nine, Harrison decided to solve his son's discipline problems by sending him to Upper Canada College in Toronto. Harrison chose the school mainly because his brother-in-law, Patrick Johnson, was principal. None of the cousins, including Michael, thought Mark would last long there. Students at Upper Canada wore ties and jackets to school and Michael laughed when he tried to picture that. He wasn't surprised when he heard that Mark had failed grade nine. He also wasn't surprised when he heard that Mark was expelled the following year by his uncle for drinking. It was an embarrassment, but Uncle Patrick had no choice—Mark had gone too far. Mark didn't come home after that. Instead, his father enrolled him in Rosseau Lake College, a small private school near Parry Sound, Ontario, where he graduated in 1973.

Uncle Bob and Aunt Rosemary's son Andrew was also older than Michael. Andrew was a stocky kid with an easygoing personality. Some kids used to call him "Gumper" after a cartoon character known for his plodding nature. Andrew was born a year to the day after A.D.'s death in 1953—hence his name—and that always seemed to stick out in his mother's mind. Aunt Rosemary would say that Andrew never had a happy birthday because his grandmother was always sad about his grandfather's death.

There were only two years between Andrew and Scott, and when their families lived next door to one another, they were best friends. They used to play in the adjoining yards and chase each other around Andrew's sister's dollhouse. Michael was rarely included in these games. He suspected it was because Andrew's mom, Aunt Rosemary, didn't like him very much. She found him too intense and too much of a smart alec. Michael didn't mind. He didn't care much for his aunt anyway. She was always telling her kids they were McCains and they'd never have to worry about getting a job. Michael didn't know why she had to say that to Andrew, because he never seemed to worry about much anyway.

Andrew enjoyed sports and would always rather have been out at the hockey rink than in school. In fact, Andrew would rather have been anywhere than school. He barely finished high school in Florenceville and was sent to a prep school in Maine to improve his grades so that he could go to university. He did well in prep school and went to the University of Southern Maine for a business program. When that didn't work out, he headed to St. Thomas University in Fredericton. He hated the school and left after a couple of semesters. Andrew had no interest in going back to university so he worked for McCain Foods for a summer while he figured out what to do.

Michael knew his father didn't think much of Andrew's work ethic. Wallace thought Andrew was lazy and had no real interest in the business—he had no drive and rarely showed up for work on time. But every time Andrew worked even briefly at McCain, Uncle Harrison gave him jobs in areas that reported to Wallace. That made Wallace angry, and he vowed never to give Andrew special treatment. Aunt Rosemary would always say it was only fair that Andrew got a job at the company. After all, Michael and Scott did odd jobs at McCain, so why shouldn't her son?

After a few months of working that summer, Andrew's father, Bob, convinced his son to give university one more try and Bob suggested an agriculture course at Nova Scotia Agricultural College in Truro. Andrew went and, finally finding a program he enjoyed, did his best to stick it out.

Michael found school boring too, but he wasn't about to quit. He was a straight-A student with a determination to complete his education as quickly as possible. At the end of grade nine, he pleaded with his grade ten teacher to pass him into grade eleven. For Michael, a grade skipped meant a year less in school. The teacher agreed but the school board didn't, and Michael had to complete grade ten. Then, in grade eleven, he did some checking around and discovered that Mount Allison University had a special program for exceptional kids. Michael thought he might be able to sneak in without completing grade twelve. Scott was already attending Mount Allison, which made it even more attractive. His parents agreed to help him apply and the next thing Michael knew he was enrolled in 1975 as a sixteen-year-old freshman. He took business courses, of course, but quickly found the program too dull. He wanted a tougher, more aggressive program, and a professor suggested he apply to the business school at the University of Western Ontario. He loved it and graduated in 1979.

While Michael was doing what he thought he should to get ready for a career at McCain Foods, he couldn't believe that most of his cousins weren't interested in a similar objective. Harrison's son Mark graduated from the University of New Brunswick in 1976, but he had no intention of going back to Florenceville. Instead, he headed to Calgary to work for a construction company and spent his weekends skiing. He'd met Brenda Smith, from Centreville, in his third year at UNB and the two stayed together for ten years. Michael, like a lot of the McCains, didn't think Brenda was the best woman for Mark and he couldn't understand why they married in 1983. Mark and Brenda divorced a few years later, after Brenda got sick of living away from home. By then, Mark was in Toronto working for a stock brokerage.

Michael could see that Peter had no more interest than his brother Mark in working for the family business. After high school, Peter wanted to go to UNB to be with his friends, but his father insisted he go to Trent University in Peterborough, Ontario. Soon he was in deep trouble with alcohol. Friends around Florenceville said Peter had some close calls at Trent, and it was a miracle he didn't kill himself because of his drinking. When he gave up on university, he came back to Florenceville and just hung around for a while, not sure what to do. Eventually, he got a job as a salesman for McCain, but after a few months his boss called Harrison to say that Peter was in trouble. Michael knew his father and Uncle Harrison struggled with how to help Peter. Finally, they decided to send him to the Donwood Institute in Toronto. It would be the first of two treatments.

Peter came home fully recovered from his first session at Donwood. He seemed rejuvenated to Michael, and he even finished his degree at Dalhousie and stayed on to take an MBA. He wore a leather jacket to class and was apparently more interested in music than French fries. Peter's lack of interest in McCain was legendary. Peter had once been given a job at the Grand Falls plant and was told it started at 7:00 a.m., but he'd routinely show up around 9:30 or 10:00 every morning. After a few days, the plant manager got after him and asked him to try and make it in earlier. Peter apparently said he would, but later as they were talking he said something like, "I hope I never see another potato again."

While Michael couldn't understand or respect his cousins' lack of motivation, his mother often talked about how much she felt all of her nieces and nephews needed the family's support. "They have problems," she would say, "they're in pain and they need our understanding, not our criticism." There did seem to be trouble all around. Peter's younger sister, Gillian, had spent much of her early teenage years battling anorexia and travelling to doctors in Halifax. Peter's other sister, Ann, was nearly killed in a car accident when she was in grade twelve. She and two friends had gone to Truro in September 1973 to visit some Florenceville boys who were attending the local college. The group went out drinking and later one of the boys lost control of the car and it crashed into a telephone pole. Ann's two friends died, and she was in hospital for weeks.

These problems were part of life and part of growing up, Michael's mother would say. They were symptoms of the pressures of fame and fortune that the McCain family never dealt with.

As Michael grew older and got closer to his goal of joining McCain, he became more and more frustrated with the McCain "family employment policy." It had always been expected by Wallace and Harrison that their sons and nephews would end up at McCain, whether they wanted to or not. It irritated Michael that neither motivation nor academic qualifications seemed to be prerequisites. It devalued something he'd worked hard all his life to achieve. If you were a McCain, Michael was learning, ability seemed to have little to do with promotion at McCain Foods.

His mother would repeatedly talk about the sexism prevalent in the company. While it was assumed that the boys would find careers there, no one considered encouraging the girls to shoot for prominent positions at McCain. Michael remembered when his sister Eleanor provocatively suggested that she might want to work at McCain after graduating from university. Wallace brushed her off and tersely replied, "I don't think that would be a good idea."

Harrison's daughter Laura seemed as motivated as Michael to join the family business. Like her namesake, Laura was bright and had a sharp business mind, but because she was a woman she was never given a senior post at McCain. She received a commerce degree from Acadia and helped Joe Palmer, who used to run Day & Ross, organize potato shipments for McCain in the Caribbean. She organized the loading of shipments and travelled with the cargo to several ports. She left McCain after a few months to take a sales and marketing course in Boston, then opened her own seafood business in Halifax called Skipper Seafoods Ltd.

Michael saw his other female cousins become successful in advertising, financial planning and teaching. And his sister, Eleanor, developed a promising career in music. But in terms of McCain Foods, the most the women could hope for was overseeing the company's charitable donations.

At first, Michael dismissed his mother's tirades about the company's sexism as just another feminist rant. But as he grew older, he began to understand why she found this ideology so offensive. It represented the prevailing politics within the company that prevented McCain children from being truly evaluated on their abilities and merits. Sons and nephews were promoted rapidly and given jobs that they would never have received at another corporation given their age and years of work experience. When hiring top executives for the company the final decision was always made jointly by Harrison and Wallace based on the candidate's qualifications, but when it came to hiring the McCain sons and nephews, Harrison sometimes placed them within the company without discussing his decision with Wallace, or even telling him that he'd made it. That seemed to happen a lot when the boys were young and needed summer jobs. His dad didn't mind much then—he was happy to see the boys working and saw it as appropriate training. But when Harrison hired cousin Allison as a full-time engineer without telling Wallace, Wallace became concerned.

Allison was the oldest child of Andrew McCain and his wife Marjorie. Born in 1949, Allison was always considered a quiet, shy kid. Many McCains thought Allison had to grow up fast because his father spent most of his time drinking. His mother was extraordinarily reserved and kept largely to herself. Allison's thick glasses and serious demeanour added to the overall impression most people had of him as a thoughtful person.

Allison graduated from the University of New Brunswick in electrical engineering in 1972. He immediately got a job with New Brunswick Telephone Co. Ltd.—his father's position as a director of NB Tel at the time might have helped. After three years with the phone company, Allison decided to ask Harrison for a job at McCain. He told his uncle that he wanted to learn everything about the business, from agronomy to sales. And he made it clear that, one day, he wanted to be the top man.

Harrison was obviously impressed and called Tim Bliss, McCain's vice president of engineering. Bliss wasn't keen on hiring Allison or any McCain kid. "Look, Harrison, I'm not looking for another engineer," Bliss said. "But if you are asking me to hire him I will. We can always use a body."

Wallace didn't find out that Harrison had hired Allison until the young engineer was already on the payroll. When he did find out, Wallace told Harrison they should groom Allison as a possible successor to Bliss. But Harrison had bigger plans for his nephew. He wanted Allison to get a much wider exposure to the overall operations.

Wallace was suspicious. Harrison's sons weren't working for the company and everyone knew Michael would join as soon as he graduated from university. Since Harrison didn't have his own

kids to groom, maybe he was trying to line up Allison as a counterbalance to Michael, Wallace thought.

"One of Harrison's favourite lines was 'You ought to have
checks and balances,'" recalls Wallace. "And I think he felt if
Allison came in maybe that would keep things balanced in the
family. It sure as Christ wouldn't have been on the basis that [he
was] going to support the Andrew McCain family. That's what
he would say, but that would be bullshit. Anything [Harrison]
did, he always had a good motive."

Harrison scoffed at the idea that he was grooming a successor.
He figured Wallace was getting too protective and maybe a little
worried that Allison might be competition for Michael.

Allison began moving quickly up the ranks. Within three
years he was production manager for the Florenceville plant. The
promotions were causing some disgruntlement among other
McCain staff. "Many of my staff engineers would have loved to
have gone so far so fast," said Bliss.

As he watched his older cousin move up the ranks, Michael
also wondered about his Uncle Harrison's motives. Allison was a
bright, capable guy, Michael thought. But even as a teenager,
Michael appreciated his father's feeling that Allison was best suited
to be the head of engineering some day, after the proper appren-
ticeship. Michael remembered the battles he'd had with Harrison
as a child and wondered if they would prevent him from reaching
his goal of one day running the company. What if Harrison *was*
grooming a counterbalance? Where would that leave Michael and
the other sons and nephews in the company's future, and how
would it be resolved? There were no immediate answers. Michael
knew his father and Harrison had never seriously discussed succession or their children's future within the company. The kids
would just wait and see how everything evolved. But Michael was
determined to learn as much as possible and be as prepared as he
could. He knew he was destined to have a career at McCain and
he wanted to make sure he was ready to go as far as possible, even
if Harrison was grooming Allison as a rival.

Michael realized that even if he never did reach his goal of
running McCain Foods some day, at least working in the business would bring him closer to his father and his brother. There

had always been a strong bond between Michael and Wallace, and it grew as Michael became more involved in McCain. Michael still remembers the first business trip he went on with his father at the age of thirteen. Wallace took him to visit a small company McCain had acquired in Vancouver. "I sat in on the management meetings with him and then went out on sales calls. He took me everywhere and just carried on with business," Michael recalls. The bond became even stronger when Wallace was ill in 1976 with the complications from his hernia. Scott and Michael spent hours at the Lahey Clinic in Boston where Wallace was treated, walking their father up and down the hallway to help build up his strength. "We just didn't want to lose our father," Michael recalls.

His father's illness made Michael even more protective of his dad and more conscious of Harrison's public profile. He once asked Wallace about it and was sharply rebuked. "If I competed with Harrison for headlines, our partnership wouldn't work," Wallace said before cutting off any further discussion.

Michael's brother Scott joined the company in 1978, after finishing his degree at Mount Allison. Wallace always believed Scott would join the company after university, but Scott wasn't as certain. He wanted to travel first and consider all his options. His father struck a compromise. Scott could travel as far as Britain, where there would be a job waiting for him at the McCain plant in Scarborough. The deal worked. Scott enjoyed working on the British plant floor—he never saw himself as a future CEO—and he soon returned to the Florenceville plant, where he became a production manager.

When Michael graduated from the University of Western Ontario his parents suggested he take an MBA. But Michael declined. "I'll learn all I need to know by working for my father," he said.

Michael joined McCain within days of the graduation ceremony. He started in sales, first in London, Ontario, and then as regional co-ordinator in Hamilton. His contact with Harrison was minimal, but in one of their first meetings, Michael bluntly told his uncle, "I want your job one day." When Wallace was later told about his son's comment, he laughed and thought it was just youthful bravado. But Harrison wasn't as dismissive, and he never forgot those words.

Different reactions from his uncle and his father were something Michael wrestled with for years to come. Several summers Michael had worked in the accounting department at McCain's Florenceville head office helping to prepare budgets. Budgeting at McCain was a ruthless process that involved hours of detailed work and constant supervision by Harrison, who personally oversaw the company's finances. The process was not a happy one. Harrison was used to grilling his accountants on every detail, and he was exceptionally hard on Michael. More than once, Michael took offence at the treatment. He invested a lot in his work and made a number of business judgments in his budgets that he firmly believed in. He challenged Harrison's own judgment, and Harrison was a man who did not like or expect to be challenged by anyone, let alone an independent-minded, arrogant teenager.

Things got so bad between the two of them that one day Michael asked Harrison why he thought they were having so many quarrels. Harrison looked at his nephew thoughtfully and replied, "Maybe it's a little old bull versus young bull." Michael and many others in the company found that an apt assessment. In many ways, Michael was just a younger version of Harrison. "They are like two peas in a pod," says former general manager Archie McLean.

Michael knew that his Uncle Harrison didn't like him, and he knew that he was one of the few McCain family members who refused to treat Harrison with unthinking deference. But as he started his career at McCain, Michael was less concerned with what Harrison thought of him and more concerned with what he thought of Harrison. He didn't trust Harrison, particularly when it came to Michael's father. In fact, Michael wasn't even sure if he respected Harrison any more.

Harrison had done nothing but challenge Michael in a way that singled him out from his brother and cousins. Michael knew that the hard feelings growing between himself and Harrison would only cause his father pain. His father was anxious for things to get better between Michael and Harrison, not worse, and would not listen to Michael's worries about his uncle. It was just too difficult for Wallace to accept.

The way Michael saw it, Harrison was continuing to build a social mythology that made him the public face of McCain Foods and the McCain family, and he was doing so at the expense of Wallace. The summer Michael was hired, Harrison organized a huge wedding for his oldest daughter, Ann, who was marrying Rick Buckingham, the son of a local store owner. It was an event people around Florenceville still talk about. More than five hundred friends, celebrities, politicians and dignitaries were invited to Harrison's home, and many were flown in on the company plane. The swimming pool was covered with planks to make room for an orchestra and dance floor. Men in tuxedos parked cars, and huge tents were filled with enough food and liquor to keep the town going for weeks. The guest list included Premier Richard Hatfield, former premier Louis Robichaud, Bank of Nova Scotia CEO Cedric Ritchie, a host of cabinet ministers, the Lieutenant-Governor and the Governor General. But several people at the wedding thought something was wrong. The bride and groom looked young and insecure, recalls Harrison's friend Claude Bursill. To Bursill, Ann and Rick looked as though they'd rather be anywhere than there. In fact, the marriage was to last only a few years. To Michael, the wedding celebration was more about Harrison than the bride. It was yet another opportunity for Harrison to promote his own public image. On that day, the world saw Harrison not just as father of the bride, but as father of McCain Foods and the McCain family.

TOP: *Hugh Henderson McCain and his wife Frances.*
BOTTOM: *Andrew Davis McCain, later known as A.D.*

TOP: *A.D. with his four boys, clockwise from top left: Andrew, Bob, Harrison and Wallace.*
BOTTOM: *Harrison's 1949 graduation photo.* (Acadia University Yearbook)

Family Enterprise

TOP: *Harrison, Wallace, Andrew and Bob celebrate the opening of their Florenceville plant in 1957 with their mother Laura.* (Telegraph-Journal)

BOTTOM: *Plant workers, farmers and friends watch as the McCains open a plant in Centreville in 1967.*

LEFT: *Frozen French fries were a tough sell at first, but as television and fast food took off in the 1960s, McCain Foods was pulled right along.*

BELOW: *Wallace shows son Scott around a company plant in 1967 with New Brunswick Premier Louis Robichaud.*

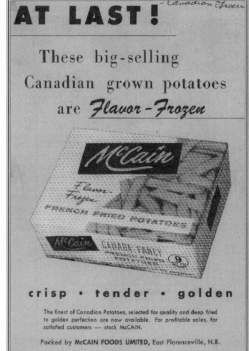

ABOVE: *Not always one big, happy family. Standing from left: Bob, Andrew, Patrick Johnson, Wallace, Jed Sutherland, Harrison. Seated from left: Margaret, Rosemary, Eleanor, Laura, Marie, Marjorie, Billie.*

LEFT: *By the company's tenth anniversary in 1967, sales topped $20 million and McCain frozen French fries were sold on three continents.*

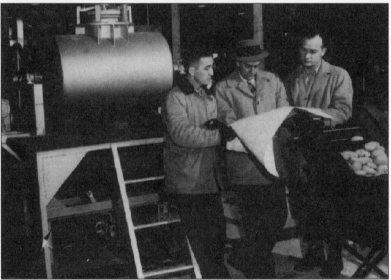

When they started out, no one expected McCain Foods to become successful: Farmers grew the wrong kind of potatoes, plant equipment routinely broke down and employee turnover was high because workers, especially women, had to endure tedious jobs.

TOP: *McCain sons and future company directors. From left: Allison, Andrew, Scott and Mark.*
BOTTOM: *Wallace and Harrison were long time friends of Premier Robichaud.*

RIGHT: *Wallace's wife, Margaret, became New Brunswick's Lieutenant Governor in 1994.*
(Peter Canton, Gerald Campbell Studios)

BOTTOM: *Eleanor, Scott, Michael and Martha with their parents Wallace and Margaret McCain.*

CHAPTER ELEVEN

Wallace fumbled with the telephone and looked quickly at the clock before answering. It was 5:00 a.m. Probably another crisis call from the Australian operation, he thought as he picked up the receiver. But before he could say hello, Wallace heard Rosemary crying into the phone. Bob was dead. It was June 13, 1977.

Wallace leapt out of bed and told Margaret to call Harrison. Then he raced the short distance down Riverside Drive to Bob's house. When he got there, Rosemary was devastated. She'd been totally unprepared for the suddenness of her husband's death. The day before, Bob had gone to church with Rosemary and attended a barbecue in the afternoon with some friends. In the evening he'd called their youngest son, Kirk, at school and made plans to visit him soon. Although the family had known since 1973 that Bob didn't have long to live, it had been a hopeful spring. A few months earlier, he and Rosemary had talked with doctors about trying another kidney transplant, and the doctors had been hopeful that it might work this time. Now, just when things were looking better than they had in years, Bob was gone.

Bob's funeral was held two days later, and just as when A.D. died, the town went into mourning. Hundreds attended the funeral, and the Florenceville United Church later dedicated a stained-glass window to Bob's memory. Bob had touched the community in a way that no other McCain ever had. Just three months earlier, hundreds of villagers and friends from across the county had paid tribute to him in a special dinner hosted by the local Liberal Party. They came to thank him for the years he spent on county council as Florenceville's representative and for the countless occasions when he used his expertise in farming to help shape provincial agricultural policy or just to help a local farmer. By the time he died, Bob had been named to the Canadian Agriculture Hall of Fame for helping with the development of Holstein cattle.

His death was a terrible loss to the family. Bob had always been the brother everyone could talk to and get along with. He was in many ways the calm go-between for his younger, more aggressive brothers. Not only had he given Harrison and Wallace the idea for McCain Foods, but he'd never begrudged them their success. Even though he was a co-owner and director, he was happy to leave the operations of the company to his younger brothers. His death in many ways dried up the glue that held the family together. As strong as their mother had always been, it was Bob that seemed to be able to keep the pressures of success from tearing things apart. His death opened the first fissures in the family.

A few months before he died, Bob had asked Rosemary which of his brothers he should name as a trustee for his family trust. The trust included his shares in McCain, which represented about one-sixth of the company. Bob's sisters, Eleanor and Marie, weren't considered because it wasn't the kind of role the McCain men expected women to play, and the sisters didn't own any McCain shares. Rosemary didn't think Bob's older brother Andrew was up to the job, and she knew she wouldn't get along with Harrison. That left Wallace. Rosemary wasn't especially fond of Wallace but she had a soft spot for him. He had brought her a dozen roses once when she was sick, and he'd stayed with her sometimes when Bob was out of town. Bob agreed and appointed Wallace as trustee. "What a mistake that turned out to be," recalls Rosemary.

From their first meeting just after Bob's funeral, Rosemary and Wallace disagreed over the terms of Bob's trust. Wallace felt the trust clearly specified that Bob's children should receive the largest share of his McCain holdings. But Rosemary said she should have a larger share. Bob wanted her taken care of, she said, and the trust was set up to protect her. "Bob said to me, 'I am setting up this trust for you because I can't get medical coverage,'" she remembers. "Wallace did everything he could to take it away from me and give it to my children. But he didn't know that they were supporting me and would just give it back."

Feelings of resentment and bitterness that had been simmering for years bubbled to the surface in the battle over the trust. Rosemary blamed Wallace for not including her son Andrew in the company. "Wallace did nothing but run down my family," she said. "He wanted his sons in the company, I could see it." Wallace turned on Rosemary, calling Andrew lazy and blaming her for spoiling him.

As Wallace and Rosemary faced off, Harrison was working behind the scenes, patching up his differences with Bob's widow. Sensing her loneliness and isolation from the family, Harrison began inviting Rosemary to functions at his house. He became close with Rosemary's son Andrew and encouraged her other son, Kirk, when he wanted to go to Humber College in Toronto to study hotel and restaurant management. Wallace was uncomfortable with Harrison's new and growing friendship with Rosemary. He didn't understand why Harrison was suddenly being so supportive. The two had never liked each other. In fact, as Wallace remembers it, when Harrison had shown up at Rosemary's house on the morning of Bob's death, Rosemary had greeted him with "What are you doing here?" and Wallace had been forced to intervene to keep the peace.

For Rosemary, the fall-out over the trusteeship was the last straw. She'd had enough of small-town Florenceville and the suffocating cocoon of the McCain family. It was time for her to get on with her own life. While vacationing in Florida, she met George Gyetvai, a retired American Chrysler executive. They married in Halifax in 1979. Many McCains saw the marriage as disrespectful to the memory of Bob, who had been dead only two years. To some it was a betrayal of Bob and the family. But Rosemary felt it was the break she needed from the McCain culture. Soon after the wedding, she moved into a house in Fredericton and began spending winters in Florida. The McCains "all wanted me to walk around Florenceville in mourning for the rest of my life," she recalls. "I was forty-nine years old and they wanted me to be a widow."

Harrison attended Rosemary's wedding and hosted a reception for the newlyweds later. He even commandeered the company plane to fly guests in from Florenceville. That didn't sit well with Wallace, who saw it as a waste of company money. But Harrison insisted that Rosemary's wedding was an important event and she deserved to have her friends and family attend. He brushed off Wallace's concerns with a terse: "The plane is leaving and whoever wants to go had better be on it." Wallace and Margaret were noticeably absent.

Bob's death also prompted the first major challenge to the ownership structure of McCain Foods. The company had no plan in place to deal with the death of a director. In fact, there were few written plans for anything involving the ownership structure of the company. There were no by-laws, no shareholder agreement that set out the powers of company directors, officers and shareholders. Corporate governance—the roles and duties of directors, shareholders and senior officers—was as foreign to the McCains as a missed sale. Wallace and Harrison made all the decisions. They hadn't even written out their own job descriptions until 1978 when the company lawyer told them it might be a good idea. Now they had to figure out who should take Bob's place on the board.

The company's board of directors hadn't changed since it was founded in 1956. The directors had always been the four brothers and their sister Marie's husband, Jed Sutherland, who lived in Woodstock. The board rarely met and had no real power. Minutes of supposed board meetings were often drawn up by Wallace and Harrison, who would meet together and call it a board meeting.

Bob's shares were split among Rosemary, her four children and her son-in-law, Elizabeth's husband, William Apold. Apold bought about $100,000 worth of McCain shares from Rosemary after Bob died in order to help pay some estate taxes. He would remain the only non-McCain ever to hold company shares directly. Now, instead of four company shareholders—Wallace, Harrison, Andrew and Bob—there were nine. And for the first time there was no one on the board representing Bob's family. Strangely, instead of inviting a member of Bob's family to fill his place, Wallace and Harrison decided to appoint the company lawyer, Roger Wilson, to the board. Ironically, that decision went against everything Wallace and Harrison stood for in terms of who should sit on company boards. "Many people think—and I am one of them—that the company lawyer and other company advisers cannot be directors—they are absolutely not impartial," Harrison wrote in a later memo to Wallace. Bob's family didn't complain about being left off the board. In fact, they didn't even ask for a board seat. They recognized that Wallace and Harrison made all the decisions at McCain and resigned themselves to that for the time being.

Wallace and Harrison did make one gesture to the shareholders. They began paying a small dividend a year after Bob's death. It was the first return the shareholders had ever received for their McCain holdings.

Bob's son Andrew returned to the Nova Scotia Agricultural College after his father's funeral. Andrew had been close to his father and suffered his loss deeply. He felt alone and uncertain about his future. While some of his other cousins banked on a career at McCain, that had never been part of his game plan. Besides, while Harrison had been supportive and willing to bring him into the company, Wallace never seemed eager to have Andrew around. Andrew started looking elsewhere for a job. Not long after he returned to school, a recruiter from Arnold Nasco Ltd., an agricultural supply company in Guelph, Ontario, came to campus looking for salesmen. Andrew applied and was hired. He was thrilled at the chance to finally get out on his own and move away from the bad memories at home.

When he arrived for his first day on the job, Andrew noticed a line of men with placards. The company was on strike. The recruiter hadn't told Andrew that he had been hired as a scab. But Andrew needed the job. He braced himself for the abuse and walked in. "I was in Ontario and I had no bloody money so I was crossing the picket line regardless," he recalls. "McCain Foods hadn't paid any dividends since day one and I was broke."

A few years later he was offered a better job at another company. He accepted it and headed home to New Brunswick for a short vacation. But when he returned the job was gone. While he was in New Brunswick, the company had decided it couldn't afford to hire him.

Andrew spent a few months looking for work with no luck and decided to return once again to New Brunswick. After a few weeks, he met up with Alan Morris, an old Florenceville friend who had a five-member folk-rock group called the Howard Brook Band. Morris said the band was looking for a manager and Andrew decided to take the job. After a few months he was enjoying the music business so much he went to Full Sale Sound in Orlando, Florida, for a course in record engineering. When he returned he helped the band record its only album, *Howard She Going?*

Things started to sour when some musicians associated with the band were arrested on drug charges, though Andrew says he had no idea what was going on. About a year after the drug bust, Morris and another band member decided to break up the band. While artistic differences among the band members had a lot to do with it, Morris was also disillusioned with Andrew's management. "We both thought Andrew was never being up front with us," says Morris. "I was doing it for the music and I don't think he ever understood that. He acted like a big shot in the music business."

Andrew says the band was barely making money and he wanted to take it in a more profitable direction. "There were some artistic differences over the direction I thought the band should go and the direction some of the players thought the band should go. So we parted company," he says.

After Howard Brook, Andrew hooked up with a band called Red Eye, a contemporary rock band out of Fredericton. They toured clubs around the Maritimes for about two years until another band hired away the lead singer. Andrew's band recruited a new singer and changed its name to Stinger, claiming modest success in the eastern Canadian pub scene.

The rock-and-roll life appealed to Andrew, and he earned a reputation for extravagance. He had taken up race-car driving when he was in Ontario and later started buying the latest Harley-Davidsons. After a few years, Andrew wanted to move the band to California and tap into a larger market, but two of the band members were married and didn't want to move. The band split, and Andrew was looking for another band to manage. He also thought of opening a recording studio in Woodstock, where he was living. When that didn't turn out he bought a Sam the Record Man franchise in Woodstock and ran it with a friend. He then met a local travel agent, got married and settled down. He even gave up car racing and slowed down on the Harleys.

At the time, Andrew expected to have a quiet life in Woodstock raising a family and running the store. Before long, however, making a living began to seem a lot less urgent: while he had no direct involvement in McCain Foods, by 1993 Andrew was earning $365,000 a year in dividends from the company.

CHAPTER TWELVE

By the early 1980s, McCain's massive expansion of the 1960s and '70s was beginning to cause problems. There were growing pains in parts of Europe and at home in New Brunswick as the company tried to keep up with its ever-expanding horizons.

Europe had been a lucrative market for McCain ever since Wallace and Harrison shipped their first package of frozen peas to Smedley's Ltd. in London in 1959. By the end of the 1960s, nearly half of McCain's total revenue was coming from Europe. From Britain to Holland, West Germany, Belgium and Spain, McCain fries were streaming into restaurants and refrigerators. Then they hit France.

Throughout the 1970s, McCain supplied the French market from its plants in Holland. But the French government started quietly urging the McCains to build a plant in France. When the government started threatening tariffs, the McCains were ready to talk. They agreed to build a plant near Harnes, in northern France, in exchange for about $5 million in government assistance.

McCain's $27-million plant was officially opened in October 1981. It immediately looked like a huge mistake. Local farmers had no idea how to grow proper processing potatoes. The company had to start a massive, and expensive, training program. And just when McCain thought the farmers might finally be prepared, the French government provided a huge grant to a local co-operative so it could open a competing frozen-food plant twenty miles down the road in Bethune. Harrison and Wallace were furious. There was barely enough product to keep one plant going, and now the government was helping to build another one. Within months of opening its plant, the co-operative slashed prices, forcing McCain to follow suit. Soon, neither company was making any money.

At the same time, McCain was having trouble launching Superfries in France. Superfries had been successfully marketed in Canada and Britain as crispy and oil-free homemade fries. But McCain discovered that the French would not compromise for convenience: they liked their fries deep-fried in oil and would eat them no other way. "The main problem in France was we wanted to grow very fast, and we took shortcuts on market research," McCain's former European CEO Paul van der Wel has said.

While the problems in France mounted, the brothers also found themselves embroiled in a nasty takeover struggle at home. In the late 1970s, Wallace and Harrison decided to take a run for control of Canada Packers Inc. It was a bold move. Based in Toronto, Canada Packers was one of the country's largest meat processors with about $2 billion in sales. It also had a large frozen vegetable business at the time, which is what really interested Wallace and Harrison.

In June 1979, the brothers spent an estimated $21.4 million for about 10 percent of the company's shares. They were now ready to seek a seat on the board. From there, they could survey the business in detail and see if it was worth a final push for control. Their cover was blown when news of their quiet power grab became public. Harrison tried to play down speculation that McCain was going for control, but Canada Packers' largest shareholder, the McLean family of Toronto, was alarmed.

The McLeans had started the company in 1927 when James Stanley McLean, a bookkeeper with a degree in mathematics and physics from the University of Toronto, took over a meat-packing warehouse from his father-in-law. McLean later merged his packing operation with two others, called it Canada Packers and ran it until a month before he died, in 1954, when he turned it over to his only son, William. The young McLean ran the business with a strong will and a keen sense of family duty. He was deeply religious and had a puritanical leadership style. Office workers were required to wear jackets at all times, and he was known to have once thrown a relative out of his home for making an improper remark. McLean retired as president in 1978 (which might have prompted the McCains to make their bid) but he still controlled the family's 26 percent stake in the company. Given his moral outlook, William no doubt saw the McCains as boorish upstarts out to grab the McLean family business from under its feet. He had no intention of agreeing to any board seats for the New Brunswickers. Along with Canada Packers' chief executive, Valentine Stock, McLean prepared to beat back the McCain challenge. Stock didn't like the McCains either. The Maritimers' brash and aggressive style clashed with the staid, conservative management at Canada Packers. Stock was also worried that if Wallace and Harrison were allowed on to the company board they would have access to confidential information, and that was untenable to Stock, since McCain and Canada Packers competed with each other in the frozen vegetable business. "Harrison was furious at Stock and the two had some real shouting matches," a source close to the deal recalled.

Stock and the McLeans began convincing other major Canada Packers shareholders to block the McCains from the board. The McCains meanwhile kept buying up shares until they'd accumulated around 12 percent. McLean finally offered Harrison and Wallace a board seat but only if they agreed not to acquire any more shares. Harrison refused. There wasn't much more the McCains could do. "We were told by our financial people that McLean had a good connection with the other shareholders and if we made an offer it wouldn't fly," recalls Wallace. "McLean and Stock outwitted them," says former McCain executive Archie McLean (no relation). Harrison and Wallace "lacked proper advice and knowledge. They didn't know how to play the game then," he adds.

Shut out of the Canada Packers board and with no chance of launching a successful takeover bid, the McCains sold their shares in 1985 for $53.6 million. The bid wasn't a complete failure—the McCains had bought the shares at $30 and sold them at $38.25—but analysts weren't impressed with the venture. "They would have done a hell of a lot better with Canada Savings Bonds," Roland Jones, an analyst with Merrill Lynch

Canada Inc., said at the time.

Four years later, McLean announced that he was selling his family's stake in the business—but not to just anyone. All bids had to be approved by the company's board, likely a ploy to stop a second McCain bid. The McCains didn't try another attempt, and within a year, McLean put together a $700-million deal that turned control of Canada Packers over to Hillsdown Holdings PLC, a British food conglomerate. Hillsdown immediately merged the company with Maple Leaf Mills Ltd. and renamed the combined firm Maple Leaf Foods Inc. Years later, the McCains would take another run at Maple Leaf. But it wouldn't be Wallace and Harrison making the offer. It would be Wallace and his sons.

Back in Florenceville, pollution charges were once again circling McCain Foods. The company had faced a barrage of criticism for years about polluting the Saint John River, but after the company had installed waste-treatment facilities, with the help of the provincial government in the 1960s and '70s, they thought their pollution troubles were over. So it came as a surprise to Wallace and Harrison when, in 1981, the company was hit with a variety of charges for polluting the river. Rather than fight the case, the company chose to plead guilty; it was fined just $1,000 and ordered to improve its water-treatment operations. Two years later, McCain was charged with eight more pollution-related offences under the Federal Fisheries Act. Federal officials claimed effluent from the company's plants at Grand Falls and Florenceville was killing fish. This time the company faced fines of up to $400,000, and Wallace and Harrison were not about to give up without a fight. After meeting with their lawyers, the McCains came up with a remarkable defence. Far from killing the fish, they argued, the effluent from the plant was helping fish because it was all food by-products. "We said we were actually putting food in the river and that there was only one ten-square-foot area with pollution," a source close to the case recalls. McCain's legal team hired experts who tested the effluent and testified that the waste wasn't entirely harmful.

The judge didn't buy the argument and found McCain guilty,

but he fined the company just $1 on each count. Federal lawyers were furious and quickly asked for an appeal, which was rejected. They got some minor comfort, however. While the federal case was before the court, McCain was fined $3,500 by the provincial government for pollution. A year later, McCain announced the construction of a $5.8-million secondary-waste-treatment facility in Florenceville. Once again, the facility was built with a federal grant, this time $2 million from the Department of Energy, Mines and Resources.

Once the pollution charges were settled, it looked like the company's growing pains were finally ending. In France, the price-cuts, competition from the co-op and the debacle over Superfries had hurt profits. But the brothers stuck it out, and by the mid-1980s things were slowly beginning to turn around. They got a major boost when McCain researchers developed a French fry that could be deep-fried on the stove and taste just the way the French liked it. It was a perfect alternative to Superfries and it was destined for success. Another big break came when the co-operative finally went broke. McCain bought their plant and added an $11.5-million expansion. The company also doubled production at its Harnes plant. All that extra production, with no competition, gave McCain a huge advantage. Soon the losses were turning into profits and McCain owned around 50 percent of the total French fry market, including food service and retail sales.

In Britain, the brothers bought another processing plant in 1982 in Grantham. They would later add a cheese-processing operation in Scotland and build two pizza plants in England. That helped boost production so much that by the late 1980s, half of all French fries served in British pubs and restaurants were made by McCain. In 1995, profit from British operations increased to $63 million from $52 million in 1994. Sales grew to $664 million from $528 million. The only weak spot in Britain was Britfish Ltd., a small fish-processing company McCain bought in 1984 that never lived up to expectations. In Japan, the growth in popularity of western culture pushed the fast-food industry to new heights, and McCain went along for the ride. The company grabbed about 20 percent of the total

French fry market and became one of the biggest suppliers to Lotteria, Japan's largest fast-food chain with nearly nine hundred restaurants in Japan and Korea.

Even in Australia, where McCain faced some of its biggest challenges, the company was showing signs of phenomenal growth. Part of the reason was the settling of a long-standing problem that had crimped sales. Australian restaurants, the McCains had discovered, preferred French fries made from Tasmanian-grown potatoes instead of spuds grown in Victoria, where McCain had its plant. It was similar to the issue McCain faced with the Russet Burbank potato in North America. To solve the problem, the brothers acquired a vegetable-processing plant in Smithton, Tasmania, in 1984, which was quickly converted into a full-fledged French fry plant. That ended the potato debate and sales rocketed. Within a short time, McCain owned nearly half the French fry market in Australia and 45 percent of the frozen pizza business. McCain would soon become Australia's second-largest overall food company, with $225 million in sales by 1993. The company later bought another plant in Penola, Australia, and expanded to New Zealand.

Canadian sales were still growing strong in the 1980s. The plants in Florenceville and Grand Falls were expanded in the early 1980s, and this time the federal government kicked in about $1.5 million in grants. After years of delay, the McCains even made some tentative moves into the United States. They had bought two small plants in Maine in the 1970s, but in 1984 they saw an opportunity to acquire one more in Presque Isle. The plant was owned by Potato Services Inc., which had gone bankrupt. Simplot owned about half of Potato Services and submitted a $5.4-million (US) bid for the plant to a U.S. bankruptcy court, beating McCain's $3.1-million (US) bid. McCain bought the plant from Simplot in 1987 after it ran into trouble again. However, even the brothers couldn't make it a success and they closed the plant in 1992. It was the first layoff in McCain history, affecting 197 workers, and one of the few times McCain ever had to close a plant. Fortunately, the workers were given jobs elsewhere at McCain.

As the company prospered, so did the McCain brothers. By

1989, Wallace and Harrison were each earning more than $600,000 a year in salary. By the early 1990s, the company was also paying 31 cents a share in annual dividends; that meant another $2.9 million a year for each brother. However, the tycoons were too busy to enjoy their growing fortune. Neither had expensive hobbies and they couldn't shake their ingrained frugality. In 1988, Wallace decided to splurge and buy himself a new green Jaguar. He agonized for weeks over the decision but finally broke down and bought the car, even though he knew it was an outrageous luxury. When the muffler broke, Wallace's old self emerged. "They told me it would cost $3,000 to fix," Wallace recalls. "I said, '$3,000 for a muffler? You've got to be kidding.' And, I walked out." He returned only after the mechanic agreed to lower the charge.

Buoyed by the company's success, Wallace and Harrison were keen to broaden their product line. In the early 1980s they expanded into the cheese business. By 1984, McCain had bought three Ontario-based cheese companies, Darigold Products Ltd. of Oakville, Tavistock Union Cheese and Butter Ltd. of Tavistock and Harrowsmith Cheese Factory Ltd. in Harrowsmith. McCain paid about $14.5 million for all three and combined them into one unit.

At the same time, the McCains were making a more daring move. In the late 1970s, Gordon Hill, the company's advertising agent, had been working on ads for some Florida juice companies, and he told Harrison and Wallace that they should think about getting into the business. Archie McLean, the company's marketing manager, thought it was a good idea and added his voice to Hill's. "They were not enthusiastic," recalls McLean. "Juice wasn't something they understood. Their feeling was 'If we can't look out the window and see it growing we're not interested.'"

After some coaxing from Hill, the McCains agreed to visit some Florida juice companies. The trip convinced them that the business was worthwhile, but they didn't want to start from scratch. The decided to buy an existing operation and picked up Sunny Orange Canada Ltd. of Toronto in 1980. Being a small juice producer, Sunny was a good way for McCain to get a feel for the business. A year later they bought another company,

Niagara Foods Ltd. based in Stoney Creek, Ontario, and some plants owned by Loblaws. Now McCain was ready to launch its own line of frozen concentrated juice. But it wasn't going to be easy.

Florida companies dominated the business, mainly because of their easy access to orange groves; some even owned their own trees. But McCain got a big boost in the early 1980s when Brazil began making concentrate much more cheaply than the Americans. That gave McCain a competitive edge, and its juice business took off. In 1987, McCain opened a new $5-million juice plant in Calgary. As usual, the federal and provincial governments were there to help out, this time with $584,925 in grants. Soon, along with frozen concentrate, McCain added chilled juices in new Tetrapak box containers. It wasn't long before the company was the second-largest juice seller in Canada, next to Minute Maid.

For Hill, the company's expansion into the juice business left a bitter taste. He felt the brothers had betrayed his contacts in Florida by not buying American concentrate. He was also having a falling out with Archie McLean at the time. Hill was convinced that McLean was planning to bring most of the company's advertising in-house in order to cut off Hill's ad agency. By the early 1980s, Hill says he was under pressure to cut his commission. A short time later, he was called to a meeting in Florenceville. "They wanted me to cut my commission from 15 percent to 5 percent," he says. "I couldn't do it so I quit. It was clear they wanted to fire me."

Hill had felt for a while that he couldn't trust the McCains. He was still angry about the time the brothers hired away one of his employees without telling him. The employee didn't work out and left McCain shortly afterward. "I could have told them he wasn't any good, if only they'd asked," recalls Hill. Hill struggled to keep his firm going for a few more years without the McCain account, but when the recession took hold in 1990 he had to close. "I didn't want to lose any more money." Now retired and living in a small apartment in Toronto, Hill is still bitter about his final years working for McCain. "They use people," he says.

With the addition of juice and cheese, McCain was getting so big that by 1984 the brothers created a holding company called McCain Inc. The arrangement was a way to shelter some of their investment from taxes. All of the families' shares were transferred to McCain Inc., which was later renamed McCain Foods Group Inc. The group's only holding was McCain Foods Ltd., which remained the operating subsidiary. Even though the holding company was little more than a tax shelter, the brothers still had to create a board of directors for the new company. Wallace and Harrison decided to keep it simple. They just used the same board as McCain Foods—Wallace, Harrison, their brother Andrew, Jed Sutherland and company lawyer Roger Wilson—for both companies.

By the end of June 1984, sales had nearly doubled over four years to $847 million. The following spring, sales were over $900 million, and Harrison was hoping they could hit $1 billion by the end of the company's fiscal year on June 30. As the date approached, Harrison became eager and pestered chief financial officer Carl Ash with questions about the final calculation. Finally, late in the day on June 30, Ash walked into Harrison's office with the good news. McCain's sales had topped $1 billion and the profit for the year would be just under $25 million, a new record. Harrison jumped, slapped Ash on the back and rushed off to tell Wallace. Ash didn't have the heart to mention that he had slightly adjusted the revenue accounts to come up with the magic number. All that mattered was that McCain Foods was now truly in the big leagues. After less than twenty years in business, the company was now a member of the billion-dollar club.

The brothers were so proud they took Ash, Carl Morris, Tim Bliss and several other senior managers on a retreat to a resort in the Caribbean. After the commemorative plaques were handed out and the Scotch bottles drained dry, Wallace and Harrison stood up for an announcement. The work was just beginning, they said. The challenge now was to double sales in five years.

No one laughed.

CHAPTER THIRTEEN

Margaret sat down on her patio chair and took a deep breath. It was dusk, and she had the house to herself. From where she sat in her back garden she could still make out the lush, rolling hills of the Saint John River valley. She loved it here. Even though she'd been looking at this view for twenty-five years she found it as lovely as the first time she'd laid eyes on it. For her it confirmed the existence of God. He was out there and He cared. Whenever she had an important decision to make, faced a crisis or felt a moment of insanity coming on, she looked to the land's harmony and beauty to help her find the right answer.

Right now the decision she was wrestling with concerned her own future. It was May 1985, and she'd just been offered the post of chancellor of Mount Allison University, her alma mater. She'd served on the board of regents for ten years, but becoming chancellor—that was a big step. She was deeply moved by the university's invitation. Her family had been active alumni of Mount Allison for decades. Her great-uncle, George Trueman, had been Mount Allison's chancellor in the 1920s, her father was a Mount Allison grad, and so were Wallace and three of her children. Margaret had done her honours thesis at Mount Allison on the history of the university. She felt that if she accepted the job she would be carrying on a family tradition. She was particularly touched by the board's request because it was the first time they'd asked a woman. And, she knew her mother, Margaret, who had taught at Mount Allison and had always been a strong advocate for womens' right, would be proud that the university had asked her daughter to be chancellor. Margaret's mother had died two years earlier but her legacy was still very much alive in Margaret. And, Margaret knew that if her mother were alive today there would be no question of her accepting the position.

Wallace was thrilled. "It's perfect," he told her. "With all the kids grown up it will give you something to do." He knew Margaret didn't like to travel with him on business trips and he'd worried about how she'd keep busy in that big house all by herself.

But in spite of her excitement, Margaret had mixed feelings about the appointment. She was going to accept it, but she worried that the job would take her focus away from home, where she felt she was still needed. As she sat enjoying the early evening air, she thought about the effect the huge expansion of McCain in the last few years had had on the relationship between Wallace and Harrison. There were real problems developing between them, and she knew they were getting worse.

She thought back to when she'd first sensed tiny fissures in the bond. It was the opening of the plant in Harnes, France in October 1981. Building the plant had been a huge project for the brothers. Aside from the months of planning and organization required, they'd had to work closely with the French government, which had contributed substantial money for the project. Margaret remembered Wallace flying back and forth across the Atlantic so many times he was never sure what time zone he was in. When the plant was finally finished, the opening ceremonies were a major event. Government and town officials joined hundreds of employees and well-wishers. Harrison was in charge of European operations, so he spoke about McCain's plans for France and how proud he was of the plant. Wallace didn't say much, deferring to what was his brother's jurisdiction. After the opening ceremonies, as Wallace and Margaret mingled with the crowd, Margaret noticed that Harrison and two other McCain executives were holding a press conference and having their picture taken by the local media. She turned to Wallace and asked him if he knew the press conference had started. "What press conference?" he replied. Margaret was furious. Wallace had spent just as much time and effort on the plant as the others had, and there was Harrison, back-slapping and taking credit for it.

The incident was small, but it was one of many that confirmed what she had always suspected about Harrison: he was determined to be the public face of both McCain Foods and the McCain family. The way Margaret saw it, Harrison could no longer separate the two. His personal and business lives were indistinguishable. He had begun using the same political and strategic tactics within the family that he had used in business for years.

Bob's death in 1977 had forced Wallace and Harrison to confront the issue of succession for the first time. But now, eight years later, there was still no plan, and Margaret was worried. Harrison and Wallace just didn't seem to be able to talk about the issue directly. Margaret had also been keeping an eye on Harrison's promotion of his nephew Allison through the ranks of the company. The first big promotion came in 1980 when Wallace was looking for a director of manufacturing for Australia. Harrison had suggested Allison. Margaret knew Wallace wasn't thrilled with the suggestion. Wallace liked Allison and knew he was a hard worker, but he didn't think he was the right man for a management job. Allison was a "first class Indian," Wallace would say. "I'm not sure he's the best chief in the world, but a good Indian." When Harrison insisted, Wallace relented. There was only one factory in Australia at the time anyway. Allison proved to be a competent worker and was promoted to production director a few years later. But even after watching Allison work, Wallace did not see him as a real leader, capable of running McCain.

Margaret trusted Wallace's instincts. He didn't feel Allison was up to the job and he didn't believe Harrison did either. Harrison must have some other reason for continuing to encourage Allison's promotion, Margaret thought. She wondered if it was a deliberate attempt by Harrison to unilaterally anoint a successor, a successor he could influence and control. Margaret knew that Harrison was concerned about her son, Michael. Michael was driven, capable and keen. She sensed that Harrison was using Allison as a counterweight to gain leverage in the succession process.

Because of the way she felt about Harrison, Margaret hadn't wanted either of her sons to work in the family business. It looked to her like a collision course—their potential would be limited and defined by Harrison, not by their own abilities. And with that in mind she worried about Michael's fixation on a senior job at McCain. His identity was too wrapped up in the company, Margaret thought. Margaret and Michael had talked about Harrison and his intense need for control, but neither found they could approach Wallace. Wallace was confident his older brother would never actively sabotage their relationship. Wallace still believed they had the power to work as a team. And whenever he raised Margaret's suspicions with Harrison, Harrison would quickly downplay them and assure Wallace that their partnership was as sound as ever. Assurances from Harrison were worth their weight in gold to Wallace. No suspicions from his wife or son were ever able to stand up to them. He refused to discuss Harrison's intentions with Margaret and Michael and he reminded them that he had known Harrison a lot longer than they had.

Things had become so difficult between Harrison and Michael in 1982 that Michael talked about starting another career. He had moved back to Florenceville to work in McCain's marketing department and married his high school friend Christine Buckingham, daughter of a local merchant, in 1981. But he soon became fed up with his job at McCain and began thinking about starting his own business on the side. Michael had been interested in computers and thought about doing some computer work in his spare time. One evening, he approached his father with the idea.

"The fuck you are," Wallace replied sharply. "I don't allow moonlighting."

Michael was crushed and spent the next few weeks trying to figure out if he should stay at McCain. Finally, he went back to Wallace and said he was quitting. Though Wallace was devastated, Margaret was quietly pleased. She felt it was the best thing Michael could do for himself. However, she could also see how much Michael's decision had upset his father. Wallace was broken-hearted to lose him because they got along so well. After a week of agonizing, Michael found the guilt of hurting his father too painful. He went to see Wallace early one morning in his office to tell him he had decided to forget the computer business and stay on at McCain.

Wallace got the message and set about finding something challenging for Michael to do. The company's computer system was a mess. It handled most of the accounting and all the billing for Day & Ross. A consultant's report had just recommended that the system needed a new manager and a complete overhaul. Wallace suggested to Harrison that they give Michael a crack at it. Harrison agreed and Michael was hired as the systems manager. He was a bit overwhelmed at the offer.

"They said to me, 'Well, you're interested in computers so here is a challenge for you,'" says Michael. "I had an Apple computer at home. That was my only computer experience."

The job reinvigorated Michael and he took it on with gusto. He managed to turn the operations around within a few months, but he also managed to create several long-time enemies. He clashed regularly with senior executives at Day & Ross, most of whom were twice his age and not eager to be pushed around by a kid just out of university.

"He was a real prick at times," says Joe Palmer, former Day & Ross president. But Michael didn't care. He was after results and that's all that counted.

Margaret wasn't pleased to see her son back at McCain. She knew that as his profile within the company rose, he'd be coming closer to a collision with Harrison, and at McCain Harrison had the upper hand. In spite of what Wallace believed, she couldn't see any strength left in the partnership that had made McCain Foods an international success. If Wallace and Harrison had such a solid partnership, Margaret thought, why was the outside world presented with only one McCain: Harrison? In 1984, Harrison, not Wallace, received the Order of Canada, largely because of the success of McCain Foods. The social ties between the brothers were almost completely gone, and now that McCain had reached $1 billion in sales and both brothers were worth millions, Margaret was certain Harrison's public image was about to outshine his younger brother's by far.

The death of Wallace and Harrison's mother Laura in 1982 only compounded the problem. Laura had a stroke in February and died on March 11. She was ninety years old and still carried a driver's licence, a pocketful of speeding tickets and the title of president of McCain Produce. Laura's funeral was a massive event taking up two churches and the prayers of the entire county. She had been the family's figurehead for decades, and her youngest sons respected and adored her. She would often call up Harrison or Wallace, scolding them for firing some poor worker and demanding that the man be rehired. The sons always obliged. She was a great defender of the family, always praising the work of her boys in public and keeping the family's problems to herself, where they belonged. She lived by the motto "Never complain, never explain." If she had something critical to say to any one of her children she wrote out a note and sent it in the mail, even though most lived only a few yards from her house. Now that she was gone, Margaret sensed that Harrison would quickly fill the vacuum she had left. Now, more than ever, Harrison would be seen as the family's patriarch.

Rosemary, especially, saw Harrison as the family leader. The problems over Bob's trust and her own remarriage had driven Rosemary closer to Harrison and opened a breach between herself and Wallace. The division was deepened when Rosemary's son Kirk died in August 1984. Kirk and two friends had been at a party in suburban Toronto celebrating their last exam at Humber College. After a round of drinks, the boys piled into a car for a ride. They crossed a railroad track, didn't see an oncoming train and were killed instantly. Rosemary was devastated by the death. Kirk had been a luckless kid who always seemed to be wondering where he fit in with the McCains. Rosemary remembered particularly how Harrison had taken Kirk under his wing after Bob died, and she was tremendously grateful for his support.

As she sat watching the dusk turn to night, Margaret thought about Rosemary and about her own birthday party a few months earlier. Wallace had organized a huge celebration. He had rented a room at the University of New Brunswick in Fredericton and invited dozens of friends from Florenceville. All of the family attended—except Rosemary. Relations between her and Wallace were too tense for Wallace to feel he could invite her. Rosemary never forgot the slight, especially since she was living only a few blocks from where the party was held.

The event went well into the night, and sometime after midnight Margaret and Wallace began to thank everyone for attending. They made a round of goodbyes and stopped by the bar to shake hands with Wallace's brother Andrew.

A few hours later, Andrew headed over to the Lord Beaverbrook Hotel where he was staying and stopped to talk to a few friends. He headed to his room, opened the door and collapsed. Wallace's doctor, Warren Nugent, was in town for the event and happened to be staying in a nearby room. Friends ran to get him and he desperately tried to revive Andrew. But there was little hope. Andrew was rushed to the hospital and died a few hours later on October 2, 1984. He was sixty-three years old. Publicly, the family would only say that Andrew died after a brief illness. But in truth his death was due to internal hemorrhaging, caused by severe liver problems related to his years of heavy drinking.

Andrew's death was a hard blow to the family, coming only a few months after the death of Kirk and Margaret's mother and only two years after Laura's. Like his mother and father, Andrew was buried in the family's small graveyard not far from the McCain family home on the west side of the river overlooking Florenceville.

The loss of Andrew also put the future of McCain Produce in question. After Bob's death in 1977, Andrew and his mother Laura had tried to keep McCain Produce going but had run into trouble. After Laura's death, the business was run entirely by Andrew, and the problems mounted. Just before he died, Andrew had blown an $8-million deal to sell seed potatoes in Algeria. The deal fell apart when the Algerians decided they could get a better price elsewhere. Andrew managed to get the Algerians to buy some of the produce, but McCain Produce ended up losing money. A few years later he made another deal to sell a shipload of potatoes to South America. The sale was arranged through Bertrell Skou, an Argentinian who had been dealing with McCain Produce ever since A.D. was alive. A.D. and Bob had always demanded a letter of credit before arranging any shipment to South America; it was a necessary, and prudent, form of security. But this time Andrew decided to send the potatoes after Skou gave his word that the letter of credit was in the mail. The letter never arrived. Skou couldn't be found and McCain Produce was stuck for a $6-million loss. The deal left the company broke. Wallace and Harrison had to step in and cover McCain Produce's debt and try to keep it afloat. By the time Andrew died, McCain Produce's annual sales were barely $1 million and the company was entirely reliant on McCain Foods for financing.

After Andrew's funeral, Wallace, to his surprise, found that he had been appointed executor of his brother's estate. This time he had better luck than he'd had helping manage Bob's trust, and he was able to work well with Allison and Marjorie. Margaret felt it was significant that both brothers had appointed Wallace to look after their affairs. She felt it was an omen. Perhaps the brothers knew something about Harrison that she didn't. Whatever their motives, they obviously felt they could trust Wallace to carry out their last wishes and protect their family's interests.

Because of the problems at McCain Produce and Andrew's death, Harrison and Wallace decided to absorb McCain Produce into McCain Foods completely. They could apply the losses to McCain Foods' profits and lower its taxes. More importantly, buying out McCain Produce would be a way to help their sisters Marie and Eleanor, who each owned one-ninth of the company. "The company was worth nothing but we felt, Jesus, we should do something," said Wallace. "So we forgot about the big losses and valued the properties. We just ignored the fact the company was broke and said 'What is the value of the land?' because they owned a lot of land, four or five thousand acres." The value came out to nearly $1 million. Instead of taking their one-ninth share of the price, Wallace and Harrison gave the money to their sisters. "They had the shares themselves, but I didn't take my [payment], I gave it to Marie and Harrison gave his to Eleanor."

With Andrew gone, Margaret knew that Wallace and Harrison would finally be forced to face the issue of succession. As with Bob's shares, Andrew's shares were now divided up among his wife Marjorie and his six children. Wallace and Harrison also had to find someone to take Andrew's place on the

McCain board. The logical choice would have been to appoint Allison or someone else from his family. But once again, the brothers opted for a quick-fix solution and appointed Mac McCarthy, their long-time manager in Britain. Neither Wallace nor Harrison really wanted a strong board usurping their control, and Mac wasn't about to rock the boat.

The quick fix, Wallace had explained to Margaret, was to buy them some time. At least they were now talking about succession, he said. She knew Wallace was looking to Michael as a successor and she knew Harrison was looking to Allison. The company had been built on the unique relationship between Wallace and Harrison at a time when power and money and image had been irrelevant to both. But this wasn't 1956, this was 1985, and Margaret's fear was that Harrison would now abuse his power in the selection of a successor. The succession would be more about Harrison and who he was than it would be about the company and the next generation. She knew that power and public image were as important to Harrison as Wallace's family was to him. She feared that neither brother would be able to budge if a compromise was needed. Her fears were well founded.

Harrison wrote a note to himself after a meeting with Wallace at which they discussed succession. In it, Harrison sums up the cross-purposes the brothers were working at.

> If for example, one of Wallace's boys is made Chief Executive and makes his brother [second in command], and they control the company and treat my kids as "country cousins" who are supposed to be "in the dark" about the company's business…I am dissatisfied. If Allison, the most experienced member of the next generation, has the same role and he decides he doesn't need Wallace's boys in any area of high responsibility, is Wallace satisfied? I doubt it. In summary, I am trying to point up that the company belongs to the shareholders of the next generation—not the Chief Executive—and we should deal with that problem now, and if we can't deal with it now, we will hemorrhage when we deal with it a few years from now.

CHAPTER FOURTEEN

Wallace had just stepped into his morning shower when he heard Margaret yelling something about a phone call.

"Take a message," he shouted back.

"He's insistent," replied Margaret as she entered the bathroom with the telephone. "He says it's important."

Wallace grumbled and stepped out of the shower. He picked up the receiver and barked "Hello." He could barely hear the voice on the other end. Whoever it was sounded as though he was calling from a train station.

"You going to Chicago today?" the caller asked above the noise.

"Yes," replied Wallace impatiently.

"You'd better be careful what you say or do, or you're not going to like what will happen to you." The caller hung up before Wallace could say a word.

"Who was that?" asked Margaret.

Wallace was stunned. After telling Margaret what had happened he quickly called the Florenceville RCMP. They called the Chicago police who got to work trying to track down the caller.

"Are you really sure you should still go?" Margaret asked anxiously. But Wallace said he'd be damned if he was going to cancel an important business trip because of some crank.

Nine months earlier, in November 1985, Wallace and Harrison had bought Bodine's Inc., a juice company based in Chicago. The deal was a big breakthrough for the brothers. While McCain's sales had topped $1 billion globally, the company was a bit player in the U.S. market. The brothers had been afraid to take on J.R. Simplot, Lamb-Weston and Ore-Ida. Now, things were different: McCain owned the biggest juice-maker in the American Midwest and the eleventh largest in the country. Better yet, they'd picked it up for a song. Just $7.3 million (US)* for the plant and a seven-acre site that the brothers saw as a perfect base from which to expand McCain's operations into the States. Everything was falling into place. The optimism was, however, short-lived. A few months after they closed the deal, Wallace and Harrison started to learn more about Bodine's and the shady character who'd owned the business. Within six months, the deal that was supposed to be a winner for McCain had turned into the biggest fiasco in the company's history.

Bodine's was started in 1955 by Ed Boden, a tough Lebanese-American who grew up on Chicago's west side, where kids learned to fight before they could walk. He left school and volunteered for the army during World War II. When he returned from the war, Boden and his brother Joe started a small juice business called Boden's. But the brothers had a falling out and Ed went off to start his own juice business down the road. He called it Bodine's, and the two brothers became fierce competitors.

Boden managed to build up a decent roster of customers for Bodine's but annual sales rarely went above $5 million. In 1978, Boden decided to push for a bigger share of the local market and hired Roger Walsh, a local food broker, as sales manager. Walsh encouraged Boden to expand into frozen orange juice concentrate. Boden had been making mainly bottled juices because for years the concentrate market had been dominated by Florida-based companies who had easy access to orange groves. But Walsh told Boden that Brazilian orange growers had begun making cut-rate concentrate that was so cheap, Bodine's could be competitive even with the extra transportation charges. The company could cut its costs even further, Walsh said, by shipping the concentrate directly from Brazil to Chicago by way of New Jersey. That would avoid going through Florida and paying a

---

*All currency figures relating to U.S. companies are in U.S. dollars.

duty that the Florida Citrus Commission put on all imported concentrate.

Boden jumped at the idea. Finally he had a chance to make Bodine's a major player in the juice business. He and Walsh got to work converting the plant and lining up shipments of concentrate from Brazil. Once they started production, Walsh found another way to cut costs even further: they could dilute the concentrate with sugar. Orange juice concentrate cost about a dollar a pound while sugar cost twenty-five cents a pound. Good idea, replied Boden, and the two started experimenting with different sugar mixtures.

Within a few weeks, Bodine's concentrate hit the shelves of grocery stores across Chicago. They called it "100% Pure Orange Juice." Walsh and Boden knew the label was misleading. By law, they were supposed to list ingredients on the label and indicate that the juice was sweetened, but if they did that, they would lose their competitive edge over the Florida-based companies. Besides, Walsh and Boden thought, who would ever find out?

Getting the sugar formula right proved to be harder than they thought. If they added too much sugar, the juice would taste too sweet and their cover would be blown. They got a scare in March 1978, when a diabetic called the local Food and Drug Administration (FDA) office to complain that he'd had a reaction after drinking Bodine's juice. George Bailey, an FDA officer, called Boden and asked if Bodine's was adding sugar to its juice. Hoping to fend off an investigation, Boden admitted he was adding some sugar but promised not to do it again without proper labelling. The assurance worked. The FDA backed off and Walsh and Boden spent the next few months perfecting their recipe. Finally they hit on a mix of cane sugar, corn sugar, monosodium glutamate, ascorbic acid, malic acid, potassium sulfate, sodium benzoate and orange pulp wash. The formula worked, and sales of Bodine's "Pure Orange Juice" took off.

From 1978 to 1982, Bodine's sales jumped from $5 million to $56.5 million. By 1984, the company was selling $101 million worth of juice a year and its plant was pumping out more than 50,000 gallons of juice a day. Thanks to the cheap concentrate and the sugar formula, Bodine's could undercut every producer in the Midwest, and the company's juice was being sold through 155 supermarket chains and wholesalers across thirty-six states. Things were growing so fast, Boden built a new 145,000-square-foot plant on a seven-acre site on Chicago's south side. He also spent $4.4 million on new equipment to make other "pure" juices, including apple, pineapple, grapefruit, lemonade and cranberry. They were all made with the same sugar mixture, and so far no one had caught on to their scam.

Boden had finally made it. He was now the business tycoon he'd always wanted to be. Profiles appeared in the local papers lauding Boden and Walsh for their business acumen and their ability to beat the Florida juice giants. Major supermarket chains were calling from across the country to put in as many orders for Bodine's juices as the company could handle. Things were just getting better and better for Boden. He hired his son, Ed Jr., as vice president and the two paid themselves a combined $600,000 a year in salary. Boden bought a yacht, a house in Florida, an exclusive condominium on Chicago's waterfront and started an expensive car collection. Walsh was promoted to chief operating officer and hired his son, Roger, as sales manager and vice president of finance. He also bought a 20 percent ownership stake in Bodine's.

Boden's success was rankling other Chicago juice-makers and the Florida Citrus Commission, which was still mad at Boden for ducking the Florida levy on foreign concentrate and getting a free ride on the Commission's advertising promoting the U.S. juice industry. Soon the commission and other juice companies began questioning how Bodine's could manage such phenomenal growth at such discount prices. No other juice-maker in Chicago or the Midwest could compete with Bodine's, even using Brazilian concentrate. There was just no way to make pure frozen orange juice that cheaply.

The grumbling found its way to Jim Mundo, an FDA inspector in Chicago. Mundo started poking around Bodine's and in May 1983 he seized 2,500 cases of juice for inspection. The FDA tested the juice and found out that it was laced with sodium benzoate. Once again, hoping to avoid a more detailed probe, Boden and Walsh agreed to recall some cases of juice.

Walsh told Mundo the sodium benzoate had come from a leak in the company's refrigeration system. To cover his tracks, Walsh ordered an employee to put a crack in a mixing vessel just in case Mundo wanted to see for himself. The story worked, and Bodine's went back to business as usual. But Mundo was suspicious and seized more cases of Bodine's juice a year later. This time he found cane sugar in the juice. He ordered more cases recalled and told Boden and Walsh that if they didn't stop marketing their juice as pure they would face charges.

Boden and Walsh were now desperate to throw Mundo off their trail. The recalls were beginning to hurt the bottom line. Bodine's lost $2.6 million in 1983, compared to a profit of $400,000 in 1982. Walsh went on a publicity offensive and assured consumers in a television interview that while mistakes had been made, Bodine's juice was now completely pure. Meanwhile, he and Boden were working feverishly to come up with a new formula that would escape detection. They decided to switch from cane sugar to beet sugar hoping it couldn't be picked up by the FDA's testing equipment. They also started mixing in distilled water because it also wouldn't likely show up on the test. And they threw in some grapefruit concentrate for good measure because it was selling at a fraction of the cost of orange juice concentrate.

The new mix worked and Bodine's "naturally pure orange juice" was once again back on the shelves. To keep the juice flowing, Boden had to buy as much beet sugar as the company could find—up to 38 million pounds in one year. He also installed a new water-distillation system in the plant. Meanwhile, Walsh made sure none of the purchases showed up on the company's financial statements. The duo thought they had finally outwitted the FDA. They were wrong.

By 1985, other juice companies had figured out the key to Bodine's success and were making their own variations of "pure juice," many of them using the cheap, untraceable beet sugar. The FDA knew the problem was widespread, especially in Chicago, and investigators worked overtime to try to keep up with the ever-changing chemical concoctions. Inspectors got a big breakthrough when researchers came up with a new method of testing for beet sugar in concentrate. The FDA investigators decided to try it out on their number-one suspect, Bodine's.

The test worked, and in April 1985, Bodine's was ordered to recall 20,000 cases of juice. Walsh tried to assure the FDA that the adulteration was a mistake and that it wouldn't happen again, but he and Boden knew the game was over. It was time to get out. The best way to do that was to sell the company.

Toronto-based John Labatt Ltd. had expressed an interest in buying the company a year earlier. Labatt already owned Everfresh Inc., another Chicago juice company, and was eager to move into the juice business on a bigger scale. Labatt officials had even toured Bodine's plant. Boden told Labatt he wanted $30 million for the company, but Walsh didn't want to sell his 20 percent stake and he talked Boden out of the deal. Now, a year later and with the FDA on their backs, Boden and Walsh called Labatt to see if the company was still interested. Just as they were about to start negotiating, however, Walsh's son, Roger Jr., got a call from a top official at Nebraska-based ConAgra Inc. The massive food conglomerate was interested in buying Bodine's. Walsh and Boden couldn't believe their luck. ConAgra had about $6 billion in sales at the time and could easily afford to pay top dollar for Bodine's. They quickly dropped Labatt and started dealing with ConAgra.

At the same time, McCain's vice president of corporate development, George McClure, was looking at Bodine's as a possible acquisition for McCain. McClure was based in Toronto. He'd worked on and off at McCain for nearly fifteen years and had spent most of his time assessing potential acquisitions for the company, mainly in Europe. By the fall of 1985, McClure was focusing on finding something for McCain to buy to increase its presence south of the border. Alex Jeffery, the general manager of Sunny Orange, a Toronto-based juice company owned by McCain, told McClure about Bodine's and suggested he take a look at the company. McClure phoned Walsh and arranged a trip to visit Bodine's on September 19. Walsh wasn't happy to hear from McClure—he was already set on ConAgra as a buyer—but he agreed to show him around.

After touring the plant, McClure asked Walsh why Bodine's

sales had dropped from $101 million to $80 million in a year. McClure didn't know about the sugar dilution or the FDA seizures and Walsh wasn't about to tell him. Instead, Walsh said the company had lost a few bulk sales.

McClure was still impressed with the operation, and after he returned to Toronto he told Wallace that McCain should pursue negotiations with Bodine's. He also asked Walsh for some more detailed financial information about the company. Walsh wasn't interested in McCain and fired off a quick handwritten report to McClure. He was focusing on his October 23 meeting with Truk Morrison, the president of ConAgra's trading division, at which time he hoped to close the sale of Bodine's to ConAgra.

Morrison arrived at Bodine's early that Monday morning with a team of lawyers—a sure sign, Walsh thought, that ConAgra was ready to deal. Walsh and Boden ushered the ConAgra officials into Bodine's tiny boardroom. Walsh was right. Morrison immediately offered to buy Boden's 80 percent interest in the company for $6 million. It wasn't the $30 million Boden had demanded from Labatt, but he knew he was in no position to reject the offer. It was only a matter of time before ConAgra and everyone else found out about the sugar dilution. Boden agreed to sell. Morrison then turned to Walsh and asked if he wanted to join ConAgra as president of a new fruit juice division the company planned to set up. Walsh could have a five-year contract and a salary of $200,000 a year plus a 20 percent profit bonus, Morrison said. And, he added, Walsh could keep his 20 percent stake in Bodine's. The offer was better than Walsh had ever expected and he quickly accepted it. With the deal done, everyone shook hands and went out for a long lunch to celebrate. They agreed to draw up the papers and officially close the deal a week later on October 31. The next morning, still flushed with excitement about his new job, Walsh called McClure and told him to forget about pursuing Bodine's. The company has been sold, he said. McClure shrugged and dropped the project.

Six days later, on October 29, Wallace was preparing for a trip to Australia when he got a call from Jose Luis Cutrale, a major supplier of orange juice concentrate in Brazil. He knew

McCain had been interested in Bodine's and he told Wallace that Boden's deal with ConAgra wasn't sealed. If Wallace was prepared to make Boden a better offer, McCain could still get Bodine's. But Wallace would have to move fast. Boden and Walsh were going to officially close the deal with ConAgra in two days. Wallace hung up and called Boden. McCain was still interested, Wallace said hurriedly, and Boden shouldn't sign any papers until they'd had a chance to meet. Boden said he would hear what McCain had to say, but the ConAgra deal was closing on October 31 as scheduled.

Walsh hit the roof when he heard Wallace had called. The ConAgra deal was as good as done, Walsh thought, and he didn't appreciate the McCains messing it up now. Walsh called McClure and blasted him for McCain's interference. McClure explained what Cutrale had told Wallace and that it was Wallace's idea to talk to Boden directly to see if a deal was still possible.

"In other words, to go around me," replied Walsh.

"I'm sorry, but that's what Wallace wanted to do," said McClure.

"I don't appreciate the tactic used by Wallace and they had better bring a cheque because I'm going to Minneapolis on the thirty-first for my meeting with ConAgra," Walsh said before slamming down the phone.

Meanwhile, Wallace was in a bind. He had already arranged to go to Australia the next day and didn't have time to go to Chicago to see Boden. He went to see Harrison early on October 30 and explained the situation. Both were concerned that losing Bodine's to ConAgra would be big mistake and a lost opportunity for McCain to set up in the American heartland. But they had to act fast—Boden's deal with ConAgra was closing in just twenty-four hours.

Harrison called Boden and said he would be in Chicago by 1:00 p.m. Then he raced to the McCain airstrip and told the pilot to head to Toronto. As the plane took off, Harrison called McClure and company lawyer Roger Wilson, who was also based in Toronto, and told them to get to the airport. They were coming with him.

On the flight to Chicago, McClure tried to fill Harrison in on Bodine's. It looked like a good business, McClure said, even though he hadn't finished his own assessment of the company. The plant and equipment appeared to be in good shape and the land was undervalued at $4.5 million. McClure said they could combine Bodine's with McCain's Canadian juice operations and save about $3 million a year in concentrate costs. As an added bonus, he said, the company was non-union. Harrison smiled.

The McCain plane landed at noon at Chicago's Midway Airport. Walsh was there to pick them up. McClure could see that Walsh was angry, but Harrison tried to warm him up with some back-slapping humour. The group arrived at Bodine's twenty minutes later and headed for a tiny conference room. Harrison shook hands with Boden, as well as his son, Ed Jr., and Walsh's son, Roger Jr. A couple of Bodine's lawyers and Ricardo Lopez, vice president of operations, were also there.

Boden left most of the negotiating to Walsh. He opened the meeting by saying they were only meeting Harrison as a courtesy since the deal with ConAgra was virtually complete. Harrison ignored the comment and pressed ahead with questions about Bodine's operations.

Walsh gave him an updated financial statement. It wasn't encouraging. Bodine's had lost $519,000 in August and overall losses for 1985 were $330,000 as of August 31. Walsh also said the company lost $280,000 in September and expected to lose up to $200,000 in October. Surprising figures for a company that was supposedly booming.

"What happened, boys?" Harrison asked. "Why the $519,000 loss in the month of August?"

Walsh said the loss was due in part to delays in concentrate shipments from Brazil. He added that competition had also increased and he noted that the FDA had recalled some product. Walsh said the company was also paying for a U.S. Department of Agriculture inspector to monitor its juice and fend off criticism from the Florida Citrus Commission. He told them the commission had been on Bodine's back for years because it was buying Brazilian concentrate.

Walsh hinted at other problems, but he gave only sketchy references and didn't tell Harrison in detail what Bodine's had been doing. "Bodine's is a poor name," he said. "Sold a lot of junk for years." Lopez, who was also promised a job at ConAgra, nodded and said, "Bodine's had a bad reputation." If the comments were intended to dissuade Harrison from making an offer, they didn't work. Nothing would quash Harrison's resolve. He was here to do a deal and a deal was going to get done.

Harrison bargained, haggled and cajoled Walsh throughout the afternoon and well into the evening. Finally, at 10:00 p.m., Harrison made an offer—$7,275,000. McCain would pay half now and the rest in annual payments over five years. Walsh could stay on as president and Lopez could remain vice president of operations. Harrison paused to let the offer sink in. Then he pulled out a bank draft and turned to Boden. "You can have $100,000 cash right now, as a deposit," Harrison said. Then he looked at Walsh. "You can have $25,000."

Boden was sold. It wasn't much more than ConAgra's bid, but Harrison was offering cash, now. Harrison did have one catch. Boden would have to repay a $400,000 loan he owed the company. Boden shrugged and agreed. ConAgra would have made the same stipulation, he thought.

Walsh wasn't as pleased, but he had little choice. Once Boden had agreed to the deal, Walsh had to take it as well or he risked being left with no job and 20 percent of a company that he knew was in trouble. Harrison smiled and slapped them both on the back as he handed out the bank drafts. The agreement was typed up on an old typewriter by Boden's secretary.

Once everyone had signed, Harrison cracked open a bottle of Canadian Club and poured a round of drinks. After a few more rounds he called Wallace in Florenceville. "You own a juice factory, Wallace, in Chicago," he said cheerily. "Thanks," Wallace replied. "Good night."

Walsh called ConAgra officials the next day to tell them about the McCain purchase. Morrison was furious. ConAgra had a commitment from Bodine's. Walsh said he realized that, but Boden had already agreed to the McCain offer. Morrison then threatened to sue McCain.

Harrison flew back to Florenceville the next day leaving

Roger Wilson and McClure to wrap up the details. Both sides agreed to close the deal a week later on November 6. Roger Wilson panicked. McCain had never closed a deal that quickly and it was up to him to finalize the legal paperwork. Then he realized with a feeling of queasiness that no one from McCain had taken a close look at Bodine's books, or the plant.

The day before the deal was to close, Harrison was in his office in Florenceville when his secretary came in and handed him a letter that had been couriered from Chicago. Probably more paperwork on the Bodine's deal, Harrison thought as he opened the envelope. Inside was a one-page letter.

> Enclosed is a portion of the FDA information on Bodine's, Inc. of Chicago, obtained through the Freedom of Information Act. In addition to adding food color, pulp wash, preservatives, grapefruit pulp wash etc. to their "100% pure orange juice" they are also known to add a very large amount of beet sugar. A conclusive test to find beet sugar in orange juice is finished and will be announced within the next six weeks. Prosecution papers have also been delivered to Bodine's because of their addition of grapefruit to orange juice. These papers will be filed with the Federal Courts in a short while. Don't believe this letter!! You have access to Bodine's purchase and sales records. Check total orange juice and sugar purchases against sales of cans and bulk concentrate. Check with the Chicago and Washington Food and Drug Administration!! A company with your good reputation doesn't want to lose it.

The letter was signed "Citizens for Pure Foods."

No information was enclosed. Harrison was perplexed. Must be a union organizer trying to make trouble, or some disgruntled employee, he thought.

He called McClure and asked him to call Citizens for Pure Foods and find out why they sent the letter. McClure talked to Walsh and Lopez, who had never heard of the outfit. Lopez checked the return address and discovered it was a vacant lot in Rockford, Illinois. McClure then asked Walsh if he knew anything about the issues raised in the letter. Walsh told him about Mundo's investigation and the product recalls. The recalls had to do with mould in the plant, poor hygiene and a cracked storage tank, he said. McClure didn't press the issue, but he decided to visit the local FDA office to find out if they knew anything about the Citizens for Pure Food.

Later that afternoon, McClure and Walsh met with Mundo, George Bailey and two other FDA investigators. Bailey told McClure about the recalls but said he'd received no complaints about the company since May. "But we made it clear to them that we were watching Bodine's and still investigating," recalls Bailey. "When they left we just looked at one another. We couldn't believe they'd bought Bodine's."

McClure left the meeting reassured by Bailey's comments. He called Harrison and told him to forget about the strange letter. Harrison agreed, and the deal closed the next day as planned. McCain changed the company name to McCain O.J. Inc. and then McCain Citrus Inc.

It wasn't long before there were signs of trouble. Days after the deal closed, the McCains discovered that Bodine's had lost $1,371,000 in October, far more than the $200,000 predicted by Walsh. A couple of weeks later, Wallace arrived from Australia for his first visit to Bodine's. As he was being shown around by Lopez, he noticed some huge water containers.

"What are those for?" he asked Lopez.

"You mean you don't know?" Lopez replied, somewhat startled.

Lopez motioned to Wallace to follow him behind a stack of barrels in the yard. He told Wallace the tanks were part of the distillation system used in the adulterating process. He explained that Bodine's had been stretching its orange juice with sugar for years. Wallace was shocked. He knew about the anonymous letter but hadn't given it any more credence than Harrison and McClure had. Wallace ran over to a telephone and called Harrison. "What the fuck is going on?" he yelled into the phone. "Did you know about this? Didn't you see those boilers?" Harrison was baffled.

Wallace then went to see Walsh and asked him about adulteration. Walsh admitted that the company had been adulterating juice but insisted that the practice had stopped. "Well, you're the general manager," Wallace replied. "You had to be involved." Walsh denied any involvement, and Wallace was stuck. He couldn't fire Walsh or Lopez because McCain needed them to run the business until it could be absorbed into the other juice businesses. In fact, Lopez was later paid a $54,000 bonus by McCain, as part of his employment contract.

Problems were cropping up at an alarming rate now. Wallace found five hundred fifty-gallon drums in the yard that were supposed to be full of concentrate. Instead they were full of water left over from the adulteration process. In December, Wallace noticed that the company's energy bills had dropped substantially. When he asked Walsh about the decrease, Walsh replied that it was the result of a price cut by Chicago gas companies. He didn't tell Wallace that the real reason for the drop in energy consumption was because the distilled water operation had taken up huge amounts of power.

By early 1986, Wallace and Harrison were getting fed up. How could they get out of paying the $3.6 million they still owed Boden and Walsh? In March 1986, the McCains hired Coopers & Lybrand to do a post-closing audit of Bodine's. They wanted to see if Boden and Walsh had inflated the value of Bodine's by lying about the adulteration. The report did find discrepancies between the financial statements provided by Bodine's and the actual state of affairs. McCain financial officer Bob McFadden used the report to calculate that the discrepancies were worth $3,771,133.00. Not surprisingly, it was almost exactly the amount McCain still owed Boden and Walsh. The brothers sent them a copy of the report along with a letter. McCain had paid enough for Bodine's and wouldn't be making any payments on the remainder they owed.

Wallace and Harrison knew they had to get rid of Walsh as soon as the letter was sent. They also decided to fire Lopez, who had admitted his involvement in the adulteration scam. But who would they make president of Bodine's? The operations were a mess. The company had almost no proper accounting system, no quality control, no marketing and a horrible reputation. They needed someone quickly and someone they could trust.

Their first choice was McCain marketing manager Archie McLean, but he didn't want to move to Chicago. Wallace then suggested Michael. Wallace knew Michael was restless and needed a new challenge. He told Harrison that they should give Michael a chance to see what he could do. Harrison reluctantly agreed. There wasn't much time to consider other candidates.

With Michael appointed as the new McCain Citrus president, Wallace and Harrison headed to Chicago on August 21. Before leaving Florenceville, Wallace had received the threatening phone call warning him, "You'd better be careful what you say or do, or you're not going to like what will happen to you." The words were still ringing in his ears as they strode into the plant at 8:30 a.m. and walked quickly to Walsh's small office. Walsh looked up, surprised, and asked what they wanted.

"I have some painful news," Harrison said. "Would you resign from your position?"

Walsh was livid. These people had promised him a job when they bought the company and now they were trying to fire him. He couldn't believe it.

"I will not, and if you are going to terminate me be prepared to pay me for the four-plus years on my contract," Walsh said angrily.

"It isn't worth the paper it's written on," Harrison replied. "Our attorney has recommended that you should not work for McCain's in view of the problems with inventory and we concur with our attorney and want to get you out first before we have to deal with Boden."

"I will not resign," Walsh said firmly.

"Vacate your office immediately and we will tell the employees that you have resigned," Harrison said.

On his way out, Walsh threatened to sue for wrongful dismissal.

The next day, Wallace met Boden and his lawyer as scheduled to talk about the Coopers & Lybrand report. Wallace was fuming. He was convinced that Boden had made the threatening phone call, and he'd passed on his suspicions to the Chicago police. As the meeting started, Boden and his lawyer insisted that Wallace was wrong, and the lawyer told Wallace he was facing serious trouble if he kept accusing Boden. Wallace blew up. He leapt to his feet and leaned over the table, within inches of Boden's face.

"Yes, I called the police you son of a whore. I called the fucking police because you threatened me," he yelled. He added that the McCains had no intention of paying Boden another dime for his company.

The lawyer told the McCains they'd better think twice about not paying, or he'd take them to court. Wallace and Harrison laughed.

On August 30, McCain Citrus employees were officially told that Walsh had resigned and that Michael McCain was the new president. Lopez was fired that day and left without protest. Three months later, McCain withheld the first installment of the amount owed Boden and Walsh.

Boden and Walsh retaliated with a lawsuit demanding full payment. McCain fired back with a counterclaim saying it didn't have to make any further payments because Boden and Walsh had defrauded the company by not disclosing the adulteration. McCain also demanded immediate full payment on the $400,000 Boden owed.

Meanwhile, the FDA went after Boden and Walsh vigorously. Juice adulteration had become a major problem in Chicago and the FDA was desperate to convict the two. A criminal conviction would send a strong signal to other companies. McCain was eager to help. They wanted to clean up the company's image, and by helping the FDA convict Boden and Walsh, the McCains thought it would strengthen their own lawsuit against the pair. Wallace and Harrison began handing over mountains of documents to Bailey and other FDA investigators. They showed the officials purchase orders for water-distillation equipment, beet sugar and other ingredients. The information was critical. Now, for the first time, the FDA had enough hard evidence to go after the duo with criminal charges. In July 1989, a federal grand jury indicted Boden, his son Ed Jr. and Walsh's son Roger Jr. on nineteen charges related to mislabelling products and adulterating

food. The FDA didn't prosecute Roger Walsh, Sr. He was terminally ill with cancer and died in October 1989.

Boden, his son and Walsh Jr. pleaded guilty a few weeks later.
Boden was sentenced to two and a half years in prison and
ordered to pay a $250,000 fine. His son was fined $200,000,
given two years' probation and ordered to do two hundred hours
of community service. Walsh Jr. was also given two years' probation and ordered to do two hundred hours of community service. The investigators were surprised and pleased by the severity
of the sentence. The FDA now had some teeth to its investigation and used it to go after other Chicago-area juice-makers.

While Boden was behind bars, his second wife sold the house
in Florida, the Chicago condominium and his car collection. She
later filed for divorce. His lawyer also told him his suit against
McCain, which was still active, was hopeless. In fact, the lawyer
said, McCain had a solid case against Boden and he should try to
settle it by offering them $550,000. "No way," replied Boden.
"Those McCain bastards are trying to steal my company."

Boden was released in 1991 after serving eighteen months in
a prison camp in Wisconsin. He headed straight to Chicago to
find a new lawyer to restart the McCain suit. A friend suggested
Douglas Morrison, a lawyer familiar with the rough-and-tumble
world of small business.

Boden met Morrison in his small office on Lasalle Street just
a block from the Cook County courthouse. Towers of paper
were piled on the floor. A fish bowl that could barely accommodate two goldfish sat next to a radiator stacked with books.
Beside that was an old television set. Morrison listened to Boden
carefully. He didn't know anything about Bodine's and had never
head of McCain. He looked at Boden's lawsuit, the McCains'
counterclaim and the report from McCain, which included the
Coopers & Lybrand review. The McCain report didn't look right
to him. It seemed odd to Morrison that the adulteration undervalued Bodine's by exactly the amount McCain owed. He took it
to an accountant friend who also said it looked suspicious. With
that, Morrison decided to take a shot. "I felt this case was worth
a roll of the dice," he recalls.

Morrison had no idea what he was up against when he filed

the papers to restart Boden's case. McCain hired Sachnoff & Wever Ltd., one of Chicago's biggest and most prestigious law firms. The firm lined up a stream of expert witnesses including accountants, financial experts and the FDA's investigators. Morrison would be essentially on his own. Morrison didn't have any experts. Worse, his client was a convicted criminal and had few friends in the juice industry. One of the few witnesses Morrison had was the accountant who'd looked at the report, but he hadn't practised accounting for years.

Seeing what he was up against, Morrison first tried for an out-of-court settlement. He told McCain's lawyers he would drop the suit if the company paid Boden $3 million. That was an outrageous offer, McCain's lawyers said before refusing to discuss any settlement. Even the judge appointed to handle the case found Morrison's offer unrealistic. During a later pretrial conference the judge asked Morrison again what he wanted as a settlement. "We want $3 million," Morrison said with a smile. Without even looking to McCain's lawyers for a reply, the judge threw up his hands and said, "That's it, we're going to trial."

For four years the case dragged through Chicago's cluttered court system and it wasn't until April 1995 that it finally got before a jury. McCain's lawyers were ready with piles of studies and a long list of experts ready to testify. Morrison was joined by his lone accountant. The Walsh family was represented by its own lawyer, Chris Gair. Gair regarded Boden as something of a liability and wanted to keep the focus of his work on his own client.

However, Morrison and Gair did agree to forget about trying to contest McCain's claim that Boden and Walsh had adulterated juice. It would be pretty hard to fight, considering the criminal convictions. Instead, their strategy was to argue that Harrison and Wallace knew Bodine's was adulterating juice when they bought the plant and didn't care. All McCain was after was a new plant on a big piece of land in the middle of America. McCain was just trying to rip off Boden by refusing to pay the money it owed. McCain's lawyers stuck to their argument that Boden and Walsh lied about Bodine's true value and the adulteration. Had McCain known what Bodine's was doing, they added, the deal never would have gone ahead.

Harrison and Wallace were called to testify soon after the trial started. Morrison didn't know what to expect, but as soon as they hit the stand, Morrison knew he couldn't have asked for two better witnesses. "I didn't think we had a chance until they showed up," he said later. "They were amazingly good, for us."

Harrison testified first. Gair went after him about the anonymous letter he had received a day before the Bodine's deal closed. How could McCain argue it didn't know about the adulteration when it had received that letter outlining everything Bodine's had been doing?

"My question to you is: You could hardly claim that the reason you didn't pay [the amount owed] was sugar substitution if you already knew about the sugar substitution before the deal closed, is that correct?" Gair asked.

"I don't, I don't, I don't follow it. You've got a couple of double negatives in there. Just try it, try it again," Harrison replied.

"Okay. One of the reasons that you claim that you did not pay on the notes is because you were unaware of the sugar substitution before the deal closed, correct?" Gair said.

"I believe—no. I believe the—I don't have that in front of me, and it was ten years ago. But I believe the, I believe—and I haven't reviewed that, but I believe the, I believe the, I believe the investigator's report at Coopers & Lybrand showed—," Harrison said before the two got into a shouting match.

"Sir—"

"—that the company's assets were substantially overstated."

"Sir, didn't you—"

"Whether, whether—I want to finish this answer. Well, whether or not, whether or not they were—"

"Well, excuse me, sir. The way this works in court, I'm not the chairman of the board, but I ask the questions, the judge decides, and you answer the questions…. So in other words, the letter makes repeated references to the addition of sugar, the introduction of sugar into Bodine's orange juice, does it not?"

"Well, two. Let me repeat it, two," Harrison said.

"It makes three references, sir," said Gair.

"Well, I see two."

"All right. Well, whether it is two or three, Mr. McCain, it—"

"Let's find out."

"—is two more than are in your affidavit, isn't that correct?"

Later Gair angered Harrison again when he referred to a comment made about him in a *Maclean's* magazine article:

"Sir, tell me whether this statement is true about you, 'I made a mistake once, but I was in the sixth grade.' Is that something you tell people?"

"No."

"That's not…that's something you've never told anyone?"

"How could I say that?"

"Have you ever read…"

"How could I say that?"

"…*Maclean's* magazine?"

"Yes, I've read lots of *Maclean's*."

"Did you read the issue when it said that your colleagues say that one of your favourite sayings is, 'I made a mistake once, but I was in the sixth grade?'"

"That is not one of my favourite sayings. It is not one of my favourite sayings. I might have said it one time, and you might have. It is not one of my favourite sayings, and I don't, I don't, I don't, I don't wish to be identified by that."

Wallace testified a few days later and kept his composure a bit better. However, at times he also came across as arrogant, which only helped Morrison and Gair.

"At one point he was talking about some business trip to Australia," recalls Morrison. "And he says, 'Well, when I go to Australia I normally go on a Friday.' I mean, here is a jury of twelve people who have probably never been outside of Chicago and here's a guy saying not only that he goes to Australia all the time, but when he goes it's always on a *Friday!* Who cares?"

By now Morrison felt that the case had turned in his favour, but Gair wasn't so confident. Just ten minutes before closing arguments, Gair reached a settlement with McCain and Walsh dropped out of the suit. Morrison was on his own. He summed up his case quickly and waited for the jury's decision. It came four hours later. Boden won.

McCain was ordered to pay Boden and his son, Ed Jr.,

$2,432,042 each. The amount included interest dating back to the day the deal closed. The jury also ordered McCain to pay $418,188.47 to cover Boden's legal costs. Boden had to pay McCain $680,584 to cover the outstanding loan he owed Bodine's. Gair, who had settled for far less, immediately tried to undo his deal with McCain but the judge rejected the motion. If he hadn't cut the deal, Morrison estimates that Walsh's estate would have won about $1 million.

Wallace and Harrison were stunned. "I can't believe that criminal won," Wallace said after he heard about the verdict. George Bailey of the FDA couldn't stop laughing when told of Boden's victory. "He won? No way. I just can't believe it."

McCain lawyers were so perplexed at the verdict that they questioned jurors afterward to find out what went wrong. In a confidential report, the jurors said one reason for their decision was Harrison's arrogance on the stand. McCain's lawyers appealed the decision on February 20, 1996, and tried a flurry of post-trial motions to have the award thrown out, without success. The appeal court upheld the verdict on April 17, 1996. The delays only increased the award to Boden. By law, the court charges 6.7 percent interest on awards as they work through the appeal process. Boden's award climbed from $4.2 million to $5 million after the appeal. By Morrison's calculations, the McCains have paid more for lawyers than the amount they owed Boden. At ten years, the case is the longest-running civil suit in Chicago's history.

Ed Boden isn't celebrating. He lives in a small house close to his old neighbourhood on Chicago's west side. He's now in his early seventies and he's flat broke. The house belongs to his daughter. Boden lives in a spare room. It's been a long fall from the days of a six-figure income, a house in Florida and a car collection. He's angry at the system and at his greedy ex-wife, but Boden saves most of his aging wrath for the McCains. "Those bastards," he says gruffly. "I've been battling them for years and now I've won. They owe me and now they have to pay."

CHAPTER FIFTEEN

From the hot, muggy August day in 1986 when he started at McCain Citrus, Michael knew the job would be hard, but not this hard. "Cluster fuck" was how he described the business to his father whenever he asked. McCain Citrus had no proper accounting systems, no marketing, a weak sales network and few customers. Grocery stores wanted nothing to do with Citrus because of its past life as Bodine's.

But Michael was excited by the job. He'd been yearning for a real challenge at McCain ever since he got out of university. Now here he was, twenty-seven years old and running a McCain business in the United States. His mother was worried. The death threat Wallace had received during the Bodine's takeover had frightened Margaret, and Chicago was a long way from Florenceville. But she knew nothing would stop her son from going.

Michael was under pressure from the day he arrived at the Citrus plant on Kilbourn Avenue. McCain had a lot riding on the project. The United States had been a wasteland for Wallace and Harrison and the Bodine's acquisition hadn't helped. Michael knew, however, that he had his father's support, and he knew his dad would never have given him the job if he didn't have confidence in him. To Michael's surprise, even Harrison had offered some words of encouragement and had flown with Michael to Chicago for his first day on the job. During the flight he'd told Michael not to worry, just to do his best. For a moment, Michael put his suspicions about his uncle aside. For a moment, it seemed all the McCains were pulling together.

Michael needed all the support he could get. In his first eight months as president, McCain Citrus lost over $1 million (US).* Sales plummeted to $32.9 million, less than a third of sales during Bodine's heyday. Michael tried everything to turn things around. He cleared out the entire senior staff and overhauled virtually every plant operation. It didn't work. In 1987, his second full year in Chicago, Citrus lost $1.4 million.

Michael was getting discouraged, but he kept pushing everyone around him for a solution. The problem was that Citrus was stuck with just one plant in Chicago and a tainted one at that. Citrus would never be profitable unless it got bigger, he thought. It had to be bigger to take on the Florida giants, and one of the best ways to do that was to buy other juice companies. Over the next three years, Michael bought International Fruit of Massachusetts Inc. for just under $7 million; Dell Products Corp. of Hillside, New Jersey, which cost $6.9 million (McCain also had to take over $7.1 million in liabilities) and Cliffstar Corp. of Dunkirk, New York, for less than $7 million. The acquisitions gave Citrus six plants in various conditions. Michael merged all the operations into one unit with three plants. He also modernized the New Jersey plant with about $2.5 million in new equipment, and he built a new $8.1-million juice plant in Fontana, California. Now he had to hope that his $31 million worth of deals and expansions would pay off. Every deal had to be approved by Wallace and Harrison, and so far both had given Michael a lot of room. They would start to have second thoughts, however, if Citrus's losses didn't end soon.

Fortunately for Michael, McCain Foods was making record profits overall and could afford to wait for a turnaround at Citrus. McCain's profits doubled in 1986 to $50.6 million from just under $25 million in 1985. In 1987, profits were up again to $54.8 million and sales were closing in on $2 billion.

Michael's position at Citrus was small relative to the overall McCain operation. But he was the only son or nephew running any McCain division. To Wallace, that was more evidence that Michael might have what it takes to one day run McCain. But

---

*All currency figures relating to U.S. companies are in U.S. dollars.

Wallace knew Harrison didn't feel the same way. And he knew that the more responsibility Michael took on, the more of a challenge Harrison would feel. Michael's position was also clouding the succession issue. By early 1988, Wallace and Harrison were no closer to resolving succession or the whole problem of involving the other families in the company. Wallace and Harrison knew that the existing board was untenable—as long as there were no representatives from the families of their older brothers, the board could never fairly represent the interests of the family as a whole. The brothers had made a few half-hearted attempts to discuss changes, but nothing was ever decided.

Michael didn't have time to care. By 1988, Citrus's new plants were finally paying off. At the end of McCain's fiscal year on June 30, Citrus's sales increased to $103.5 million and the company had an operating profit of $25,000. It wasn't much, but at least the company had stemmed the losses in terms of daily operations. The overall loss, however, was still nearly $1.3 million, mainly because of the cost of the expansion program.

Now that he had a bigger, more cohesive operation, Michael felt the company needed a change in direction. Marketing studies had shown him that consumers' tastes were changing. People weren't buying as much frozen concentrate juice. They preferred bottled juice. "Here we were, 92 percent of our business was private label frozen concentrate," Michael recalls, referring to juice made for grocery stores. "And that, in a sense, was like riding a dinosaur because [concentrate] was declining in favour of the chilled juices."

Michael wanted Citrus to have its own brand of bottled juice. In early 1989, he began some market research to develop a new product. A few months later, the research team came up with a fruit juice cooler for adults called Boku and a small boxed juice for kids between the ages of two and six called Junior Juice. Michael liked the ideas and he took them to Wallace and Harrison. Wallace was enthusiastic. Harrison wasn't.

Harrison felt the McCain name should be front and centre, not Boku or Junior Juice. How could the company ever build up a profile in the States, Harrison argued, unless every product consistently used the McCain name? Michael argued that because

McCain was so unknown in the U.S., the name wasn't an advantage, and therefore the company should use another name if it made better marketing sense. He also said that adults wouldn't buy a brand of juice that had the same name as a juice for kids. "It would be like Gerber making wine or beer. How many people are going to buy that?" But Harrison was adamant. The two battled for weeks. Here we go again, thought Michael. Harrison was just trying to bully him to prove who was boss. This wasn't about Harrison not liking the products, it was about Harrison not liking him. After a few more days of warring, Michael simply ignored Harrison and went ahead with the project.

"I wasn't going to kiss his ass just because he was chairman," Michael recalls. "He was wrong."

A few months later the two were at it again, only this time Wallace entered the fray. On August 30, 1989, Harrison sent a letter to the shareholders, all family members, outlining McCain's financial results for the 1989 fiscal year. In terms of sales, the news was better than expected. Sales had reached $2.1 billion, more than doubling in just four years. That had surpassed even Wallace and Harrison's expectations (they hadn't expected sales to top $2 billion until 1990). But the news on profit wasn't as good. Overall profits had dropped sharply to $35.5 million from $66.6 million in 1988. "We lost heavily in both the Day & Ross Transportation Group and in McCain Citrus," Harrison wrote. He added that while profits had declined in Europe, an area he managed, the drop was due to weaker European currencies.

Wallace and Michael were furious. They felt Harrison had unfairly singled out Michael's operations to make him look bad. Citrus's results were poor but the company was showing signs of turning around. Losses had climbed to $6.6 million in 1989 from $1.3 million in 1988, but that was mainly due to the costs associated with the new juices, plant renovations and the new California plant. The company had also been hit with rising concentrate prices, but that was part of a temporary cycle. Sales had risen by 23 percent to $127.2 million from $103.5 million. In three years, Michael had not only managed to turn a slight operating profit but he had taken a company that was blacklisted by most grocers and turned it into a respectable competitor. Why didn't Harrison include all that in his letter? Michael fumed.

For years, while France lost money, Harrison had explained the losses in terms of McCain's overall business strategy. It was the same with the plant in Spain. By 1986, in order to avoid import tariffs, Spain was moving into the European Economic Community and was dropping its own hefty tariffs. The McCain plant was becoming uncompetitive as cheaper products flooded in from other countries. Without the tariffs, McCain could supply Spain more cheaply from somewhere else. Yet the brothers were determined to keep the Spanish plant, at least for now. It was simply "the McCain way." (The company eventually sold the plant.)

"I had a really good feeling about what we were doing," Michael recalls. "We'd got our brand launched and this commodity cycle was just a month or two. We had the building blocks and the turnaround was done. Then Harrison goes around and starts telling everybody, 'Oh, they're losing money.'"

For Michael it was the last straw. He'd had enough of the battles with Harrison. He told his father he was resigning. It was clear to Michael that Harrison would always block his every move. He couldn't go on under a constant shadow of disapproval. He wrote Harrison a bitter letter announcing his resignation. He had no intention of working at McCain Foods for ten to fifteen years only to find out that he had no chance at CEO because of family politics.

Harrison felt Michael was overreacting. Yes, the report had been blunt but Citrus had lost money and the shareholders needed to know. Michael was just being too sensitive and hotheaded, Harrison told Wallace. Harrison offered to send another report to shareholders explaining what Michael was doing at Citrus. He also asked to meet in Toronto to discuss their differences and clear the air. Michael went reluctantly. He wasn't sure there was much point to the meeting, but at least he could confront his uncle and present his concerns.

After the meeting, both thought some progress had been made and Michael was leaning towards remaining with the company. Harrison sent Michael a letter a few days later that included a summary of how he saw the meeting. "I couldn't believe it," recalls Michael. "The notes didn't reflect anything I said."

Michael sent off a stinging letter to Harrison blasting him for trying to control Wallace and his family. One thing, at least, had become clear to Michael: if he left now, he would be abandoning his father at a time when Wallace needed him most. Michael could see that his father and Harrison were heading for a battle over the future of McCain, and he wanted to be there. Harrison's son Peter had rejoined the company in 1988 after finishing his MBA at Dalhousie. Harrison was already clearly backing Allison as a potential future CEO, and with Peter now on board, he would have even more options.

Michael called Harrison and told him he was withdrawing his resignation. He would be staying at Citrus. "My father needs me now more than ever," he said.

Wallace sat in his office staring at the piece of paper on his desk. He'd already paced the length of his office several times—a sure sign he was agitated. He had plenty of work to do and calls to make but he just couldn't concentrate. Every time he tried to start working he'd find his eyes and attention pulled back to the piece of paper sitting on his desk. It was a memo from Harrison.

"Jesus Christ," Wallace said, shaking his head as he read the letter again. He stared at the closed door near his desk. It was the door to Harrison's office. He remembered the days when the door was always open and they would yell back and forth while they worked. Those days had been over for a long time. Now they rarely saw each other, and most of their communication was through inter-office memos.

The page in front of him outlined for the umpteenth time Harrison's plans to change the McCain board of directors. Among the options, Harrison wanted the company to have two boards. One would be made up of the sons and nephews of the four brothers—Wallace, Harrison, Andrew and Bob. This family board would reflect the interests of the McCains as shareholders in the company. The second board would be made up mainly of McCain executives—including Wallace and Harrison—and it would oversee the day-to-day operations of the business. Under

Harrison's plan, he and Wallace would sit only on the operating board and leave the children to run the family board. Harrison felt that would give them a chance to oversee the operations without actually compromising the brothers' control over the company. He believed strongly in a two-board system and felt that the family board was the best way to resolve shareholder issues. "The only completely safe board is probably a board made up of McCains who own shares—outsiders sooner or later get weaker or entangled, and it is extremely difficult to find people who really would have a deep commitment to McCain Foods' future," Harrison had written.

Wallace knew where the idea for two boards had come from. Roger Wilson had spent years working with Harrison in Britain and Europe and had seen two-tiered boards at several family-owned businesses. Harrison and Wilson had become close friends, and Wallace was suspicious of Wilson's loyalties. Wallace sensed that Wilson's allegiance was exclusive to Harrison. After all, Harrison had suggested putting Wilson on the McCain board when Andrew died.

To Wallace, Harrison's two-board proposal was a recipe for disaster. An all-family board would only enshrine the family's problems within the corporate structure. The sons would perpetuate the jealousies and bitterness that were already dividing the family. Two-tiered boards might be popular with European companies, but they were rare in North America.

McCain needed only one strong board, Wallace said to his brother. It should be made up of ten people, six family and four non-family members. Sons and nephews appointed to the board would get a better understanding of the company's operations. The non-family members should be non-McCain employees as well, so that they could provide a sober outsider perspective on the company.

Wallace was anxious to resolve the succession issue. It was no secret that Wallace felt Michael, of all the children, had the most potential to run the company, and Wallace wanted a McCain to take over one day. Only a family member, he thought, would have the drive and loyalty to keep McCain going at any cost. It was in their blood: from their grandfather, Hugh Henderson

McCain, to their father, A.D., the family business was in their genes. But Harrison wasn't convinced. He wanted the two-board system and he didn't necessarily feel a McCain had to run the company.

"The proposal you gave me for immediate decision is the same proposal you have been making for two years," Harrison had written Wallace. "I.e.: 1. Let's keep the company private, 2. We have to have a McCain run it, 3. It has to be Harrison's family or Wallace's family, 4. Michael has the most experience of the three McCains, Michael, Scott and Peter, 5. Therefore, Michael is named the new boss for McCain Foods 'in waiting' for his father or his uncle to die or quit. In summary, your formula just fits the decision you want to arrive at."

What was bothering Wallace now as he read the latest memo was that Harrison didn't seem open to discussion. And from Wallace's point of view, every proposal that Harrison came up with was bound to dilute Wallace's own power and that of his family. Wallace had been stunned at one point when Harrison suggested splitting the company in four and putting one son from each family in charge of an operation. There would still be a single chief financial officer and all marketing and budgeting would be handled by one office, Harrison had explained. There would also be a strong board, "to say No to the head of each segment." "Why would I agree to that?" Wallace had asked at the time. Under a four-way split, Wallace's family would end up with control over one-quarter of the company even though they owned one-third of the shares. Besides, Wallace didn't want to give up running half the operations. Harrison had also suggested splitting the company in half. Each brother would own two-thirds of his half and the remainder would be held by the other families. Wallace rejected the idea: the real issue, he insisted, was succession, not how to divide the company up.

Harrison was making suggestions out of exasperation. He'd been trying to find some middle ground with Wallace with no success. Harrison wanted both brothers to agree to a new board and, eventually, to a succession plan. But every idea he put forward was shot down by Wallace, who seemed interested only in promoting his son Michael.

As the brothers wrestled over each other's suggestions, Wallace stopped to try and figure out what was going on. In the three decades they had worked together, this kind of protracted argument had never happened before. Maybe it wasn't worth carrying on the relationship. Maybe they should sell McCain.

The stress of the negotiations with Harrison and the problems in the United States were taking their toll on Wallace physically. In early 1988 he noticed a lump and felt some pain in his abdomen. "God, no," he said to himself. He couldn't afford any more trouble with his intestine. He flew to the Lahey Clinic and the doctors told him it wasn't a hernia, it was an abscess from a stitch that hadn't been removed during his last operation. Wallace was relieved when the doctors said it would be a simple procedure. But once again what started out as routine surgery ended in another mess of adhesions that clogged up his small intestine as soon as he was opened up. A team of doctors operated for seven hours trying to cut out the adhesions while still keeping what was left of Wallace's small intestine together.

Once again, Margaret feared Wallace wouldn't make it. He was fifty-eight years old. How many more major surgeries could he withstand? But Wallace beat the odds again. He made it through the surgery and spent the next four months recovering. The operation wasn't a total success, however: the doctors told him that they had missed one tiny area of adhesions. A further operation would be too risky. Wallace would just have to live with it until a special laser surgery procedure was perfected. Both Wallace and Margaret were relieved. Neither could bear another gruelling operation.

After weeks of recuperation, Wallace returned to Florenceville to pick up where he had left off. The discussions over succession were sucking both brothers dry. They seemed to be taking priority over everything, including business. And they were preventing Harrison and Wallace from working effectively as a team. Wallace knew Harrison deeply resented the way Wallace worked with Michael, but what did he expect? Michael was the next generation and represented the future of the company. Harrison's hostility to Michael was so intense that it seemed, in Wallace's eyes, to be clouding his business judgment. Margaret had been telling him this routinely, but Wallace hadn't wanted to believe it. In his experience, if Harrison had reasons for doing something or not doing something they were always sound. However, as Wallace recovered from his surgery, he found it hard not to blame Harrison for the biggest mistake in McCain Foods' history. All he could see was that Harrison had thrown an unbelievable opportunity out the window.

It happened in early 1988. Lamb-Weston was put up for sale by its owner at the time, Amfac Inc., a diversified company based in San Francisco. Lamb-Weston had become one of the largest French fry producers in the United States, but its five plants were inefficient and the company was barely breaking even.

Wallace saw the sale as an unbelievable opportunity. Lamb had been a tough competitor for McCain for years and it had been one of the reasons McCain had stayed out of the United States. Now, instead of starting from scratch and building a French fry business in the States, they could just buy one. In one stroke McCain could establish itself as a major player south of the border. "It would fix us up just right," he told Harrison. Lamb-Weston's plants were also in the U.S. northwest, next to some of the best potato-growing areas in North America.

Lamb-Weston did have a lot of problems, and turning it around would be harder than anything McCain had ever attempted. Wallace estimated that McCain would have to cut hundreds of jobs to make the company competitive. But it was worth a shot, and Wallace worked on a bid with Harrison, Carl Morris and Tim Bliss.

Wallace thought the company was worth about $270 million (US) and he thought McCain should put in a bid of about $260 million. Several other companies, including ConAgra Inc., were also placing bids. ConAgra was still smarting over the way the McCains had handled the Bodine's purchase—never mind that the deal had probably worked out better for ConAgra than McCain.

Wallace and Harrison worked on their bid for weeks. But as the deadline drew closer, Harrison became more cautious. He began to reconsider the purchase. It would be the largest purchase ever by McCain and Harrison wasn't sure the company was ready to handle it. McCain didn't have any experienced management in the U.S. French fry business, he told Wallace. The two pored over the facts and figures for days. Wallace still felt it was worth a try, but after weeks of hearing no from Harrison, he finally gave in and McCain withdrew from the auction.

Lamb-Weston was sold on April 4, 1988 for $276 million to a joint bid by ConAgra and Golden Valley Microwave Foods Inc., a Minnesota-based company that specialized in microwave food. It was the worst possible scenario for the McCains. Not only had McCain lost a chance to establish a presence in the States, but Lamb-Weston was now part of the one company that could take on McCain worldwide. ConAgra was more than six times larger than McCain and was eager to get into the frozen French fry business.

Wallace and Harrison tried to recover from the Lamb-Weston loss by buying two plants owned by P.J. Taggares Co. for $55 million a few weeks later. The plants were in Othello, Washington, and Clark, South Dakota, which were good potato-growing locations. It was the biggest acquisition ever by McCain and it would double their French fry production in the United States. But the Taggares plants weren't going to get McCain even close to competing with Lamb-Weston. After all, Taggares was selling the plants because they were losing money. The Othello plant was in such bad shape that McCain had to spend about $50 million installing a new processing line and equipment.

There was no masking the fact that by not bidding for Lamb-Weston, the McCains had made a huge mistake. Under ConAgra, Lamb-Weston soon became McCain's biggest competitor globally, grabbing about 19 percent of the world French fry market compared to McCain's 24 percent share. In the States, Lamb-Weston became an even bigger player, with about one-third of the food service market while McCain had less than one-tenth. Just two years after buying Lamb-Weston, ConAgra bought out the 50 percent share owned by Golden Valley for around $500 million, nearly five times what Golden Valley had paid in 1988. To make things worse, within two years of the purchase, ConAgra hired Robert Cowan as president of Lamb-Weston. Cowan was the man Harrison had called a "stupid fucking farmer" more than twenty years earlier. Cowan hadn't forgotten the jibe and he'd been promising himself for years to go after McCain. Soon he'd have his chance.

With business relations breaking down and succession planning going nowhere, Wallace decided to reach outside the family for help. In March 1988, he wrote Leon Danco, an American expert on family businesses. Wallace had read about Danco in a magazine and wondered what advice he might have for McCain. Danco had received an MBA from Harvard in 1947 and worked in a variety of industries before settling on a teaching job at a college in Cleveland. But the school closed down a few years later, and "when you're an unemployed academic you can do two things, drive a cab or consult," he says. Danco decided to become a marketing consultant. Many of the businesses he worked with were family-owned, and the proprietors seemed to always want to talk about what to do with their kids and succession planning. From those discussions, Danco pioneered the new field of family business consulting, and in 1962 he opened the Centre for Family Business in Cleveland.

Wallace didn't tell Danco much about McCain in the letter. "Since I am one of the owners of a family business, I would be interested in hearing from you," he wrote. He didn't mention that McCain was a $2-billion-a-year company. Danco had never heard of McCain, but he wrote back saying he would be happy to see what he could do. A few weeks later, Wallace arranged for Danco to come to Florenceville for a meeting.

When Danco arrived, he was amazed at the size of McCain. This was no ordinary family business, he thought to himself as he looked at a map of their operations around the world. Wallace brought him to his home for dinner and told him about the brothers' problems. It wasn't easy for Wallace to open up. He had fought his wife and son for years over what he was now admitting to Danco.

Danco listened carefully. He disagreed with Harrison's two-board idea. Family businesses need one strong board, he told Wallace. And succession shouldn't be dictated by family members.

The board should handle it, and the owners should stay out of it.

Danco later met Harrison and offered much the same assessment. He then asked for more information on the family and the business. "The company is private," Harrison and Wallace replied firmly, refusing to offer any financial details. Danco was surprised. "They were so secretive," Danco said later. "If you asked them what time it was they would say, 'Why do you need to know?'"

Danco then spent the next few days meeting with a parade of McCain family members and looking for the key to the family dynamics. Specifically, he wanted to get their thoughts on succession and on the board proposals.

One of Danco's first meetings was with Rosemary. By the time she met Danco, Rosemary's second husband, George, was terminally ill with cancer. He had been sick for years, and Rosemary was feeling beaten down. She had just been through all of this with Bob and wasn't sure how she could cope with another death. Rosemary let Danco know how bitter she was about the way Bob had been treated by the other McCains. She told him about how she felt Bob's contribution to McCain had never been fully recognized by the other members of the family. "Bob was beaten out by Wallace and Harrison," she told Danco. She felt that, after Bob's death, her family, and especially her son Andrew, had been excluded from any meaningful role in McCain. She told Danco how alienated and angry Wallace had made her and her son, Andrew, feel. Andrew, she said, was "brilliant and misunderstood."

Danco met Andrew next. He was still running the record store in Woodstock and he was married and had a son, whom he'd named after his father. Andrew felt more settled and secure; his rock-and-roll days were behind him. He'd started taking more of an interest in McCain, attending annual shareholders' meetings and following the company's fortunes with interest. His direct involvement in McCain, however, was still minimal. He told Danco that he supported Harrison's two-board plan. The company should have a board that included members from all four families. Danco saw Andrew as a disgruntled shareholder eager for a more important role. Andrew "thinks he is a good

judge of business, and seems to be the man of the family,"
Danco noted after their meeting. Andrew was also a potential
troublemaker, Danco wrote in a note to himself. He "could be
dangerous in protecting his interests."

Allison was Danco's next appointment. The two talked about
the business and Allison's family, which had also been shut out
of the McCain board. For that reason, Allison also favoured radical change to McCain's board structure, including more input
from the minority shareholders. Danco was impressed with
Allison. "Good prospect," Danco noted. "A team player, couldn't
rule him out" as a possible successor.

Michael was one of Danco's last appointments. Like his
father, Michael was also uncomfortable talking about the problems of succession and the board with a stranger. He had also
just quit smoking and spent the entire meeting wolfing down
mints. Danco knew that Wallace saw Michael as a potential successor, "the crown prince." Michael didn't hide his aspirations
either. In their meeting, Michael said he wanted "to be the CEO
of the world's largest food business." Danco could tell Michael
was suspicious and concerned about Harrison's motives and the
way he felt Harrison was controlling other family members. The
tensions within the family became evident near the end of the
meeting. Michael was talking about the succession issue when
Allison's three sisters arrived for their meeting with Danco.
When Michael saw them, he immediately changed the subject.

Danco returned to Cleveland to sort out his interviews and
prepare some ideas. To Danco, McCain was a textbook example
of how not to manage a family business. McCain had no succession plan, no real board of directors and no outsiders to tell the
brothers what to do. Most family businesses fail to survive past
the first generation because the owner doesn't plan properly for
succession. Instead, the owner keeps complete control and cre-
ates an irrelevant board stacked with family members of varying
capabilities. Once the owner dies, the family, and the business, is
pulled apart by in-fighting over who should take over. McCain,
Danco thought, was headed for a similar fate. The family-con-
trolled board proposed by Harrison would simply perpetuate the
brothers' current squabble after their deaths.

Danco proposed one seven-member board made up of Wallace, Harrison and five outsiders. He also recommended that the brothers buy out the other families in order to simplify the company's ownership. Danco added that he could come up with a workable board and succession plan within twenty months for a fee of $300,000 (US).

Danco sent the brothers a letter in March 1989 outlining his proposals but he didn't hear back. "I called a couple of times but they didn't reply so I left it." A few weeks later, Harrison wrote to Danco asking him for a copy of one of his books. "I was so upset I told my secretary to charge him for it," says Danco. Along with the book, he sent the McCains a $60,000 (US) bill for his services.

Harrison didn't think much of Danco's proposal and certainly didn't want to pay the consultant money for what the family could do itself. Wallace wasn't that taken with Danco either. He did agree with Danco's one-board suggestion, but he still wanted the succession issue decided between himself and Harrison.

With Danco out of the picture, Harrison went back to work on his plan for two boards. Harrison's adamance on the issue was forcing Wallace to reevaluate the years they'd worked together. Wallace knew Harrison's stubbornness well and had regularly given in to it, but only because Harrison was right. Whatever their differences might be in business or personal matters, Wallace had always felt that they shared an unrelenting commitment to McCain and wanted to do what was best for the company. The only reason Wallace was so interested in promoting his son Michael was because he felt Michael was the best man to lead McCain. Wallace believed that if Michael had been Harrison's son, Andrew's son or Bob's son, he would have felt the same way. After all, Wallace did not have the same expectations of his eldest son. He loved Scott dearly, but Scott didn't have the edge or the guts that Michael had to bring McCain into the next century. Wallace knew in his heart that this was one time he couldn't compromise. It alarmed Wallace that Harrison was closing himself off. Harrison was becoming more and more like a stranger to Wallace at a time when Harrison's face was becoming more and more familiar to the outside world.

In June 1988, Wallace was in his office in Florenceville when a call came in from the executive offices of the Bank of Nova Scotia. "Would McCain Foods like to buy a table for the Harvard Business School Club of Toronto's awards dinner?" a secretary asked. "Why would we want to do that?" Wallace replied.

"Well, the club is awarding Harrison its Canadian Business Statesman Award," the secretary said. Wallace was surprised. He knew the award was a distinguished honour. Former recipients included Paul Paré, chairman of Imasco Ltd., and A. Jean de Grandpré, chairman and CEO of BCE Inc. Wallace wondered why Harrison hadn't told him about the award. He told the secretary he would buy a table and sent a personal cheque for $10,000.

The awards dinner was held in Toronto a few weeks later and was attended by four hundred of Canada's most important leaders. Because the dinner was a business event, Wallace invited a group of McCain executives to join him. But when he arrived at the dinner, Wallace was shocked to find that Harrison had already arranged a table for McCain family members, excluding Wallace.

Tom Woods, president of the club, got up and introduced Harrison, praising his exceptional leadership during a period of rapid growth at McCain. As the crowd applauded, Harrison thanked Woods and introduced the people sitting at the family table. He didn't mention Wallace. Then Harrison gave a speech about the success of McCain and the importance of international expansion for Canadian companies. Not once during the speech did he mention Wallace, who was sitting only a few feet away. By the time Harrison sat down, Wallace was boiling. "He didn't say one word about me the whole evening. Not one," he told Margaret later. "It's a good thing you weren't there." Wallace felt humiliated and embarrassed. He couldn't rationalize Harrison's behaviour. It was painful, but he had to acknowledge at last that Margaret and Michael were right. Like the husband of an unfaithful wife, Wallace felt he was the last to know. His relationship with Harrison was crumbling, and it was dawning on Wallace that Harrison had no interest in repairing it. Ironically, Harrison reveals in a note he wrote to himself in 1992 that he, too, was feeling like the betrayed spouse in a threesome.

The position today between Wallace and me is nicely analogous to a divorce. For about thirty-five years, he and I got along splendidly—supporting each other, accepting the other's veto on important matters and made an excellent, mutually supportive team. As one person said, "if you scratch one of them, you are scratching the other one too." That was correct. Enter a third party—Wallace's son Michael—who has ambitions to be the CEO of the Group and says so openly. That is not a Federal offence, except, that his father now becomes his ally to accomplish this goal, and unfortunately that must be at Harrison's expense....

Wallace felt cursed as he stood in the snow early on December 31, 1989, and stared at the smouldering McCain plant. A spark from an acetylene torch had ignited some old insulation in the Florenceville plant. The fire had quickly spread throughout the building and it took ten regional fire departments several hours to put it out. By the time it had run its course, the fire had caused $25 million in damage and destroyed much of the plant's cold storage system. "Happy New Year," Wallace thought to himself.

Wallace and Harrison had other fires to put out that year. K.C. Irving was beginning to flex his muscles in the potato processing industry. In 1979, he'd purchased a Prince Edward Island company called C.M. McLean Ltd. and renamed it Cavendish Farms. The McCains kept a close eye on Cavendish Farms for years but they didn't see the company as much of a threat. Which was just as well since the Irving boys were long-time friends of the McCains.

Then, while Wallace and Harrison were rebuilding the plant in January 1990, Harrison got a tip from Peter van Nieuwenhuizen, president of the PEI Potato Producers Association. Cavendish was planning a new $72-million processing plant in O'Leary, a town in western PEI The plant would reportedly receive up to $40 million in government assistance because it was seen as compensation for the federal government's earlier closure of the Summerland military base. Harrison and Wallace were furious. McCain plants were running at 63 percent capacity, and now Irving was proposing to build a plant larger than McCain's Florenceville operation? Harrison issued a press release condemning the Irving plan. "We are extremely concerned about media reports that a huge subsidy is planned," he told the press. "Such a move will attract countervailing duties from the United States and could close any possible U.S. markets for the entire Canadian potato industry."

It was a strange position for the McCains to take. Nearly every McCain plant in Canada, France and Australia had been built or expanded with the help of government money. As for the trade argument, the McCains had opposed the Canada-U.S. Free Trade Agreement and now were pointing to subsidies for Irving as a threat to free trade with the United States. Even U.S. trade officials had assured the provincial government that the subsidy was all right.

None of that mattered to the McCains. Their objective was to stop the Irving plant, period. Wallace and Harrison put aside their recent troubles and agreed to move quickly. First, they hired Simon Reisman, the Canadian negotiator for the 1988 Canada-U.S. Free Trade Agreement, to push the countervail issue and the trade issue. Then they turned to Archie McLean and told him to start lobbying the federal government to get the subsidy for Irving stopped. McLean was picked because he was a long-time Conservative and had close ties with the reigning Mulroney government.

McLean was in a tough spot. He'd campaigned actively against free trade in the 1988 election. In particular, McLean had targeted one of Mulroney's senior cabinet ministers, Charlie Mayer, whose riding included the McCain plant in Portage la Prairie. Mayer was reelected and now, two years later, McLean needed Mayer as an ally in McCain's fight against the Irvings, who also had good Tory ties. McLean did have some leverage, though. McCain employed hundreds of people in Mayer's riding and bought thousands of tons of potatoes every year from Manitoba farmers. Mayer agreed to help.

Mayer told McLean the only way the government could back out of subsidizing Irving was if McCain offered to build a factory on the island without any government support. Good idea, thought McLean. The company was planning to build a new line at the Florenceville plant anyway to start producing specialty fries to compete with some new products Lamb-Weston had introduced. A new plant might be more expensive, but in one move they could cut off Irving and still create a new product. "Our first and cheaper choice was to produce them in Florenceville. But PEI would work out fine," recalls McLean.

On January 22, McCain announced that if the government scrapped the Irving plan, McCain would build a $36-million processing plant on PEI with no government assistance. Well, almost none. The McCains did ask for $14.5 million to help build a waste-treatment facility. But, they argued, that program was open to any business in the province and McCain would pay a user fee. The tactic worked. The federal government withdrew its support for the Irving plant and Irving shelved its plans. McLean was so appreciative of Mayer's help that he put up a bill-board in Portage La Prairie that said simply: "Thanks Charlie." A few weeks later, McLean was flipping through the Woodstock *Bugle* when he saw a half-page advertisement: "You're Welcome Archie."

The Irvings were furious at the McCains and threaten to build a $50-million plant across from the McCain plant in Grand Falls. They even managed to win $29 million in financial backing from the New Brunswick and federal governments. To prove their point, the Irvings bought up acres of land around the McCain plant. But the plans were dropped a year later because of what Irving called "soft market conditions." Instead of building in Grand Falls, Irving made a $30-million upgrade to its existing plant in PEI. Meanwhile, the McCain PEI plant opened in September 1991.

For the media, the McCain-Irving spat was a colourful feud along the lines of the Hatfields and McCoys. But to the McCains, the battle was about competition, not family. "It wasn't a personal feud, it was business," says Wallace. "It could have been any-body." In fact, the effects of the feud were short-lived. Both fami-lies still socialize with one another and their respective companies supply each other: McCain French fries line the shelves of Irving convenience stores, and Irving gas fuels many McCain trucks. In business terms, Cavendish never became much of a threat to McCain. Cavendish has about 20 percent of the Canadian food service market while McCain has 60 percent, and Canada accounts for just 20 percent of McCain's total sales. Cavendish also didn't hurt McCain's bottom line during the tussle in 1990. McCain's profit jumped to $56.1 million for the year ending June 30, 1990, up from $35.5 million a year earlier.

The real upside of the skirmish with the Irvings was that it united Wallace and Harrison in a way they hadn't been for years. For a few months, it was as if they were twenty years younger, using their drive and smarts together for one common goal. And it showed that when the brothers worked as a team they could outwit anybody.

Barely a month after the Irving skirmish, Harrison named Allison managing director of British operations. The promotion put him second in command to Mac McCarthy, who was anxious to retire. Wallace was opposed to the appointment. Allison wasn't up to the job, he told Harrison. He doesn't have the personality or the drive. Tim Bliss, who was on the company's management board, backed Wallace up. Bliss remembers the time Allison was attending a reception with some local farmers in Britain.

"Allison stood back and wasn't mingling," says Bliss. "Harrison came over to him and said, 'Look Allison, these people are the lifeblood of the company, go and meet them.' Allison did for a little bit but then went back into the corner."

Harrison was adamant. Allison had the most experience and was a capable executive, he argued. And Wallace backed down. After all, Harrison was responsible for British operations and it was his decision. But Wallace was not happy about the move. Once again, Harrison seemed to be setting up Allison as a possible successor. And a few months later, Harrison did in fact put forward a list of three possible successors: Mac McCarthy, Paul van der Wel, who ran European operations, and Allison.

"I am only putting him in because I want a 'McCain' on the list, and he has the longest and best record. We have other Executives as good, and we have others who possibly may pass him—I don't know the answers to these questions at this moment," he wrote to Wallace. But Harrison also made it clear that he did not favour a family member as CEO. In an obvious reference to Michael, Harrison said: "If we had a family member as CEO with a dual role, he will tend to look after his own family first, tend to be jealous of his cousins, his cousins will tend to be jealous of him, and he will be sorely tempted to use his inside information to increase his strength inside the company. 'Politics' inside the company will grow at an increasing rate, and in my opinion, the Company will split."

Meanwhile, Harrison and Roger Wilson were also fleshing out details of the two-board proposal. The family board would be established for the holding company, McCain Foods Group Inc., which had never had a separate board of directors. The operating board would be set up for McCain Foods Ltd., the only holding in the holding company. As for succession, Harrison suggested that each brother submit a list of three candidates to the family board, which would ultimately decide.

Wallace was never going to be able to accept a two-board system, but Harrison's current plan posed further problems. Harrison would put the succession decision in the hands of people who Wallace knew were opposed to Michael. He insisted that the brothers decide the succession issue between themselves, and he proposed a single, eleven-member company board made up of family and non-family members.

Harrison was getting tired of Wallace's delaying tactics. "It is not fair for you to continue your veto of enlarging our Board of Directors," Harrison wrote Wallace. "We have talked about this for two years and now it is time to do it." But Wallace felt the only person who had talked about it for two years was Harrison. It also appeared to him that this battle would be larger than he'd ever imagined, and that he would need the complete involvement of his immediate family.

Over Christmas 1988, Wallace's family gathered at their vacation home in Jamaica. He and Margaret had bought the home a few months earlier almost on a lark. They liked Jamaica and during one visit they'd gone to look at some properties with a real estate agent. Though they'd had no intention of buying, they fell in love with the first home they saw. It was a long, white bungalow with a massive wall of floor-to-ceiling windows that looked out over Montego Bay. The house was in the exclusive Round Hill complex, and the neighbours included Paul McCartney and Ralph Lauren. Wallace and Margaret made an offer which, to their shock, was accepted. The place had been owned by a New York socialite who had a reputation for holding the best parties on the island. As the real estate agent handed them the keys she kidded Wallace about keeping up the house's social image. "This house has seen its last party," he replied sternly.

With his family all in one place, Wallace pulled Michael and Scott aside and told them about his ongoing battle with Harrison. It was the first time Wallace had talked openly about his problems with his children, though they'd been getting information all along from their mother. "Dad just wouldn't talk about it at home," says Wallace's daughter Eleanor. "He didn't know Mom was keeping me up to date."

Wallace told them how concerned he was about the future. "Hang on," he said. "I can see what's coming down the pike, and it's going to be rough."

CHAPTER SIXTEEN

Wallace braced himself as he stepped into Harrison's office and prepared for another round of arguments. It was August 1990, and by now nearly every major decision was a struggle, especially if it involved something Michael was doing. The latest issue was the appointment of a new CEO for McCain's U.S. operations. Harrison and Wallace had identified six regional divisions within the company, in order to decentralize McCain, and had agreed to appoint a CEO for each one. Five of the appointments had already been settled—Australia, UK, Europe, Day & Ross and the potato division, which included McCain Produce. But they couldn't agree on a CEO for the U.S. operations. By 1990, McCain had three U.S. businesses: McCain Citrus; Ellio's Pizza, a small New Jersey-based pizza company they'd bought in 1988; and the French fry division, which included plants in Maine, Washington and South Dakota. The brothers wanted one CEO to oversee all three divisions, which up until then had been operating separately.

Wallace wanted Michael for the job. Michael was already in charge of Citrus, which was the largest of the three divisions. And he'd finished a major turnaround of Citrus's business: the company's losses had fallen to $2.3 million (US)* by the end of June 1990, from $6.6 million a year earlier. Citrus had also posted an operating profit of $251,000, compared to an operating loss of $4 million in 1989. Sales had climbed to $133.6 million from $127.2 million. The numbers spoke for themselves, Wallace told Harrison. Besides, a year earlier Wallace had

---

*All currency figures relating to U.S. companies are in U.S. dollars.

promised Michael the CEO job if he managed to turn the company around. Now that the operations had improved, Wallace said, Michael deserved the job.

Harrison was vehemently opposed. "I can't believe that [Wallace] is going to try to extricate Michael from any responsibility for profit," Harrison wrote in notes to himself after talking to Wallace. "Michael has never made a nickel for us in his life. [Not all his fault either], but he hasn't and now he never will have to—Any time any company doesn't go well, it will be that [manager's] fault, not Michael's."

Michael didn't have enough experience, Harrison told Wallace. He'd only been at Citrus for four years, and he was just thirty-one years old. But Wallace felt that wasn't the real problem. He knew Harrison was leery of the business relationship between Wallace and Michael. It was Wallace's responsibility to oversee the U.S. operations and now he was putting Michael into the biggest job in that region. Wallace knew Harrison was worried that if Michael became CEO of the U.S. operations, the two would have a big power base to make a move for control of McCain someday. Even the media had picked up on the idea of Michael as a likely successor. Earlier that year, in a lengthy profile of the company, *The Financial Post* wrote: "Wallace's two sons seem best placed to succeed their father and uncle. Leading candidate is thirty-one-year-old Michael McCain, the photogenic president of the Chicago-based U.S. frozen juice business."

Harrison told Wallace that none of the top executives in the States were fit to be the regional CEO; Wallace should look outside the company. Wallace was furious. All the other regional CEO jobs had been filled by internal candidates—Mac McCarthy in Britain, Paul van der Wel in Europe, John Clements in Australia, Tony van Leerson for potatoes and John Schiller at Day & Ross. Why should the States be any different? Besides, this was Wallace's area of responsibility and Harrison should acquiesce, just as Wallace had backed down when Harrison insisted on Allison's appointment as managing director in Britain.

By late September, Wallace was getting tired of all the waiting and arguing and decided it was time to go ahead and appoint Michael. He sent Harrison a note saying he'd had enough and was naming Michael to the position. He was sorry that Harrison objected, but it was the right business decision. Harrison again told him to hold off and to keep looking for someone else.

Later that month, Harrison asked to meet Michael alone during a McCain sales conference in Quebec City. The two hadn't spoken much since Michael had threatened to resign a year earlier. Michael didn't really want to meet Harrison but once again he agreed, hoping a frank discussion might clear the air a little. Predictably, the meeting ended in an argument. "This is going to blow up, kid, and it's going to be on your shoulders," Harrison told Michael. "Don't you lay this on me," Michael yelled back.

A few days later, on the Friday of the Thanksgiving weekend, Wallace left Harrison a message saying that Michael's appointment would be announced later that day. He waited for a reply, but when none came, Wallace sent out a notice formally naming Michael the new CEO of McCain's U.S. operations. Wallace was surprised that he hadn't heard from Harrison. Maybe he'd finally relented, Wallace hoped. He even called Michael to tell him that it looked like Harrison had given in.

Michael was sceptical. He knew Harrison would never accept the appointment. Running a juice business was one thing, but Harrison would never agree to allow Wallace's son to run a French fry division. "You could walk on water in the juice division of the McCain organization and never go anywhere," says Michael. "But running a potato division was something else. That was far too close to home for Harrison."

Michael's instincts were right. Harrison was out of town on business and didn't receive Wallace's message until later that evening when he was flying home. He exploded. He felt betrayed. The brothers had never made such a major decision without agreeing first, he thought to himself. How could Wallace break that trust?

Harrison called Wallace from the plane and told him to cancel the appointment. Afterwards, he made a quick transcript of their conversation.

"I have already done it," Wallace said.

"Just walk out to the fax machine and stop that. You know I

don't agree to that," Harrison replied.

"You have disagreed with that five or eight times in a row and I am going to do it anyway."

"It is wrong. Just put it off until we have straightened some other things out. Call the other directors and tell them you favour it and I don't, and if they take your side, it is perfectly okay with me to proceed."

"I don't have to ask the directors who I am going to appoint or what I am going to do. I am going to do whatever I want to do."

"Wallace, you are undoing something—it is the first time in our lives that you have split from me. Just keep cool, hang in for a while."

"You've turned that down five or eight times and you will keep turning it down forever."

"Even Michael must be embarrassed," said Harrison.

"He is the smartest executive we have in the entire company in the entire world, and why would he be embarrassed? If I have made a mistake, I will take the responsibility."

"You don't have the responsibility or the authority to even make the decision," Wallace insisted. "It is not a question of taking the blame for doing it or not doing it. You are making a very serious mistake and I would like you to retract it."

"I will not do any such thing."

"You are going to have to be held accountable for this and you are going to regret it."

"Is that a threat?" Wallace asked.

"No it is not a threat, it is just a statement of fact. You are making a very bad mistake and you can't get off with it."

Harrison got home still burning with rage. He replayed the conversation over and over in his mind until he was consumed with bitterness. How could Wallace do this?

For the entire Thanksgiving weekend, Harrison shut himself up at home and called family members. By now he knew that most felt the same way he did about Michael and Wallace. It was time to rally everyone together to fight what Harrison saw as an obvious power grab by Wallace's family. If Wallace and Michael were bent on trying to wield more power inside McCain, they would have to fight for it.

One of Harrison's many calls was to Rosemary, who was living alone in Fredericton. Her second husband, George, had died nearly a year earlier, in December 1989. Harrison sent his sympathies, but Rosemary says she didn't receive any condolences from Wallace or his family. Rosemary was now close to Harrison and agreed with everything he was trying to do. His idea for an all-family board of directors appealed to her—finally her family would have some say in the company. Rosemary was also no fan of Michael's, and she was outraged when Harrison called to tell her about the appointment. She felt sick for the company, she told Harrison. Michael "is too young, inexperienced and arrogant," she added. In her heart, though, she knew the appointment marked the start of open warfare between Harrison and Wallace. "I knew the split was coming, then," she said later. She called her son Andrew, who agreed that Michael's appointment was about to become a serious problem.

Harrison reached Allison at home in England. Allison also backed Harrison's ideas for the board of directors and, like Rosemary, he wasn't fond of Michael. "My personal belief is that Michael has been a rather disruptive and divisive factor," he said later in court. Allison wondered if Margaret was behind Michael's appointment. Allison had always felt Margaret was quietly pushing Michael. "It was always my view that I thought my Aunt Margie had a very, very strong view about succession. And, specifically about Michael becoming CEO."

Harrison called his son Peter as well, who lived just down the road. After working for a while as Harrison's executive assistant, Peter was now vice president of export sales. He was furious when Harrison told him about Michael's appointment. Peter resented Michael's unbending ambition and said he was "90 percent responsible for the problems of the family." Peter never got along well with Wallace either. Wallace had never felt that Peter was committed to, or even interested in, the company. The way Wallace saw it, Harrison had created a position for Peter at McCain—the company had never had a vice president of export sales before—and Peter refused to take direction from anyone but Harrison. As vice president of export sales, Peter should have reported to Archie McLean, who was now vice president in charge of Canadian operations and had headed McCain's marketing for years. He refused.

"I said [to Harrison], for personal reasons and because I didn't think [McLean] could really bring anything to the international table, I didn't want to report to him," Peter said later in court. "Archie McLean is a very good executive, but it's his nature to be involved in all facets of the operation, and to maybe swing in and out of town and do the big deals. And for me in my position that was obviously not attractive. I would prefer to do that myself."

Wallace was also concerned about Peter's visits to a treatment centre for alcoholism, remembering his nephew's time at the Donwood Institute in Toronto when he was in his mid-twenties. Shortly before Michael's appointment in 1990, Peter had come to Wallace's office one morning to say he was in trouble again. He told Wallace he felt he should resign and go back for more treatment. Harrison was away on a trip, so Wallace told Peter not to resign but to go and get help. When he returned several weeks later he had recovered, but the treatment convinced Wallace that Peter didn't have what it took to run a company like McCain, or even to hold a senior position.

On Monday, Wallace decided to walk over to Harrison's house to see how he was doing. He hadn't heard from him over the weekend. Wallace had no idea that Harrison had been calling other family members about the appointment. In fact, he was convinced that Harrison had calmed down and accepted it. But when Wallace got to Harrison's house, his older brother was far from calm. If anything, the weekend of stewing and phoning had made Harrison even angrier. The two got into a vicious shouting match, exchanging insults, accusations and, Wallace claimed later, threats.

Wallace returned home ashen and shaken. He collapsed in a chair and sunk his head in his hands. He had never seen Harrison so upset. Something had snapped, he told Margaret. But Margaret wasn't surprised. As she sat talking to Wallace about what happened, she leaned over to him and said, "Harrison is going to fire you." For the first time, Wallace didn't scoff.

Harrison returned to work the next day vowing to solve the

"Michael problem." He went to see Archie McLean. McLean was also upset: he had been with the company for nearly twenty years and he was sick of watching McCain kids get promotions before they deserved them. Harrison pulled up a chair in McLean's office and the two started sharing their grievances and fuelling each other's anger. Then Harrison told McLean what he was going to do.

"During that conversation [Harrison] said three things to me that stick out in my mind," McLean would later tell a court. "Number one, Wallace McCain was going to pay for appointing Michael McCain as CEO of the United States without his blessing; and number two, Harrison was going to change the way the company was being managed and run; and number three, he was going to use a board structure in the future to make key decisions."

Harrison got to work on all three objectives. He called a board meeting for October 16 to discuss Michael's appointment.

Wallace was shocked when he got the notice for the meeting: the board had never held a formal meeting before. Wallace stormed into Harrison's office to ask why the meeting was being called. "If you set me up, I'm going to defend myself," he told Harrison, who brushed off the comments. Wallace headed home and called Michael. The two spent the next weekend drafting a presentation for Wallace to make during the meeting to explain the promotion. Wallace was sick at the thought of even having to explain. For nearly thirty years, the brothers had made decisions and got on with business. Now here he was wasting time trying to explain a decision that he felt needed no explanation, especially to a board that had no authority to overrule him.

Wallace arrived in the McCain Foods boardroom early on the day of the meeting. He was clutching his prepared remarks as he took a seat at the long table. As the other directors gathered around the boardroom table, Wallace glanced over at Harrison. He was smiling and shaking hands as if nothing was wrong.

As the meeting dragged on, Wallace could see that Harrison wasn't going to raise the issue of Michael's appointment. Maybe he'd had second thoughts, Wallace wondered, or maybe this was just an attempt by Harrison to show the directors who was boss.

As the meeting wound down, Wallace grew more determined to get his comments on the record. He wasn't going to let this opportunity slip by. When Harrison reached the end of the agenda he asked if there was any other business.

"Yes," said Wallace. He began to read his statement.

Wallace wanted the board to know just how serious the split between the brothers had become. He told them the trust between himself and Harrison that had built the company was gone. Then he defended his right to unilaterally select the CEO of the United States. "You gentlemen understand that Harrison and I have divided regions of responsibility. United States is my region," he said. He followed up with a rundown of Michael's resumé and a report of the turnaround at Citrus.

The other directors were shocked. Even though they were all close to the brothers, few knew the extent of the bitterness between them. Wallace had made sure they knew now. None of the directors said a word.

Wallace took their silence as an endorsement of his decision, but Harrison was furious. "That was a personal attack," he told Wallace after the meeting. Wallace replied that it wasn't meant as a personal attack. "You called the meeting," Wallace said, "against my wishes and my judgment" in order to "bring me under control. I am still hopeful that our relationship can be saved." Harrison looked at his brother hard and replied: "You've only won one round."

Harrison decided that if he couldn't undo the appointment, he had to get the two-board plan in place quickly. Creating a board made up of family members would dilute Wallace's power and slow down Michael's advancement. Harrison wrote Andrew, Allison, Rosemary and several other family members, urging them to help him put the new board in place within two months. The family board would be made up of six McCains representing all four families. It would also include one non-family member selected by the board members. The board would protect the interests of all family members, he added, while leaving the day-to-day operations to the operating board, which would include family members and company executives.

"The two-tier system is as sound as a nut and the corporate

structure involves checks and balances which slow things down 5 percent but increase security 200 percent, and that is a good tradeoff," Harrison wrote. "We do not want our company badly screwed up." As for succession, Harrison said he opposed considering only a McCain. But that could come later. Right now, they had to get the new board in place.

Harrison's letter marked the first time either brother had ever sent family members any information about the company, other than annual reports. Some family members didn't even know the board structure was up for discussion. Wallace was surprised when he saw Harrison's letter. At the very least, Wallace thought, Harrison should have sent his proposal to the board of directors first.

While Wallace pondered a reply, *The Financial Post* called Harrison to tell him they were nominating him "CEO of the Year." Wallace was in Toronto when Harrison called with the news. "They want to name me 'CEO of the Year,'" Harrison said. "Look, I realize we work together, but it's embarrassing to get out of." Wallace could barely contain his anger. Once again, he felt, Harrison was being awarded for work they'd done as a team. It was bad enough that the two were in a pitched battle over Michael's appointment, but now the outside world would once again see only one McCain brother as the brains behind the company. "I don't give a fuck what you do!" Wallace shouted before slamming down the phone.

The award got national attention. Harrison was honoured at a gala dinner and featured in a cover story in *The Financial Post Magazine.* Ironically, Harrison wasn't in fact the company's CEO; the brothers had never used the term. Instead, Harrison was chairman and Wallace was president. They had divided McCain's global operations in half and each brother functioned as a kind of CEO in his region, but they had never officially named themselves CEOs. Wallace simmered as Harrison collected the award. As a further insult to Wallace, the issue with the article on Harrison also included a special section called "Canada's Corporate Elite," billed as a guide to "Who's calling the shots at Canada's 200 leading companies." Under McCain Foods, the magazine listed Harrison as the man who called the shots.

Wallace now knew an all-out fight was coming. He needed to prepare for battle. He could see Harrison was pulling the other family members around him and he knew he didn't have many allies of his own in the family. They all respected him, but his bluntness, his ruthless assessment of some of their talents, had left him few friends. With no one inside the family to turn to, Wallace called his old friend Purdy Crawford, CEO of Imasco. Ltd. Crawford had been at Mount Allison with Wallace and the two had remained friends ever since. Wallace gave Crawford a brief overview of the situation and asked for the name of a good lawyer. Crawford suggested a few corporate lawyers, including Jack Petch, a senior partner at Osler Hoskin & Harcourt in Toronto. The two later met in Petch's office.

Wallace then called John Ward, another family business expert. Michael had heard Ward speak in Chicago and told Wallace that Ward had some interesting ideas.

Ward was just forty-four years old but he had been on the business faculty of Loyola University in Chicago for nearly twenty years. After earning a Ph.D. at Stanford in business strategy, Ward had become fascinated with the mechanics of family-owned businesses. He soon became a researcher, consultant, author and teacher on family business dynamics and structure.

From the first time he spoke to Ward, Wallace was impressed with his directness and no-nonsense style. Ward said he would be happy to see if he could help, but he had one condition. He would only work with *both* Wallace and Harrison. If Harrison didn't agree to work with Ward as well, there was no point in him getting involved. Wallace wasn't sure if Harrison would agree. Harrison hadn't cared much for Leon Danco, and Danco had an easygoing personality. Ward was like a surgeon who wasn't afraid to tell his patient he was dying.

To Wallace's surprise, Harrison agreed to meet with Ward and hear what he had to say. The meeting came a few days later.

As Ward walked in he noticed a copy of *The Financial Post Magazine* with Harrison's picture on the cover. He cringed. He knew how damaging that kind of publicity can be for one player in a two-brother team. The meeting, like many afterwards, was tense and at times tough. Ward didn't pull any punches. He told

Harrison bluntly that his two-board system wouldn't work. By selecting directors as representatives from each of the four families, the family would create a "constituency board" that would put the interests of their family above everything else. The family board would only work, Ward said, if it also included a group of four or five strong outside directors who could overrule family members.

Ward was equally blunt with Wallace. He told him to stop pushing Michael as a successor. Ward could see that Harrison would never accept Wallace's son as CEO. Harrison thought of himself as the head of the company and the family and he was determined to control the succession issue, just as he was determined to control almost everything else. There was no way the brothers would ever agree on a successor. Instead, they should throw the issue to a group of outside directors they trusted. Let them assess the talents and abilities of family and non-family and draw up a list of potential candidates. That wasn't what Wallace wanted to hear, but after days of wrestling with Ward over the issue, he finally agreed.

Harrison also didn't like the idea of turning the succession issue over to a committee. It sounded too bureaucratic and slow to him. He wanted a successor named within three months, and he didn't want it to be Michael or any other family member. "There is no McCain available to be CEO at this time, and I want a man named. If we don't have him, then we should go hire him," he told Ward. "The fastest way for us to get politics, bickering, etc., put to bed is to make a decision and then get on with the business. When we do that, we will have peace, because everyone knows exactly where they stand, and as long as that question remains open, there will be constant manoeuvring and politics."

Ward told Harrison there was no way of finding a successor that quickly. McCain had few executives that could step into the top job because Wallace and Harrison had consistently made all the major decisions. McCain was highly decentralized, which was crucial to its success, but it also meant that only Wallace and Harrison had an overall perspective. If Harrison ruled out family members, he would have to look outside the company, and that was a job for a strong board made up of outsiders, Ward said.

With little trust between Wallace and Harrison, Ward found

it impossible to come up with an agreed-upon board structure. The brothers tried to draw up a roster of potential candidates to serve as outside directors, but every time one of them proposed a name, the other rejected it, suspecting that the candidate would be a potential conspirator with the other. Not surprisingly, Ward lasted only a few months.

In the United States, Michael was still struggling to make a success of the operations under his management. The three businesses accounted for about $350 million (US) in sales and no profit. McCain Citrus was turning around slowly but was still struggling with net losses. The pizza business was also hurting. But the biggest problems were in the French fry division.

The United States was a $2-billion market for French fries, and McCain was up against its biggest rivals—Lamb-Weston, J.R. Simplot and Ore-Ida. Lamb-Weston had 35 percent of the food service market and Simplot had about 23 percent. Ore-Ida had the biggest retail brand name and had about 50 percent of the retail market.

McCain's entry into the States had been problematic from the start. Wallace and Harrison had picked up a couple of small French fry plants in Maine in the 1970s and tried to establish a foothold in New England. It seemed like a promising move at first. New England's population nearly matched Canada's, and even if McCain only snared a fraction of the market it would be enough. But McCain didn't get very far. Its U.S. rivals operated across the nation and found it easy to target McCain, which was limited to one region. All Ore-Ida or Lamb-Weston had to do was divert a fraction of their national marketing effort towards New England and McCain was swamped. Wallace and Harrison learned that they had to develop a national presence in the United States so that they weren't such easy targets, but that was expensive and time-consuming. And so far, their efforts hadn't worked. They'd lost the chance to buy Lamb-Weston, and the plants they'd bought from Taggares were too small to mount a challenge. McCain's marketing was marginal and the company was virtually unknown. Shortly after becoming CEO, Michael sent a survey to forty major players in the food service industry across the United States just to see how much they knew about McCain. Only one had even heard of the company.

Not only was McCain unknown, its products also weren't very profitable. The United States had four recognized grades of fries: premium, extra long, long and line flow. Premium fries were the best and most lucrative. They were generally made for major fast-food chains like McDonald's, who wanted long, thin fries with consistent colouring. Some premium products were also seasoned with spices. In 1990, processors charged about 34 cents a pound for premium fries and earned as much as a 40 percent gross profit margin. Extra long and long varieties were the mid-range products and were sold to other restaurants and retail stores. They cost a few cents a pound less than premium and delivered a slightly lower profit margin. Line flow fries were the discount variety. They were used mainly for private label customers—grocery stores who packaged fries under their own brand name. Line flow fries cost about 22 cents a pound and processors were lucky to see a 5 percent profit margin.

All of McCain's five U.S. plants produced mainly line flow fries. Even with the two plants acquired from Taggares, McCain was still stuck in the low-profit, private label market. The company had spent about $50 million fixing up Taggares's plants, but they had lost as much as $15 million in the first few years under McCain.

Adding to Michael's problems was a big drop in prices and in demand. From 1988 to 1990, a drought in the northwestern United States had coincided with a big increase in demand for French fries as fast-food chains expanded across the continent. That drove up prices, and every processing plant in the States was running flat out to supply customers with any grade of fries they could get. Even McCain could barely keep up with orders and sold everything it produced. But the boom ended just months before Michael was appointed CEO. The potato crop recovered, prices dropped, and demand began to fall as the recession took hold.

Michael's first priority was to figure out a way for McCain to break out of its low-profit product line. He wanted to start making and selling high-return premium products, but that meant buying new equipment to make the fries and hiring a sales team to sell them. Getting the sales team was easy. Michael replaced the entire existing organization and hired seven new regional managers and a vice president of sales. Getting the equipment to make the fries was much harder.

Most of the successful premium products had been developed, and patented, by Robert Cowan, McCain's arch-rival, who headed Lamb-Weston for several years. Before coming to Lamb-Weston in 1988, Cowan had worked on specialty products for the frozen-food division of Universal Foods Corp., a conglomerate based in Milwaukee. Cowan and his researchers perfected a system for making "curlicue," or spiral-shaped, fries. They also developed a series of battered, wedged and spicy fries. The products were a huge success. By 1990, specialty fries accounted for nearly 25 per-cent of Lamb-Weston's business. Universal Foods also got into the act by using the ideas Cowan had left behind. Soon, about 40 per-cent of its production consisted of specialty fries.

Wallace and Harrison tried to get McCain into the business around the same time, but they didn't have a machine or idea to patent. Instead, they resorted to one of Wallace's old tricks: they asked some Lamb-Weston researchers how their machines worked. It was the same tactic Wallace had used years earlier to gain access to competitors' plants just to see what kind of equip-ment they had. But it didn't work this time. Cowan shut them down and ordered his people not to talk to McCain. Wallace and Harrison then contacted Richard Livermore, a former Lamb-Weston employee who was now a consultant in Oregon. "We asked this guy if he could help us build this machine and he said sure," recalls Tim Bliss.

Livermore had helped invent Lamb-Weston's machine, and he gave McCain a copy of Lamb-Weston's confidential patent application. He also approached his friend Jerry Ross, an inde-pendent contractor in Oregon, to design a blade that would cut spiral fries for McCain. Livermore didn't give Ross any specifica-tions or plans for the blades, he just told Ross to see what he could do. Ross was already making blades for Lamb-Weston's machine and he used the same plans to make McCain's. But Lamb-Weston's plans were supposed to be kept confidential because the company was applying for a patent. "We didn't know Livermore hired Ross," says Bliss. "We just left it up to him. I suppose we should have been more hands-on."

A few months later, Lamb-Weston received a patent on its cutting process. Cowan then found out that Ross was making the same blades for McCain. He demanded that Ross stop and sign a confidentiality agreement. Cowan fired off a letter to McCain warning that it was stealing trade secrets. With Ross now unable to complete his project for McCain, Wallace and Harrison asked for the plans so they could have the equipment finished somewhere else. Six months later, McCain had its own cutting system and began making spiral fries. When Cowan found out, he hit McCain with a blizzard of lawsuits for patent infringement. As Cowan started winning the legal battles, he pressed McCain even harder. At last he was getting his revenge for Harrison's "stupid fucking farmer" remark!

By the time Michael was named CEO, McCain was mired in lawsuits. Then, a few months later, Cowan scored a knockout. In March 1991, a court in Oregon hit McCain with an eight-month injunction barring the company from using any of the machines based on the plans developed by Ross or Livermore. The judgment shut down Michael's plan to enter the lucrative premium French fry market.

At the end of the fiscal year on June 30, 1991, McCain's U.S. French fry operations had lost about $10 million for the year. That didn't look good when McCain's overall profit had increased to $66.4 million from $56.1 million in 1990. There was one bright spot for Michael, though. After four years of losses, McCain Citrus finally turned a profit of $7.4 million.

Michael's problems in the French fry division gave Harrison more ammunition to challenge his nephew's competence. How could Michael be considered as a potential successor when he couldn't even run one division?

By the spring of 1991, Harrison was clearly winning. Even Wallace could now see that the other family members were sold on his two-board idea and he'd better try and make the best of it. His lawyer, Jack Petch, told Wallace to give it a try for a few years and see how it worked. If it didn't work out, Petch said, they could change it. Petch thought Harrison would eventually agree to changes anyway. Harrison was also trying to ease Wallace's anxieties. "Harrison kept reassuring me that it would work out. It was a reasonable plan. We should go ahead with it. If it didn't suit, we could change it. We controlled the company. We could change it back. I accepted it. I didn't really accept it, because I was scared of it," Wallace said later.

Wallace was willing to back down, but insisted on some changes. He wanted the brothers to adopt Ward's suggestion and appoint four outside directors to serve as a committee to find a successor. The committee could take as long as it needed to find someone, he added. Once a candidate was found he could work in the company until Wallace and Harrison were ready to step down. Wallace also promised that he would stop advocating Michael as a successor and would leave the decision to the outside directors. However, he wanted only himself and Harrison to pick the directors. And he said the committee should consider family members and give them preference if it came down to a choice between a McCain and someone else. Wallace also wanted the company's by-laws changed to guarantee that he and Harrison could hold their jobs until the age of seventy-five.

Harrison reluctantly agreed to the outside committee of directors but not to the other changes. He didn't want any preference given to family members and he felt the other families should have a say in selecting the directors. He also wasn't keen on a retirement age of seventy-five. He and Wallace were in their early sixties—it would be years before a successor could take over. And, since Harrison was older than Wallace, it also guaranteed that Wallace would be the sole McCain chief executive when Harrison hit retirement age.

Wallace insisted that all of his proposals were crucial safeguards. Harrison said they weren't needed. The two battled throughout the spring. Finally, Harrison called a board meeting for June 6 to vote on his plan. Wallace knew it was all over. Two of Harrison's closest colleagues sat on the board: Mac McCarthy and Roger Wilson. The only other director besides Wallace was their brother-in-law Jed Sutherland, and he was in the early stages of Alzheimer's.

As the board meeting began, Wallace introduced a series of amendments to Harrison's plan. Each one was voted down. Finally, a vote was taken on the overall proposal. Wallace was the lone dissenter. Once the plan was approved, the directors called a shareholders' meeting for July 23 so that they could vote on the proposal. Wallace wanted the meeting delayed. Why not give the brothers more time to try to find a compromise? he asked. But that suggestion was voted down as well.

"Wallace asked that it be noted in the minutes that if the directors go forward to a shareholders meeting without an agreement by Harrison and Wallace on all points in the [board plan] it will signal the end of the company as we know it," said the minutes of the meeting.

With the shareholder meeting just weeks away, Wallace knew he had to take his case to the other family members and rally support. He knew he was on thin ice. The way most of the family saw it, he had been delaying changes that would give them some say in the company. Harrison, meanwhile, was promoting their interests, and they felt it was time to put his plan in place. But Wallace thought it was worth a try. He called Allison, Andrew and their brothers and sisters and asked for a meeting.

Wallace was blunt. He told them he opposed the dual board because it wouldn't work for McCain. He now envisioned a board made up of thirteen family and non-family members. However, the real issue, he said, was succession. "The best candidate to run this company long-term is Michael McCain," he told them. "But the time isn't right for that today. So, I am supporting, for this new set of by-laws, that we have a committee of outside directors and I wash my hands completely of picking a successor. Whoever they pick, whether it's Michael or John Jones or Sam Smith, I'll support."

If Wallace thought his honesty would impress his nieces and nephews he was wrong. His comments only confirmed what Allison and Andrew had suspected—that he was out to make Michael chief executive of McCain some day. In his heart, Wallace realized he'd made a huge mistake. He knew Harrison was warning the others about Michael and he had played into

Harrison's hand. "I shouldn't have said that," Wallace says looking back on the meeting. "I did say it, I believed it, I still believe it. I didn't give a shit, I was just being truthful with them. I have heard [Harrison] make this statement before: 'If Michael ever gets to run this company he'd fire all of you cousins. He doesn't like any of you.' I gave them good reason not to [support me]."

Wallace could also see even now that his brother had enormous control over his nieces and nephews. For example, he noticed how Rosemary's daughter Elizabeth always seemed to fall into line. "Harrison has given shit to Bethie many times," he recalled. "I've heard him, she's scared of him. And her mother [Rosemary] had a big influence on her, and Moma wanted to make sure Andrew was being looked after. Beth just got pulled into the trap."

As the date for the shareholders' meeting approached, Wallace held out some hope that maybe he could win over a few family members at the meeting. Andrew's sister Elizabeth had expressed concerns about the two-board system and Allison's sister Kathy had also said it was unnecessary.

At 10:00 a.m. on July 23, twenty family members gathered in the company's third-floor boardroom. It was one of the largest family gatherings in years. Wallace arrived with Scott, Michael and Eleanor. Margaret decided not to go. She had a pretty good idea what would happen and she felt her presence might just make things worse. Harrison came with Peter, Mark, Ann and Laura. Rosemary sat with her children, Andrew, Mary, Elizabeth and Elizabeth's husband William. Allison came with his brother Stephen and their sisters Kathy, Linda and Margaret. There was little chit-chat. Everyone was tense.

Harrison opened the meeting and explained why it had been called. As he sat down, Allison's sister Linda immediately moved for the adoption of Harrison's board proposal. Allison seconded the motion and Harrison offered a brief outline of his plan. He then addressed a question Andrew's sister Elizabeth had raised earlier about the marketability of McCain shares if the new board system were approved. Would potential buyers find the two board system confusing and be reluctant to buy the shares? It was a good question. Harrison had also raised the issue with

Austin Taylor, chief executive of the Bank of Nova Scotia. Taylor wrote back saying he didn't see a problem, and Harrison distributed the letter to the shareholders. Wallace shook his head. What else would Taylor say? Wallace thought to himself. Harrison sat on his board.

Roger Wilson then got up and explained that normally such a sweeping change would necessitate an amendment to the company's by-laws. But amending the by-laws required a majority of two-thirds of the shareholders, and it was clear that Wallace's family was opposed to the plan. Since Wallace held just over one-third of the company's shares and could kill any amendment, Wilson explained that Harrison's board plan would be voted on only as a proposal. That way the changes would require a simple majority for approval. Wilson assured the meeting that even if the plan was adopted only as a proposal, the changes could be implemented as if they were changes to the by-laws. Wallace shook his head in disbelief. How could the new system have any legitimacy if it wasn't in the by-laws? It was all just a clever ploy to get around him.

When Wilson finished, Wallace stood up and introduced several amendments. They were similar to the ones he'd tried to introduce at the June board meeting. His hope of any support among the other families vanished. Every amendment but one was defeated. Only his proposal concerning a retirement age for himself and Harrison was approved, but even that was changed by Andrew. He insisted that Harrison and Wallace remain eligible as board members until the age of seventy-five but their appointment would have to be approved by the board on a year-by-year basis. With all but one of his amendments defeated, Wallace tried one last manoeuvre. He asked to introduce a proposal for one thirteen-member McCain Foods board. Harrison ruled him out of order. A vote was called on the two-board proposal. It passed: three families to one.

The new board system was now in place almost exactly as Harrison had envisioned it. The company would now have two boards of directors: a seven-member family board and a nine-member operating board.

Nominations were then made to the family board. Harrison

nominated his two sons, Peter and Mark. Wallace put forward Michael and Scott, while Rosemary named her son Andrew. Allison was nominated by his sisters and brother. The new McCain generation was about to take its place. Andrew was named chairman of the board because, under Harrison's plan, the chairman could not come from Wallace or Harrison's family since they already each had one-third of the seats. The group later selected George McClure as the seventh member of the board, the one McCain executive the whole family could agree on.

All of the family board members except Andrew worked for McCain. Allison was managing director in Britain, Peter was vice president of export sales, Scott was a vice president of operations, and Michael was CEO of McCain USA. Mark was about to rejoin the company in Toronto after working for a few years for a brokerage firm. He was slated to be an assistant to George McClure, the vice president of corporate development.

The operating board was to be selected later. It would consist of Harrison, as chairman, Wallace, one nephew from the family board, two McCain Foods executives and four outside directors. The four outsiders would form a committee to search for a McCain CEO to replace Wallace and Harrison. The committee would recommend a candidate to the family board for its approval.

As Wallace prepared to leave the meeting, he thought about what had just happened. After more than thirty years, he and Harrison were no longer in charge of McCain Foods. They were now responsible to a board made up of their children and nephews. Wallace and Harrison would remain on the operating board and share equal powers as chief executives. But Wallace knew something fundamental had happened. The truth took a while to sink in, and when it did, it left him angry and depressed. He cringed when Andrew was named chairman of the family board. Wallace's worst nightmare was coming true. Andrew, the kid Wallace wouldn't hire for any job at McCain, was now chairman of McCain. And, at least technically, Andrew was now Wallace's boss.

Andrew relished the job. For years his family had been shut out of McCain. Andrew felt he had a right to a position on the board and to be chairman of the company that had been his father's idea. A few days after the meeting, Andrew had business cards printed with his new title. Later he opened an office on Woodstock's main street and hired a secretary. His mother, Rosemary, also felt vindicated. Her son had been shunned for years and was now getting what he deserved. She felt that her family was finally being taken seriously.

When he got home, Wallace told Margaret about the meeting. He was worried about what lay ahead. He knew the family board would simply be an extension of the battles the brothers were having. Margaret agreed. But she also knew that Wallace was losing the battles because he hadn't spent time cultivating close ties with the other family members. He had spent his free time at home with his family, not trying to assuage Rosemary or Andrew or Allison.

A few weeks after the shareholders' meeting, most of the McCains attended the annual McCain company barbecue. It was a beautiful day. The sun was shining, the drinks were cold and the children of McCain workers played in the open fields. As the event wound down, Harrison stood up to give a speech. After a few remarks about the company and its success, Harrison veered off into a discussion of national unity. Another round of constitutional talks were underway at the time and Harrison supported many of the changes that were being considered by the federal government to keep Quebec within Confederation. As Harrison spoke about the importance of unity and family harmony, Margaret became enraged. "How can he talk about compromise and keeping family together given what's just happened?" she thought to herself. Just as Harrison finished, Margaret scribbled out a note and handed it to him. "You hypocrite," it said.

A few days later, Harrison called Margaret at home and said he wanted to talk to her about her note. She agreed and hoped it would be a chance to clear the air. She felt Harrison treated her as an outsider with no opinions to offer on the board structure. And she was tired of being portrayed as a domineering mother who was pushing her son. She'd been the one encouraging Michael *not* to join the company. The two sat outside and talked for two hours. But far from clearing the air, the meeting ended in a shouting match. As he got up to leave, Harrison said, "I've now come to the conclusion that you are part of the problem." Margaret nodded and replied, "Of course I'm part of the problem, I am part of the family, too, just like Wallace."

Now that the two-board system was in place, the brothers had to find four outside directors. It proved to be an arduous process. They weren't sure how much they should tell prospective directors about the family dispute. If they told them too much, they wouldn't take the job, and if they told them too little they might quit. After weeks of haggling, they decided to approach three men: Arden Haynes, Kendall Cork and David Morton.

Haynes was former chairman of Imperial Oil and sat with Wallace on the board of the Royal Bank. Cork and Morton were on the Bank of Nova Scotia board with Harrison. Cork was also former managing director of a Toronto-based investment company, while Morton was former CEO of Alcan Aluminum Ltd.

Wallace and Harrison approached Haynes first and told him a little about the family problems. He agreed to join the board, and he would later become chairman of the committee to find a successor. Morton was next and he bluntly asked if there were any problems. Again the brothers downplayed the issues and Morton agreed to join.

Wallace was against appointing Cork at first. Cork had done some consulting work for McCain and Wallace didn't feel directors should have any ties to the company. However, Harrison wanted Cork, and when he agreed to take the job, Wallace backed down.

The fourth director was Vic Young, CEO of FPI Ltd. He was also a director of the Royal Bank. The brothers talked to Young on the phone and he agreed to take the job, but Wallace felt uncomfortable about not telling Young all the details of the family's problems. He called him back and gave him a broader overview of the succession issue. Wallace worried that Young might back out, but he didn't.

With the outside directors selected, Wallace tried one final move to bolster his position on the operating board. One member of the operating board was supposed to be selected from among the directors of the family board. Wallace suggested Michael. He was the best candidate for the operating board, Wallace said, because he was a regional CEO. But Harrison blocked the move and suggested Allison instead. He won again, and Allison was appointed to the operating company board. When Wallace accused Harrison of again slighting Michael, Harrison fired off an angry letter:

"Am I knifing Michael in any way?... You insinuated that Michael thinks he had been ripped off? You say that I have been playing politics with the shareholders for twenty-five years. Absolutely ridiculous. A joke," he wrote, adding that he had the support of all the other family members.

Wallace hit back, saying Harrison only had that support because of his power and control over them. "Your power. Your muscle. Their fear. You lined them all up in a row, and cracked the whip. I feel ripped off. We were once equal partners. We were once close friends. We once trusted each other. That is all gone."

CHAPTER SEVENTEEN

Harrison grimaced slightly. He was feeling some nagging pains in his chest again. He'd had some heart problems a few years ago, but he didn't think these pains were anything to worry about. Besides, he had a checkup scheduled soon—it could wait till then.

It was March 1992, and life was going pretty well for Harrison. The company was booming, the board changes he'd proposed were in place and a few weeks earlier he had received another major award. On January 7, 1992, he'd been promoted in the ranks of the Order of Canada from Officer to Companion, the highest level of the honour, for his outstanding work at McCain.

If Harrison wasn't concerned about the chest pains, however, other family members were. Wallace told Harrison not to wait for the checkup. Having been through three close calls with his own medical problems, Wallace advised Harrison to get the pain checked out right away. After some coaxing, Harrison agreed and flew to the Lahey Clinic near Boston.

The next day, Wallace was in Toronto on the way to the funeral of a business colleague with a friend when the car phone rang. It was an urgent message for Wallace. Harrison had just had a heart attack and was in a coma. The attack had come has doctors performed a double bypass operation.

Wallace flew back to Florenceville immediately and then left for Boston the next day with Peter. When they got to the hospital, the news was grim. Doctors told them Harrison was under heavy sedation and was still in a coma. Harrison's wife, Billie, was white with fear—no one seemed to think he was going to make it. For more than a week they kept a death-watch, hardly daring to leave the hospital. But miraculously, after ten days, Harrison came out of the coma.

Within a few weeks he was well enough to go home and Billie took him to a summer home in Saint Andrews they had bought a few months earlier. Billie loved the house, which looked over ocean, and she felt it was the best place for Harrison to recover.

Wallace ran the company while Harrison recovered. With Harrison away, Wallace also had the chance to work more freely with Michael, who was still facing huge problems with the U.S. operations. Michael was relieved to have the break from Harrison.

"Relations between Harrison and I were like oil and water," recalls Michael. "As cold as you can imagine. [Harrison] didn't know a fucking thing about the [U.S.] market and he'd come down [and say] 'I'm the king and I'm going to tell you my views and you're going to latch on to them like flies on shit.' I said, 'Well that's very nice, but...'"

Wallace and Michael had a lot to work on. McCain's U.S. French fry operations were a mess. Part of the problem was the lawsuits Lamb-Weston had launched over the alleged patent infringements. Robert Cowan and Lamb-Weston were winning the legal war. Cowan had already been granted a temporary injunction stopping McCain from using the specialty-fry production equipment. And, just before Harrison's illness, Lamb had won a $1.5-million judgment against McCain.

McCain's attempts to fight back were going nowhere. A court in Maine threw out a motion by McCain to have a counterclaim against Lamb-Weston heard there, where McCain had plants, instead of in Washington, where Lamb-Weston's operations were concentrated. McCain did manage to win one round involving another cutting system, but that case was now tied up in appeal. Wallace and Michael knew they had to cut their losses and settle the case out of court, but that wouldn't be easy given the bad blood between the McCains and Cowan. Cowan also had little use for Michael, calling him "an arrogant asshole."

The lawsuits were only part of McCain's problems. In January 1992, Michael had confidently predicted that McCain's U.S. plants would break even within six months. Even with the lawsuits, he felt sure the company could still produce enough of the profitable premium products to stem its losses. Lamb-Weston had shifted a large part of its production to premium fries and was piling up profits. Surely if McCain followed the same strategy, its financial picture would also improve. But it wasn't working out that way. By spring, McCain's U.S. French fry losses were mounting. Michael couldn't understand what was wrong. Costs at the McCain plants had been stripped to the bone, and the sales team had been raked over the coals for not delivering customers. And yet the company seemed to be losing ground rather than gaining on Lamb-Weston. Just as Michael and Wallace were banging their heads against the wall trying to figure out what Lamb-Weston was doing, Michael got the biggest inside tip of his life.

A source at Lamb-Weston gave Michael a copy of the company's confidential inside price list. It was like finding the key to a treasure chest. According to the information, Lamb-Weston was charging a fortune for its specialty products and using the profits from those sales to undercut prices on its other fries. For example, Lamb-Weston had convinced fast-food chains such as Burger King and Hardees to put two kinds of French fries on their menu, conventional premium fries and specialty products such as seasoned, battered or curlicue fries. Lamb-Weston charged 55 cents (US) a pound for the specialty products and slashed the price for the other fries to 29 cents from the going rate of 34 cents. The price difference pummelled Lamb-Weston's competitors, who didn't have a lot of specialty products and relied on the other fries for most of their business.

McCain was hit especially hard because specialty products accounted for just 1 percent of its sales in the United States. As long as Lamb-Weston could keep the price of its non-specialty fries down, McCain couldn't compete.

After reviewing Lamb-Weston's price system, Michael figured there were a couple of ways to fight back. McCain could make an all-out push to develop specialty products and take advantage of the high prices, just like Lamb-Weston. But that would be expensive and it could take years, especially since McCain was still fending off lawsuits on machines to make the products. A better option was to buy a company that was already established in the specialty market. In May 1992, Michael learned that Universal Foods Corp. of Milwaukee might be willing to sell its frozen-food division. Universal's French fry operation had become the fourth-largest potato processor in the United States, with three French fry plants in Idaho and Washington. Better still for McCain, about 40 percent of Universal's sales consisted of specialty products similar to Lamb-Weston's.

Michael told Wallace about Universal and he flew out to Milwaukee to talk about a possible deal with the company. When he returned home, Wallace told Michael that Universal might sell the plants for between $250 million (US)* and $270 million. They got to work on the details of a bid and code-named the project "Orange." Wallace ran over the figures with George McClure and Carl Morris, who agreed that it looked like a good deal. No one wanted to repeat the mistake McCain had made in 1988 when they'd failed to buy Lamb-Weston.

In June, Wallace and McClure went to see Harrison in Saint Andrews. They wanted to see how he was doing and bring him up to date on "Project Orange."

Harrison was supposed to be recovering but he had been restless and eager to get back to work. The heart attack had made him all too aware of his own mortality, and he now wanted the succession issue sorted out quickly. He knew the outside directors were supposed to make the selection, but Harrison didn't want them taking years. What if he had another heart attack and died? Then Wallace would be in control and could influence the succession process. "Did I think that I could influence those directors? No," Harrison said later when asked about his mood at the time. "Did I think that if I were six feet under the ground, our affairs could be represented, so that Wallace could influence the attitude and decision of those directors in matters such as personnel? Absolutely, yes."

---

*All currency figures relating to U.S. companies are in U.S. dollars.

As McClure and Wallace arrived at the house, Wallace could tell Harrison was preoccupied. He seemed gruff and angry. After Wallace outlined the Universal bid, Harrison raised a number of questions. How could Michael manage more plants when the operations he was already running were losing money? How could the company take on more plants in the States when it didn't have the management to run a bigger operation? After debating the issue for a while, Harrison said he was against the idea. Wallace backed off and the deal fell through. (Two years later, Universal's plants were bought by Lamb-Weston for around $200 million.)

With the Universal bid dead, Michael decided to try another, far riskier move. If McCain couldn't join the specialty market, why not destroy it? McCain could drop the price of the few specialty products it sold and try to force Lamb-Weston into a price war. That might push Lamb-Weston to increase the price of its conventional fries to make up the difference, allowing McCain to raise the price of its own regular fries. In order to sustain a price war, McCain would have to make more specialty products, but, by the summer of 1992 that was starting to look more possible. Cowan was no longer president of Lamb-Weston and Michael was making headway on a settlement with the company over the patent lawsuits. Eventually, he worked out a deal in which McCain paid Lamb-Weston $5 million (US) for a licensing agreement to use the equipment. With the lawsuits ended, McCain was on its way into the specialty market.

But could they make enough specialty fries to sustain a price war with Lamb-Weston? McCain had only one plant making specialty products, and it was in PEI. As part of the lawsuits, Lamb-Weston officials had been given access to the PEI plant to view the equipment and they knew its capacity. If McCain announced it was starting a price war with only that plant producing specialty fries, Lamb officials could simply ignore the move, knowing the plant couldn't handle the increased production for long.

Michael proposed a $7-million expansion of McCain's plant in Othello, Washington. For a $7-million expenditure, the company could see an extra $20 million in annual sales, if the plan worked. Wallace approved the plan and told Harrison they were going ahead with it. On July 21, Michael called a reporter at *The Wall Street Journal* to announce that McCain USA was cutting the price of its specialty products by 10 percent.

"We're counting on competition not following our lead," Michael told the *Journal*. "The longer it takes them to respond, the more opportunity we'll have to capture share."

A few days after the announcement, Wallace was talking to Tim Bliss when Harrison called. He wanted the price-cut and the Othello expansion delayed for a while so they could better analyse the impact. Michael hit the roof. "I was furious, it would have hurt the whole plan," he said. But Harrison felt the PEI plant could handle the extra production on its own, and he didn't believe it was worth spending money to expand the Othello facility. "My father's point of view was, why risk capital?" Peter would later say. "Why risk an investment on new products that were humming along quite well there, but nobody had any crystal ball saying that those new products were going to enjoy a demand forever. Harrison's point of view was simply that even if we cut back on our profits a little bit, by continuing to service that market out of Prince Edward Island, we are not putting at risk any capital."

Wallace was angry at what he saw as an about-face by Harrison. He told Harrison it was too late. The price-cut would go ahead as planned.

Harrison had another reason for wanting to delay the Othello plan. He'd received McCain's earnings for the fiscal year ended June 30, 1992, and they didn't look good. Profits had fallen 38 percent to $41.2 million from $66.4 million in 1991. The drop was mainly due to Day & Ross and McCain USA. Harrison wasn't surprised at the Day & Ross results. The trucking company had been in trouble for years, just like every other trucking line across Canada. Federal deregulation of the industry, as well as the recession, was hurting everybody, and there wasn't much McCain could do. Day & Ross had lost about $20 million over the last five years, but everyone was confident that once the recession was over the business would pick up. If not, Wallace and Harrison were already mulling over the possibility of selling that division. McCain's U.S. results, however, were another matter. The company had lost $7.6 million in total in the United States. The American French fry business had lost $15 million and McCain Citrus's profits had dropped to $6.5 million from $7.4 million in 1991. Harrison was livid. In the two years Michael had been in charge of the U.S. operations, the French fry business had lost more than $20 million, and now Citrus was falling back as well.

Harrison was convinced that Wallace had been trying to cover for Michael. For example, Wallace had put Michael in charge of buying orange juice concentrate for all of McCain's North American needs. Harrison suspected that Michael was cutting better deals on concentrate for his business in the United States than for McCain's juice operations in Canada, in order to make his own division look better. Michael scoffed at the suggestion, saying each country used different pricing formulas. Besides, he added, Harrison was looking at only a short time frame that happened to show differences in price. Over the long term, both countries received the same price. Harrison wasn't convinced.

Michael ignored Harrison's concerns and concentrated on the price-cut strategy. By the end of the summer, there were signs that it was working. The announcement had attracted good press and the discount was having an effect. Prices for conventional fries were also slowly edging up. Now, Michael wanted to tackle another long-running problem—McDonald's.

McCain's relations with McDonald's had never been great, but they'd hit a low point in the mid 1980s, when McDonald's officials in the States complained that some supplies of McCain fries were substandard. McDonald's had always been partial to Simplot and fries made from western-grown potatoes. Maybe this was just an excuse to take McCain out of the running. In any case, the damage had been done, and McCain was virtually out of luck when it came to supplying the American McDonald's.

Michael was determined to win back some of that business. He built McCain's U.S. headquarters a few blocks from McDonald's headquarters in Oak Brook, Illinois, just outside of

Chicago. Michael even moved into the same neighbourhood as several McDonald's executives and coached a local hockey team that included many of their kids. He hired a senior staff person, Phil Williams, to work exclusively on building bridges with McDonald's.

In the summer of 1992, Michael went to a McDonald's presentation about a new global supply strategy the company was developing. McDonald's was planning major expansions into new countries and it wanted better international co-ordination among its main suppliers. The program was being developed by Lynal Root, McDonald's vice president of purchasing. For its main French fry suppliers, McDonald's wanted Lamb-Weston to supply new restaurants in India and Russia; Simplot would expand with McDonald's into China and some other parts of Asia; and McCain would work with the new restaurants in eastern Europe. McDonald's offered South America to both Simplot and McCain, but McCain was favoured because of its better track record working abroad.

Michael sent Root's proposal to Wallace, who forwarded a copy to Harrison. Harrison then wrote Root a letter with some ideas about how McCain could supply McDonald's restaurants in the northeastern U.S. from New Brunswick, Maine and PEI. Wallace didn't appreciate Harrison's interference in U.S. operations. He sent Harrison an angry memo:

> I'm not sure I agree with your proposition as I don't know what will be gained from it. I don't know what you are trying to do or trying to prove. A typical scenario, Harrison, when you write a letter to Lynal Root, you don't discuss it with me. Second, you don't even have the courtesy to copy either Michael or Phil Williams, or ask their advice. I think this continues to reinforce my comments that you wish to run your own show and to hell with anybody else, and your resentment against the organization, and what we are trying to do in the USA. Since it's not your deal, then it's a bad deal.

Later that month, Michael invited Root and two other McDonald's executives to a McCain fishing camp near Grand Falls to talk about the global supply plan. Michael invited Wallace and asked if Harrison should attend as well. Wallace said there was no need for himself or Harrison to be there—it was a U.S. gathering and Michael could handle it. When Harrison called Root in Chicago to arrange a meeting to discuss the McDonald's purchasing plan, Root said he would be in New Brunswick in a couple of days and they could talk about it then. Harrison was furious. He'd had no idea Root was coming and he felt embarrassed and humiliated. He called Wallace and demanded to know why he hadn't been told about Root's visit. Wallace explained that it was Michael's turf and they should butt out. But Harrison was fuming.

By the end of August, relations between Wallace and Harrison were beyond repair. Nearly every time they met they argued. At one point Harrison said to Wallace: "You or I or both of us are going to go if you don't behave yourself."

Harrison often complained to his sons, especially Peter, who lived close by, about the endless fights with Wallace. "I was aware that the tone of their communication continued to deteriorate," Peter said later in court. "I live about a mile down the road from my father. I visit him often. And he complained almost at every meeting we had that he and Wallace just were not getting along."

Things got so bad that Wallace and Harrison talked about dividing the company between them. "I said I wanted peace and quiet and would he consider taking a share of the world and he and Michael running it for their own profit, and the rest of us doing the best we could with the other companies," Harrison wrote in a note to himself at the time. "I said I hoped he wouldn't take out the entire one-third of his shares because I thought the problem would work itself out over a few years and that the company should be one company and not fragmented."

Wallace didn't like the idea of dividing the company. He took it to mean that Harrison was trying to get rid of him. "Harrison casually offered to piece me off with 'maybe a plant somewhere' or 'maybe a business in the U.S. somewhere.' This borders on insulting…," he wrote later in a letter to the board.

Wallace felt he should keep the discussion going with some sort of counter-proposal. In the last week of August, he made three suggestions. The first was a geographic split. The brothers had already divided management of the company in half, with Wallace running North America, South America, Australia and New Zealand and Harrison running the UK, Europe and Day & Ross. Why not simply formalize the split and let each brother act as an independent CEO of his division and report only to the company board.

Wallace's second idea was a "shotgun" sale of shares between the brothers. Under a "single trigger" shotgun, Wallace would set a price and Harrison could decide whether to sell his McCain shares to Wallace at that price, or buy Wallace's shares at that price. Under a "double trigger" shotgun both would submit bids and whoever had the highest bid could decide to buy or sell shares.

Wallace's final option was an outright sale of McCain. But this was a last resort, he added. "I believe that if we keep probing why we are not getting along better, we can possibly isolate the problems and deal with them, with a far happier solution than breaking up the company or selling it," he told Harrison. "I honestly believe you and I could get our act together again."

None of Wallace's suggestions interested Harrison. To Harrison, there was only one solution. "[I]f Wallace really wanted to settle the problem, the move wasn't a very dramatic move. Move Michael," Harrison said later in court. "So I thought he really didn't want to settle the problem. He really wanted to force a breakup of the company."

Harrison's resentment towards Wallace and Michael's close relationship was now more profound than ever.

"Wallace's closer liaison with his son—is perfectly understandable," he wrote in notes to himself at the time. "The fact that it has 'gone too far' and become cruel, and probably expensive to the other shareholders is another matter.... Naturally, [Michael] and Wallace busy themselves plotting and fantasizing about 'how wonderful it would be if "just they" were together instead of with Harrison.' This is to be accomplished by making Michael look better, and Harrison look worse. It is not strange at all—we are witnessing the breakup of a commercial relationship on about the same basis as many marriages fail."

By the end of August, Harrison was more convinced than ever that the company had to find a successor as quickly as possible. On September 3, Harrison wrote Andrew, chairman of the family board, and told him something had to be done.

"It is with regret and guilt that I advise you that Wallace and I are no longer a single team running the McCain Group of Companies," Harrison wrote. "A happy situation which for thirty years saw us agreeing and letting each have a veto over important decisions has been substantially fractured. The discomfort level is so high that I believe some action must be taken."

Harrison then mentioned Wallace's three suggestions. "I think your Board has to decide which of, or if any of, these three courses would be equitable and in the best interests of the all the [sic] shareholders. I see this as primarily, but not completely, a family problem, so your Board is exactly the right forum to discuss and deal with the problem, in my opinion."

Harrison didn't say what action he expected, and Andrew didn't know either.

What could the family board do? As much as he sympathized with Harrison, Andrew wasn't sure if his board had the power to kick Wallace out or force the succession issue. The board did have one option, though. It could refuse to approve Wallace's appointment as president of McCain when it came up for annual review in October. For now, Andrew sent a copy of the letter to the other directors and thought about his next move.

Wallace and Margaret were in France on a week-long holiday. They returned to their hotel late one evening and took a phone call from Scott. Scott read them Harrison's letter over the phone and Wallace sank heavily into a chair. He knew exactly what it meant. Harrison was trying to force him out. Their relationship was over. After nearly forty years working side by side, his older brother wanted him fired. Wallace thought about flying back that night to mount a defence, but Margaret convinced him to stay put for the rest of the week. They might as well enjoy a bit of a holiday, especially if everything was going to turn ugly at home.

Michael was in Brazil scouting around for a site for a new McCain plant when his secretary called from Chicago. She faxed him a copy of Harrison's letter. Like his father, Michael immediately recognized the letter as a move to dump Wallace. He got on the phone to his father and brother. They all agreed to meet and plan a strategy when Wallace returned.

Meanwhile, Harrison began contacting McCain's outside directors. He wanted them to know what was going on and that they should be prepared to pick a successor fast. Harrison also called his friend Mac McCarthy.

"I am going to help resolve the problem while I am here and not leave it for my children or outside directors to resolve," he told McCarthy. "It is naïve to think that the company can be held together by a vote of the outside directors on anything that is not, repeat not, acceptable to the shareholders."

Harrison and Andrew also met to figure out a plan of attack. Andrew decided to call a meeting of the family board for September 11 to go over Harrison's letter.

By week's end, Wallace had returned from France and flown to Chicago to meet Michael and Scott. Wallace wanted to stop Harrison from using the family board as his executioner by bringing the issue to the operating board instead. This was a management issue, Wallace felt, not a shareholder issue. He also knew that he had more supporters on the operating board than on the family board. Maybe he could convince the operating directors to ignore Harrison's letter and let the outside directors continue at their own pace with the succession process.

Wallace also wanted some more legal advice in case things got messy. He brought his lawyer, Jack Petch up to date and they agreed to meet to discuss some options. After briefing Petch, Wallace called Tony Fell, the CEO of RBC Dominion Securities Inc. in Toronto, and asked him to come to Chicago that day. Wallace felt he needed some financial advice since his stake in McCain could be up for grabs. Fell arrived and discussed some overall options. He then put them in touch with Tom Muir.

Muir was just thirty-six years old at the time but he was already vice president and director of mergers and acquisitions for RBC Dominion. He had a wry smile and a tall, slender build that was still fit from his years as a world-class badminton player. Muir had been in the finance business for years, but it was his grandmother who got him interested in mergers and acquisitions. She had held some shares in a small printing company for years. One day the company's owners offered to buy back her shares for $500 each. Muir did some digging around and discovered that the shares were worth about $20,000 each. She refused the offer and didn't sell until the company offered $15,000 per share.

Muir was also one of the few people on Bay Street who actually knew something about McCain. A year earlier he'd been part of a team that made a pitch to McCain for some business. The group offered to help McCain restructure and prepare for the future. Without knowing anything about the internal family wrangling, Muir's team had even offered to help draw up a succession plan. Harrison and Wallace listened but politely declined.

Wallace, Michael and Scott met Muir in Toronto. They told Muir what was happening and asked for some suggestions. Muir laid out several options, including the possibility of buying out other family members to win control of McCain. It might be ugly, Muir said, but it might also be the only way around Harrison. Everyone took a deep breath and decided to wait and see what happened.

Wallace returned to Florenceville and sent Andrew a formal response to Harrison's letter. "Since Harrison's traumatic illness in March, he appears to have lost desire to understand the details of the operation of this business which has been a source of frustration [for both of us]," Wallace wrote. "Again, since his illness, Harrison has developed an extreme sense of urgency that things have changed. He has repeatedly proposed to me that we: 1) Don't have time to get the [company] Board involved and 2) We should appoint a new outside manager for an undefined position in the company, right now. I have rejected this proposal each time."

Wallace added that the outside directors should be left to pick a successor at their pace. As he had said before, the candidate could come on board and work for the company until the

brothers were ready to retire. But he had no intention of stepping down. If Harrison wanted to leave, that was fine by
Wallace.

The family board met early on September 11. Everyone was
uncomfortable. They had only met as a board a half dozen times
and were still unsure of the process. Andrew, Allison, Peter and
Mark said they agreed with Harrison that their board should
address the issues he'd raised. Scott and Michael disagreed. Like
Wallace, they felt the operating board should deal with
Harrison's concerns. But the others pressed ahead. Peter made a
motion proposing four options: Harrison and Wallace could
stay; both could be ordered to leave; Harrison could go; or
Wallace could go. He argued that the motion was necessary
because Wallace and Harrison were going through a kind of
divorce.

"Wallace McCain was looking at alimony and property settlement prior to the divorce," he said during the meeting, referring
to Wallace's suggestions about dividing up the company. He
added that "the problem calls for a hard-headed solution." Mark
agreed and said "time is of the essence…three to five years has
been wasted."

Allison and Andrew also favoured a quick solution to the
problem. "It is appropriate that the directors get on with a solution," said Allison referring to the succession process. He added
that "if those options [in Peter's motion] were viewed as a threat,
maybe they needed to be." Andrew agreed and felt the board had
no other option. "The problem, as I saw it, was we had two co-
CEOs who were involved in a war in the middle of our company," Andrew said later. "My objective [was] to have a smoothly
functioning executive office. If these two guys are at each other's
throats, obviously we [didn't] have one."

Scott and Michael opposed Peter's motion. They felt Peter's
real objective was his final option—the removal of Wallace. Scott
suggested hiring a mediator to help the brothers find a solution.
Michael said the board should get some advice before considering any drastic move. George McClure also urged caution. He
was the only non-family member on the board and he felt
squeezed from all sides. But he called the motion "a desperate

move" and said he was not prepared to vote for it. When the discussion ended, Andrew called for a vote. Peter's motion passed 4 to 3.

Wallace was indignant when he heard about the vote. Here were Andrew, Peter and Mark, people he had little respect for as businessmen, threatening to fire him. "I hasten to remind you that all your wealth today is due singularly to the intense effort and sweat equity in this business by Harrison and myself over thirty-five years," Wallace wrote in a letter to the board a week after the meeting. "For you to even threaten to discharge either or both Harrison or myself, shows extraordinary ingratitude, for which you should be ashamed. For the sake of the company, I hope and trust your character is infinitely stronger than what you displayed here. In my entire career, I have never responded to threats and have no intention of starting now."

Wallace knew there wasn't much he could do. Harrison was clearly orchestrating the manoeuvres and lining up his sons and nephews for the fight. "At the time I was very, very angry at the directors," Wallace said later in court. "After I simmered down and thought about it a while, I came to a conclusion and I am satisfied it was correct, that I blame my brother for it. And I do. I hate to say that.... Because I don't believe his sons, or those nephews, would have proposed my discharge without his influence."

After the family board meeting Harrison and his sons began to plan their next move with Andrew and Allison. No one really wanted to fire Wallace outright. Instead, they decided that a better route would be to demote Wallace to non-executive vice chairman. Harrison could remain chairman and oversee the succession process. The outside directors would also be instructed to find a successor within a few months. Once a successor was found, Harrison could then step down from his executive duties.

Wallace and his sons were also planning their next move. First, Wallace decided to call the outside directors to give them his side of events. He also wanted to make them an offer. The directors should hire a consultant to review Michael's performance. "[I]f this evaluation comes back and says that Michael is capable of handling his current position and more, then the company pays for the study, and the issue is put to rest," Wallace wrote. "If the study says that Michael is not capable of handling his current position, then I will pay for the study personally and ask for Michael's immediate resignation." The directors had no interest in the idea. They didn't want to become involved in the fight between Wallace and Harrison over Michael.

After the directors turned down the idea, Wallace met Petch to review his legal options. Petch told Wallace that he had to move quickly. He drafted a letter to the family board making it clear that Wallace was prepared to take them to court. Peter's resolution should be revoked, Petch said, because the dispute between Wallace and Harrison was an issue for the operating board, not the family board. The outside directors had been appointed to handle the succession issue and they should be left alone to do it.

Wallace then suggested a meeting between himself, Harrison, Andrew and Allison to state his position to all four families. The meeting was arranged for October 5 at McCain headquarters in Florenceville.

At 9:00 a.m. sharp, Andrew and Allison's brother Stephen walked in to the boardroom, Wallace and Harrison were there waiting for them. Allison couldn't make it and had sent his brother instead. Stephen was a vice president of McCain Produce but he had kept out of the family problems up until now and he generally left Allison to speak for his brothers and sisters.

Wallace began by reading a three-page statement outlining his proposals. First, he suggested splitting the company geographically, with each brother running his half independently. Failing that, Wallace proposed that the brothers hire a mediator or consider some kind of buy-sell arrangement as a last resort.

"I will compromise everything except for three issues," Wallace's statement said. "I will not be thrown out of this business or demoted after what I've done for all of you [including Harrison]. I'll fight that [with every resource] to my grave, and my sons I think will carry on after. I will not allow Harrison to make the management succession decision [including evaluation of my sons]. His interest is biased. I will not play second fiddle to Harrison in this organization. This has been a fifty-fifty partnership and it's going to stay that way or hang on for the ride."

Wallace's words infuriated Harrison. As soon as he finished, Harrison shot back that the problems were caused by the relationship between Michael and Wallace. He didn't agree with what Michael was doing in the United States and losses were piling up. Wallace was blind when it came to Michael and was only out to see that his son took over one day. Harrison also chided Wallace for threatening legal action, and he rejected Wallace's suggestion to split the company. The family board's resolution was perfectly reasonable, Harrison added, and if it chose to fire both brothers it was okay with him. "You *should* like the resolution," Wallace replied angrily, "it was your idea."

Andrew listened carefully and then said he agreed with Harrison. The operating board wasn't able to deal with a problem between the brothers. He also rejected a split of the company because his family would be in a minority position in both companies. Then he asked Wallace if he would consider any solution that involved both brothers stepping down within a few months. "No way," Wallace replied firmly.

As he left the meeting, Wallace could see there was no hope for a negotiated solution. He talked to Michael and Scott and they agreed that it was time to see Tom Muir and talk about a bid for control. Wallace owned just over 33 percent of McCain's shares. He needed another 17 percent for majority control. Wallace and his sons knew Harrison, Andrew and Allison would never sell their shares. But what about Andrew's sisters Elizabeth and Mary, or Allison's mother Marjorie? They weren't particularly involved in the company and maybe they would consider selling if the price was right. If even a few family members agreed to sell, Wallace might just be able to win control. It was worth a shot. Muir code-named the plan "Project Baker," after a former colleague, and started drafting an offer.

Muir's first problem was figuring out how much Wallace should offer. No one knew what each McCain share was worth. The company was private and no family member had ever sold shares before. Muir knew that coming up with a price wouldn't be easy. Most valuations are done with extensive information from the company, but Wallace didn't want Harrison to know anything about the bid until it was launched, so Muir wouldn't have much to work with.

Next, Muir had to find the money to pay for the shares. It would probably take about $300 million to buy enough shares for control, and even Wallace McCain didn't have that kind of money. Muir would have to find some financial backers. But who? Banks would want detailed information about the company before putting up any money. He also knew that the banks wouldn't be eager to get involved in a messy family squabble, especially if it was headed for court. Another problem was the company's 1992 results. McCain's profits had slid to $41.2 million from $66.4 million in 1991. That wouldn't look very attractive to banks or investors, no matter how rosy the company's past. A final stumbling-block was McCain's dual-board system. Despite what Austin Taylor of the Bank of Nova Scotia had told Harrison in 1991, Muir knew that two boards would confuse investors and make them reluctant to get involved.

As Muir figured out a way of launching "Project Baker," Andrew and Harrison increased the pressure. They called meetings of the family and operating boards in Toronto to deal with Peter's resolution. The family board would meet on October 28 and the operating board would meet on October 29. Then the family board would meet again on October 30. During the second family board meeting, for the first time directors would be asked to approve a list of senior McCain Foods officers, including Wallace and Michael, submitted by the operating board. Wallace was worried that he and Michael would not be approved. He had Petch send another letter to the directors warning them about a possible lawsuit. "Our client will pursue his remedies, for damages or otherwise, personally as against any individual director who participates in any oppressive or otherwise unlawful conduct," Petch wrote.

During the first family board meeting, Peter reiterated the importance of his motion. "Harrison McCain had the only sense of urgency and…Wallace McCain is happy to go on as they had been," he said. "Wallace's appointment of Michael ignored the historic right of veto, which had existed between Harrison and Wallace. And, second, the recent $7-million capital expenditure in Othello again ignored the historic veto. Harrison McCain realizes he can no longer work with Wallace McCain. Their partnership [is] over. And the company no longer operate[s] on their mutual agreement." The meeting ended after a short discussion. Everyone agreed to wait and see what the operating board did at its meeting the next day.

Wallace sat uncomfortably in the spacious boardroom high above Toronto's financial district. The operating board meeting began with a routine, three-hour overview of operations. Finally, near the end of the day, the directors turned to Peter's resolution. Just as Wallace was about to present his case, Mac McCarthy introduced a motion effectively ordering the outside directors to begin their search for a new CEO immediately so that the candidate could take over within a year. Wallace was angry and launched into a defence of his position. McCarthy's motion, Wallace said, presumed that the brothers were stepping down within a year. And he wasn't planning on leaving.

Arden Haynes, who was chairing the outside directors' committee, was also uncomfortable with the motion. He didn't want to get caught in the middle of a battle to dump Wallace or Harrison. He said the committee would not speed up its work unless specifically ordered to do so by Wallace, Harrison or the family board. As the meeting wound down, Harrison tried another tactic. He proposed that the board consider splitting the U.S. operations into two groups, with the French fry business in one and the juice and pizza businesses in the other. Michael could run the pizza and juice business, he said, but the company should find "a mature, experienced potato executive as the CEO of the U.S. potato business." Wallace saw the suggestion as an obvious attempt to undercut Michael and he managed to convince the other directors to drop the idea.

Late that night, Harrison held a strategy meeting in his suite at the King Edward Hotel with his sons, Andrew, Allison and their lawyer. George McClure was also there.

McClure had been wavering, unsure which brother to support. He felt awkward having to make the choice, but as a key vote on the family board, neutrality wasn't an option. McClure had been close to both brothers over the years. Everyone trusted his opinion, which is why no one had opposed his appointment.

Wallace especially considered McClure a confidant. Before appointing Michael as CEO of McCain USA, Wallace had called McClure for his opinion. McClure said he understood why Wallace was making the appointment and promised to help smooth things over with Harrison. McClure had worked with Michael on ways to improve his rocky relations with his cousins. And McClure had also voted against Peter's resolution, along with Michael and Scott, at the family board meeting in September. Wallace now saw him as a potential ally.

As much as McClure had been struggling over his loyalty, in 1988 he'd hinted to Leon Danco, the family business consultant, that if there was ever a struggle for power between the brothers he would side with Harrison. A month before Harrison's letter to Andrew, McClure had also made his position known to Archie McLean. The two met late in August 1992 and started talking about the brothers' feud. McClure "made some comments that he was going to side with Harrison in dumping Wallace," recalled McLean. "I could sense a change in direction." A few days later, McLean tried to warn Wallace about McClure's allegiance. Wallace had come to McLean's office to talk about the feud. As Wallace was leaving, McLean told him to beware: "A man you trust is going to put a knife in you back." Wallace thought about McLean's comment and tried to think who he was referring to. The next morning he saw McLean again and asked who he meant. "I think I said something to the effect that there were three men involved in the operation of the company that were on one or the other boards and it should be easy to figure out," Archie recalls. "At that point Wallace said to me, 'Well, Mac McCarthy is clearly in Harrison's corner. John Clements [manager of Australian operations] is in my corner, and George McClure has told me he won't take sides.'" McLean didn't say anything at the mention of McClure's name. He just shook his head as Wallace left.

Now, as he sat in Harrison's suite, McClure had made up his mind. He would stick with Harrison.

The group sat around the living area and talked about the day's meeting and what to do at the family board meeting the next day. They knew the family board would have to pass some motion to satisfy Haynes, who had said that the outside directors wouldn't speed up their work on succession unless they were ordered to hurry by the family board. After several drafts, the group finally settled on a motion. Gary Girvan, a lawyer for Mark and Peter, ran over to his office nearby and had the motion typed up by a secretary. When he returned, he handed it to Allison. He would introduce it at the meeting the next morning.

The family board meeting started at 9:00 a.m. The first item of business was the approval of the senior officers. Michael and Scott braced for a showdown, but every officer, including Wallace and Michael, was reappointed. Peter didn't really want to approve Michael's appointment. "I believed that Michael deserved to be fired," he said later. "But I also believed that it would create further friction between Harrison and Wallace. And make some sort of—any possibility of an amicable settlement, impossible. I thought we should focus on the problem between Harrison and Wallace."

Allison also only grudgingly approved Michael's reappointment. "I said I definitely have some questions about the U.S. But I think the overriding reason for [voting for Michael] was that this was a serious family problem. And, quite frankly, it was—embarrassing. And, so I said if Michael was not approved at that meeting, Wallace would be extremely upset, and we would be very unlikely to try to get a resolution to the problem."

With appointments finished, Allison introduced his motion. It started with an outline of the breakdown between Harrison and Wallace. It then urged the outside directors to "proceed on the basis that a new Chief Executive Officer shall take office as quickly as possible..." The directors should also "consider and consult with this board and the board of McCain Foods Ltd. as to appropriate non-executive roles for the present Chairman and President."

Michael and Scott were caught off guard. They realized immediately that the resolution was designed to dump Wallace into some non-executive role. They quickly asked for a break and called Petch. He rushed over, but the others refused to let him address the meeting. Michael then tried to amend the motion but was outvoted. Running out of options, Scott and Michael threatened to sue if the motion was approved. Wallace "would only leave kicking and screaming," Scott said. But Andrew called for a vote. "Those in favour," he asked. One by one, Peter, Mark, Allison and Andrew put up their hands. Scott and Michael looked at George McClure. They didn't know about McClure's meeting the night before and expected him to vote with them.

But his hand went up as well. The motion carried, five to two.

Michael and Scott were stunned by McClure's vote. He had supported them a month earlier and called the suggestion of either Wallace or Harrison stepping down ridiculous. Now he was endorsing a motion that would require just that. A few days after the meeting, Michael went to see McClure in Toronto. "I just want to know, why?" Michael asked. "I can't talk about it," McClure replied.

McClure's vote was a devastating setback for Wallace and his sons. Wallace felt betrayed. Harrison had now won over five of the seven family board members. How could they fight on? Maybe they should just quit. One weekend after the meeting, the three talked about resigning. At one point they were ready to give notice, but they decided they couldn't surrender now. Not that easily. They still had "Project Baker."

By December, Harrison was getting impatient with the sluggishness of the outside directors. They had been given the instruction they needed to get going, so what was taking so long? The committee had hired two executive-search specialists, including Grant Nutall, who had worked for Haynes at Imperial Oil. Nutall was charging the company $1,000 a day plus expenses. Haynes, meanwhile, was drafting a list of CEO duties before starting a formal search. He also asked for an indemnity for the directors to protect them from any legal action. Harrison agreed but Wallace didn't; he believed that the directors were already adequately protected.

In early January 1993, Harrison called Haynes about the delay and got the sense that Haynes wanted more direction. Harrison called Andrew and together they drafted another resolution to get the committee going. This time the motion was clear: Wallace and Harrison would not again be approved for their positions by the family board. The implication was that the committee had to find a successor within a year. When he saw the motion, Haynes was upset and called Harrison to complain. Harrison misunderstood, he said. The committee didn't want any more prompting. Harrison was exasperated and called Andrew to talk about the motion.

Harrison "phoned me up and he told me that he had a subsequent conversation with Arden Haynes," Andrew said later. "And Harrison actually was quite angry because he said, 'I recall very distinctly what Arden Haynes told me in the first instance and now it appears that he [has] changed his mind or he is getting cold feet.'"

Andrew was also angry at what he felt was backtracking by Haynes and delays by the committee. "I didn't give a damn what Arden Haynes or the rest of the [committee]…wanted as far as the resolution. My objective here was to get the [committee] working, and I was trying to make an effort to get them working. They…didn't seem to be willing to start." Andrew called another family board meeting and the resolution passed.

When Wallace saw the resolution he immediately called Petch. It was the last straw. Petch sent Harrison and the directors notice of a lawsuit and a draft statement of claim. In it, Wallace said the resolution was oppressive to him as a shareholder because it was forcing him to step down before he wanted to leave. Wallace told Harrison the suit would be filed in court in two days unless the board reconsidered its motion. The directors were worried. A messy lawsuit would hurt the company and the family. They wanted to back off. Harrison and Andrew agreed to rescind the motion, for now.

After winning what they knew was only a temporary victory, Wallace, Michael and Scott headed to Toronto to check with Muir on "Project Baker." He had come up with a price of $55 a share. That meant it would cost Wallace $270 million to buy enough McCain shares to get majority control. But Muir was still having trouble finding financial backers. No one wanted to get involved. His last source was George Engman at the Ontario Teachers' Pension Plan Board. "Teachers'," was Canada's second-largest pension fund, with nearly $40 billion in assets. Engman headed investments for the board and had a reputation for innovation. Muir gave his usual pitch about what Wallace was trying to do and the future of the company. To Muir's surprise, Engman was interested. He was concerned about the family issues and the lack of concrete information, but Wallace was a proven executive. And, despite the bad year in 1992, Engman thought McCain's finances were impressive. After several meetings, Engman agreed to put up $100 million. In return, Teachers' would get a seat on both McCain boards if Wallace was successful.

Muir still needed another $170 million. He went to three different banks but found little interest. They were all afraid of the family problem. Muir's last call was the Royal Bank. Even though Wallace sat on the bank's board and it owned Muir's employer, RBC Dominion, Muir was grilled about the offer, Wallace and the family situation. Finally the backing from Teachers' helped him win the bank over and Royal agreed to extend a loan. With the bank on board, Wallace coughed up another $1 million to cover the financing and legal fees. "Project Baker" was ready to go.

Late in the afternoon of May 5, 1993, Tom Muir and his boss, Tony Fell, divided up a list of McCain family members. They were about to call everyone who held McCain shares to tell them that Wallace was offering to buy their stock. They didn't have to make the calls—a package of material was already on its way to every shareholder—but they felt a phone call might help cushion the impact. Both were antsy as they picked up the phones and started to dial. McCain was a $3-billion company, but it was part of a family tradition that went back four generations. Now Muir and Fell were about to tell family members that one McCain wanted to buy them out and take control.

Fell made the first call. It was to Harrison.

CHAPTER EIGHTEEN

It was around 6:30 p.m. when Harrison's secretary, Marilyn Strong, put through the call from Tony Fell. Harrison was just about to go home, but he knew Fell and he didn't mind staying and chatting for a bit.

Fell began by saying this was a business call. He explained that Wallace was making an offer to buy 4.9 million McCain shares from any family member who wanted to sell. Harrison didn't have to do the math. That was enough shares to give Wallace just over 50 percent ownership of McCain. Harrison thanked Fell for calling and hung up. He sat for a moment at his desk and stared blankly at the wall. He couldn't believe it. His own brother was trying to launch a takeover bid for the family firm. Harrison was so upset he would later equate the bid with Pearl Harbor. In a note to Wallace, Harrison described Fell's call "telling me that my brother and long-time and closest associate is making a bid to take control of our company—that night! That was May 5/93. Dazed, I thought it was December 7/41."

As he drove home that night, Harrison knew he had to fight back. He began a round of phone calls to as many family members as he could reach. Harrison was fairly confident that no one in the family was going to take up the offer, but he needed to be sure. One of his first calls was to Andrew, who had already been called by his mother, Rosemary. Andrew was hurt and furious. McCain Foods was part of his heritage and he had no intention of ever selling his shares. Rosemary was also livid. How could Wallace ever think they would be stupid enough to sell their shares to him? When Harrison reached Allison, he was just as determined to fight back and promised Harrison the full support of his family. As an added humiliation for Allison, his letter from Muir outlining the offer was addressed to "*Ms.* Allison McCain."

The next morning, Harrison, his sons and Andrew met to review their options. By then, they had all received a written outline of Wallace's bid. It included a letter from Wallace that said the offer was a way of avoiding litigation. Wallace added that if he was successful, Teachers' would end up with a 10 percent stake of McCain and a seat on the family and operating boards. McCain might also go public. The addition of non-family shareholders, Wallace felt, might act as a check on family conflicts, and having McCain shares listed publicly on the Toronto Stock Exchange would make it easier for other family members to sell their shares if they wanted to. In his letter, Wallace said the other families could keep their seats on the family board but he would become the sole chief executive head of McCain.

To Harrison, the letter was an insult. Wallace was not only going for control of the company, he was also trying to kick Harrison out. After nearly forty years, how could Wallace end their business relationship so callously? Harrison was also opposed to taking McCain public. He didn't want public shareholders or a pension fund like Teachers' taking such a large ownership position in the company. McCain was stronger as a family-owned business, Harrison believed, and it should stay that way. Andrew, Peter and Mark agreed.

That morning they drafted an agreement committing the members of Harrison's, Andrew's and Allison's families not to sell their shares to Wallace without the unanimous consent of the group. The agreement effectively killed Wallace's bid. Harrison was pleased. Not one family member was going to take Wallace's offer, even though for some, like Rosemary, it meant turning down $50 million in cash. Harrison could now point to the agreement as proof that the family had lost all faith and trust in Wallace.

Wallace wasn't shocked by the reaction of Harrison, Andrew or Allison, but he was surprised that no other family members took the offer. It was more evidence of just how powerful Harrison's hold on the family really was. Who would dare defy him and sell their shares? He tried to talk to Harrison and explain the letter and the reason for naming himself the single chief executive. It was a technical requirement, Wallace explained. The banks and Teachers' were too confused by joint leadership and wanted a clear understanding of who would be in charge. Wallace had no intention of removing Harrison as chairman or co-chief executive, he said, but Harrison didn't buy it. He told Wallace he should resign for even considering such an offer. "I don't believe it could ever be in the best interests of the shareholders of a family-owned company to have their CEO continue in office while trying to gain control of their own company from them," Harrison said.

Harrison didn't expect Wallace to quit, so he decided to make Wallace an offer for his shares. Surely, Wallace knew he didn't have the support of the family, so maybe he and his family should just sell their shares and leave. Now Harrison faced the same problem Muir had run up against—how much should he offer? Harrison could match Wallace's offer of $55 a share, but why go that high? Harrison had the family in his corner—Wallace might be forced to accept a lot less. After getting some advice from Goldman Sachs & Co. in New York, Harrison and the others started drafting a bid. Wallace was offered $40 a share, half down and half over a fifteen-year period. It was a $374-million offer. Harrison also wanted a five-year agreement committing Wallace not to work for any company that competed with McCain Foods.

Wallace wasn't biting. Not only was it $15 a share lower than his bid, but he feared the deal would cripple McCain. Wallace had financed his offer outside the company, but Harrison would be using company money to pay off Wallace. Under Harrison's offer, Wallace calculated that the company's debt would soar from $796 million to $1.17 billion. The extra interest costs alone would cut McCain's profits to $48 million. After rejecting Harrison's offer, Wallace said he would consider dropping his own bid for control on one condition: "All you have to do, Harrison, is tell me I'm not going to get fired, and this conversation is all over and the problem is all over," he said.

Wallace knew that wouldn't happen. With his offer rejected

and Harrison committed to pushing for a successor to take over within a year, Wallace felt he had no option. He had to go to court. He realized that a lawsuit would bring the feud out into the public, and that worried him almost more than the legal action itself. Wallace had shied away from the media and hadn't granted an interview in nearly twenty-five years. The press would have a field day with the feud and turn the McCains into a soap opera. Margaret wasn't as concerned. She felt media attention was the only way the real truth about what was going on would come out. At the very least, she thought, the public would realize that there was another McCain brother.

Jack Petch suggested the family consider hiring a public relations firm to give them advice on how to handle the media. Hill and Knowlton in Toronto was one of the biggest and it had a reputation for playing hard ball. Petch called and spoke to John Lute, a former business reporter who had been with the firm only a short while. Petch didn't give Lute many details of what Wallace was up to, but he asked Lute to meet the family, who were in Toronto for a short time.

Lute didn't know much about the McCains and he'd never heard of Wallace. As he caught the elevator to Wallace's suite in the Four Seasons Hotel, he tried to guess what the McCains were after. Wallace answered the door, and Lute was greeted by Michael and Scott and their sister Eleanor. Margaret joined them shortly afterwards, and for the next three hours, the family gave Lute a summary of what had been going on over the last thirty years and explained the circumstances surrounding the upcoming lawsuit. By the time he got back to his office, Lute's head was spinning from information overload, and he still wasn't really sure what the family wanted him to do. No one knew when the case would be launched. Everything was on hold for a few months while Wallace and Harrison haggled over share prices. In the meantime, Lute decided that Wallace could use some media training. "I asked him what his relationship with the media was like," remembers Lute. "He said, 'It's okay, but I get myself into trouble.'" Lute suggested they try a few practice interviews just to see. Lute played the reporter and fired a series of tough questions at Wallace. He fumbled nearly every answer, giving long, rambling responses that sometimes contained so much information he hurt his own cause.

As he worked with Wallace, Lute was astounded that none of the family's problems had ever leaked out to the media. Even close company colleagues had no idea what was going on. During a particularly angry spell in the spring of 1993, Harrison and Wallace were nominated to the Canadian Business Hall of Fame. Both were invited to attend a gala dinner in Toronto during which they would be presented with the honour together. Both agreed to attend the event. At the time the only communication between Wallace and Harrison was in memos and through lawyers. Wallace went to the dinner straight from a meeting with his lawyers and Lute to prepare the lawsuit against Harrison and the other family members. "It was strange," recalls Lute. "Here he was plotting all day against Harrison and all of a sudden he says, 'I've got to go to some awards dinner with Harrison.'"

Any one of the 1,200 people attending the dinner would have been convinced that Wallace and Harrison were the best of partners and enjoying the pinnacle of their success. They sat near each other and had their picture taken together with the award. Both were beaming. There was no hint of the bitter struggle that was being waged between them over the future of McCain. Fittingly, the date of the awards presentation was April 1.

While Wallace prepared for the legal fight, Harrison was also meeting with a public relations consultant. Harrison didn't know Wallace was planning a lawsuit, but he was certain the family would end up in court and he wanted to be ready for any public attacks by Wallace. Harrison hired Pat McGee of OEB International Ltd. in Toronto and told him to develop a reactive strategy. Harrison did not want to get into a mud-slinging match with Wallace. His side would react to whatever Wallace did, nothing more. McGee worked with Andrew and Mark for a few days and they settled on a game plan of waiting and watching.

Harrison was also meeting regularly with his lawyers and Andrew to come up with another board resolution to speed up the succession process. Harrison was moving so quickly that he appeared to ignore Andrew altogether at times, even though

Andrew was chairman of the family board. Some letters Andrew was supposed to sign were drafted and sent to lawyers negotiating with Wallace without Andrew's knowledge. Allison, meanwhile, was working on some of the outside directors, and he found some support. Kendall Cork told Allison that if Wallace didn't sell his shares something would have to be done. "We need to make some 'decisions.'" Cork told Allison. He added that "we should...pay Michael three and a half years and be done with it."

By the end of May, Harrison had upped his offer to Wallace. McCain would pay $46 a share. It was a $430-million offer, but Wallace again turned it down.

As the brothers haggled over share prices and plotted legal strategy, the outside directors made a suggestion. Since the January board meeting, the directors had become confused about what they were supposed to be doing. Should they be looking for someone to take over from both brothers in a matter of months, or would Wallace still be around for many more years? In a memo to Harrison and Wallace, the outside directors suggested that both brothers step down and take non-executive roles. The outside directors would then find a new CEO for McCain without any input from the family board. The proposal went nowhere. Harrison could never accept a succession plan that took the family out of the decision-making process. And Wallace didn't want to leave his job, period.

With the directors' proposal rejected, the brothers continued their bickering and scheming into June. Then, just when everyone expected the battle to head to court, they were called on to put aside their differences and deal with a crisis, as a family.

Harrison's wife Billie had kept herself apart from the feud in the family. Once her children had grown up and moved away, Billie had returned to her one great passion—art. She started an art competition at the Beaverbrook Gallery in Fredericton and took courses on art and antiques at Sotheby's in London. She spent so much time in London that she bought a small flat there. Now the rheumatoid arthritis she'd been battling for years was preventing her from enjoying her studies and her own painting. She'd been to doctors at the Lahey Clinic and in Fredericton several times for treatment, but by early 1993 the pain was growing worse. Her brother, John McNair, kept telling her to see another doctor. Finally, she checked into a Fredericton hospital for more tests and treatment. She spent four months in and out of hospital trying different medications and hoping something would ease her pain. In June more tests were done, but by now the doctors were concerned about something more serious than arthritis. Billie was told she had ovarian cancer and she didn't have long to live.

"I went to see her on a Tuesday before her tests came back and she said she was planning to go to St. Andrews," said one of Billie's best friends. "On Thursday she got the tests back and she was flown to Halifax for surgery on Friday. It was that sudden."

Everyone in the family was shocked. And, for a moment, they forgot their squabbling and focused on Billie's health. Wallace offered to put all talk of buy-outs and lawsuits on hold until Billie's condition improved. Harrison dropped the negotiations with Wallace and spent weeks with Billie at the hospital as doctors operated and treated her. Six weeks later, Billie returned home, buoyed by the assessment from the surgeons. "The surgery got most of it," remembers her brother, John McNair. "But there was a little bit left, maybe the size of a thumbnail. She had to have chemotherapy in Fredericton for months. It was very hard on the family. But Harrison managed to stay positive. He kept a brave face."

Even Billie's illness couldn't keep the McCains united for long, however. By mid-summer, Harrison and Andrew were back to planning another board resolution while Wallace was finalizing his lawsuit.

In August, Michael and Wallace decided to try a new tactic— publicity. McCain's price-cut in the United States was working well and it had raised the company's profile. Now Michael thought it was time to work on his own image. Why not encourage some press coverage on Michael and Wallace's role in the company? At first the P.R. campaign began primarily in Chicago business magazines and industry publications. Then *Forbes* magazine published a long article on McCain USA, complete with a glowing portrait of Michael. "Impressed by the job his son Michael has done in the U.S.," the article said, "Wallace McCain reportedly wants to anoint him as heir apparent." That article was followed two weeks later by a two-page feature in *The Financial Post*. The article included the first interview with Wallace in twenty-five years. *Post* reporter Eric Reguly had no idea Harrison and Wallace were waging war against one another at the time, but he asked Wallace about succession. The question was brushed aside. "We don't have an heir apparent," was all Wallace said. The publicity campaign went better than Michael had ever expected. If nothing else, he thought, it would drive Harrison mad. Michael even called Reguly to thank him for the story. "I remember him saying he was so happy he would kiss my ass in public," remembers Reguly.

A few days after the *Post* story, Andrew called a family board meeting for August 13. There was only one item of business: a resolution to remove Wallace as president of McCain and name him non-executive vice chairman. Harrison would remain chairman and the only chief executive of McCain until a new CEO was found. Once passed by the board, the resolution would be submitted for approval to all family members as shareholders. If they approved, the changes would take effect on September 30.

Wallace wasn't surprised when he saw the resolution. He'd been expecting it. He also had no doubt the resolution would receive majority support from the family. There wasn't much Wallace could do. He tried to organize some support among the directors of the operating company and found a few allies. Vic Young, one of the outside directors, worried about the effects of the resolution on McCain. A board can't just remove the president, co-founder and one-third owner without causing serious turmoil, he said. Young told Andrew to hold off on the resolution and give the brothers more time to find a solution. But Andrew was tired of waiting. Delay would only make things worse, he told Young.

"I said, 'Well look, Vic, you know, we have been going through this thing for some time. Nothing seems to be happening,'" Andrew said later in recounting the conversation. "'What are you talking about here?' And [Young] said to me,

'Look, I have tried everything I can. I will continue to try it.'"
Young and the other outside directors were "a bit timid in
assisting us with the problem," Andrew added. "I think [Young's]
a bit confused about where his duties really lie. His duties lie
with the interests of the company, not Wallace McCain, not
Harrison McCain, not Andrew McCain."

Wallace tried one final move to hang on to his job. He made
another offer to buy McCain shares, but this time, instead of
offering to buy just enough shares to win majority control,
Wallace proposed buying out every family member. His price
was still $55 a share. Instead of costing him $270 million, the
new offer would take more than $1 billion. Ontario Teachers'
agreed to back the new bid for the same $100 million they'd
pledged for the earlier offer. The Royal Bank was also still prepared to arrange financing. This time Wallace said that if he was
successful, he and Harrison would remain co-chief executives of
McCain. Harrison could also remain chairman. His sons and
Allison would keep their jobs at the company.

The offer caught the other families off guard. Andrew delayed
the board meeting until August 17, but his reaction to the offer
was the same. He wouldn't sell. Neither would Harrison or any
other family member. To all of them it was further evidence of
why Wallace had to go.

"The McCain Group is an asset of the McCain family, [it] is
not for sale as far as I am concerned, and I am told as far as the
families of [Allison's mother] Marjorie McCain and Rosemary
McCain-McMillan are concerned," Harrison wrote Wallace.
"Your latest offer is a further hostile act so far as the family is
concerned, and I believe will strengthen the family's resolve to
get on with the management succession issue."

August 17 was a typical warm summer day in New
Brunswick. The family board meeting was held in Fredericton at
the office of Bruce Eddy, one of the lawyers representing Andrew
and Allison. As tourists strolled through the historic neighbourhood, the McCains sat around a small boardroom table ready to
vote out one of the founders of the company. Peter, Mark,
Andrew, Allison and George McClure were hoping for a quick
meeting with little debate, but Michael and Scott weren't about

to give in that easily. They handed out a three-page statement outlining their opposition to the resolution. "It appears that Harrison McCain [is] exercising his influence over certain members of this board," they said. "We are quite frankly shocked that members of this board would seriously contemplate firing a co-founder of the business on the basis of no evidence of a so-called 'serious management issue.'"

Michael and Scott pointed to the record 1993 profit as proof that removing Wallace made no business sense. McCain's profit had jumped to $76 million by the end of fiscal 1993 from $41.2 million a year earlier. Sales were up nearly 10 percent to $2.9 billion. Even the United States, under Wallace and Michael, was turning around. McCain's 10 percent price-cut on specialty fries was working. Lamb-Weston was matching the price-cut and jacking up its prices on conventional fries, just as Michael had hoped. By early 1993, prices for conventional fries had increased to 32 cents (US) a pound from as low as 26 cents before McCain's announcement. The price-hike boosted McCain's bottom line in the United States. By the end of fiscal 1993, the U.S. division had an operating profit of $3.4 million (US)* compared to a loss of $7.6 million in 1992. Better still, the perennially troubled U.S. French fry business cut its losses to $4.6 million (US) from $15 million.

Their glowing report had no effect. It was too late. Nothing was going to turn the tide now. Just after Michael and Scott finished, Andrew called for a vote. The resolution to remove Wallace McCain as president was approved, five to two.

The next day, Andrew sent other family members a letter explaining the resolution and asking for their consent. "It is the opinion of your board of directors that, in view of the age and health of the two incumbent chief executives and the fact that they cannot agree to work together, action must be taken now to resolve the situation as contemplated by the resolution," he wrote. Excepting Wallace's family, every family member agreed to the resolution. Wallace was now nothing more than a figure-head in the company he had helped to found.

---

*All currency figures relating to U.S. companies are in U.S. dollars.

    Harrison decided to make one final offer for Wallace's shares. "I will recommend as follows," he told Wallace in a handwritten note. "Cash offer $429,571,184. Safe income included: $150,000,000. Value per share recognizing safe income: $53.91 per share. Cash offer per share: $46.00."

    Wallace read the note quickly. He picked up a pen and scrawled across the bottom: "I reject this." Then he called Petch and told him to file the lawsuit.

John Lute sat in Jack Petch's office high above Toronto's King Street reviewing plans for the day with Petch and Alan Lenczner, another lawyer who would handle Wallace's case in court. It was August 23, 1993, and Wallace's thirty-nine-page statement of claim was ready. To keep the other side guessing, it wouldn't be filed in court until just before the Court of Queen's Bench office closed that afternoon in Fredericton. Once the case was filed, Lute was to start calling the media. They all agreed that Wallace needed a good first crack at publicity because no one knew who he was or why he was going to court. "The whole communications strategy was 'Wallace who?'" recalls Lute. "We didn't want him to be seen as a whiney junior partner, he was co-chief executive. We had to get out of the gate early with our story."

    Lute planned to call only a few media outlets, including *The Financial Post, The Globe and Mail,* Southam news and two of the major papers in New Brunswick, *The Daily Gleaner* in Fredericton and *The Telegraph-Journal* in Saint John. Early that afternoon he got the okay from Petch: the papers were filed in the court office. Lute's first call was to the *Post.* He explained the suit briefly to assignment editor Michael Babad and said there would a briefing with Lenczner later that afternoon.

    Just as Lute was about to call the next newspaper on his list, Lenczner's partner Peter Griffin relayed a frantic message. Something went wrong in Fredericton and the papers wouldn't be filed until tomorrow. Lute's face dropped. The *Post* was already on to the story and was making calls around New Brunswick trying to find out what was going on. Lenczner wanted the media called off until Wallace's statement of claim was officially filed in court. It wouldn't look good if Wallace's lawyers were seen leaking court documents before they were properly filed. Lenczner told Lute to call the *Post* and tell them to hold off on the story for a day, but it was too late. News was already spreading across New Brunswick that something was up between the McCain brothers. Lute knew they had to keep going now and he convinced Lenczner to hold a short briefing. Angry at the *Post* for refusing to hold off on the story, Lenczner called Karen Howlett, a reporter in the *Globe's Report on Business* and invited her to the briefing as well.

By the time the meeting was held around 4:30 p.m., Lenczner and Petch had been able to notify the court that the papers would indeed be filed. The boardroom was empty except for two reporters, two lawyers and Lute. A small McCain chocolate cake sat in one corner along with some boxes of McCain juice. Lute handed out a short summary of McCain's history and Lenczner began going over Wallace's statement of claim, in which he characterized the board's resolution as both oppressive and illegal.

Harrison got word of the suit late in the afternoon from his lawyer, who had been served with a copy of the action. He started a barrage of phone calls, including one to Andrew, who was away on a fishing trip and had to be tracked down in the middle of the bush. Andrew rushed back to Woodstock and sent Wallace a letter urging him to reconsider his lawsuit. He then met with his lawyer to figure out what to do. Andrew was petrified about the publicity the suit would cause. He was also worried that Wallace might leak sensitive company information, and that news of the case would threaten his family's safety. His lawyers had a suggestion. Shortly after 7:00 p.m., they called Judge Ronald Stevenson at his home in Fredericton. They told Stevenson about Andrew's concerns and asked if they could request a publicity ban on Wallace's suit. Stevenson agreed to hold an impromptu hearing in his chambers that night and told them to tell David Hashey, Wallace's local lawyer. Before heading over to Stevenson's office, Hashey called Petch in Toronto to tell him about Andrew's request. Petch and Lenczner laughed. There was no way a judge would grant a publication ban, they said.

As Hashey took a chair in Stevenson's office, he went over

Andrew's affidavit. "I believe that the sensitive information disclosed in the statement of claim exposes the members of the McCain family to public scrutiny and associated potential risk to their personal safety," Andrew said. "I humbly request that the court file in this action be sealed and publication of any information concerning this action be prohibited until members of the McCain family are able to make security arrangements for the safely of their families."

The hearing lasted less than an hour. Incredibly, Stevenson agreed to the request and issued an order banning any reporting on the case. He also barred all public access to Wallace's statement of claim. Andrew's lawyer faxed a copy of the handwritten ruling to Harrison's media consultant, Pat McGee. He frantically began calling *The Financial Post* and *The Globe and Mail* and faxed them a copy of the ruling only minutes before their final deadlines. The ruling forced both papers to withhold details of the suit in their stories. But it didn't matter. News that the McCain brothers were suing dominated media across the country. By the next day, the *Globe* and *Post* had figured out a way around the ban. The ruling applied only to New Brunswick, which meant that media outside the province were free to report on the case in detail. The *Post* and the *Globe* started running detailed stories about the suit in editions outside New Brunswick. Papers sold in the province either had the story removed or contained a more general report. But the ban couldn't stop New Brunswickers from hearing details of the suit on national television and radio. Local reporters were also getting faxed copies of stories from out-of-province newspapers. It was a ludicrous arrangement, and commentators across the country denounced the publicity ban as a move by a judge to protect the powerful. The *Post,* the *Globe* and the CBC also hired lawyers to fight the ban in court.

On August 26, three days after the ban was ordered, Stevenson lifted it. In a short ruling, he explained that it was only meant as a temporary measure to allow Andrew to make some security arrangements. Stevenson also took a shot at the press, which had ridiculed him for days. "Freedom of expression and freedom of the press do not guarantee freedom of access to information," he said. In general, he added, it is unfair for reporters to have access to one side of a lawsuit before the other side has had a chance to file a defence.

As soon as the ban was lifted, Lute sent Wallace's statement of claim far and wide. To counter him, McGee drafted a statement for Harrison: "As successful as we have been at running this business the last thirty-five years the fact remains that Wallace and I are two businessmen in our sixties sitting atop a three-billion-dollar global enterprise that is in great shape. To make sure that it stays that way in the future, we need to find a new CEO to take over. It's time for transition. There are lots of reasons. Three families that include most of the shareholders think so. Wallace's family has a different opinion. I have reconciled myself to changing my role in the company. I think it's time Wallace did too."

While the media blitz continued, Wallace and Harrison prepared for the coming court case. Wallace's suit was complex. He argued that the family board's resolution removing him as co-chief executive was oppressive to him as a director and shareholder of McCain Foods. He also challenged the family board's authority, saying it didn't have the power to kick him out: the proposal that had created the board was never officially incorporated into the company by-laws. He added that there was no business reason to force him out of his job. McCain's profits had never been higher, and the businesses that he ran were on track to break more records. Wallace also asked for an injunction barring the August 17 resolution from taking effect until a trial was held. If he won that trial, Wallace suggested the court order McCain Foods divided along geographic lines or sold.

In his statement of defence, Harrison reiterated that it was Wallace's appointment of Michael that had caused all of the problems. "From the day Wallace appointed Michael as CEO of the U.S. operations to this day, an atmosphere of distrust, intrigue and manoeuvring has existed." He argued the board's resolution was not oppressive because the directors were acting in the interests of the majority of shareholders. The board was created to represent the shareholders, Harrison said, and it had the right to fire both brothers.

A hearing on Wallace's suit was set for September 23 in Fredericton, with Justice Ronald Stevenson presiding. In the meantime, both brothers began lining up supporters inside and outside the company. Harrison got supporting affidavits from Andrew, Peter, Mark, George McClure, Mac McCarthy, Allison and his sister Linda. Each said that the board was only abiding by the wishes of the family, who wanted the feuding between Wallace and Harrison to stop.

Wallace had no family support other than his own. But he knew there were people in the company that backed him, and he needed them to come forward now. One of Wallace's first calls was to Archie McLean.

McLean was at a McCain sales conference in Quebec when Wallace called. He had tried to stay out of the dispute between the brothers. For his own protection, he'd even started making notes after every meeting with Harrison or Wallace. "It was crazy, no way to run a business," McLean later recalled. "But it was gang warfare."

Wallace asked McLean to read over some of the affidavits filed by Harrison's side. Most said the feud was hurting the company's operations. McLean didn't understand what they were talking about. McCain Foods was enjoying record profits and he hadn't seen any operational problems. "I thought [the affidavits] were out in left field about the impact on company operations," remembers McLean. "I wrote an affidavit that day expressing Wallace's contribution to the company. I called every vice president that reports to me and said, 'I would like to say you support me,' and they all agreed."

Wallace rounded up other executives, including John Clements, who ran McCain's Australian operations, and Alden Lunn, manager of the company's field department and Wallace's friend since childhood. Other supporting affidavits came from the heads of the U.S. divisions, as well as the presidents of McCain Fertilizer, Thomas Equipment and McCain's meat business in Quebec, called Bilopage Inc. They all said that the problems between Harrison and Wallace had not affected their operations. Wallace hoped that the affidavits would help strengthen his argument that there was no business reason to let him go.

A week before the hearing, both camps set up in Fredericton. Nearly two dozen lawyers, many from some of Toronto's top law firms, descended on the city with teams of advisers and assistants. So many lawyers showed up that court officials had to move the hearing from the Court of Queen's Bench in the city's main courthouse to a federal courtroom a few blocks away, because it had more chairs. Wallace's side set up shop in the Sheraton Hotel. Harrison's team stayed across town at the Lord Beaverbrook Hotel.

A few days before the hearing was to start, Thomas O'Neil, a lawyer for Harrison's sons Mark and Peter, got a call from New Brunswick Premier Frank McKenna. The Premier offered to help Wallace and Harrison negotiate a settlement. McCain Foods was one of New Brunswick's largest employers, and McKenna knew there was a risk that the lawsuit could result in the company being divided or sold, and possibly moving out of the province. He wanted both sides to try one last attempt at an out-of-court settlement. McKenna suggested representatives from each side meet. He would be available to help keep the peace.

Wallace sent Petch and Tom Muir. Harrison sent Gary Girvan, a lawyer representing Mark and Peter, and Fred McElman, a lawyer representing Andrew. They met McKenna in his office. "He said, 'Guys, this should never go to court,'" recalls Girvan. "Here's my home phone number. We've got a place in Kingsclear for you to go to and a retired judge to sit as a mediator. Good luck.'"

The four headed off to the Mactaquac Inn, a resort outside Fredericton that had been booked by McKenna's office. They met for the next four days. The negotiations centred around finding an acceptable price for Wallace's shares. Although Wallace had offered to buy the others' shares for $55 a share, he now wanted far more. Muir argued that the shares were worth more because the company's profits had jumped 85 percent to $76 million in 1993. At one point, Wallace wanted as much as $75 a share for his block, or $700 million. Girvan was prepared to get close to $55 a share but no higher. Both sides also talked about splitting the company. Wallace was still insisting on a geographic split but Harrison was opposed. He would consider giving Wallace a few plants but no French fry operations. The day before the hearing was to begin, the talks ended where they'd begun, with no settlement, and both sides headed back to their hotels.

With no deal in sight, Wallace came under intense pressure to settle the dispute in a private hearing. Company executives, including Archie McLean, urged Wallace not to go ahead with a public trial but to consider a private arbitration. Harrison's side had suggested the idea earlier but Wallace had refused. He and his family felt that a public trial was the only way to guarantee that their side would be heard. A private trial would only keep everything hidden, and Wallace was tired of sacrificing everything to the McCain family code of secrecy.

The night before the hearing was to begin, Wallace and his family sat around the living room of their suite debating the idea of a private hearing once again. Wallace was having second thoughts, and Lenczner and Petch were pushing him towards it. Finally, late that night, Wallace asked Margaret. She was aching to say no. She knew an open trial would be difficult for the family, but it was the only way the public could ever come to understand what had been going on inside the family for years. On the other hand, she could also see the strain the past few months had caused Wallace, Michael, Scott and her daughters. Even some of her close friends were telling her not to push for a public trial. Margaret turned to Wallace and nodded. "Yes," she said.

The next morning, Petch called Girvan and the two met for breakfast at 7:00 a.m. Petch offered to withdraw Wallace's suit and hold a private hearing before a judge. Girvan was exasperated. He'd been pushing for a private hearing for weeks, and Petch had refused. Now, on the day of the hearing, Petch had changed his mind. "No chance," Girvan said. "We're ready to go, it's too late."

By 9:00 a.m., the main courtroom in the Federal Court building was packed. Reporters pulled in chairs from other courtrooms and the security guards left the courtroom doors open so onlookers could watch from the foyer. Harrison and Wallace sat on opposite sides of the room surrounded by their families and lawyers. While the brothers waited for the hearing to begin, lawyers bustled in and out, still trying to see if the case could be dropped and settled in private. Girvan was still refusing but was willing to talk. "This is crazy," Wallace said with a laugh as he watched a pack of lawyers scurry from one room to another trying to pin down a deal.

With just minutes to go before the hearing was to start, McCain Foods lawyer, John Campion, asked for an adjournment for one day. There was still some room for negotiation, he told Judge Stevenson. The adjournment was granted and a stream of lawyers and family members headed to hotels and law offices throughout Fredericton's downtown. By late afternoon, everyone had agreed to a private hearing, but they still had to work out the terms. Who would be the arbitrator? How would the hearing be structured? What would be included? What about an appeal process?

Harrison's side wanted the arbitration over quickly and they pushed to have everything finished by the end of October. Wallace wanted a commitment that the board wouldn't take any action to remove him until the hearing was complete. Then, just before 9:00 p.m., Lenczner and Petch walked over to meet Harrison's lawyers with yet another revised draft. When more objections were raised, Lenczner and Petch walked out in exasperation. "It's up to you," Lenczner said gruffly as he walked briskly out of the office. He and Petch hailed a taxi to return to the Sheraton Hotel to meet Wallace. "We're going for a drink," Lenczner said as he got in the cab.

A few minutes later, Campion arrived in the lobby of the Sheraton with an agreement. Lenczner came out of the dining room to meet him. "Let's sign it here, right here on this table," Lenczner said laughing and pointing to a coffee table. Campion shook his head and headed for an elevator with Lenczner trailing behind. They returned a few minutes later and Campion announced to the lingering handful of reporters that an agreement for a private hearing had been struck.

The hearing would be conducted like a private trial, with a judge borrowed from the provincial government. The issues considered would be the same as those raised in Wallace's lawsuit—

oppression of Wallace as a minority shareholder. The McCains would pay all the costs of the hearing except the judge's salary. There would be no change to Wallace's position while the hearing was underway, but the company would continue its process of finding a successor.

The next day everyone filed back into court to officially withdraw Wallace's suit and present the terms of the arbitration. Judge Stevenson agreed and in less than five minutes dismissed the case.

Wallace invited Petch, Lenczner and Muir to his home in Florenceville for dinner. They piled into Wallace's green Jaguar for the ninety-minute trip. A few kilometres outside Fredericton, Wallace saw flashing lights in his rear-view mirror. "Dammit," he said. "The police." He pulled over, rolled down the window and waited for the officer to walk up to the window. Wallace knew he was way over the speed limit and resigned himself to paying yet another speeding ticket. But just as the officer was about to write out the ticket, he took a second look at Wallace. "You're Wallace McCain, aren't you?" he said. "Yes," replied Wallace. "You've got enough problems," the cop said, tearing up the ticket.

As both sides prepared their case for the arbitration, Arden Haynes, the chairman of the committee of outside directors, was getting fed up with his position on the board. The succession process he'd been hired to help oversee was at a standstill and the family was about to spend the next few months in court. Tired of the feuding and the legal wrangling, Haynes resigned from the board. The battling "just absolutely paralysed the company and I didn't want to sit there while that was going on," he recalled. "The company is going to continue to progress nevertheless, but there wasn't much of a role for a director at that point. I just didn't feel that the board of directors could be that effective under those circumstances. [McCain] has got a good strong organization out in the field. My concern was to hopefully get the thing settled quickly before some serious damage might be done."

The arbitration began on January 10, 1994, with Judge Ronald Stevenson hearing the case. Everyone had agreed on the choice of Stevenson because he was already somewhat familiar with the issues. The McCains rented the entire 166-room Wu Conference Centre at the University of New Brunswick for the hearing. Wallace again set up his team in a top-floor suite at the Sheraton. "We called it Camp McCain," remembers Margaret. Wallace even moved his dog Zack into the hotel. His daughter Eleanor flew out from Toronto and attended the hearing daily along with Michael and Scott. Margaret also moved into the hotel but decided to stay away from the Wu Centre. She couldn't face the tension and anger that she knew she would feel if she sat there listening to Harrison, Andrew, Allison and the others. Most of Harrison's team stayed at the Lord Beaverbrook Hotel. Harrison spent most evenings in Florenceville and flew in daily for the hearing. His wife, Billie, was in and out of hospital. Her condition was serious. Wallace asked Harrison if he wanted to delay the hearing, but Harrison wanted to get the whole thing over with. It became a cruel irony: while dozens of lawyers wrestled over issues of money, power and control that would end up tearing the family apart, Billie was quietly and courageously facing imminent death from cancer just a few blocks away at the Everett Chalmers Hospital.

Wallace was the first to testify and he spent over a week on the stand. His lawyers had to prove Wallace's oppression claim and convince Judge Stevenson that dividing or selling the company was the best solution. To make their case, Wallace's lawyers introduced a stack of expert evidence. They spent $500,000 on a study of McCain Foods by management consultants at McKinsey and Co. Accountants at Peat Marwick did detailed valuations of McCain shares, and David Donnan, a Toronto-based food industry consultant, did a major review of McCain's operations.

The experts and the studies were all designed to back Wallace's contention that McCain could be split in half. Wallace suggested that he take McCain's North American and Australian businesses as well as Day & Ross and Thomas Equipment. Harrison could have the European and British businesses as well as Asia and McCain Produce. It was a similar division to the way the brothers had run McCain for nearly twenty years. Both companies would use the McCain brand name in their region.

However, if either brother tried to expand into the other's territory, he would have to use another brand name. Both companies
would also share space in the existing head office in
Florenceville. Each could hire his own financial, legal and tax
help, or they might agree to share some of those services. The
two companies could also have joint purchasing agreements for
products such as juice concentrate. Co-operation agreements
might also be arranged to allow each side access to the other's
factories or research and development. Each brother would own
two-thirds of his company and one third of the other.

The split was the only practical way to solve the brothers'
feud, Wallace's lawyers argued. It was also the least painful. The
McKinsey report concluded that dividing the company would
cost only about $1.3 million a year, primarily in the duplication
of head office functions.

Wallace also reiterated his earlier proposal for a shotgun sale.
As a final solution, Wallace suggested that his and Harrison's
McCain shares could be put up for an auction. Muir put the
value of McCain shares at $82.50 a share, or $2.3 billion for all
of the family's shares.

Harrison's side rejected all of the options. His lawyers argued
that there was no oppression and, therefore, no need to consider
any of Wallace's suggestions. Even if the suggestions were considered, they were unworkable. For example, dividing the company
wasn't as easy as it sounded. Harrison's long-time friend Sir
Graham Day, former chairman of Britain's Cadbury Schweppes
PLC, testified that McCain worked best as a whole. Splitting it
in half would only weaken both sides and deteriorate the company's strong brand name. Roger Martin of the Monitor
Company, a management consulting group hired by Harrison's
lawyers, also said that Wallace's half would have a big advantage
under the split because he would own the American market,
which was the most lucrative French fry market in the world.
According to Martin, if Wallace's business became competitive in
the United States it would use that competitive advantage elsewhere against Harrison's company.

Lenczner scoffed at the testimony of Martin and Day. The
Monitor group had only spent a few weeks at McCain and

hadn't talked to any regional CEOs, he argued. And Day had only spent six days at the company, most of which involved talking to lawyers.

As the arbitration dragged on, tensions flared. At one point, Lenczner met Harrison at the Beaverbrook to discuss a possible settlement. After the meeting, Wallace and Margaret gave Lenczner a ride back to the Sheraton in Margaret's black BMW. Lenczner got in the back and started briefing them on what Harrison had said while Margaret drove. Lenczner started explaining how sorry Harrison felt that everything had been dragged into court. "He really cares for you," Lenczner told Wallace. "He's trying to do what is best for the family." Margaret nearly drove the car off the road. "Fucking hell!" she screamed as she pounded her fist on the steering wheel. "That bastard is now turning you against Wallace!"

The brothers met only once after that to try for a settlement, but no deal was reached. Another attempt was made by Allison, who told Michael that Wallace could keep his job but Michael would have to go. Michael turned the offer down.

Wallace's sister Eleanor also called and urged him to give up the lawsuit. Eleanor had always been close to both brothers. She was like them in many ways—shrewd, active and constantly on the move. But Eleanor had always treated Harrison with particular deference. He was her older brother, and she saw Harrison as the family leader. As problems mounted between Wallace and Harrison, Eleanor began to distance herself from Wallace's family.

By the time of the arbitration, Eleanor just wanted all the problems to end. "Just resign and do what Harrison wants," she told Wallace. "It isn't so bad." Wallace was angry and snapped back, "Don't choose, Eleanor. If you choose you're going to lose one of us." Wallace didn't talk to Eleanor again for ten months. When they next saw her, Eleanor was battling a brain tumour and had only weeks to live.

Ironically, McCain Foods had one of its biggest business breakthroughs during the arbitration. Every day while the hearing went on, Michael and other McCain officials worked on the negotiations with McDonald's over construction of a $25-million plant in Argentina. Three years earlier, McDonald's had approached McCain about the project because of the company's success at international expansion. Wallace and Harrison had been leery at first, because they knew McDonald's would want a joint, open-book arrangement, but the opportunity was too good to pass up.

As the arbitration wound down, McCain and McDonald's finalized the project. In return for building the plant, McCain would receive an eight-year exclusive agreement to supply McDonald's restaurants in Chile, Brazil, Argentina and Uruguay. The contract included guaranteed returns for McCain. "It's a goldmine," Michael said later. Indeed, McDonald's accounted for 40 percent of the total French fry consumption in those four countries, and now it was all McCain's business. McCain had been thinking about expanding into South America for years but had shied away because of political and economic instability. Now McDonald's had led them in.

The arbitration ended on March 21, 1994, and Judge Stevenson promised a ruling by April 22. It had taken six months and cost the family more than $10 million. As they headed home, Wallace and Margaret felt a tremendous relief. No matter which way it went, at least the ruling would finally end the turmoil.

Harrison, Andrew and Allison were also confident. No New Brunswick judge, they felt, would split McCain Foods. And no judge would second-guess the will of company shareholders. At last, Harrison could also spend some time with his wife Billie. Harrison had bought a hospital bed and set it up in the living room at home in Florenceville so that Billie could look out over the valley.

Just after the hearing ended, Billie called one of her close friends and asked her to come over for tea. "I thought she was doing really well and that this was a tea party she'd arranged," said the friend. "But when I got there, I was the only one there. She looked weak and I was really sad to see her looking so bad. She said, 'I think I'm doing better.'"

As they sat drinking tea, Billie talked about how much she enjoyed the view of the river, the farmland and the rolling hills. She also said, now that the arbitration hearing was finally over, she and Harrison planned to go to Bermuda at Easter. Billie died a few days later on March 30, 1994. It was less than two weeks after the arbitration hearing and only three days before the Easter weekend.

Her funeral was held on Good Friday. The tiny Anglican church in Florenceville was packed and the front seats were lined with dignitaries, including Frank McKenna, B.C. business tycoon Jim Pattison, J.K. and J.D. Irving, Bank of Nova Scotia CEO Cedric Ritchie and former Nova Scotia premier Gerald Regan.

Marilyn Strong, Harrison's secretary, greeted mourners as they entered the church and showed them to their assigned seats. Wallace, Margaret and their children were assigned seats at the back of the church. As Margaret sat down, she felt embarrassed. She had played the organ in this church for more than thirty years, it had been a second home. Now here she was feeling uncomfortable and unwanted. But like the rest of her family, Margaret was anxious to keep a low profile. Emotions between the families were raw and Wallace and Margaret did not want the bitterness to detract from Billie's funeral. Before the funeral, Wallace had gone to the bishop presiding over the service and asked for his guidance. The bishop suggested that, given the circumstances, Wallace's family should attend the church service but not the committal or the reception. The day before the service, Margaret arranged a bouquet of apricot-coloured roses, Billie's favourite, and took them to the funeral home where Billie was resting. It was Margaret's way of privately paying her respects.

During the service the bishop spoke eloquently of Billie. He had spent many hours with her in her final days. Then Billie's youngest daughter, Gillian, read a poem. As she listened, Margaret thought about Billie's life, which had been dedicated to Harrison from the day they were married in 1952. Billie had been the hostess for countless McCain parties and raised her children alone while Harrison worked non-stop building McCain Foods. She had always been something of an enigma to Margaret, and few people had ever been able to get close to her. Margaret searched the main body of the church in vain for Billie's closest friends but couldn't see them. Where was Sally Baxter? Margaret wondered. She had been Billie's friend since childhood. Where was Sheila McCarthy? She and her husband Mac had vacationed with Billie and Harrison every year for thirty years. Where was Carole Regan, another old friend? These were the people who really knew Billie. They should be in the main body of the church.

Margaret stared at Billie's pallbearers as they carried her coffin. It saddened her to think that even in death it was Harrison's identity Billie assumed, not her own. Four of the six men who carried Billie's casket—George McClure, Tony van Leersum, Paul Dean, Don Young—were former or current McCain Foods executives. The other two—former Trudeau aide Jim Coutts and Bank of Montreal vice president Dick O'Hagan—were friends Harrison had met through McCain. There was nothing personal about the funeral, Margaret thought, nothing private, nothing that spoke about Billie, her life, her work, her joys, her sadness. It was, like so many events in Billie's life, yet another tribute to Harrison's great achievements and personal power.

CHAPTER NINETEEN

Wallace sat nervously with his family in a small law office in Fredericton. It was April 20, 1994, and Wallace was waiting for his lawyers to bring back Stevenson's ruling, two days early. Wallace's lawyers, Alan Lenczner and Jack Petch, had been gone a long time. Maybe Stevenson called them in for some discussion.

Finally, the door opened and Lenczner and Petch walked in. "Uh-oh," Wallace thought as he looked up at them.

"We've got some good news and some bad news," Lenczner said as he handed Wallace a copy of the 110-page ruling.

As he read through it, Wallace couldn't see much good news. Stevenson had rejected Wallace's argument that Harrison and the family board were treating him unfairly. And he hadn't even considered the proposed division of McCain that Wallace's lawyers and advisers had spent months, and millions, preparing.

"On the whole of the evidence I cannot find that either the preferred shares or common shares of [McCain] will be adversely affected by the removal of Wallace McCain from his present role. On the facts as they now exist it is neither reasonable nor legitimate for Wallace McCain to expect to continue as a co-CEO with Harrison McCain," Stevenson wrote. "I find that neither the directors nor the shareholders of [the family board] acted in bad faith or that they or any of them were unduly influenced by Harrison McCain."

The only bright spot for Wallace was that Stevenson had ruled that the resolution to remove Wallace was technically invalid. Under the company's by-laws, the family board did not have the power to remove senior officers; that could only be done by the operating board. The ruling meant that Wallace would get his job back. But not for long. Stevenson also said the family could simply change its by-laws to give the family board authority to remove executives. However, Stevenson added that if Wallace was demoted to a non-executive position, he was entitled to a seat on the operating board and his full salary. The reference to salary irritated Wallace. "He thinks this is about money," he said angrily. "That's not it at all. He's missed the point."

After Wallace had reviewed the ruling, Lenczner handed him a seven-page personal letter Stevenson had written to both brothers. Wallace was surprised by the letter, as were Lenczner and Petch. Judges didn't normally offer long written rulings and then send personal letters with their own thoughts on a case. Even Stevenson conceded in the letter that it might be inappropriate. "But I am concerned about the future of the McCain business," Stevenson wrote.

In the letter, Stevenson said he didn't see any hope of Harrison or Wallace working together again. He suggested they both resign as McCain's joint chief executives but remain as directors. The outside directors should then find a new CEO. He also criticized the company's two-board system. It "has not worked and will not work for McCain." He suggested a single eleven-member board made up of Harrison, Wallace, one child from each of the four families, the CEO and four outsiders. The children should not be employees of the company but should include daughters and nieces as "the women in the family should be considered as well as the men. Eleven of the eighteen members of the second generation are women," he said, referring to the children of Wallace, Harrison, Andrew and Robert but ignoring the five children of Marie and Eleanor.

Stevenson also suggested the company consider a public share offering: "...the presence and influence of non-family shareholders, like the non-family directors, would act as a restraint on inter- and intra-family disputes."

Wallace was frustrated as he read the letter. It offered suggestions that he had been fighting for for years. He had always opposed the two-board system and was a strong proponent of McCain making a public share offering. But since Stevenson's letter wasn't part of his official ruling, his proposals carried no weight.

That evening Wallace and his family met in their suite at the Sheraton for dinner. The family was dejected. The ruling solved nothing. It only restarted the process of removing Wallace. And, while Stevenson's letter offered a viable solution, it wouldn't be taken seriously. "It was an emotional dinner," recalls Wallace's daughter Eleanor. "We were prepared for anything, any solution. But we weren't prepared for a ruling that solved nothing."

David MacNaughton, CEO of Hill and Knowlton and a Liberal Party strategist, joined the family for dinner that night. He had taken over as public relations consultant from John Lute. MacNaughton wasn't ready to concede defeat yet. He suggested they go on a publicity offensive. At the very least, the ruling gave Wallace his job back and a seat on the company board, so in that way it was a victory. Calls went out that night to the media. The strategy worked. Stories the next day in several papers focused on Wallace getting his job back. To readers, it appeared Wallace had won.

Harrison was furious. Not only was the ruling supposed to be confidential, but Wallace was leaking only part of the story. Harrison decided to ignore the reports and focus on his next move.

The ruling was clear: the shareholders had the right to remove Wallace. Within a few days of the decision, Harrison and Andrew called in their lawyers and got to work on changing the company's by-laws.

Wallace knew it was just a matter of time. But what were his options? There was no hope of making another bid for shares and he was running out of legal angles. With nothing to lose, Wallace and his lawyers seized on Stevenson's letter. Wallace said he would agree to step down, but only after the company scrapped the two-board system and made a public share offering. The share offering was more important to Wallace now, because he felt it was the only way he could get fair value for his McCain shares.

Harrison wasn't interested in the idea. "As I have told you, I believe the lack of confidence and trust between us precludes us continuing as co-Chief Executives for any extended period of time. I have no time for a single board system in this family company. I unequivocally support the present two board system," he told Wallace in a letter. Harrison added that he would only consider a public share offering if Wallace sold some of his shares at the time of the offering. That way, Wallace couldn't mount a takeover bid as a one-third owner.

Wallace was getting more and more dejected. He kept up his usual gruelling pace at the company but his interest was waning. He started thinking about selling his shares to Harrison at almost any price, just to get out. Convinced it was his only option, Wallace went to see Tom Muir in Toronto to talk about a deal.

"Forget it," Muir said bluntly. "You'll never get a fair price from Harrison. Learn to live with keeping your stake in McCain and finding something else to do." But Muir could see how despondent Wallace was becoming and he decided now was the time to start coming up with some new projects.

During the arbitration Muir had told Wallace and Michael that the majority owner of Maple Leaf Foods Inc. might be interested in selling the business. It was déjà vu for Wallace. Maple Leaf's predecessor was Canada Packers, the company Wallace and Harrison took a run at in the late 1970s only to be shut out by the McLean family, which controlled the company at the time. Muir was familiar with Maple Leaf because he had worked on the purchase of Canada Packers in 1990 by a British conglomerate called Hillsdown Holdings PLC. Hillsdown now owned 45.3 million shares, representing 56 percent of the company. Maple Leaf's sales were now over $3 billion annually and it had been turning a consistent profit of around $75 million a year. But the company had become much more diverse. Along with meat processing, Maple Leaf now had a chain of doughnut shops called Country Style Donuts; a line of bakery products, including Dempster's, Homestead and Baker's Choice; a range of seafood products; and majority control of Corporate Foods Ltd., a frozen-food business.

Now that Wallace was sure he'd soon be forced out of McCain, his interest was piqued by the possibility of buying another company. Muir told Wallace they couldn't make an offer for Maple Leaf until they'd figured out how to structure a bid and lined up some financing. Muir didn't want Wallace to sell any of his McCain shares to pay for Maple Leaf. The bid would have to be arranged in a way that would give Wallace the best of both worlds—continued involvement in McCain, as a shareholder and director, and a new company for Wallace to run. The only problem was financing. Muir knew it would take at least $1 billion to take over Maple Leaf, and if Wallace didn't sell his McCain shares, where would he get the money?

Muir decided to make another call to George Engman at Ontario Teachers'. Muir knew Engman was sold on Wallace as a manager and might be interested in working with him on another deal. Muir, Michael and Engman went for lunch at an Italian restaurant in downtown Toronto to talk about Maple Leaf. Engman was intrigued and said he would think it over. Two weeks later, he called Muir and said he was in. Now the bid was starting to look feasible. Wallace's future was shaping up after all.

A week after Stevenson's ruling, Margaret was working in her garden when the phone rang. It was the Prime Minister's Office. Prime Minister Jean Chrétien wanted to know if Margaret was interested in becoming Lieutenant-Governor of New Brunswick. She was stunned by the offer. Wallace wasn't. In the last eight years, while serving as chancellor of Mount Allison University, Margaret had become actively involved in a host of non-profit causes, especially agencies that helped battered women. Margaret hesitated. She wasn't sure if she should take on anything so major when her family was in such turmoil. How could she assume such a high-profile position in the province when she doubted Wallace would be at McCain, and in Florenceville, much longer? Wallace's plan to bid for Maple Leaf meant moving to Toronto, where the company was based. And if that offer didn't work out, Wallace was thinking about moving to the United States where there were more opportunities in the food industry. Wallace urged Margaret to take the position. "There wasn't any question about her being able to do it," Wallace recalled. "I pressed her to take it because I knew she could do it easily. But it was no sure-fire deal that she would accept it."

Their children also urged Margaret to take on the job. "We all told her this kind of opportunity doesn't come around very often and she should take it," says her daughter Eleanor. Margaret agreed but vowed to relinquish the role if she ever felt it was compromising her family. She also promised to donate her salary to the Muriel McQueen Fergusson Centre for Family Violence Research.

Margaret was officially installed as Lieutenant-Governor on June 21, but she refused to invite Harrison, Andrew or many other family members to the event. "Not one of them offered any congratulations," she said. "So I said 'Forget them.'" To Harrison and the others, it was a slight they would never forget.

Over the spring and summer, Muir kept working on the Maple Leaf bid. By mid summer, he was ready to see if Hillsdown was interested in what he had to offer. The answer was no. Plans had changed and the shares were no longer for sale. It was a stunning setback. Muir had spent weeks lining up financing and laying the groundwork for a bid. Now all bets were off. Wallace was discouraged. But he had accepted the idea of trying to find another company to buy while still keeping his McCain shares, and he told Muir to look for another opportunity. "As the summer went on, Wallace began thinking, for the first time, about a new life away from McCain," recalls Muir. Wallace was even thinking about moving to Toronto and he asked his daughter Eleanor, who had moved to Toronto with her husband, to start looking around for a house.

Meanwhile, Scott and Michael were using every trick they could as members of the family board to delay Andrew's attempts to introduce a motion to dismiss Wallace. They also challenged the work of the committee of outside directors that was trying to come up with a short list of candidates to take over from Wallace and Harrison. The outside directors had interviewed forty people for the job and spent $500,000 so far on the search. Michael and Scott demanded access to a list of the candidates, even though the board had voted to keep the names confidential. They also demanded to know how the committee could continue when it hadn't yet replaced its chairman, Arden Haynes. At one point, they even tried to introduce a motion calling on the family board to sue the outside directors and the operating board for withholding information.

Harrison was getting tired of their tactics: "As businessmen, I ask you to be practical and not legalistic in this matter and not lean on some frivolous use of by-laws, agreements, etc., to upset the protection of a third party's identity…"

While Michael and Scott tried to tie up the board, Andrew forged ahead with another try at ousting Wallace as co-chief executive. He consulted extensively with his lawyers on the drafting of a resolution. He wanted to make sure the resolution complied with Stevenson's ruling and wouldn't give Wallace any room to launch a lawsuit. Finally, in late July, he called a family board meeting for August 9. The directors would consider a resolution giving the board the power to "remove from office, at any time and from time to time, any senior executive of [McCain]…with or without cause and without the appointment of a successor…"

The meeting was angry and tense. Michael and Scott opposed the motion and again demanded information about the candidates under consideration for CEO. Peter, Mark and Allison asked Michael why he wanted the information. "I don't have to justify the request," he shot back. "I'm a director and I'm entitled to it." The motion passed, five to two. Three days later, Andrew called a special meeting of all shareholders to endorse the resolution.

The family was to meet on September 13, which gave Wallace barely a month to block the resolution. He didn't expect to win any support among the family, so, he took his case to the operating board at a meeting in late August. Wallace told the other directors that the family board's resolution had only one objective: to remove him as president and co-chief executive. He didn't want to leave, he said. And it was unfair to remove him as co-chief executive when Harrison would remain chairman and CEO until a successor was found. "I am most dissatisfied with a situation where Harrison has been allowed to participate in the process while I have been excluded," Wallace told the board. "I cannot support a search for a new president who will become Harrison's second-in-command for an indeterminate grooming period while Harrison continues as the sole CEO."

Wallace also tried to stir up the issue of moving McCain's headquarters. There was already concern in Florenceville that once a new CEO was in place McCain would move its head office out of the village. Wallace tried to introduce a motion that would require the new CEO to keep the headquarters in Florenceville, but the motion was outvoted. Wallace then tried a final attempt at incorporating Stevenson's letter into a possible solution. Harrison agreed to talk about it, but the two got nowhere. "I did not learn much because he was highly abusive of most people concerned," Harrison wrote later.

Knowing they would lose the family vote in September, Wallace and his sons went back to court. This time, Michael and Scott asked the court to stop the CEO selection process and Wallace's removal until they'd received more information about the candidates. They argued that they were entitled to the information as directors.

Wallace filed a more complicated suit. First, he wanted an injunction to stop the company from removing him until a trial was held. He also wanted the court to recognize that the partnership between the brothers had broken down and a court-ordered solution was required. He asked the court to consider the remedies suggested by Stevenson in his letter—a public share offering and a new board. It was an unusual case. Courts are often asked to "wind up" partnerships that have broken down, but most cases involve small companies like a garage or corner store. It was rare for a company the size of McCain to ask for similar treatment. It was also risky. The court didn't have to consider Wallace's suggestions. A judge could come up with his own remedy if he agreed that the partnership had broken down, including an outright sale of McCain to a third party.

Harrison dismissed the lawsuits as another delaying tactic. The family, as shareholders in McCain, would determine Wallace's fate, not the courts. Wallace's lawyers had tipped off the media again, which further angered Harrison. During one testy exchange, Harrison blew up when a letter he had just received from Wallace was already in the hands of reporters. "The press had the Goddamn letter in an hour and a half and I'm still writing my notes to reply," he told Canadian Press. "The letter was written to go to the press. It had my name on it, and it told me they were going to start a court action today, but all the preamble is stuff for the [the media] to suck in and sell to all the readers you can."

In a terse letter to Wallace, Harrison added: "You are trying to mislead the Judiciary, our employees and the public in general. You put your own self-interest before our family, our company and our province." Wallace shot back that he was only providing a true picture of events: "I can understand you're upset that a more balanced picture is now emerging. Everything you have said about me is exposed as inaccurate. To accuse me of trying to manipulate people is [like] the pot calling the kettle black in the extreme."

Wallace and Harrison then took their cases to the company employees. In an open letter Wallace explained that a public share offering was in the best interests of the company. He added that he was committed to keeping McCain in Florenceville.

In his letter, Harrison explained that Wallace was not being fired but moved to a new position. Once that happens, "I will continue as Chairman and CEO but only for a month or two until the new CEO has been introduced and briefed." He then said the new CEO might work out of Toronto instead of Florenceville but the move would only involve a few people. Harrison added that Wallace's proposal for a public share offering was a bigger threat to Florenceville because it would water down the ownership with large institutional investors: "These shareholders would simply see us as a stock certificate to be bought or sold."

Andrew was also fed up with Wallace's legal wrangling. "It's clouding the issue to suggest that somehow mysteriously if the public becomes involved [through a share offering] in this company that the management problems will go away. It won't. All Wallace's proposal would do, in my opinion, would be to include the public in the squabble," he said at the time. Like Harrison, Andrew was tired of the constant publicity and the leaks by

Wallace to the media. "This is just a fucking embarrassment. It really is," he said.

As the lawsuits moved through the courts, Muir kept working quietly on another investment opportunity for Wallace. In September 1994, Wallace, Muir and Michael flew to New York to meet with David Jacobs of Morgan Stanley & Co. Jacobs gave Wallace and Michael a day-long presentation on several companies that were up for sale. The companies included Continental Baking Co., a subsidiary of Ralston Purina. Continental was based in St. Louis and had sales of around $2 billion (US) and 23,000 employees. But it had run into trouble lately, and Ralston was now shopping it around. Wallace and Michael were interested. After returning to Toronto, they decided to make a bid. Once again, Muir got to work lining up the financing. He code-named the bid "Project Breakfast," referring to the company's line of breakfast cereal.

A few days after the New York meeting, Wallace and Michael flew to Moncton for a hearing on the lawsuits. The case had been moved to Moncton because of a backlog of cases in Fredericton and it was before Justice Paul Creaghan.

The Court of Queen's Bench in Moncton is on the second floor of the city's largest office tower. The building is adjacent to the City Hall and the Beausejour Hotel. This time lawyers from all sides stayed at the Beausejour, which is connected to the office tower by a walkway. The hearing was held in one of the largest of the four courtrooms that take up the entire floor. And, once again, Wallace and Harrison sat on opposite sides of the room, surrounded by their families. "Each family on opposite sides of the aisle," one lawyer said before the hearing started. "It looks like a wedding, or a funeral."

The hearing attracted about a dozen reporters and several onlookers. During one break, June Hayes, a sixty-eight-year-old taxi driver from Petitcodiac, stopped Harrison in the hallway. Hayes had run a small canteen in the late 1950s and had met the McCains during one of their wild sales trips across the province when they were first flogging their new frozen fries. Hayes never forgot their enthusiasm and drive. Dressed in an old coat and rumpled clothes, she grabbed Harrison by the elbow and handed him a crumpled-up piece of paper. On it, she had scribbled an offer to mediate the dispute for free. Harrison thanked her and walked off, sticking the paper in his pocket. "I don't want them to give their money to lawyers," she told reporters later. "I want them to straighten this out."

At the end of the first day of the hearing, both sides met separately in the hotel to plan strategy. The family meeting to approve the board resolution was to be held the next morning at McCain headquarters in Florenceville. Wallace and his family decided to skip the meeting and stay in Moncton for the hearing, which was scheduled to last one more day. There was no need to go to the meeting anyway, they thought. They all knew how the vote would turn out. But Wallace asked Petch to go and vote the family's shares by proxy. Wallace also wanted Petch to try to get the meeting delayed, at least until after the hearing. Petch left that night with a law student in a rented car. It was a four-hour drive to Florenceville and, as Petch left, Wallace threw him the keys to his house and told him to stay there for the night.

Harrison and his sons, along with Andrew and Allison, flew back to Florenceville on the company plane. They had no intention of missing the meeting and couldn't wait to finally have the resolution approved.

The next morning, just before 10:00 a.m., Harrison and his family arrived at the McCain Foods' third-floor boardroom. Most of the family was already there. Andrew sat at the head of the table. Allison sat nearby, along with his brother Stephen and his sister Margaret. A few other family members sat or stood around the long wooden table. Everyone was waiting to see if Wallace or his family would show up. Then, just as Andrew was about to start the meeting, Petch burst in with the law student and declared that he was there to vote Wallace's shares by proxy. Harrison shook his head angrily. He knew Petch's only purpose was to disrupt things. Sure enough, the meeting dragged on for two hours as Petch threw up a myriad of roadblocks and challenges to votes. Finally, by noon, the family had endorsed the resolution and the family board was granted the power to remove senior executives. The vote went as expected: every family member, except Wallace, as represented by Petch, voted in favour of the resolution.

While the meeting was being held in Florenceville, Wallace sat with his family in the first row of seats in the courtroom. He had a bit of arthritis in his left knee, and the constant sitting was starting to hurt. Petch's call with the results of the vote came during a break. Wallace wasn't surprised. He shrugged and sat down to hear the rest of the arguments.

During the hearing, Wallace's lawyer, Alan Lenczner, argued that the suit was the only way Wallace could protect his investment. The brothers had a de facto partnership which had broken down, and Harrison wasn't able to run the whole business on his own. Wallace had a right to participate in the selection of his successor since his actions would have an impact on the value of Wallace's shares. A public offering, Lenczner added, was also the only way Wallace could get fair value for his shares.

Company lawyer John Campion said it was unfair to force the family to keep a chief executive it didn't want. He pointed to Stevenson's ruling, which made it clear that the family was within its rights to remove Wallace as co-chief executive because the entire McCain family owned the company, not just Wallace or just Harrison. Campion also took direct aim at Wallace's claim that the brothers had a partnership. There was no partnership, Campion said. Four brothers, not two, had founded McCain, and four families now owned it, to varying degrees. Besides, how could Wallace claim that a partnership existed when the family as a whole had agreed to the 1991 board changes? Wallace had voted against the changes but they were approved and adopted anyway. How could that happen in a partnership? Campion summed up by calling Wallace's latest suit nothing more than a delaying tactic to prevent other McCains from doing what they had every right to do. "The battle has been fought, the smoke has cleared and Wallace and his family have lost," Campion said.

Two weeks later, Justice Creaghan made his decision. He rejected Wallace's request for an injunction and expressed his doubt that any further legal action would succeed. "While it is true that Wallace McCain has made a significant if not essential contribution to the success of the company in the past that is not to say the company cannot successfully operate in the present without guidance from Wallace McCain acting as a co-chief executive officer," Creaghan said. Wallace could still proceed with his lawsuit but there was nothing stopping the family from removing him as chief executive in the interim.

Wallace knew it was game over. There was little point pursuing the lawsuit if he was out of McCain. Wallace, Michael and Scott were disappointed but not devastated. Muir was still working on "Project Breakfast," and the family was already resigned to planning a new future.

Harrison was relieved by the ruling. Now the family board could finally put an end to this drama. Within two days of the ruling, Andrew called a board meeting for October 12 at the office of Fasken Campbell Godfrey, McCain Foods' law firm, in Toronto. Andrew hoped it would be a quick and painless exercise. Coincidentally, the day before the board meeting, McCain's public relations staff sent out a news release announcing the acquisition of a new cheese company in New Zealand. The company was called Wallace Dairy and the announcement was made by Wallace McCain. It would be his last official act as company president.

Michael and Scott walked quickly across the broad entranceway of the Toronto Dominion Centre off King Street in the heart of Toronto's financial district. It was shortly after 9:00 a.m. on October 12. When they entered the Fasken Campbell boardroom, Michael and Scott quickly started rearranging the chairs. Andrew asked what they were doing. Michael said he needed a slide projector. When Andrew asked why, Michael replied, "I want to make a presentation." Andrew rolled his eyes and ordered the machine. As Peter, Mark, Allison and George McClure strolled in, Michael began arranging a set of slides. This was Michael and Scott's last chance to save their father's job, and they were going all out. Michael began by telling the directors they should view Wallace's removal like any other business decision. "Does it make sense to remove Wallace from a business perspective?" Michael asked.

The company had enjoyed another record year in 1994. By the end of the fiscal year on June 30, profits had increased to $105.6 million from $76 million in 1993. Through a series of slides, Michael broke down those results by the companies Wallace and Harrison managed. In 1994, the divisions managed by Wallace and Harrison accounted for nearly an equal split of the company's overall $3.2 billion in sales. But Wallace's side contributed 54 percent of the profit while Harrison's contributed 46 percent. Furthermore, Wallace's sales had increased 15 percent while companies under Harrison's management had increased by 5 percent. As for profits, Wallace's division had increased earnings by 104 percent while the profit in Harrison's division increased by 19 percent.

Pointing to the slides, Michael insisted that removing Wallace was a bad business move. Wallace had superior results and better sales growth than Harrison. Wallace also had a closer relationship with McDonald's, and he was in better health than Harrison. "What if Harrison falls prey to a heart attack?" Michael asked. "What if the new CEO is not satisfactory? What if ConAgra declares war?"

The presentation lasted well into the afternoon. The only relief for the other directors came when Andrew ordered several short breaks so that he and Peter could go outside for a cigarette. But in the end, no one was swayed. To the other directors, Michael had missed the point—the shareholders wanted Wallace out. By about 4:30 p.m., a vote was taken on the resolution. It passed, five to two.

Michael and Scott left quickly and called Wallace with the result. Wallace was shaken. He'd had no delusions about how the vote would turn out, but now that it was official, the impact sank in. He was no longer president and co-chief executive of McCain Foods, a position he'd held for nearly forty years. David MacNaughton immediately sent out a blistering press release in which Wallace attacked Harrison as rigid and vindictive. "...[T]his action has more to do with personal acrimony than business acumen," Wallace said in the release. "Given that this is a termination without cause based solely on family politics, not only do I consider this poor business judgment, but a flagrant display of ingratitude and disrespect."

The board vote lingered in Wallace's mind for days. He felt listless and distraught. He was no longer allowed to do what he'd been doing his entire adult life—helping to build one of the world's largest food processing companies. The board had made him non-executive vice chairman and he still had his seat on the operating board, but that meant little to Wallace. He couldn't go through plants any more barking out orders and making decisions. He couldn't fret over a contract or go out on sales trips. He couldn't do what he loved.

Wallace's daughter Eleanor called him one morning shortly after the vote. "There was a regular management meeting at the company that day and he couldn't go," she said. "He wasn't invited and it really hit him. He couldn't talk he was so depressed." A few days later, Wallace sent a letter to the employees. "I claim each of you as friend and family," he wrote. "This marks an end to a chapter in the McCain history books."

CHAPTER TWENTY

Wallace and Margaret's hearts ached as they drove out of Florenceville. It was late fall, 1994. They had no idea if or when they would return to their home, but they knew it wouldn't be for a very long time. They took a long look at their house, the white pillars standing proudly across the front, and the glorious view of the Saint John River valley. To the south across the river, steam was billowing up from the McCain plant. The big star on the roof looked a little weather worn but it still shone out amid the rolling hills.

As they drove down Riverside Drive, they stared at the McCain family home where Wallace and Harrison had grown up and shared a bed as kids. Derek, the son of Wallace's sister Eleanor, now lived there. It had been painted beige and renovated, but it looked much the same as it had when Wallace was a boy. He could see the kitchen door and remembered pulling up a chair by the massive wood-burning stove to watch his mother cook. Across the road was the tiny house Wallace and Margaret had rented in June 1956 when they'd returned from Saint John to help start McCain Foods. The house was owned by the company now.

Farther up the road stood the house of Wallace's grandfather, Hugh Henderson McCain. Michael had bought the house years ago and renovated it before moving to Chicago to run McCain Citrus. He rented it to his cousin Stephen now, but he'd always hoped to one day live there with his family. As Wallace passed by the sturdy white house, he knew his son would never live there again. Scott's house was already up for sale.

Through the trees, Wallace could still make out the buildings that lined Florenceville's Main Street. Right in the middle, standing where it had stood for decades, was the low, brick McCain Produce Co. building. Wallace remembered his father sitting behind a desk in the office, wearing his three-piece suit, trying to arrange a shipment of potatoes to somewhere in South America.

Sixty-four years of Wallace's life and nearly one hundred and fifty years of McCain family history had been played out on this road in this village. For Wallace, saying goodbye to Florenceville meant saying goodbye to the only life and world he'd ever known, or had ever wanted to know. But right now he and Margaret couldn't stay. To stay was to be reminded every day of what had happened, what had been destroyed and what they no longer had. Banishment from the company meant banishment from the family, and the only way Wallace and Margaret could cope with the pain was by leaving.

Now their home was a condominium in downtown Toronto. Margaret would commute weekly to Fredericton for her work as Lieutenant-Governor. They hadn't planned much beyond that. Wallace's bid for Maple Leaf was still up in the air. If it fell through, they might move to the States to find another company to buy.

The fallout from Wallace's removal from McCain was quick. Within two weeks, the company announced Harrison's son Peter would become president of a new McCain division called McCain Foods International. The appointment had been planned for months but the timing demonstrated the clear shift of power inside the company. McCain's corporate headquarters was moved to BCE Place in downtown Toronto. George McClure quit his job as vice president; he remained, however, on the family board. And a few months after Wallace's removal, Allison was named CEO of British operations replacing Mac McCarthy, who took the job as chairman in Britain. Wallace was furious when the announcement was made at a McCain board meeting. "I said, 'Mac, you must be retiring.' Harrison said, 'No he's not.' I said, 'Jesus, you're making him chairman. Mac, how old are you?' He said, 'Sixty-eight.' 'Well,' I said, 'Pretty good.

You want to fire me at sixty-two, you son of a bitch. He's sixty-eight and he's going to stay.'"

Adding to Wallace's anger over the appointment was that he had been pushing Harrison for years to name McCarthy chairman of UK operations as a reward for his years of service. "Being a corporate chairman in England is like being God. I always had a soft spot for Mac, he'd made a lot of money for us and did a good job of running the company for us and I always wanted to make him chairman. But Harrison was the chairman so no god damn way. He would say, 'I'm not making him chairman, I'm the chairman.' I said, 'Come on Harrison, give it to him. You couldn't raise his pay enough to make it equivalent to being chairman.' He'd say, 'No sir.'"

With Wallace no longer overseeing U.S. operations, Michael also began to feel the heat. According to court documents, Harrison arrived in Chicago a week after the October board meeting to meet with McCain's U.S. executives and Michael wasn't invited to the meeting, even though he was still the regional CEO. Harrison told the executives that Michael's career was in jeopardy. At Harrison's urging, Michael was later put on probation by the company's operating board.

In the Florenceville office, Archie McLean also felt the effects of Wallace's absence. He'd been a friend of Harrison's for years but had openly supported Wallace during the legal wrangling. McLean wanted a shot at the McCain CEO job, which he knew would be decided soon now that Wallace was gone. He had been with the company for nearly twenty-five years and felt he knew the overall operations as well as any other insider. But he also knew that his support for Wallace wouldn't put him in a favourable light.

A few weeks after Wallace was demoted, McLean wrote to Harrison about the McCain CEO job. He talked about his long association with both Harrison and Wallace and said he was the best person to become CEO and bring harmony among all the McCain families. When Harrison didn't reply, McLean wrote again. Finally, McLean cornered Harrison in a hallway and asked about the job. "The issue is before the board," Harrison said. McLean shook his head and replied, "No, I'm looking at the man who will make the decision." Harrison nodded and the two met in his office. Then he said, "Archie, you have caused this family a lot of grief and you won't be considered for the job." McLean was angry but at least he knew where he stood. He returned to his office and wrote out his resignation.

In November 1994, just a month after the family board meeting, Wallace decided to attend a McCain operating board meeting in London. He was still a director and he was determined to go, even though he knew he wouldn't be welcomed by Harrison. Wallace and Margaret left for London on November 15. They didn't want to stay at the Dorchester or Britannia Hotels because that's where Harrison and the other directors normally stayed, so they booked a room at the Connaught. They didn't know until they opened the curtains in their room that the hotel was across the street from the Britannia.

The next day, Wallace found himself thinking about Sir John Knott, the chairman of Hillsdown Holdings. Wallace had given up making a bid for Hillsdown's ownership stake in Maple Leaf Foods months ago when he'd been told it was not for sale, but it still nagged at him. He really wanted Maple Leaf. It was about the same size as McCain, it was in the food processing business, and it was Canadian. Why not give Knott a call? Wallace thought to himself. But what would he say? Wallace didn't know Knott very well, even though Hillsdown was a large potato supplier for McCain in Europe. In fact, Wallace didn't even have his number—he'd have to call Muir in Toronto first. This indecision and second-guessing was new for Wallace. After all, he'd spent his life making decisions and cutting deals. But this was different. Throughout all his years at McCain, Harrison had coordinated the financial side of major transactions. Harrison got involved in the wheeling and dealing on all their bids for companies or factories. Wallace had done some deal-making, but nothing this big, and nothing that had so much riding on it personally.

"Should I call him?" Wallace asked Margaret. "Yes," she replied. "Are you sure?" he asked again. "Yes," she answered. "No, I don't think I should," he said. "Of course you should," she said. "You *know* you should."

Wallace called Muir for Knott's number. "It's worth a try," Muir told Wallace. Then Wallace picked up the phone and called Knott's office. Knott would be happy to meet Wallace that afternoon. Wallace was thrilled. On the way over, Wallace mulled over what he was going to say. He thought he had a pretty good idea how the conversation was likely to go. But when he arrived in Knott's office, Wallace was taken aback. Knott wanted to talk about buying Wallace's shares in McCain!

"I met Wallace McCain to chat really about his share holding in McCain Foods. I thought if there was some way in which Maple Leaf and McCain foods could get together that would be interesting from everybody's point of view," Knott recalls.

Wallace didn't know what to say at first. "I said, 'Fine.' I wasn't sure if he could buy them, but I said 'Fine.'" Wallace then eased the discussion towards Maple Leaf. By the end of the meeting, Knott had dropped the idea of buying Wallace's McCain shares and was hinting that a deal for Hillsdown's shares in Maple Leaf might be possible after all. Wallace couldn't believe it. As he returned to his hotel he could barely contain his glee. He called Margaret before he left and told her to meet him at the front door. They had tickets to a show, but Wallace was almost too excited to go now.

"When I got in the car his eyes were the size of two small melons," said Margaret. "All he said was, 'Maple Leaf is possible.'"

Later that night, Wallace called Michael, then Scott, and then Muir to tell them the good news: Maple Leaf was back on. Muir called Morgan Stanley, the investment banker helping with the Continental Baking bid, to tell them Wallace wasn't interested in Continental any more. Muir invited the team at Morgan Stanley that had been working on the bid to help with the new Maple Leaf bid. Michael code-named the project "Marla" after famed developer Donald Trump's then mistress, Marla Maples. Now all they needed was about $1 billion.

Muir said they had to arrange all their financing before they could go back to Knott with a bid. Engman from Ontario Teachers' was still interested, but Muir doubted Teachers' would kick in more than the $100 million they'd already committed for the failed McCain bids. Wallace could come up with another

$150 million or so on his own, but that still left at least $750 million. Since Muir was adamant that Wallace not sell his McCain shares, where would that money come from?

Over the next few weeks, Muir and David Jacobs from Morgan Stanley worked on a detailed presentation to take to various Canadian and American banks. They expected a tough sell. Wallace was still an unknown in the financial community. Harrison had been the point man on finances at McCain, not Wallace. Wallace had also just been embroiled in a bitter family feud, and he was turning sixty-five—not exactly the age when most people try to start a new career with a $1-billion buy-out.

Muir and Jacobs planned to make their pitch to all the big Canadian banks first, except the Bank of Nova Scotia. Harrison was still a member of its board and Wallace didn't want him to know what he had in mind. Their first few presentations were received coolly, and their hopes were flagging by the time they made one of their final stops: the Toronto-Dominion Bank. Wallace called bank president Richard Thomson for an appointment. The two had never met, but Thomson was curious about Wallace. The banker had a reputation as a wiley manager who was not afraid to take risks or go with his instincts. In early December 1994, Wallace, Michael, Scott, Muir and Jacobs filed into Thomson's office. Wallace told the president he was planning a bid for Maple Leaf Foods.

"Isn't that interesting," Thomson interrupted. "You called a week ago, and for the last week we've been trying to think which company you were interested in and we didn't think of that one."

Wallace was in the middle of outlining what he had in mind when Thomson interrupted him again. "How much do you need?" he asked. Wallace said he was looking for about $600 million in term debt and $100 million in an operating line of credit.

"You've got this bank's commitment," Thomson said. "But you'll need more than that. We'll give you $650 million and $150 million."

Wallace and the others were stunned. They hadn't even finished their presentation and here was Thomson offering more money than they'd requested. Dazed, Muir said, "We're interested in getting firm commitments in a week." Thomson leaned over the table to Muir and replied, "Tom, I don't think you understand, you have a commitment now from this bank." Thomson explained that he didn't need to hear any more. It was people who counted in a deal like this, and he'd spent a week checking out Wallace. All of the reports were impressive. "I've done my homework on you," Thomson said to Wallace. "Would it be satisfactory if we had a term sheet drawn up by Saturday?"

Muir and Jacobs were stilled stunned when they walked out. They had never arranged that kind of financing so quickly from a bank. Now it was time to move. With the T-D's commitment, Muir wanted to see if he could squeeze a bit more out of Teachers'. He knew there was nothing more humiliating to a pension fund like Teachers' than to be shown up by a bank on a risky venture.

Engman said he was still mulling over the deal and how much Teachers' could commit. Muir said that was too bad, because he had just gotten back from T-D and they were ready to commit $700 million by the weekend. Engman was silent for a moment and said he would call back. A few hours later, he phoned to say that Teachers' would put up $150 million. It was $50 million more than Muir had expected. With the financing in place, Wallace and Margaret started to get excited. So much was riding on this bid.

"At the time, nobody really understood the depth of hurt and humiliation we'd suffered," Margaret recalls. "When he got involved in this, there was an air of excitement. We moved out of Harrison's orbit of power and control. This was a chance to be productive and pro-active."

Still, the Maple Leaf deal was far from certain. Wallace had to come up with a price for Hillsdown's shares, and there were plenty of legal details to arrange with Teachers'. The fund insisted the deal had to be arranged so that there was absolutely no chance of a lawsuit from disgruntled minority shareholders. Teachers' was already in the midst of a messy lawsuit over the acquisition of Maple Leaf Gardens Ltd. in 1994 by grocery tycoon Steve Stavro. Wallace, Michael, Scott, Muir and Engman wrestled with the details over Christmas. Soon everything was bogged down. By New Year's Day, it looked like the deal was off. Teachers' conditions were too strict and the financing was falling apart. At one point, "Wallace could barely hold back tears," recalls Margaret. His big opportunity was slipping away.

Wallace, Michael, Muir and Engman kept negotiating. To solve Teachers' concerns about legal issues, a special meeting of Maple Leaf shareholders would be held to vote on the offer and a series of conditions before it expired. Other legal arrangements were worked out and the deal fell back into place. In mid January, Wallace called Knott and arranged a meeting.

Michael, Scott, Muir and Jacobs went to London with Wallace. Muir also invited Engman. He wanted to prove to Knott that the bid was serious. Wallace first met Knott alone. He offered Knott about $15 per share for the Hillsdown stake. But the deal involved new shares in Maple Leaf and little cash. Knott wasn't interested. He wanted more cash and he wasn't sure now if Hillsdown was interested in selling. Wallace was shaken but said he would call Knott again the next day. Wallace returned to the hotel to tell the others. He was embarrassed. He felt he had completely misread his November meeting with Knott. The next day, Muir, Jacobs, Engman and Wallace met Knott again. They wanted to find out what he wanted, but Knott was firm. "The basic message was, the asset is not for sale," recalls Muir. The group headed back to Toronto depressed. But Wallace was determined that a deal could still be struck. It just had to be the right deal, that's all.

While Wallace was working on the Maple Leaf bid, lawyers for McCain Foods, Harrison, Andrew and the family board were preparing another round of legal action. This time the company was taking Wallace to court to have his lawsuit thrown out. Justice Creaghan had dismissed Wallace's application for an injunction, but Wallace's suit over partnership breakdown was still before the court. A hearing was set for January 30, a couple of weeks after Wallace's second meeting with Knott. The hearing would also be in Moncton before Creaghan.

Wallace again sat at the front of the courtroom with Michael and Scott. They were having a hard time focusing on the hearing. Their minds were on the Maple Leaf bid and trying to figure out how much to offer. Harrison sat two rows down on the opposite side surrounded by Peter, Mark, Andrew and McClure. The arguments were much the same as during the first hearing before Creaghan, and so was the result. Creaghan threw out the case. Wallace immediately filed an appeal but he knew the legal route was closing. Now more than ever, the family had to concentrate on making a future with Maple Leaf.

Within weeks of the decision, McCain's committee of outside directors finally put forward a candidate to succeed the brothers as chief executive. Harrison supported the choice and was ready to have the candidate officially approved by both McCain boards. He called an operating board meeting for February 28 to announce the appointment. Wallace had no idea who had been chosen and sent Harrison a memo asking for some background information before the meeting. "As a co-founder of the business, I'd like to have the opportunity to meet the man and spend some time with him," Wallace said.

"Wallace, you are a non-executive director and you are going to receive exactly the same information as any other director," Harrison replied. "I can arrange for the candidate to meet you on a one-on-one basis at 8:45 a.m. [before the meeting].... At that time I will give you his cv and help progress the conversation."

To Wallace, the offer was an insult. Harrison was offering him just over an hour to meet the man who would take over the McCain family business. "In addition to being a director of this company, I am a co-founder, co-builder and a 35 percent shareholder," he wrote back. "My entire fortune and my life's work is tied up in this company and I believe it entitles me to meaningful participation and input into the selection of the person who will take that business into the next century."

Harrison couldn't understand his brother's sensitivity. "[Wallace] said, 'I need a day.' Well I said, 'Jesus Wallace, you got fourteen directors, thirteen directors at the moment, we really can't take thirteen days to interview this guy, we can't all do that. But if you want to talk to him a while later, no problem. But as far as the scheduling time, the guy is coming in here from the west coast he's going to get in the night before, I got about four directors to see and you can have him at 8:45. You can have him until 10:00."

The squabble overshadowed the new CEO's official appointment, which was announced at the board meeting as Harrison had planned. Wallace was there and met the new chief executive just before the meeting. He was Howard Mann, a forty-eight-year-old managing director of the food products division for Rank Hovis McDougall, a British food conglomerate. Mann tried to brush off the controversy over his appointment and spoke to the media about how eager he was to work with both brothers. "It's a dream job," he said after his appointment. "I have the greatest respect for them as food professionals."

Wallace continued to work on his Maple Leaf bid. By early March 1995, they finally had an offer to take to Knott and Maple Leaf's other shareholders. It was a complex bid made up of cash and shares in the new company. Shareholders could get up to $15 per share in cash—not a bad price considering that Maple Leaf's shares had traded around $12 a share for most of the year on the Toronto Stock Exchange. Hillsdown was guaranteed up to $680 million in cash for its 45.3 million shares. If successful, Wallace and Teachers' would each own one-third of the new company and the remainder would be held by public shareholders. Hillsdown agreed to accept the bid providing no better offer came along before Wallace's offer expired.

Wallace was now ready to make the offer public. But first, he called Archie McLean. Wallace knew McLean had given his resignation to McCain, effective in July. He'd told McLean about the Maple Leaf bid in January and now asked him to join the new company as CEO. McLean agreed and called Harrison that night. "I said I was taking tomorrow off to look at a job offer in Toronto," recalled McLean.

Just a few days before the announcement, Wallace and Michael began having second thoughts about the deal. They hadn't been given access to Maple Leaf's operations in order to see if their price reflected the company's true value. "We had Arthur Andersen ready to go in," recalls Michael "and we were going to go through the normal practice of any transaction. In any transaction that I have been involved in you get an opportunity to come in and kick the tires." But this wasn't any normal transaction and Maple Leaf's board refused to provide any information. "They

told us, 'It's a public company, read the public documents,'"
remembers Michael. "I was pissed off. I didn't accept that
because I thought it was irresponsible."

Maple Leaf's board relented. They agreed to let the McCains
review the company's books and operations, but they had just
one weekend. Wallace, Michael, Scott and Muir got started late
on Friday. McLean joined them as soon as he arrived from New
Brunswick.

Around midnight Sunday, March 5, after two days and nights
immersed in the details of Maple Leaf, the group met at
Wallace's condominium for a final decision. "We just looked at
one another and said, 'Do we want to go or not?'" remembers
Michael. "'Here's what we know, here's what we don't know.'
Everyone said, 'Let's go for it.'"

At 9:00 a.m. on Monday, a press release went out over financial news wires. The Wallace McCain family was making a bid
for Maple Leaf Foods. To launch the bid, Wallace incorporated a
company called Castlefin Inc., named after a town in Ireland in
the area his ancestors came from. Hillsdown announced that it
would take the offer unless a better bid came forward. If successful, Wallace would become chairman of Maple Leaf and
McLean CEO. It was a $1.1-billion offer; Wallace was putting
up $150 million and Teachers' another $150 million. Wallace
also planned to use $140 million from Maple Leaf's treasury to
help pay for the deal, along with $575 million in financing from
the T-D Bank. He had another $75 million available from the
bank just in case another bidder came forward and he had to up
his bid. It was the biggest deal of the year.

The offer was open until April 20. Margaret noticed the date
and laughed. That was the first anniversary of Justice Stevenson's
ruling, she told Wallace. "God, don't tell me that," he replied
shaking his head. With the news release out, all Wallace could do
now was to try and sell his offer to as many Maple Leaf shareholders as possible and hope like hell no one else came up with a
better bid.

Most shareholders and analysts were lukewarm about the bid.
Maple Leaf had been an under-performer as far as many shareholders were concerned and they were happy for someone to

take it off their hands. "They'll get my shares," said one share-holder at the time. "I'm not too fond of the company." But some analysts speculated that the bid wouldn't be enough to ward off potential rivals. "I believe there is at least a decent chance of interest in Maple Leaf by most likely some of the major U.S. food companies and that this is not necessarily a done deal," said analyst Steve Garmaise of First Marathon. Maple Leaf would be worse off under McCain, said Brian Lomas of Scotia McLeod. Before the bid, Maple Leaf had no debt and at least $150 million in cash. If Wallace won, the company would end up with no cash and a $575-million debt. "It's not the best thing that could have happened to Maple Leaf's shareholders," Lomas said. He added that the company's current management had done a good job but it looked like most would be replaced by Wallace, Michael, Scott and Archie McLean.

A week after the announcement, Wallace held a news confer-ence to provide more details of his bid. The meeting was held in the King Edward Hotel in downtown Toronto. As he walked into the packed room, Wallace felt a twinge in his stomach. He had never held a news conference like this before, and this was no ordinary announcement. Wallace stepped up to the micro-phone as Michael, McLean, Muir, Engman and Jacobs took their seats behind him at a long table. Scott wasn't there. He was at Wallace's home in Jamaica for a vacation he had planned with his family months earlier.

Wallace took a deep breath and began reading a prepared statement about his plans for Maple Leaf. Archie McLean and Tom Muir also spoke briefly before the meeting was opened for questions.

The first question was blunt. "Have you resolved the differ-ences with your brother over McCain?" "We're here to talk about Maple Leaf today," Wallace gamely replied. More questions fol-lowed about McCain and competition between McCain and Maple Leaf. "I don't see any conflict at all," Wallace said. He added that the overlap between Maple Leaf and McCain amounted to just 1 percent of the annual sales of both companies.

Then came questions about how he could remain on the board of McCain. "I have an investment in McCain and I'd like to keep it. I'm on the board and it's non-competitive. There is no reason why I shouldn't stay," Wallace said. For much of the press conference, Wallace didn't even refer to McCain by name; instead he called it "that other company."

When asked why someone who was turning sixty-five would get into such a complex venture instead of just retiring, Wallace laughed and said: "I wanted something to do. I was asked to retire [by McCain], I didn't want to and I'm not going to. When I choose that I want to retire, I'll retire. I'm one of those who believe that if you keep an active mind and keep building, you can keep growing longer. I really wanted something more to do. That may sound childish, maybe stupid, but it's a fact."

What about the role of his sons in Maple Leaf? "Isn't this just nepotism?" asked Bernard Simon, Toronto reporter for *The Financial Times* of London. Wallace shook his head. "I'm very proud of my sons and their executive abilities. They both have real proven track records," he said.

The takeover was major news and Wallace became an instant celebrity. He was profiled in dozens of newspapers, magazines and on television. All the attention made Wallace more careful than ever to follow Margaret's numbering scheme for his ties and suits. The irony wasn't lost on him. For forty years the only McCain most people ever heard of was Harrison. Now, everyone was talking about Wallace McCain. "The end result of what happened with [Harrison] got me into what I'm doing now," he said a few days after the press conference.

Back in Florenceville, Harrison was still trying to work out the impact of Wallace's bid. He was surprised when he heard that Wallace was making a bid for Maple Leaf, and immediately called Wallace to wish him good luck. Then he called his lawyers to inquire about Wallace's status on the McCain board. There is "a lot of potential conflict and suspected conflict with everything else going on," he told reporters at the time. "Our lawyers say [Wallace] will be walking a high tight wire. I'm not saying he can't do it, I'm just saying in my opinion it would be a hard job to do both." But there wasn't much the lawyers could do. Judge Stevenson's ruling had guaranteed Wallace a seat on the board. And, under New Brunswick law, Wallace's family, as significant minority shareholders, were guaranteed board seats in proportion to the number of shares they held. That meant that as long as Wallace's family owned one-third of McCain, it was guaranteed roughly one-third of the family board seats.

Harrison was having a harder time accepting the role of Michael and Scott in the bid. He was incredulous that, as McCain executives, Michael and Scott would help launch a takeover of a McCain competitor without first resigning or at least telling him. Within hours of Wallace's announcement, Harrison ordered the locks changed on their office doors. The locks were changed on Archie McLean's office as well, just for good measure, even though he had already resigned. Harrison was especially angry at Michael. He must have spent hours working on the bid, Harrison thought, instead of working for McCain. The more Harrison thought about it the angrier he became. The next day, Harrison fired Michael. "Since Wallace McCain was removed as president and co-CEO of McCain Foods Ltd., you have engaged in and continue to engage in acts of insubordination…" Harrison wrote Michael in a brief letter. "As of the date of this letter, your employment with the McCain Group, specifically McCain USA Inc., is hereby terminated."

Harrison sent another letter to McCain's senior staff in the United States explaining the firing. "For some months, Michael has declined to take my specific direction on various things I wanted done," he wrote. He added that Wallace's bid put Michael in a clear conflict with McCain. "I believe Michael was treated exactly the same as if an executive of McDonald's decided he was going to invest, and probably help run a KFC franchise…. It just won't fly and I could not stand for it any longer."

The actual removal of Michael turned into a comedy of errors. Harrison's office couldn't find Michael that day because he was en route from Toronto to Chicago. They needed to send him Harrison's letter, but where? It couldn't be sent to Michael's office because he had been locked out. Instead, they faxed a copy to Michael's home in Chicago. Meanwhile copies of both letters had already been sent to the media.

Before boarding his flight, Michael checked his answering machine at his office in Chicago for messages. The first two messages were from reporters asking him to comment on his firing from McCain. The third message was from his wife, Chris, telling him to call home because he'd received a letter from Harrison. Michael called Chris and she read him the letter. He was furious and immediately called the reporters. "If being a man of my own mind makes me insubordinate then I plead guilty," he said, adding that he was thinking about suing. Referring to Harrison he added: "This is the action of a frustrated man."

A week later, Michael did sue Harrison in Chicago for wrongful dismissal. In the suit Michael asked for more than $1 million (US) in compensation. He said he had taken a pay-cut because he'd been assured he was in line for more senior jobs at McCain. And he threw in a defamation claim, suggesting that Harrison had "engaged in extreme and outrageous conduct…with the intent of causing Michael McCain severe emotional distress."

Harrison didn't fire Scott. Instead, the two agreed to meet when Scott returned from his vacation to work out a time line for Scott's resignation. The arrangement was a sign of Scott's popularity within the family and the company. If he had taken any other action, Harrison would have risked alienating hundreds of McCain plant workers who adored Scott. Indeed, on the day Scott left, nearly three hundred McCain employees held a going-away party for him. Another event was held at the plant in P.E.I. and a third at the dairy operations in Toronto. Harrison had never seen Scott as a threat in the way that Michael was. To Harrison, Scott must have seemed like a "good fellow" who was only sticking with his father and his brother. But Scott had also been a loyal and public supporter of his father and his brother. At a huge retirement party for McCain vice president Tim Bliss in October 1994, just days after the board meeting had removed Wallace from his position at McCain, Scott had given a speech honouring Bliss's service to the company. With Harrison sitting only a few feet away, Scott had remarked on the size of the crowd and on the respect everyone shared for Bliss. "I only wish my father would be able to leave with such honour," he'd said.

Two weeks after launching his offer for Maple Leaf, Wallace went to see his sister Eleanor in the hospital. Eleanor had been diagnosed with a brain tumour following bouts of dizziness on a trip to Britain. She'd been receiving treatments for nearly a year. When the McCain family found out they were devastated. Eleanor was a lively, joyous person, but the tumour left her barely able to speak. Margaret and Wallace were especially upset. They had been very close with Eleanor, and had named their daughter after her. And Eleanor had joined them on vacations and kept in touch weekly by phone. But Eleanor had kept her distance from them ever since she and Wallace had argued during the arbitration hearings. Margaret had missed Eleanor terribly but knew Eleanor felt she had no choice but to side with Harrison. There was no room for neutrality in the fight between Harrison and Wallace—and it was Harrison that Margaret blamed.

A few months earlier, in November 1994, Eleanor's husband, Patrick Johnson, had died suddenly of a heart attack. The funeral was held in Toronto on December 2, at Saint Michael and All Angels Church. Hundreds attended the service, and it was one of the few family gatherings attended by all the McCains, including Harrison and Wallace. But the brothers sat on opposite sides of the church, and at a reception later at Upper Canada College, they stayed on opposite sides of the room.

During Eleanor's last few weeks, Margaret sat at her bedside for hours. Wallace also visited Eleanor as often as he could. "Eleanor's face lit up when we arrived," remembers Margaret. "She kept asking her nurse, 'Are they coming, are they coming?'" But it saddened Margaret that so much time, time they could have been together, had been stolen because of the battling between Wallace and Harrison.

March 20, 1995, was the last time Margaret and Wallace saw Eleanor. When they visited her they could tell she was not doing well. "She kept saying, 'I love you, I love you,'" remembers Margaret. Eleanor died a few hours later. Her funeral was held four days later on March 24, in the same church where her husband's funeral had been held three months earlier. Once again, nearly all the McCains attended the service and again all sides avoided one another.

Throughout April, Michael and Scott returned to Toronto to be with Wallace as he waited out the final days before the offer for Maple Leaf expired. There wasn't much they could do but wait. Wallace had made the rounds of analysts, shareholders and journalists and everyone was now wondering if another bidder might emerge. With a week to go, Wallace headed to Jamaica for what he thought would be a break. But all he could do was talk on the phone and worry. What if there was a more lucrative offer from a U.S. company? Could Wallace match or better it?

Nothing happened for days. Wallace was beginning to breathe easier. Then, just days before the offer was set to expire, Wallace got a call from Muir. IBP Inc., a U.S. meat-processing company with about $11.6 billion in sales, was poking around and expressing interest in making a bid. Maple Leaf had scheduled a shareholders meeting for April 19 to vote on Wallace's offer. There was still time for IBP to pull something off. Wallace worried. Muir kept trying to see if there was any more information. Finally, the night before the shareholders' meeting, IBP backed off.

The next morning, Wallace, Michael and Scott smiled as they walked into a special meeting of Maple Leaf shareholders in the Crown Plaza Hotel in Toronto. Wallace's daughters Eleanor and Martha, who both lived in Toronto, were also there. They all laughed and joked with shareholders and Maple Leaf Foods executives. Everyone was finally relaxing. A few minutes later, shareholders were asked to vote on Wallace's offer. It was approved by 99 percent of the shareholders.

Wallace, Michael, Scott and Archie McLean met in Jack Petch's office the next morning to sign documents and tie up the deal. In the corner sat a small box of Country Style Donuts, a restaurant chain owned by Maple Leaf. "Well," Petch said after the papers were signed, "you'd better not stick around here, you're not making any money for Maple Leaf here."

A few weeks later, Wallace held a party at the Rosedale Golf and Country Club to celebrate the takeover. About 130 people attended, including several from Florenceville. For Wallace and his family it was an emotional celebration. They had finally made a break with McCain and were starting a new life.

Margaret held back tears as Michael and Scott spoke about the deal and how honoured they were to work on it with their father. Wallace joked about how much the party was costing, considering all the other fees the takeover had involved. T-D Bank president Richard Thomson was given a sweatshirt commemorating the amount of money his bank had put up. And everyone took up a collection for a shelter for battered women that Margaret sponsored. "They were relieved and really happy," says Suzanne McLean, a family friend who was at the event. "It was the first event where they had been truly happy in a long time."

Around the same time, Harrison was hosting his own party in Fredericton. The event was to commemorate the opening of a new wing of the Beaverbrook Art Gallery. The wing was named in honour of Billie, and Harrison had put up about $1.5 million for its construction. As always, Harrison invited the political and business elite to the party. The Irvings were there, along with Premier Frank McKenna and nearly his entire cabinet. Harrison was led around the room by his daughter Laura. He then gave a rambling speech about "pictures" and how much the wing cost. But to some at the event, Harrison didn't seem to have the same spark. He looked tired and sad. "He never mentioned his wife by name in the speech," says one person who was there. "And he looked really ill."

A few weeks later, McCain Foods recorded a 13 percent jump in profit for fiscal 1995 to a record $130 million. Sales topped $4 billion.

EPILOGUE

June 6, 1995

Harrison is leaning back in his chair in the boardroom at McCain Foods. In keeping with the McCain corporate culture, his dress is casual, an open-necked shirt and a light sweater. But there is nothing casual about his manner. He is reluctant to talk, and this meeting has been arranged only after months of negotiations through lawyers.

The fire still burns when he is asked about Wallace and why he had to go. "The basic problem has been that Wallace and his family have favoured maintaining control of the company through his family in management roles that the rest of the families don't support. And 34 percent [Wallace's ownership stake] doesn't beat 66 percent [the other families' share], it's that simple. Nobody else wants to do that, they want it run on the basis of a meritocracy."

Harrison recalls how much he and the other families gave in to Wallace. They negotiated for years to change the board structure, and every time Wallace objected. They agreed to bring in outside directors, at his insistence, and let them find a new chief executive. And when Wallace took everyone to court they agreed to an outside arbitrator—a sitting judge—who said the shareholders had a right to decide the future of their company.

"We felt the changes we had made to satisfy Wallace meant that we would have unanimous agreement and we were surprised, absolutely surprised, to find that it was not unanimous."

Harrison knows the situation can never be fully resolved as long as Wallace, Michael and Scott are still board members and shareholders of McCain. "I wish that it were resolved more permanently than it is," Harrison says firmly.

November 17, 1995

Wallace swivels around in his white chair and looks out the living-room window of his condominium. It isn't much of a view, just a drained pool in a city reservoir surrounded by highrise apartment buildings. Wallace's condominium takes up most of the sixth floor of the building, but it's still a far cry from the space and openness of his Florenceville home. For now, though, Wallace doesn't mind. There's a reason for where he's living and a purpose to his life. The condo is a five-minute walk from Maple Leaf's head office at Yonge Street and St Clair Avenue.

That's where Wallace would be right now if he wasn't feeling so dizzy. A few weeks ago he went hunting, and the noise from the gunshots has caused him an inner-ear problem. For days, he's been too dizzy to walk. Even reading is difficult. Toronto doctors haven't been able to figure out what's wrong and neither have physicians at the Lahey Clinic. In the meantime, Wallace has been told to stay home and sit still. He's going crazy. He has too much to do and too many decisions to make at Maple Leaf. Poultry prices are down, the meat processing division is a mess, and something has to be done about the milling and seafood businesses. As he sits swivelling, the phone beside him rings again and again. McCain employees call, offering to jump ship and join him at Maple Leaf. A former RCMP officer from Florenceville calls just to wish him well. An old family friend calls to tell Wallace he's in town for a few days. Then Tom Muir calls wanting to go over some papers. Muir has quit RBC Dominion Securities and is now Wallace's chief financial officer at Maple Leaf Foods.

Being stuck at home gives Wallace time to reflect, something he doesn't particularly want to do. It's been a year since the McCain family board voted to remove him as co-chief executive of McCain. In June 1995, Howard Mann officially began his job as McCain CEO. Wallace laughed when he received a memo from Harrison a few days after Mann started. The memo outlined Mann's responsibilities: at first he would be in charge of North America, Australia and New Zealand while Harrison would continue to run Europe and Japan. It was the same basic breakdown Harrison and Wallace had shared for years. The memo said Mann would assume more duties over time. But to Wallace the message was clear: Harrison planned to keep his management role for as long as possible.

Wallace still attends operating board meetings at McCain but he doesn't participate very much. "I couldn't get a motion passed on what day of the week it was," he says. But the irony of his position is not lost on him. Because of Judge Stevenson's ruling, Wallace is guaranteed a spot on the McCain board and a job—as non-executive vice chairman—at his full salary. That salary and his dividends from McCain—about $3 million a year—are helping to pay for his takeover of Maple Leaf.

The family board has assigned Wallace some duties as non-executive vice chairman. He's been asked to research a new phone system for the company's head office and told to analyse whether McCain should sell Thomas Equipment, McCain's farm equipment business. Wallace handled the first job by calling New Brunswick Telephone and asking for some brochures on phone systems. He sent the brochures to Harrison and the board. As for the second assignment, he held a brief meeting with Archie McLean and the two decided McCain shouldn't sell Thomas Equipment.

Over the summer of 1995, Wallace and Harrison tried to formally end their legal wrangling. Wallace agreed to drop his lawsuit, and in return Harrison agreed to pay some of Wallace's share of the costs for the arbitration. But hours after a verbal commitment was made, Wallace's lawyers refused to sign the deal. In the final draft of the agreement, Harrison had added a stipulation that Wallace never again sue the company on the same grounds, a breakdown in partnership. Harrison didn't want a replay of the arbitration and the court battles. Wallace's lawyers saw the added wording as a move to cut off potential legal options Wallace might need in the future. Wallace is still a one-third owner of McCain, and his lawyers don't want him giving up any legal weapons. Harrison's side refused to change the wording and the deal was scrapped. But Wallace decided to drop his lawsuit anyway. He couldn't be bothered any more and it seems meaningless now. Maple Leaf is taking up all Wallace's time—within months of the takeover, the company was plagued by adverse market conditions resulting in losses of $43.7 million. He really doesn't care what Harrison or the others might do. There's little they can do that would hurt Wallace more than they already have. They've publicly removed him from the one job he cherished.

Wallace has made his peace. He's forgiven his nephews for what's happened. It was Harrison who put them up to it, he says. Harrison broke the trust and bond the brothers shared since childhood, and he knows they will never be close again.

On January 5, 1996, Wallace was named an Officer of the Order of Canada, an honour Harrison received in 1984. It was the first time Wallace had been publicly recognized for his own business abilities. He is no longer working in Harrison's shadow and has his own public image and business profile.

Margaret, too, has a public image. As she enters the spacious hallway of the lieutenant-governor's mansion in Fredericton her assistants chorus, "Good afternoon, your honour." Margaret still gets a kick out of the greeting. Her staff continue to call her "Your honour," even though she has repeatedly asked them to call her Margaret. She still finds it hard to adjust to the official protocol her position as requires.

Most of Margaret's weeks are spent at the official residence in New Brunswick. She's served only one year of her five-year term and she already misses her family miserably. She has also purchased a house in Toronto's Rosedale neighbourhood, reportedly for $2 million, and she hopes that one day she and Wallace will be able to move into the house and make it a home. They are also planning to build a house in Nova Scotia near Peggy's Cove.

Margaret treasures the peace she has now. Yes, there is life after McCain and Florenceville. Despite the fact that her children want her and Wallace to keep the family house in Florenceville, in her heart, Margaret knows they can't.

In recent months, Margaret has had to make several trips back to Florenceville to pack up the family's possessions and send them to Toronto. Every one of these trips has been excruciating. People in the village are afraid to talk to her. Some won't even look at her as she walks down the street. Friends who are too afraid to socialize with her in Florenceville have called her in Toronto to explain their distance. They told her that in a McCain Foods management meeting held in the fall of 1995, company lawyer Michael Campbell read a notice to senior executives. The notice, Margaret was told, instructed employees not to communicate or socialize with anybody from Maple Leaf Foods or the Wallace McCain family because they were competitors. When one executive challenged the notice, arguing that McCain had never had a policy like this before and that it was ridiculous for the company to decide who its employees could socialize with, he was asked by Howard Mann, McCain's CEO, how much he valued his job.

"Coming back to Florenceville is like looking at an open grave," says Margaret. "It's horrible."

January 6, 1996

Michael pulls into the parking lot of the Leaside Arena in Toronto and slams on the brakes. It's a cold Saturday afternoon and he's late for his son Jonathan's hockey game. Michael's black BMW still has Illinois plates, even though he's been living in Toronto for nearly a year and they've long since expired. "I've been too busy to get them changed," he says as he helps ten-year-old Jonathan pull his hockey bag out of the trunk. "Hope like hell I don't get caught." The two walk quickly into the arena and down a flight of stairs to the small dressing room. Michael helps his son dress for the game and then barks out a few friendly words of encouragement to the rest of the team. As the players file out onto the ice, Michael climbs up into the stands to watch.

He will never forgive his cousins for the way they have treated his father. And he will never forget. He and his brother Scott are still on the McCain family board and neither has any intention of leaving. "I don't want my son going through what our family went through," he says. "I don't want to ever be in a position of having to choose between my son and Scott's or Eleanor's."

The bitter experiences at McCain have got them working out a strategy for their families. They have hired family business consultant John Ward to work on plans for a new company board.

"Never let the family decide on succession," Michael says, outlining the strategy they've developed with Ward. "Give it to outsiders. And always have an exit strategy—a way for someone to leave the family business without ever having to ask."

Privately, though, Michael has moments of intense guilt. "For the rest of my life," he has told his mother, "I will have to wear the albatross, the albatross that took away Dad's life and Scott's future."

INDEX